DEC 07 2021

ARTISAN BOOKS | NEW YORK

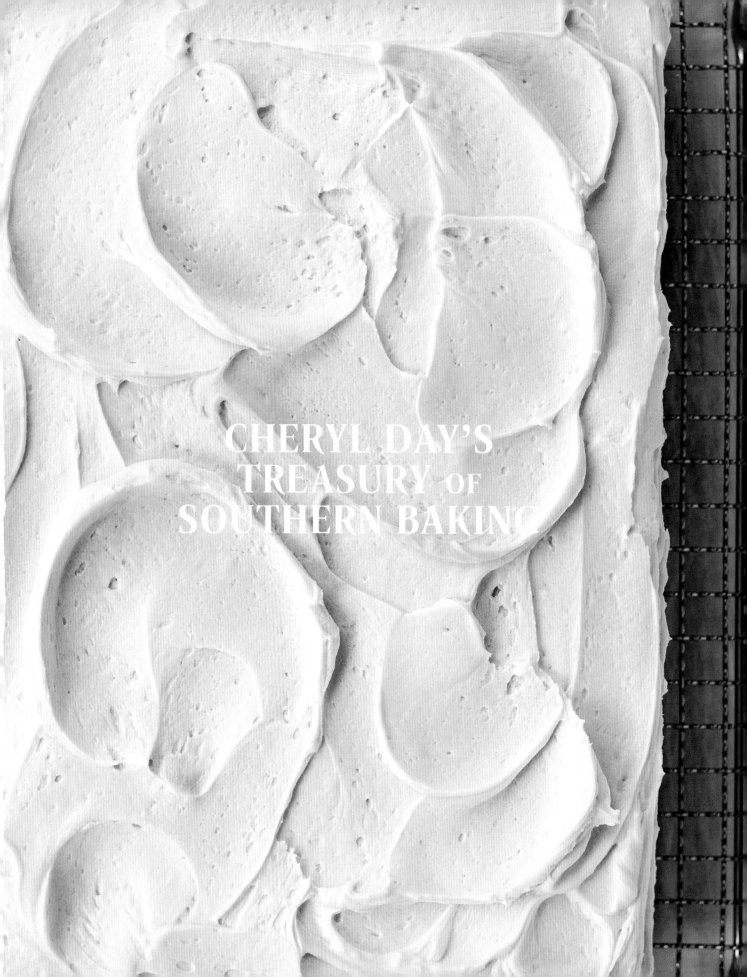

CHERYL DAY'S TREASURY of SOUTHERN BAKING

Cheryl Day's Treasury of Southern Baking

PHOTOGRAPHS BY ANGIE MOSIER

Library of Congress Cataloging-in-Publication Data

Names: Day, Cheryl, author.
Title: Cheryl Day's treasury of Southern baking / Cheryl Day.
Description: New York : Artisan, a division of Workman Publishing Co., Inc.
 [2021] | Includes index.
Identifiers: LCCN 2021004795 | ISBN 9781579658410 (hardcover)
Subjects: LCSH: Cooking, American—Southern style. | Baking. | Back in the
 Day Bakery (Savannah, Ga.) | LCGFT: Cookbooks.
Classification: LCC TX715.2.S68 D436 2021 | DDC 641.81/50975—dc23
LC record available at https://lccn.loc.gov/2021004795

Design by Nina Simoneaux
Photo styling by Haylie Waring

ISBN 978-1-57965-841-0 (hardcover)
ISBN 978-1-64829-146-3 (B&N Exclusive Edition)

Artisan books are available at special discounts when purchased in
bulk for premiums and sales promotions as well as for fundraising or
educational use. Special editions or book excerpts also can be created
to specification. For details, contact the Special Sales Director at the
address below, or send an e-mail to specialmarkets@workman.com.

For speaking engagements, contact speakersbureau@workman.com.

Published by Artisan
A division of Workman Publishing Co., Inc.
225 Varick Street
New York, NY 10014-4381
artisanbooks.com

Artisan is a registered trademark of Workman Publishing Co., Inc.

Published simultaneously in Canada by Thomas Allen & Son, Limited

Printed in China
First printing, September 2021

10 9 8 7 6 5 4 3 2 1

For my mother, Janie Queen. When you have
the opportunity to do what you love, you should
count your blessings one by one—and I do every day.
My love affair with baking and the American
South began while making pie with you.

———

This book would not have been possible without the
millions of enslaved laborers who worked in the fields,
plantations, and kitchens of the United States. My great-
great-grandmother Hannah Queen Grubbs was born
enslaved in 1838 and was among the women who created
many of these Southern recipes. My story has a direct
connection to her life experience and expertise. With
reverence for her and so many like her, I carry this
history forward in sharing recipes that I love.

CONTENTS

*Every great dream begins with
a dreamer. Always remember,
you have within you the strength,
the patience, and the passion to reach
for the stars to change the world.*

—HARRIET TUBMAN

INTRODUCTION

THERE MUST BE SOMETHING etched upon the genes of people whose lineage is rooted in the South, something that compels the sweet tooth and the handmade, that when passed on from generation to generation never wavers, just like a penchant for "y'all" and "yes, ma'am." It's in the faint handwriting of heirloom "receipts," written without measurements but with instructions to add less buttermilk to the biscuit dough if the day is humid or to dust the dough with a little more flour if it is too sticky. It's found in the batter-splattered pages of spiral-bound community cookbooks filled with family recipes gathered to raise money for church fellowship halls, school plays, and even a bus boycott in Montgomery, Alabama. We love the scratch-made, and creating food that nourishes and honors our past yet keeps us firmly planted in the here and now.

In the South, every day is worthy of a special treat from the kitchen. Southerners are famous for their hospitality, and they dine with casual elegance any day of the week, all year long. You feel the pride and craft of Southern baking at every part of the meal; there is always an abundance of fresh baked goods made by caring hands. Southern food is a mélange of cultural influences. Tastes and flavor profiles vary from region to region, and yet it all represents love and treasured memories of our mosaic heritage. Food is our currency. It is our legacy. The first thing to drop down on the table in front of you is a small plate of hot bread billowing with steam, served with softened butter or something sweet like preserves,

likely put up last summer. Offered alongside the meal are fluffy or flaky buttermilk biscuits, light and crisp fritters, or buttery cornbread made in a well-seasoned cast-iron skillet. And whether it's a silky custard pie or thick slices of cake served with homemade ice cream, dessert is never an afterthought.

Southern bakers are celebrated as some of the best in the world, and they are also known to be resourceful. When cane sugar was scarce, they made syrup from cane or sorghum, or they kept bees to collect their honey, which sated the sweet tooth. They "put up" wild berries found on their land to bring sweetness to a long winter. Southerners are known for creating delicious

recipes simply from whatever ingredients they have on hand. Legend has it that when a former slave selling her pastries was asked about the delicious sugar pie she'd made, she replied, "Oh, it's jes' pie!" And that "chess pie" remains the most iconic pie in the South today.

In the South, we love to compare recipes and debate what makes a recipe truly "Southern." Would a Southerner ever put sugar in her cornbread? Possibly. History shows us that until sugarcane from Louisiana and Georgia became scarce during the Civil War, there was a good chance that most cast-iron-skillet cornbreads had some sugar in them. When unsweetened, hoecakes and johnnycakes tasted just fine slathered in sorghum syrup. And biscuits: There is no one right texture. Every kind of biscuit, whether layered and flaky or tender and soft, has its place on the table. How many Southern

grandmothers are there? That is perhaps how many ways there are to bake a biscuit. As with many cultures, the pace of modern life has taken a toll, rendering the passing down of food traditions ephemeral like the faint handwriting of old recipes—not gone, yet faded. Every family has a recipe and a story that goes along with it. Those family stories keep our history from being erased or forgotten.

MY SOUTHERN ROOTS

I come from a long line of women who cooked and dared to follow their dreams. I did not know my own genetic code was engraved with a Southern baker's talents until I discovered my mother's journal after she'd passed away. Filled with the notes, letters, poetry, songs, and recipes through which my mother, Janie Queen, shared

the valuable stories of my ancestors, it guided me to open my own bakery, Back in the Day Bakery, in Savannah, Georgia, in 2002. In my mother's journal, I met my great-great-grandmother Hannah Queen Grubbs, who was born enslaved in 1838 in Alabama. Although Hannah was unschooled—she did not learn to read or write until she was fifty years old—she had a special gift for baking, and that is how she made a living for herself and for her family. She was the cook in the kitchen of a prominent politician. At that time, the cooking in middle- and upper-class Southern homes was always done by Black women. Most of the Southern recipes we know and love today were created by enslaved or formerly enslaved women who were cooks and bakers just like my great-great-grandmother. Their recipes were passed down through oral accounts and eventually made their way onto the page, but that is where

the origin stories often got twisted, and to this day, unraveling the details can only be described as a delicate dance on eggshells. It's been said that history is written by the victors, and when it came to the recipe books from that era, they were written by white women who took credit for the creations of their Black cooks. I'm fortunate to have Hannah's handwritten recipes to show me their true origins.

Hannah became well known to folks all across Dale County for making the tastiest buttermilk biscuits, sweet potato pies, lemon pound cakes, and coconut layer cakes. She catered parties, picnics, social functions, and family weddings, and she made box suppers for folks in her own community too. Although small in stature, she was a powerhouse in the kitchen. Hannah's daughter, my great-grandmother Queen, followed in her mother's footsteps and went on to open a general store in Clopton, Alabama, where she sold her famous gingerbread squares, lemon meringue pies, and small cakes frosted in what my mother described as "delightful pastel colors."

As I've traced my own family history, I've uncovered the stories of other women of color who forged a life in food. There was Sally Seymour, a free Black pastry cook who founded a cooking dynasty in Charleston; the resilient Malinda Russell, a free woman of color who published the first known cookbook written by a Black woman in the United States; inspirational pastry cook and caterer Cleora Butler; the courageous Georgia Gilmore, who fed and funded the Montgomery, Alabama, bus boycott with her Club from Nowhere; queen of Creole cuisine and entrepreneur chef Leah Chase; and legendary chef and cookbook author Edna Lewis, who founded the Society for the Revival and Preservation of Southern Food. All innovators and pioneers in their own right, and the creators of Southern food as we know it now. All of these women have influenced me in some way and given me the courage to follow my own dreams. It is that passed-down wisdom that has made me the woman and baker I am today.

People often ask me how I became a Southern baker despite the fact that I grew up in Los Angeles. My mother left Alabama on a train on April 18, 1943, joining the Great Migration, the way millions of pioneering Black folks left the American South for cities about which they'd heard whispers of equal opportunities for all. She was brutally honest with me about growing up during segregation, yet she also knew how important it was for me to experience life in the South firsthand. And so because of my mother's courage in leaving the South, I had the opportunity to return. I spent two years at Stillman College, a small historically Black college in Tuscaloosa, Alabama, following proudly in the footsteps of other women in my family—it was

like a homecoming for me. My roots run deep in this fertile soil.

My mother brought her culture and a box of family recipes with her on the train she took to Los Angeles, and the memories she shared had a major impact on me. I can still remember the connection I felt when as a young girl, I first visited my grandma Hannah's kitchen in Dothan, Alabama, with my family. My grandmother was clearly the woman in charge of all the pots and pans, and her heart and soul were dished out on every plate. There was always a lot of preparation going on, picking up ingredients from multiple local shops or farmers, then coming home to peel, pick, and shell whatever we'd pulled from the garden. There were chores to do. Tables to set. Napkins to fold.

At first, I thought the celebration that greeted us was because of our arrival, but every day of every summer I spent at my grandmother's felt this way. It was simply her way of life. We sat down to a table set with beautiful linens and covered with plates and bowls that would be passed. And passed. And passed again. Whenever I came to visit, I found the Black folks I encountered to be welcoming and kind and very connected to one another, like one big extended family. Acknowledgment and respect were omnipresent, whether we were at church or at the grocery store.

I could not help but notice that the people in my grandmother's neighborhood were various shades of brown, just like me, and that was worlds apart from my life back in Los Angeles, where nobody in my neighborhood looked like me. In my grandmother's community, people greeted one another by name, and cared for one another in a genuine way by sharing food as they would a warm hug. For events from baptisms to memorials, they gathered together often. With church socials, potluck suppers, and cookie swaps, it seemed life went along at a much slower pace there. You could actually hear the sounds of

cicadas, and catch lightning bugs in glass jars. I fell in love with the South. Terms like "sustainability" and "local" were not words we used back then, but it was the way of life. I learned how to "put up" the summer harvest and make delicious vinegars and pickles out of things that other folks would just toss in the trash, like watermelon rinds and other fruit scraps.

At summer's end, I would return home to Los Angeles with Mason jars of jam and other preserves just in time to share my bounty for show-and-tell at school. I'd tucked away the sense memory of the smell of honeysuckle and jasmine in the late-afternoon air as we shelled peas on Grandma Hannah's big front porch and of one of my favorite experiences—sampling the farm-stand haul, especially peaches always perfectly ripe and often warm from the sun. I still imagine the smell of her famous peach pies baking on a warm summer's day whenever I savor a sweet bite of peach with its juices dripping down my chin. Ever since those days of my youth, I have been fascinated with the beauty, history, and food culture of the South; these feelings keep me connected to my family and to the place I now call home.

SOUTHERN BAKING TODAY

Southern baking is an important part of American culinary history, but it is not stuck in time. It has endured and evolved. The diversity of the South is increasing every day, and that has made the region a melting pot of cultures from many communities that clearly presents itself on the plate. The culture that is found there today has been shaped not only by the agriculture and historic foodways but also by the creativity of the folks who live in the different microregions of the South. Thanks to the influences of new generations of immigrants and their children who share their own traditional ingredients and recipes with us, our hearts and our palates have expanded. The South is far more inspiring and colorful than it was when I first visited as a child. And baking in the South is more exciting than ever. While the undaunted spirit of enslaved cooks and grandmothers lives on in our gathering cakes and mile-high meringue pies, we embrace the new in recipes with ingredients and flavors that were unknown to our ancestors.

I feel like there is no better baking than that happening in Southern kitchens, but you can bake like a Southerner no matter where you live. And that's where this book comes in. Here you will find more than two hundred tried-and-true recipes that share the pride of craft of from-scratch Southern baking and highlight the ingredients and regional specialties that make Southern foodways unique. I was lucky enough to have that box of recipes that set me off on my baking journey handed down to me. But that was only the starting point. I am an avid collector of old Southern cookbooks, to the point of obsession. Researching and discovering new recipes is my passion. So the recipes in this book were inspired by many sources. These include cooks and bakers like Abby Fisher, one of the first Black cookbook authors, and the book she published in 1881, *What Mrs. Fisher Knows About Old Southern Cooking*, which includes meticulous details for her recipes for pastries, pies, biscuits, ice creams, jams, and preserves (unlike most cookbooks of that time, which offered only a sentence or two about the method, assuming knowledge on the part of the reader). They also include church cookbooks. In the South, these are not simply records of an olden-day fundraising effort, but rather historic references from an important publishing network for women passing down hundreds of years of pastry traditions. I've often found handwritten recipes tucked inside the pages of these books too. I also talked to Southern grandmothers, sisters, great-aunts, and sister-bakers, listening to their stories and soaking up everything I could, giving me an oral history I could share.

We live in a time where it is commonplace for folks to restore old houses and to revitalize urban neighborhoods, but we cannot overlook the importance of preserving the heritage of the South found in its recipes and its agrarian past. As a baker, I find those recipes and their origins inspiring, and I honor their heritage here. But I've also taken the liberty of breathing new life into the older recipes, updating them where necessary to reflect modern baking techniques and equipment.

With this book, you will learn to create buttery multilayered biscuits, light and crisp fritters, delicate cake layers and creamy frostings, silky puddings and custards, and many other specialties that are the foundation of our rich and varied culture. These are the recipes that celebrate the fine art of Southern baking. You will learn to bake with Southern ingredients like benne, corn, rice, sorghum, and peaches; to master the pies, both sweet and savory, that are the hallmark of any true Southern baker; and to build cakes worthy of any Sunday supper.

For me, life in the South is about hospitality, community, celebration, and preservation. I am honored to be able to share my own story here because of the courage of my ancestors who lived long enough to share their stories, and also the stories of those who did not. We Southerners acknowledge our complicated history, but we also move forward with a renewed sense of excitement as we write the next chapters of our culinary history. I hope you'll find this book as valuable as I found my inherited recipe box and that you'll use it as a trusted baking companion, a resource that you can depend on for the very best Southern baking recipes, and a starting point for the creation of family traditions and memories of your own.

SOUTHERN BAKING RULES

THERE IS NOTHING MORE SATISFYING and comforting than tying on your favorite apron and getting into the kitchen to bake something delicious for yourself—and to share with others. Southern baking recipes are steeped in passed-down tradition. If you are lucky enough to stand next to a seasoned baker, you will learn the nuances that make this style of baking so special. And learning to bake that way is a confidence builder. But not all of us have someone to stand alongside, so use the well-honed tips that follow to guide you with gentle support and a knowing hand as you mix your way to Southern baking mastery, no matter where you live.

1. Read the Recipe

Always read the recipe from start to finish before you begin to make sure you have a clear understanding of all the steps. Think of the recipe as your guide to success. Read through the ingredients list and the method to ensure that you have the tools and ingredients and time needed to complete the recipe. One of the most common kitchen errors is to not realize that an ingredient—say, sugar—should be added in two separate increments rather than all at once. If you don't read the instructions carefully, you are not setting yourself up for success.

2. Organize Your Work Space

Your most important baking tool is a clean and organized work space. Set out all of your ingredients and utensils so they are ready to go before you start baking, and prep the ingredients as necessary. The French term *mise en place* means, literally, "put in place." Measure out the flour, sugar, and spices; peel, slice, grate, chop, or otherwise prepare the other ingredients. Have your baking pans ready as well. Preparing cake pans correctly guarantees successful removal of baked cakes or bars. With many baking techniques being time-sensitive, it can be disastrous to start mixing only to realize that your butter and eggs should have been at room temperature—which brings us to our next rule.

3. Temperature Matters

It is essential to have your ingredients at the temperatures called for in the recipe. For example, if your eggs are too cold when they are added to your perfectly creamed butter and sugar, the butter will seize up, deflating the air bubbles that you worked hard to create, and the batter will resist being completely mixed. If that happens, the air bubbles will not expand during baking, and the result will be a flat, dense cake, not one with a light, fluffy, tender crumb.

The quickest way to get your eggs to room temperature is to simply put the whole eggs in a small bowl of hot tap water and swish them around for a minute or so, being careful not to bang their delicate shells against one another. Don't leave them in the hot water too long, though, or they will begin to cook.

If a recipe calls for "room-temperature" butter, that means it should be between 65°F and 68°F (18°C and 20°C). A few visual and tactile clues can also help you determine the proper temperature. You should be able to make an indentation in the butter with your finger, but it should still be slightly firm, and it should definitely not be squishy. If the butter gets too warm, label it with the date and return it to the refrigerator for future use that does not require creaming, then start again with fresh butter. Aim to pull the butter out of the refrigerator about an hour before you are going to start baking. Another option is to cut the butter into ½-inch (1.5 cm) cubes and add it to the sugar, then cream until you reach the proper temperature as specified above. Butter will not cream properly if it is warmer than 70°F (20°C), and you should also take into account that the other ingredients, like sugar and flour, may be at warm room temperature, so stay in the specified range for the best outcome.

4. Preheat Your Oven

Unless you are making the Cold-Oven Pound Cake (page 80), you need to start preheating your oven at least 20 minutes before baking to make sure it has time to come to the correct temperature. All ovens are not created equal, and baking temperature will make a big difference in the result. If you put biscuits in an oven that has not been heated properly, they will not rise to their full flaky potential. On the other hand, if the oven is too hot, the result can be disastrous.

Ovens cycle on and off during baking, and every time you open the oven door, the temperature will drop slightly. This is why baking times are given as a range. But always check at the earliest time (e.g., if the recipe says to bake for 20 to 25 minutes, first check at 20 minutes). Don't worry, though, if what you are baking takes 5 minutes longer than suggested. Use the visual clues for doneness given in the recipe as well, and always note your baking time, which will be helpful the next time you make that recipe. Baking requires that you use your senses as well: Sight, touch, and smell are critical indicators. We call this "baker's intuition."

5. Know Your Ingredients

It is important to understand the role of each ingredient in baking. Remember that baking is a science. You can't just substitute ingredients and think it will all work out in the end.

Take the unassuming egg: It performs many important functions in baked goods and other desserts, such as custards and soufflés. Eggs can leaven, thicken, moisturize, and enhance flavors. Whole eggs, as well as yolks on their own, are great emulsifiers. The lecithin in yolks binds fats and water, which normally would resist each other. Eggs also provide structure: When egg whites are whipped to stiff peaks and folded into a batter, the air trapped in the whites expands in the heat of the oven during baking, acting as a leavening agent to produce light, airy chiffon and other cakes.

Baking soda and baking powder are both leaveners. They create chemical reactions in doughs or batters that release carbon dioxide bubbles and allow biscuits or cake layers to rise. Baking soda requires the presence of an acid, such as sour cream, buttermilk, molasses, or non-alkalized cocoa powder, to activate it.

Baking powder does not require the presence of an added acid; it reacts once it is combined with a liquid, such as milk. Baking powders made with aluminum compounds have a chemical aftertaste, so I urge you to use aluminum-free baking powder in these recipes.

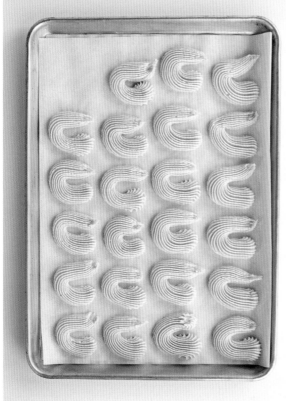

6. To Weigh or Not to Weigh

The recipes in this book give ingredient measurements as both volume and weight (in grams). Weighing ingredients on a kitchen scale will provide the most accuracy in your recipe. But I realize that not all home bakers keep a scale on their kitchen counter, so the recipes can be made successfully using measuring cups—as long as you use them correctly.

7. Measuring Dry Ingredients

When you measure flour or sugar, either weigh it or use this no-fail technique for measuring by volume. First, though, always store flour and sugar in canisters rather than the sacks they came in, so that you have plenty of space to dip and scoop. Loosen up or fluff the flour or sugar a bit with your measuring cup or a spoon. Then scoop the flour or sugar into your measuring cup until it is heaping, and sweep a straight edge, such as the back of a table knife, across the top to level it. Do not tap the cup to settle the contents. (Note that brown sugar should be packed into the cup.)

8. Cream the Butter Properly

In order to produce the perfect texture in cakes and cookies, you must master the technique that is the foundation of so many recipes: creaming butter. Most cookie and cake recipes start with the words "Cream the butter and sugar," or "Beat the butter and sugar together," without any explanation of what that actually means. But if you don't do this properly, your recipe will not turn out well. When creamed correctly, butter and sugar provide much of the structure of baked goods. Because it is so important, it bears repeating that butter will not cream properly if it is warmer than 70°F (20°C), and you should also take into account that the other ingredients, like sugar and flour, may be at warm room temperature. If your butter is too cold, the sugar mixture won't be strong enough to create those all-important air bubbles, but if it is too warm, the sugar will get buried in the butter and separate, without creating any air bubbles at all. In short, the most important factor in creaming butter and sugar is the temperature of the butter (see "Temperature Matters" on page 19).

When creaming butter, you want to beat the room-temperature butter and the sugar together until the mixture is very light in color, fluffy in texture, and almost doubled in volume; this step aerates the butter, as air bubbles are literally forced into the butter mixture. These air bubbles expand during baking, giving your baked goods the texture you want. I've included time estimates in all the recipes to give you a sense of how long this step will take. You can use these estimates as guidelines, but it is also important to know what the result should look like. Once you master this technique, you will be amazed at what a difference it makes. Your cakes will have a light, delicate crumb, and you will enjoy crisp, chewy cookies with a tall glass of milk.

9. Separate Eggs Properly

Eggs are easier to separate when cold. When a recipe calls for eggs to be separated, gather your eggs and two bowls: one for the egg yolks and the other for the egg whites. Lay a piece of plastic wrap on your work space for easier cleanup. Carefully tap one egg on the countertop in the very middle of the shell—not on the edge of the bowl—to avoid pushing shells into the bowl and bacteria into the egg. The easiest way to separate eggs is to use your extremely clean hands. Crack

the egg and turn the whole egg out into the palm of your hand, letting the white fall through your fingers right into the bowl. Be careful not to break the egg yolk into the white. Whites with even the tiniest trace of yolk will not whip properly. Put the egg yolk in the second bowl. Repeat with the remaining eggs. Let the egg whites come up to room temperature before beating them, which will result in more volume when whipped.

To store egg whites, refrigerate in a clean airtight container for up to 2 days, or freeze for up to 3 months. Be sure to make a note of how many egg whites you have. (To use the whites for meringues, for example, you can weigh out the amount you need: One large egg white weighs 30 grams.)

To store egg yolks, beat them lightly with a fork and refrigerate in an airtight container for up to 3 days. Be sure to make a note of how many egg yolks you have. (You can also weigh out what you need to make a pastry cream or custard, for example: One large egg yolk weighs 19 grams.)

10. Take One Final Step When Mixing a Batter or Dough

Mixers are fantastic tools, but sometimes the beaters don't quite reach the very bottom of the bowl. There is nothing worse than finding a trail of butter or flour at the bottom of the bowl when you are scraping out the last bit of batter or dough. Many of the recipes in this book that use an electric mixer tell you to finish mixing the batter or dough by hand to make sure it is completely mixed. Batters and doughs are often time-sensitive, and you certainly don't want to overmix, but doing a few final folds by hand to blend in all the dry ingredients will ensure that mixing is complete. This simple step can save the day.

BAKING TOOLS AND EQUIPMENT

YOU CAN START BAKING with just a few basic tools and pieces of equipment—bowls, measuring spoons, measuring cups, rubber spatulas, whisks, and baking pans—and then add others as needed. This list will help you determine what you need.

Baking Pans

For cakes, pies, and muffins, you want good-quality, sturdy aluminum pans that provide even heat. Avoid thin, lightweight pans that can cause your baked goods to burn. For bread pans, invest in heavy stainless-steel pans. These pans will allow the loaves to develop a good crust all over.

Copper Jam Pot

You can make jam in almost any heavy-bottomed pot, but if you plan on making jam frequently, a copper one is well worth the investment. Copper conducts heat more evenly than stainless steel. A copper pot is also a great choice for making caramel, which requires even heat.

Be sure to always combine your fruit, lemon juice, and sugar in a separate container as noted in the recipes of this book. Putting the fruit in the pan on its own will cause the fruit to react with the copper and can be dangerous. The high concentration of sugar in the mixture prevents toxicity.

Food Processor

A food processor can quickly and easily puree, slice, chop, shred, or grind almost any ingredient.

Kitchen Scale

Weighing ingredients is more precise than measuring them by volume. A scale gives you the ability to weigh ingredients in either grams or ounces. The recipes in this book include gram weights.

Knives

If you haven't already done so, I urge you to invest in good-quality knives, along with a steel and a sharpener to maintain them. A paring knife, 3 to 4 inches (8 to 10 cm) in length, is best for peeling and slicing fruits and scoring piecrusts. A chef's knife that is 6 to 8 inches (15 to 20 cm) in length can be considered a utility knife, best suited for chopping nuts and dried fruit, among other tasks. A serrated bread knife, 8 to 9 inches (20 to 23 cm) in length, is great for chopping blocks of chocolate, cutting cakes into layers, and, of course, slicing bread. Local kitchen supply shops often offer knife skill classes. Take one. The knowledge you acquire can save you from unfortunate accidents.

Measuring Cups and Spoons

Measuring spoons are one of those tools so underrated that you never stop to think about how important they are. Before measuring spoons, Grandma's handwritten recipe would tell you to use a pinch of this and a dash of that to make her lemon pound cake extra special. We can credit Fannie Farmer, the author of *The Boston Cooking School Cookbook*, for introducing measuring cups and spoons to the home cook in 1896. She helped standardize the measuring of ingredients.

Measuring cups fall into two categories: dry and wet. They are not meant to be used interchangeably. Dry measuring cups come in a standard set of four—1 cup (237 ml), ½ cup (118 ml), ⅓ cup (79 ml), and ¼ cup (59 ml)—and are designed to hold precise amounts of flour, sugar, oats, nuts, berries, and other such ingredients. Fill them to the top and then level off the ingredient with a straight edge, such as the back of a knife. Wet, or liquid, measuring cups, which are usually glass or plastic (I recommend glass), have a pour spout. Add the liquid to the cup to come up to the appropriate measuring line. I suggest you have a few different sizes of wet measuring cups—1-cup (237 ml), 2-cup (473 ml), and 4-cup (946 ml).

Mixing Bowls

Mixing bowls come in many different sizes and materials, including glass, ceramic, and stainless steel. I like heavy-duty stainless-steel bowls; they make mixing easy. Look for bowls that are wider than they are deep. You can usually pick these up for a great price at your local restaurant supply store. Stainless-steel bowls are very durable, and they are also nonreactive. A set of six mixing bowls from small to large will cover most baking needs. Use heatproof glass bowls for melting chocolate and for anything you need to pop into the microwave to warm.

Oven Thermometer

Whenever someone asks me about a baking problem, I always reply, "Do you have an oven thermometer?" All ovens are not the same. It's important to know where your oven stands when it comes to maintaining temperature. A properly calibrated oven is essential for both baking and cooking. To check your oven (even if it is new), place an oven thermometer in the oven, turn the oven on to 350°F (175°C), and check to make sure the temperature is what it's supposed to be. If it is not, adjust your baking times accordingly or have the oven calibrated by a professional.

Parchment Paper

I can't say enough about the wonders of parchment paper. It's perfect for lining baking sheets, cake pans, and brownie pans for easy cleanup. And it also creates a nonstick surface, if you want to avoid using cooking spray.

Rimmed Baking Sheets

All you really need are two 12-by-17-inch (30 by 43 cm) heavy-duty rimmed aluminum baking sheets (aka half sheet pans) for cookies and one 15-by-10-inch (38 by 25 cm) rimmed jelly roll pan for sheet cakes and slab pies and bars. The debates about the merits of nonstick, dark-colored, or insulated pans may seem endless, but when lined with parchment or sprayed with nonstick spray, good heavy-duty baking sheets will outperform all others, and they will last a long time. You can find them at your local restaurant or kitchen supply store or online.

Rolling Pin

Southern bakers often collect rolling pins, and everyone has a favorite. In most Southern kitchens, you will find either a hand-turned wooden pin or a standard 18-inch (46 cm) heavy pin with two sturdy handles on ball bearings. Both offer a nice weight and maneuverability, making them great for rolling out cookie and pie doughs, biscuit doughs, and yeasted doughs. A French rolling pin is lighter, is tapered at both ends, and does not have handles. Take good care of your pin, and it will last for generations of baking and become a treasured family heirloom. To clean it, lightly remove any remaining dough with a bench scraper and wipe with a damp cloth; it may need an occasional treatment with beeswax salve (see Resources, page 389).

Rubber Spatula, Plastic Bowl Scraper, and Metal Bench Scraper

A flexible spatula is your best tool for getting every bit of cake batter into your pan (leaving just a little bit behind in the bowl to taste, of course!). Make sure you have at least one heatproof spatula. You can also use it to fold other ingredients into a batter. A plastic bowl scraper is handy, of course, for scraping out bowls, but you can also use it to scoop measured dry ingredients that you have whisked together into the mixing bowl. A metal bench scraper is best for lifting up sticking biscuits from your work surface, for dividing bread doughs, and for scraping your work surface clean.

Sifter

A sifter is great for mixing and aerating dry ingredients, and it also helps break up any clumps of ingredients. A sifter (or a fine-mesh sieve) is specified in some of the recipes in this book. Other times, using a whisk to aerate the dry ingredients is good enough.

Stand Mixer or Handheld Mixer

You can use a hand mixer for many of these recipes, but if you plan on baking frequently, a stand mixer is one of the best investments you can make. A good stand mixer will allow you to cream butter, whip egg whites, mix bread or cookie doughs, and blend delicate cake batters. It will give your batters and doughs a better consistency and make easy work out of long mix times. The recipes in this book use the paddle attachment, the whisk attachment, and the dough hook.

Whisks

Whisks are good for stirring batters, whipping meringues and creams by hand, and stirring custards into a smooth consistency. The open design of a whisk makes it a handy tool for mixing and aerating dry ingredients if you don't have a sifter—in fact, sifting is easier with a whisk. Whisks come in various shapes and sizes, so having a few will help you do many different tasks in the kitchen.

ADDITIONAL BAKING EQUIPMENT

Pots, Cake Pans, Baking Pans, and Pie Plates (and a Cast-Iron Skillet)

One 6- to 8-quart (5.7 to 7.6 L) heavy-bottomed nonreactive stockpot

One 2- to 3-quart (1.9 to 2.8 L) heavy-bottomed nonreactive saucepan

Three 8-inch (20 cm) round cake pans

Three 9-inch (23 cm) round cake pans

One 10-cup (2.3 L) Bundt pan

One 9-inch (23 cm) springform pan

One 9-by-13-by-2-inch (23 by 33 by 5 cm) baking pan

One 9-by-9-by-2-inch (23 by 23 by 5 cm) baking pan

One 8-by-8-by-2-inch (20 by 20 by 5 cm) baking pan

Two 12-cup muffin pans

Two 9-by-5-by-3-inch (23 by 13 by 8 cm) loaf pans

One 9-inch (23 cm) pie plate

One 9-inch (23 cm) deep-dish pie plate

One 10-inch (25 cm) cast-iron skillet

Other Handy Tools

Apple peeler

Box grater

Candy or digital thermometer

Canvas pastry cloth

Colander

Digital instant-read thermometer

Fine-mesh sieve

Fine-mesh sugar duster

Heat-resistant spoons

Kitchen blowtorch

Kitchen scissors

Microplane

Oven gloves or mitts

Pastry bags and assorted tips

Pastry blender

Pizza cutter

Silicone baking mats

Silicone-bristle pastry brush

Spatulas: small, medium, and large offset spatulas and small, medium, and large straight spatulas

Spider skimmer

Stainless-steel ice cream scoops: 1-ounce (30 ml), 2-ounce (59 ml), and 3-ounce (89 ml)

Strainer

Timer

Wire cooling racks

Hot Breads and Crackers

I like the country foods: the greens and the beans and the cornbreads and the biscuits. Not just for the taste, but because it infuses the house with an aroma that says, "You are welcome. You're going to have some good food. It's going to take some time. And once you eat it you won't want to leave."

—MAYA ANGELOU

BISCUITS HOT FROM THE OVEN, cornbread served right out of the skillet, dainty crisp cheese straws, pillowy beignets, and comforting spoonbreads are all hallmarks of Southern baking. When it comes to Southern cuisine, there is a juxtaposition between making do with what you have and the desire for abundance. The recipes in this chapter come together quickly with pantry ingredients you likely have on hand, but they are some of the most time-honored, cherished recipes in the Southern baking canon. Yet while they have been passed down through generations, only a select few bakers are able to master their nuances. These recipes will provide all the guidelines you need to make them your own.

Southern bakers pride themselves on serving hot breads hot. The breads are best eaten with butter or a dollop of jam, cane or sorghum syrup, or honey. On the off chance you have leftover biscuits, save them to make the Southern Party Mix. Leftover cornbread can be toasted in a skillet for a crumble topping for a savory cobbler, or cut into 1-inch (3 cm) cubes and lightly toasted in the oven for croutons. Once you have mastered the Flaky Butter Biscuits with their delicate pull-apart layers, Buttermilk Beignets, Raised Yeast Waffles, and Skillet Cornbread, you will understand the true pride and craft of Southern baking and will want to serve these warm comforting breads often.

Flaky Butter Biscuits

PICTURED ON PAGE 41

Biscuits are an icon of Southern baking, and some say it takes a lifetime to learn to make a really good one. To learn the feel of the biscuit dough is a skill that requires experience, but anyone can become a biscuit master if they are willing to put in the practice. Your hands and eyes are your best tools as you mix the dough. For this recipe, you fold and stack the dough to create the flaky layers. How you punch out the biscuits is also important. Never twist the cutter; the biscuits will have more loft if you don't compress and seal the edges. Use any leftover biscuits for lunch or breakfast sandwiches or to make Southern Party Mix (page 58).

MAKES ABOUT 12 BISCUITS

1½ cups (188 g) cake flour (not self-rising)

4 cups (500 g) unbleached all-purpose flour

4 teaspoons fine sea salt

3½ teaspoons (15 g) baking powder, preferably
    aluminum-free

1½ teaspoons granulated sugar

½ teaspoon (3 g) baking soda

¾ pound (3 sticks/340 g) cold unsalted butter, cut into
    ½-inch (1.5 cm) cubes, plus 4 tablespoons (57 g)
    unsalted butter, melted, for brushing

2 cups (473 ml) buttermilk

Flaky sea salt, such as Maldon, for sprinkling

SPECIAL EQUIPMENT

2¼-inch (6 cm) biscuit cutter

Position a rack in the middle of the oven and preheat the oven to 375°F (190°C). Line a baking sheet with parchment.

In a large mixing bowl, whisk together both flours, the fine sea salt, baking powder, sugar, and baking soda. Add the cold butter cubes and toss to coat. Working quickly, cut in the butter with a pastry blender, or pinch the cubes with your fingertips, smearing them into the flour. You should have various-sized pieces of butter ranging from coarse sandy patches to flat shaggy shards to pea-sized chunks. Give the ingredients a good toss with your hands to make sure all the pieces of butter are completely coated in flour.

Make a well in the center of the dry ingredients, pour in the buttermilk, and use your hands to mix the dry ingredients into the buttermilk until you have a shaggy dough. Gently turn the dough out onto a clean work surface. The dough should still look crumbly. Now be prepared to get messy! Using the heel of your hand, smear the butter into the flour—that is how you build those flaky layers. Bring the dough together by smearing, folding, and turning it, then repeat until there are no more dry bits of flour remaining and the dough comes together in a mass.

Flour a rolling pin and lightly dust your work surface with flour. Roll the dough into a 12-by-14-inch (30 by 36 cm) rectangle, with a long side toward you. Begin by doing a tri-fold, starting from the right: Fold the right side of the dough over the center and then fold the left side over the first fold, lining up the edges and pressing the layers together. Rotate the dough 90 degrees and roll it out again into a rectangle, then fold the dough in half from the top down, pressing the layers together. Roll the dough out again into a rectangle and fold it in half once more, pressing the layers down again. Then, using a bench scraper or a sharp knife, cut the dough in half and stack the bottom half on the top half, pressing the layers together. Dust the dough lightly with flour, and roll the dough out again into a rectangle about 1 inch (3 cm) thick.

Dip the edges of a 2¼-inch (6 cm) biscuit cutter in flour and punch out the biscuits; do not twist the cutter, or you will seal the layers of the dough you have worked so hard to create, and the biscuits will not rise as high. Make sure to dip the cutter in flour after every cut, and arrange the biscuits 1 inch (3 cm) apart on the prepared baking sheet. Then carefully gather up your scraps, press them together until you have a cohesive mass, roll them out again, and cut more biscuits. The scrap biscuits may bake a little topsy-turvy, but that's okay; they will still be flaky and delicious. (*If you don't want to bake all the biscuits at once, you can freeze some on a baking sheet until solid, then wrap and freeze them to bake at a later date. You can bake them directly from the freezer; just give them 5 to 7 extra minutes in the oven.*) You can bake the biscuits now or refrigerate them for up to 1 hour before baking.

Brush the tops of the biscuits with the melted butter and give each one a sprinkle of flaky sea salt. Bake, rotating the pan halfway through for even baking, for 25 to 30 minutes, until golden brown. The biscuits are best served hot out of the oven (you will want to taste one immediately, and give yourself a pat on the back).

If you have any leftovers, store them in an airtight container for up to 1 day. To reheat, place the biscuits on a wire rack in a preheated 350°F (175°C) oven for 5 to 6 minutes. To freeze leftover biscuits, wrap in foil and place in a large ziplock bag. To reheat the biscuits, place the foil-wrapped biscuits in a 350°F (175°C) oven for 18 to 20 minutes, then carefully open the foil and bake for an additional 5 minutes.

Scallion and Cheddar Cathead Biscuits

PICTURED ON PAGE 41

Southerners are known to give their recipes colorful names. This one is so called because the extra-large drop biscuits are as big as a cat's head. They are crisp and golden on the outside, soft and pillowy inside, and filled with scallions and cheddar cheese and just the right amount of black pepper. They are quick to fix and simple to make—you don't even have to roll out the dough.

MAKES ABOUT 12 BISCUITS

1½ cups (188 g) unbleached all-purpose flour

1½ cups (188 g) cake flour (not self-rising)

¼ teaspoon granulated sugar

2 tablespoons (26 g) baking powder, preferably
    aluminum-free

1 teaspoon fine sea salt

½ pound (2 sticks/227 g) cold unsalted butter,
    cut into ½-inch (1.5 cm) cubes

½ cup (30 g) chopped scallions

2 cups (8 ounces/227 g) grated sharp cheddar cheese

1 teaspoon freshly ground black pepper

1½ to 2 cups (355 to 473 ml) buttermilk

1 egg, beaten with a pinch of fine sea salt, for egg wash

SPECIAL EQUIPMENT

3-ounce (89 ml) ice cream scoop

Position a rack in the middle of the oven and preheat the oven to 375°F (190°C). Line a baking sheet with parchment.

In a large mixing bowl, combine both flours, the sugar, baking powder, and salt and whisk until completely blended. Add the butter cubes and toss to coat. Working quickly, cut in the butter with a pastry blender, or pinch it with your fingertips, smearing it into the flour. You should have various-sized pieces of butter ranging from coarse sandy patches to flat shaggy pieces to pea-sized chunks, with some larger bits as well. Add the scallions, cheese, and black pepper, tossing to mix well.

Make a well in the center of the dry ingredients, pour in 1½ cups (355 ml) of the buttermilk, and gently mix with one hand or a rubber spatula until the mixture is crumbly but starting to come together into a shaggy mass. If the dough still looks too dry during this process, add up to ½ cup (118 ml) more buttermilk. The dough should be moist and slightly sticky.

Finish mixing the dough in the bowl, turning the dough onto itself a few times until it comes together into a mass. (Remember, biscuit making is all about touch, so work gently but with purpose.) Gently pat down the dough until it resembles a loaf of bread. Dust the top of the dough lightly with flour.

Using a 3-ounce (89 ml) ice cream scoop, scoop big mounds of dough onto the prepared baking sheet, arranging them about 1 inch (3 cm) apart so that the biscuits have room to puff up and rise. With lightly floured hands, gently flatten the biscuits.

Lightly brush the tops of the biscuits with the egg wash. Place the biscuits in the oven and bake, rotating the pan halfway through for even baking, for 25 to 30 minutes, until golden brown. Serve hot out of the oven or at room temperature.

Honestly, I can't imagine that you will have any biscuits left over by the end of the day, but if you do, you can store them in an airtight container overnight. To reheat, place the biscuits on a wire rack in a preheated 350°F (175°C) oven for 5 to 6 minutes. To freeze leftover biscuits, wrap in foil and place in a large ziplock bag. To reheat the biscuits, place the foil-wrapped biscuits in a 350°F (175°C) oven for 15 minutes, then carefully open the foil and bake for an additional 5 to 10 minutes.

Heavenly Angel Biscuits

These are as soft as a pillow and as light as a feather; some folks call them Bride Biscuits. They're made with self-rising flour, yeast, and baking soda—a little extra insurance that the biscuits will rise high. Pile these up on a party tray next to the deviled-egg platter, or split and sandwich with a sliver of country ham and a little strawberry jam (see page 350) for a sweet and savory bite.

MAKES ABOUT 16 BISCUITS

One ¼-ounce (7 g) package active
    dry yeast
1 teaspoon granulated sugar
¼ cup (59 ml) warm water
3 cups (375 g) self-rising flour
1 teaspoon (6 g) baking soda
½ teaspoon fine sea salt
¼ cup (59 ml) cold vegetable shortening

8 tablespoons (1 stick/113 g) cold unsalted butter, cut into
    ½-inch (1.5 cm) cubes, plus 3 tablespoons unsalted
    butter, melted, for brushing
1 cup (237 ml) buttermilk

SPECIAL EQUIPMENT
2-inch (5 cm) biscuit cutter

Position a rack in the middle of the oven and preheat the oven to 425°F (220°C). Lightly butter a baking sheet.

In a small bowl, stir the yeast, sugar, and warm water together. Set the bowl aside in a warm place for about 5 minutes. The mixture will start to bubble, bloom, and lightly foam as the yeast activates.

In a large mixing bowl, whisk together the flour, baking soda, and salt. Add the shortening and cold butter cubes and, working quickly, cut them in with a pastry blender, or pinch them with your fingertips, smearing the butter into the flour. You should have various-sized pieces of butter ranging from coarse sandy patches to flat shaggy shards to pea-sized chunks, with some larger bits as well.

Add the buttermilk and the yeast mixture to the flour mixture and stir with a rubber spatula until the dough just starts to come together. Turn the dough out onto a lightly floured surface and knead until it forms a ball. You may need to add just a light dusting of flour to keep the dough from sticking, but do not add more flour than is needed. Less flour and a gentle touch when handling the dough will ensure light and flaky biscuits.

Flour a rolling pin and lightly dust your work surface with flour. Roll the dough out to a 1-inch (3 cm) thickness. Dip the edges of a 2-inch (5 cm) biscuit cutter into flour and punch out the biscuits as close together as possible, without twisting the cutter, making sure to dip the cutter in flour after every cut, and arrange them on the prepared baking sheet: For softer biscuits, place them close together so that they just barely kiss; for crisper biscuits, leave 1 inch (3 cm) between them. Then carefully gather the scraps together, gently roll them out again (just once), and cut more biscuits.

Place the biscuits in the oven and bake for 20 to 25 minutes, until golden brown. Remove the biscuits from the oven and immediately brush the tops with the melted butter. Serve hot, warm, or at room temperature.

Leftover biscuits can be stored in an airtight container for up to 1 day. To reheat, place the biscuits on a wire rack in a preheated 350°F (175°C) oven for 5 to 6 minutes. To freeze leftover biscuits, wrap in foil and place in a large ziplock bag. To reheat the biscuits, place the foil-wrapped biscuits in a 350°F (175°C) oven for 18 to 20 minutes, then carefully open the foil and bake for an additional 5 minutes or so.

Sweet Potato Biscuits

PICTURED ON PAGE 41

Sweet potatoes are a Southern staple. Naturally sweet, they have a great texture and flavor and are loaded with vitamins too. Adding mashed roasted sweet potatoes to biscuit dough raises the bar, lending an appealing caramelized flavor to classic buttermilk biscuits.

MAKES ABOUT 16 BISCUITS

2 sweet potatoes
2¼ cups (281 g) cake flour (not self-rising)
6 cups (750 g) unbleached all-purpose flour
1½ tablespoons fine sea salt
½ teaspoon freshly ground black pepper
2 tablespoons plus 1 teaspoon (30 g) baking powder, preferably aluminum-free

2½ teaspoons granulated sugar
½ teaspoon (3 g) baking soda
14 ounces (3½ sticks/397 g) cold unsalted butter, cut into ½-inch (1.5 cm) cubes, plus 4 tablespoons (57 g) unsalted butter, melted, for brushing
2 to 2½ cups (473 to 592 ml) buttermilk
Flaky sea salt, such as Maldon, for sprinkling

SPECIAL EQUIPMENT
2-inch (5 cm) biscuit cutter

To roast the sweet potatoes: Position a rack in the middle of the oven and preheat the oven to 400°F (205°C). Line a baking sheet with parchment and spray the parchment with nonstick spray.

Peel the sweet potatoes and cut into 1-inch (3 cm) cubes. Place the cubes on the prepared pan and bake for about 1 hour, until fork-tender.

Transfer the roasted potatoes to a bowl and mash them with a potato masher. Measure out 1½ cups (328 g) for this recipe (any leftovers are yours for snacking) and let cool.

When you are ready to make the biscuits, position a rack in the middle of the oven and preheat the oven to 375°F (190°C). Line a baking sheet with parchment.

In a large mixing bowl, whisk together both flours, the fine sea salt, pepper, baking powder, sugar, and baking soda. Add the cold butter cubes and toss them to coat. Working quickly, cut them in with a pastry blender, or pinch with your fingertips, smearing the butter into the flour. You should have various-sized pieces of butter ranging from coarse sandy patches to flat shaggy pieces to pea-sized chunks, with some larger bits as well.

Make a well in the center of the dry ingredients, add the sweet potatoes, and mix with a rubber spatula just to incorporate. Add 1½ cups (355 ml) of the buttermilk, gently mixing with the spatula; the dough will start to look shaggy. Gradually add about ½ cup (118 ml) more buttermilk. Gently mix the ingredients with your hands until you have a shaggy dough.

Turn the dough out onto a clean work surface. Using the heel of your hand, smear the butter into the flour—that is how you build those flaky layers.

Bring the dough together by smearing, folding, and turning it, then repeat until there are no more dry bits of flour remaining in the bottom of the bowl and the dough comes together in a mass. If the dough looks dry during this process, add some more of the remaining buttermilk and continue folding until it comes together.

Flour a rolling pin and lightly dust your work surface and the top of the dough with flour. Roll the dough into a 1-inch-thick (3 cm) rectangle. Dip the edges of a 2-inch (5 cm) biscuit cutter into flour and punch out the biscuits (do not twist the cutter, or you will compress the layers of dough and the biscuits will not rise as high) as close together as possible, making sure to dip the cutter in flour after every cut. Arrange on the prepared baking sheet, leaving about 1 inch (3 cm) between them. Then carefully gather the scraps together, gently roll them out again, and cut more biscuits. (*You can refrigerate the biscuits for up to 1 hour before baking.*)

Brush the tops of the biscuits with the melted butter and sprinkle lightly with flaky sea salt. Place the biscuits in the oven and bake, rotating the pan halfway through for even baking, for 25 to 30 minutes, until golden brown. The biscuits are best served hot out of the oven. Go ahead and add a pat of butter, and watch it melt.

Leftover biscuits can be stored in an airtight container for up to 1 day. To reheat, place the biscuits on a wire rack in a preheated 350°F (175°C) oven for 5 to 6 minutes.

Buttermilk Beignets

PICTURED OPPOSITE

A visit to New Orleans isn't complete without a stop at the legendary Café du Monde for beignets and coffee. That first bite of soft billowy pastry is a true delight. It's easy enough to fry up some beignets at home. Serve them warm with a heavy dusting of confectioners' sugar and a cup of coffee, and be transported to the Big Easy.

MAKES ABOUT 24 BEIGNETS

3½ cups (438 g) unbleached all-purpose flour

⅓ cup (66 g) granulated sugar

1½ teaspoons (5 g) instant yeast

½ teaspoon fine sea salt

½ teaspoon freshly grated nutmeg

¾ cup (177 ml) water, at room temperature

½ cup (118 ml) buttermilk

1 large (50 g) egg, at room temperature

2 tablespoons unsalted butter, softened

1 teaspoon pure vanilla extract

Vegetable oil for deep-frying

Confectioners' sugar for dusting

SPECIAL EQUIPMENT

Spider skimmer or slotted spoon

Candy or digital thermometer

In a medium bowl, whisk together the flour, sugar, yeast, salt, and nutmeg. Set aside.

In the bowl of a stand mixer fitted with the dough hook (or in a large mixing bowl, using a handheld mixer), mix the water, buttermilk, egg, butter, and vanilla on medium-low speed until combined. Add the flour mixture and mix on medium-low speed until well blended, 2 to 3 minutes. Stop the mixer and, using a rubber spatula, scrape down the sides and bottom of the bowl, then continue to mix for 5 minutes, or until the dough comes together, stopping to scrape down the sides and bottom of the bowl. The dough will be loose and sticky.

Turn the dough out onto a liberally floured work surface and lightly dust the top of the dough with flour. Shape the dough into an 8-inch (20 cm) square. Fold the dough in half, then rotate it a quarter turn and fold it in half again. Repeat two more times, then shape into a ball and place in a large lightly oiled bowl.

Cover the bowl with plastic wrap and set aside in a warm place for 1½ to 2 hours, until the dough has doubled in size (timing will depend on your ambient room temperature). The dough will be very soft and slightly sticky.

Doing your best not to deflate the dough, gently turn it out onto a liberally floured work surface. Gently lift and stretch and pat the dough with floured fingers to shape it into a 10-by-16-inch (25 by 40 cm) rectangle about ½ inch (1.5 cm) thick. After this workout, let the dough rest for 2 minutes, then cut the dough into 24 equal squares with a sharp knife or pizza wheel.

Set up your frying station: Line a baking sheet with paper towels or a clean kitchen towel. Have a spider skimmer or slotted spoon ready. Heat about 3 inches (8 cm) of vegetable oil to 370°F (185°C) in a large heavy-bottomed pot, such as a Dutch oven, or a countertop fryer. Test the oil by dropping in a tiny piece of dough: The oil should sizzle and the dough should brown within 30 to 40 seconds.

Gently add the beignets to the oil: You can fry a few at a time, but be sure not to crowd the pot, or the temperature will drop too much. Fry until puffed and lightly golden on each side, flipping them with the spider or slotted spoon, 1 to 2 minutes per side. Remove with the skimmer or spoon and place on the prepared pan. Repeat until all the dough has been fried, making sure the oil returns to the proper temperature before adding more.

Dust the beignets liberally with confectioners' sugar and serve piping hot.

CLOCKWISE FROM TOP LEFT: FLAKY BUTTER BISCUITS (PAGE 33), SCALLION AND CHEDDAR CATHEAD BISCUITS (PAGE 34), BUTTERMILK BEIGNETS (OPPOSITE), SWEET POTATO BISCUITS (PAGE 36)

Calas

This dainty sugary pastry made with cooked rice and sprinkled with confectioners' sugar is the perfect accompaniment to a cup of café au lait. Legend has it that these rice fritters became the currency of freedom for many African Creole women, who carried linen-covered bowls or baskets of them on their heads after church as they roamed the streets of New Orleans calling, "Belle calas, tout chauds!" (Beautiful calas, still hot!)

MAKES ABOUT 16 CALAS

¼ cup (32 g) unbleached all-purpose flour

2 tablespoons rice flour

3 tablespoons granulated sugar

2 teaspoons (9 g) baking powder, preferably aluminum-free

1½ teaspoons fine sea salt

⅛ teaspoon freshly grated nutmeg

6 cups (1.4 L) cold water

1 cup (185 g) Carolina Gold rice

2 large (100 g) eggs, lightly beaten

1 teaspoon pure vanilla extract

Vegetable oil for deep-frying

Confectioners' sugar for dusting

SPECIAL EQUIPMENT

Candy or digital thermometer

1-ounce (30 ml) ice cream scoop

Spider skimmer or slotted spoon

In a small bowl, whisk together both flours, the sugar, baking powder, ½ teaspoon of the salt, and the nutmeg. Set aside.

Place the water and rice in a medium saucepan and stir in the remaining 1 teaspoon salt. Bring to a rolling boil over medium-high heat, then lower the heat and cook at a gentle boil for about 15 minutes, until the rice is tender. Drain the rice and set aside to cool.

In a medium bowl, combine the cooked rice, eggs, and vanilla and gently mix together, being careful not to mash the rice too much. Gently fold in the dry ingredients.

Set up your frying station: Line a baking sheet with paper towels or a clean kitchen towel. Have a spider skimmer or slotted spoon ready. Heat about 3 inches (8 cm) of vegetable oil to 375°F (190°C) in a large heavy-bottomed pot, such as a Dutch oven, or a countertop fryer. You can test the oil by dropping in a tiny piece of dough: The oil should sizzle and the dough should brown within 30 to 40 seconds.

Use a 1-ounce (30 ml) ice cream scoop to portion a few fritters onto the skimmer or spoon and carefully lower them into the oil. Work in small batches to avoid crowding, so the temperature of the oil does not drop too much. Fry, turning the calas occasionally for even cooking, until golden brown on all sides, about 3 minutes. Using the skimmer or spoon, transfer the calas to the paper towels to drain. Make sure the oil returns to 375°F (190°C) before cooking each successive batch.

Dust the calas generously with confectioners' sugar and serve hot.

Popovers

You may be surprised at how easy popovers are to make. Keep in mind that it's fine if the batter looks a little lumpy; avoid overmixing, and the batter will smooth out as it bakes.

MAKES 12 POPOVERS

1½ cups (355 ml) whole milk, at room temperature

3 large (150 g) eggs, at room temperature

1½ cups (188 g) unbleached all-purpose flour

1¼ teaspoons flaky sea salt, such as Maldon

2 tablespoons finely chopped shallots

½ cup (55 g) finely grated Gruyère cheese

Butter for serving

SPECIAL EQUIPMENT

12-well popover pan, preferably nonstick

Position a rack in the lower third of the oven and preheat the oven to 450°F (230°C). Place a 12-well popover pan in the oven to preheat.

In a large bowl, vigorously whisk the milk and eggs until frothy, about 1 minute. Add the flour and salt and whisk until incorporated (there will still be some small lumps in the batter, and that's fine). Stir in the shallots and cheese.

Remove the hot popover pan from the oven and spray with nonstick spray (even if the pan is nonstick). Fill each well two-thirds full with batter.

Bake the popovers for 15 minutes, then reduce the oven temperature to 350°F (175°C) and bake for another 20 to 25 minutes, until they are puffed and golden brown.

Transfer the popover pan to a wire rack. With a small knife, cut a hole in the side of each popover; this will allow the steam to escape and prevent the popovers from collapsing. Popovers are best eaten while they are still warm, with a dab of butter.

Sunday Pancakes

PICTURED ON PAGE 47

Make these on a hot griddle and watch them rise and bubble, then flip them over to reveal that deep golden color—pancake perfection. This batter is as light and delicate as a chiffon cake, thanks to the addition of fluffy whipped egg whites. Serve with butter and cane or maple syrup.

MAKES ABOUT 8 PANCAKES

2 cups (250 g) unbleached all-purpose flour

4 teaspoons granulated sugar

1 tablespoon (13 g) baking powder, preferably aluminum-free

1 teaspoon (6 g) baking soda

1½ teaspoons fine sea salt

¼ teaspoon freshly grated nutmeg

2 cups (473 ml) buttermilk

½ pound (2 sticks/227 g) unsalted butter, melted, plus (optional) 1 tablespoon butter, melted, for cooking the pancakes

4 large (200 g) eggs, separated

1 teaspoon pure vanilla extract

In a large bowl, whisk together the flour, sugar, baking powder, baking soda, salt, and nutmeg. Set aside.

(Continued)

In another large bowl, whisk together the buttermilk, melted butter, egg yolks, and vanilla.

In the bowl of a stand mixer fitted with the whisk attachment (or in a medium mixing bowl, using a handheld mixer), beat the egg whites until soft peaks form.

Add the egg yolk mixture to the flour mixture and mix well. Fold about one-quarter of the egg whites into the batter to lighten it, then fold in the rest of the whites.

If desired, put a heatproof platter in a 200°F (95°C) oven to keep the first batches of pancakes warm while you cook the remaining batches.

Heat a griddle or heavy skillet over medium-high heat; if using an electric griddle, the temperature should reach 350°F to 375°F (175°C to 190°C). Spray the griddle with nonstick spray or brush with some of the 1 tablespoon melted butter. Working in batches of about 3 pancakes each, pour about ½ cup (118 ml) of batter for each pancake onto the hot griddle and cook until the edges begin to set and small bubbles appear on the top. Peek underneath a pancake to make sure it is golden in color. Flip and cook the pancakes for about another minute. Serve immediately.

Cornmeal Griddle Cakes

These tender, fluffy cornmeal cakes go well with any meal as a side.

MAKES 8 GRIDDLE CAKES

1½ cups (188 g) unbleached all-purpose flour

1 cup (128 g) cornmeal

2 teaspoons (11 g) baking soda

2 tablespoons granulated sugar

1 teaspoon fine sea salt

2½ cups (592 ml) buttermilk

2 large (100 g) eggs, lightly beaten

6 tablespoons (85 g) unsalted butter, melted, plus 1 to 2 tablespoons butter for cooking the griddle cakes

In a large bowl, whisk together the flour, cornmeal, baking soda, sugar, and salt. Set aside.

In a large measuring cup or medium bowl, whisk together the buttermilk, eggs, and melted butter. Whisk the wet mixture into the dry mixture until just combined.

If desired, put a heatproof platter in a 200°F (95°C) oven to keep the first batches of griddle cakes warm while you cook the remaining batches.

Heat a large griddle or heavy skillet over medium-high heat; if using an electric griddle, the temperature should reach 350°F to 375°C (175°C to 190°C). Grease the hot griddle with butter.

Working in batches of 3 or 4 griddle cakes each, pour ¼ cup (59 ml) of batter for each cake onto the hot griddle. Bubbles will start to form on the tops and around the edges. After 2 to 3 minutes, lift one of the cakes up with a spatula to see if it is golden brown and the edges are crispy; if so, the cake is ready to turn. Flip the griddle cakes over and cook for 2 to 3 minutes more, until the underside is golden brown. Serve immediately, or keep warm in the oven while you cook the remaining cakes.

Buttermilk Waffles

A Belgian waffle makes its way to the South with the addition of buttermilk to the batter. The deep honeycombed landscape provides the perfect home for melted butter and real cane syrup, for a traditional Southern breakfast. You can use this same batter to make a savory meal complete too—serve the waffles as a bed for fried chicken or pulled pork.

MAKES 8 WAFFLES

2 cups (250 g) unbleached all-purpose flour

¼ cup (50 g) packed light brown sugar

1½ teaspoons (7 g) baking powder, preferably
    aluminum-free

1 teaspoon (6 g) baking soda

½ teaspoon fine sea salt

2 cups (473 ml) buttermilk

3 large (150 g) eggs, separated, at room temperature

8 tablespoons (1 stick/113 g) unsalted butter, melted,
    plus more (optional) for cooking the waffles

1 teaspoon pure vanilla extract

In a large bowl, whisk together the flour, sugar, baking powder, baking soda, and salt. In a medium bowl, whisk together the buttermilk, egg yolks, melted butter, and vanilla.

In the bowl of a stand mixer fitted with the whisk attachment (or in a medium mixing bowl, using a handheld mixer), beat the egg whites until soft peaks form.

Add the egg yolk mixture to the flour mixture and mix well. Fold in the egg whites.

Preheat a waffle iron and grease it with a little melted butter or spray with nonstick spray.

If desired, put a heatproof platter in a 200°F (95°C) oven to keep the first waffles warm while you cook the remaining waffles.

For each waffle, ladle about ⅓ cup (79 ml) of the batter onto the preheated waffle iron, spreading it almost to the edges. Close the lid and cook for 3 to 5 minutes, or according to the manufacturer's instructions. Serve immediately, or keep warm in the oven while you cook the remaining waffles.

Raised Yeast Waffles

PICTURED ON PAGE 47

The magic to these old-fashioned waffles is a batter that gets an overnight rest in the refrigerator, so you'll need to plan ahead. The long rest helps the waffles develop flavor and texture. When cooked, they have a light, custardy interior and a lightly golden brown exterior. Serve them for breakfast with butter and syrup, or serve for dessert, topped with fresh cream and berries and dusted with confectioners' sugar. You could even eat them cold dipped in glaze, just like a doughnut.

MAKES 8 WAFFLES

2½ cups (592 ml) whole milk

½ pound (2 sticks/227 g) unsalted butter, cut into
    ½-inch (1.5 cm) cubes, plus melted butter for
    cooking the waffles

4 large (200 g) eggs, at room temperature

1 tablespoon pure vanilla extract

3 cups (375 g) unbleached all-purpose flour

1 cup (125 g) whole wheat flour

2 tablespoons granulated sugar

2 teaspoons fine sea salt

1 tablespoon (10 g) instant yeast

Any of the Doughnut Glazes (page 117; optional)

(Continued)

The day before you're going to make the waffles, heat the milk and butter in a medium saucepan over low heat until the butter melts. Set aside to cool to room temperature.

In a small bowl, whisk together the eggs and vanilla. Set aside.

In a large bowl, whisk together both flours, the sugar, salt, and yeast. Add the cooled milk mixture along with the egg mixture and mix until combined. Scrape down the sides and bottom of the bowl with a rubber spatula to make sure all the ingredients are completely incorporated and there are no bits of flour hiding at the bottom of the bowl. Cover the bowl with plastic wrap and refrigerate overnight.

When you are ready to cook the waffles, preheat a waffle iron and brush it with butter.

If desired, put a heatproof platter in a 200°F (95°C) oven to keep the first waffles warm while you cook the remaining waffles.

Ladle about ½ cup (118 ml) of the batter onto the waffle maker, spreading it almost to the edges. Close the lid and cook for 3 to 5 minutes, or according to the manufacturer's instructions. Serve immediately, or keep warm in the oven while you cook the remaining waffles.

Cornmeal Cheese Waffles

PICTURED OPPOSITE

Buttermilk and cornmeal are a match made in heaven in these savory waffles. Enjoy them for breakfast, top them with pulled pork for supper, or serve alongside bowls of gumbo or tomato soup for lunch.

MAKES 8 WAFFLES

1 cup (125 g) unbleached all-purpose flour

½ cup (64 g) cornmeal

3 tablespoons granulated sugar

4 teaspoons (18 g) baking powder, preferably
    aluminum-free

1 teaspoon fine sea salt

½ teaspoon freshly ground black pepper

2 large (100 g) eggs

1½ cups (355 ml) buttermilk

⅓ cup (79 ml) vegetable oil

6 tablespoons (85 g) unsalted butter, melted,
    plus more for cooking the waffles

½ cup (50 g) finely grated Parmesan cheese

In a medium bowl, whisk together the flour, cornmeal, sugar, baking powder, salt, and pepper. Set aside.

In a large measuring cup or medium bowl, whisk together the eggs, buttermilk, and oil.

Make a well in the middle of the dry ingredients and pour in the egg mixture, stirring until incorporated. Add the melted butter, stirring gently until just combined. Fold in the Parmesan.

Preheat a waffle iron and brush it with butter.

If desired, put a heatproof platter in a 200°F (95°C) oven to keep the first waffles warm while you cook the remaining waffles.

Ladle about ⅓ cup (79 ml) of the batter onto the waffle maker, spreading it almost to the edges. Close the lid and cook for 3 to 5 minutes, or according to the manufacturer's instructions. Serve immediately, or keep warm in the oven while you cook the remaining waffles.

CLOCKWISE FROM TOP LEFT: SUNDAY PANCAKES (PAGE 43), RAISED YEAST WAFFLES (PAGE 45), PAIN PERDU WITH JAM (PAGE 48), CORNMEAL CHEESE WAFFLES (OPPOSITE)

Pain Perdu with Jam

PICTURED ON PAGE 47

Pain perdu literally means "lost bread," and this version is a New Orleans–style French toast recipe that is made with day-old or stale bread. The thick slices get saturated in an egg custard, browned in butter in a skillet, and then baked in the oven. Serve with a generous dusting of confectioners' sugar and jam. You can gild the lily and pass warm maple syrup too!

SERVES 4

6 large (300 g) eggs
½ cup (118 ml) heavy cream
1 tablespoon granulated sugar
1 teaspoon pure vanilla extract
½ teaspoon fine sea salt
4 extra-thick (1½-inch/4 cm) slices day-old bread, such as brioche or challah
4 tablespoons (57 g) unsalted butter
Confectioners' sugar for dusting
Jam for serving

Preheat the oven to 350°F (175°C).

In a large mixing bowl, whisk the eggs, cream, sugar, vanilla, and salt together until the mixture is light and pale yellow.

Place the bread slices in a baking dish large enough to hold them in a single layer. Pour the egg mixture over the bread and let soak for about 5 minutes. Flip the bread over to make sure it is completely soaked in the liquid.

In a large heavy-bottomed ovenproof skillet, heat the butter over medium heat until it begins to sizzle. Gently place the soaked bread in the hot skillet and cook for 1 to 2 minutes on the first side, until golden brown; peek underneath to make sure all the slices are browned.

Flip the slices of bread over, transfer the skillet to the oven, and bake for 4 to 6 minutes. The toasts should be puffed up and golden on the second side.

Transfer the toast to plates and sprinkle generously with confectioners' sugar. Serve with a big dollop of jam.

Hush Puppies

No one is certain how these fried cornmeal nuggets got their name, but most stories say it has something to do with getting the dogs to "hush." You will find these tasty little bites at fish camps and barbecue joints, and just about any restaurant serving Southern fare. The addition of sweet corn kernels gives them a tender, almost custardy texture on the inside, with a crisp, delicate crunch on the outside. Serve piping hot.

MAKES ABOUT 30 HUSH PUPPIES

2 cups (256 g) cornmeal
2 tablespoons unbleached all-purpose flour
1 teaspoon (6 g) baking soda
1 teaspoon (4 g) baking powder, preferably aluminum-free
1 teaspoon fine sea salt
¼ teaspoon freshly ground black pepper
¼ cup (35 g) finely chopped sweet onion
¼ cup (15 g) finely chopped scallions
1 large (19 g) egg yolk
1½ cups (355 ml) buttermilk
One 11-ounce (312 g) can corn kernels, drained
3 large (90 g) egg whites
Vegetable oil for deep-frying

Candy or digital thermometer

1-ounce (30 ml) ice cream scoop or a large soupspoon

Spider skimmer or slotted spoon

In a medium bowl, whisk together the cornmeal, flour, baking soda, baking powder, salt, and pepper. Add the onion, scallions, egg yolk, and buttermilk, stirring briskly with a large spoon until the batter is thoroughly mixed. Add the corn, stirring until just combined.

In a large bowl, whisk the egg whites until they hold soft peaks. (You can use a handheld mixer to do this job, but it's easy enough to do by hand.) Gently fold the egg whites into the batter, being careful not to knock out all the air you've just worked so hard to incorporate.

Line a large plate with paper towels. If desired, put a heatproof platter in a 200°F (95°C) oven to keep the first batches of hush puppies warm while you cook the remaining batches.

Heat about 3 inches (8 cm) of vegetable oil to 360°F (180°C) in a large heavy-bottomed pot, such as a Dutch oven, or a countertop fryer. You can test the oil by dropping in a tiny piece of dough: The oil should sizzle and the dough should brown within 30 to 40 seconds.

When the oil is hot, working in small batches so the temperature of the oil does not drop too much, dip a 1-ounce (30 ml) ice cream scoop or a large soupspoon into the hot oil to coat it, then fill it with batter, hold it about 1 inch (3 cm) above the oil, and carefully release the batter into the oil. Fry, turning as needed, until the hush puppies are golden brown on all sides, 3 to 5 minutes. These puppies are so light they will usually float, bob around, and roll over when they are done, but be sure to check that they are golden on all sides before removing them. Use a spider skimmer or slotted spoon to transfer the hush puppies to the plate lined with paper towels to drain. Serve immediately, or keep warm in the oven while you fry the remaining batches.

Skillet Cornbread

Cornbread may be a very simple mix of ingredients, but it is revered by Southerners. Folks argue over whether sugar should ever be an ingredient in cornbread, but I believe there is no harm in adding a *skosh* of sugar to the batter, which helps with browning and balances the flavor of the cornmeal. You can certainly omit it if you prefer. Bake the cornbread until it is deep golden brown, sprinkle the top with some flaky sea salt, and serve hot right out of the skillet. Serve with good fresh butter or a flavored butter (see page 375).

SERVES 8 TO 12

1 cup (128 g) cornmeal

1 cup (125 g) unbleached all-purpose flour

1 tablespoon fine sea salt

2 teaspoons (9 g) baking powder, preferably aluminum-free

2 teaspoons granulated sugar

2 cups (473 ml) buttermilk

2 large (100 g) eggs

4 tablespoons (57 g) unsalted butter, melted

Flaky sea salt, such as Maldon, for sprinkling

Preheat the oven to 400°F (205°C). Butter a 9- or 10-inch (23 or 25 cm) cast-iron skillet and put it in the oven to preheat while you mix the batter.

(Continued)

In a large bowl, whisk together the cornmeal, flour, fine sea salt, baking powder, and sugar.

In a medium bowl, whisk together the buttermilk, eggs, and melted butter. Make a well in the center of the dry ingredients and gradually pour in the buttermilk mixture, mixing just until thoroughly combined. Do not overmix; it's fine if the batter is still a bit lumpy.

Carefully remove the hot skillet from the oven. Pour the batter into the skillet, return the skillet to the oven, and bake for 40 to 45 minutes, until the cornbread is golden brown and a cake tester inserted in the center comes out clean.

Sprinkle the cornbread with flaky sea salt and serve hot right out of the skillet, cut into wedges.

Sweet Corn Cornbread

Make this recipe when fresh summer corn is in the market. A touch of honey accentuates the sweet flavor of the corn in the very best way.

SERVES 8

1 cup (128 g) cornmeal

1 cup (125 g) unbleached all-purpose flour

½ cup (100 g) granulated sugar

1 tablespoon (13 g) baking powder, preferably aluminum-free

2 teaspoons fine sea salt

¼ teaspoon (1 g) baking soda

1½ cups (355 ml) buttermilk

¾ cup (177 ml) vegetable oil

6 tablespoons (85 g) unsalted butter, melted

2 tablespoons honey

4 large (200 g) eggs

1½ cups (218 g) fresh corn kernels (from about 2 ears)

Position a rack in the middle of the oven and preheat the oven to 350°F (175°C). Butter an 8-inch (20 cm) square baking pan.

In a large mixing bowl, whisk together the cornmeal, flour, sugar, baking powder, salt, and baking soda.

In a medium bowl, whisk together the buttermilk, oil, melted butter, honey, and eggs. Make a well in the center of the dry ingredients, pour in the liquid ingredients, and mix until just combined. Gently fold in the corn, using as few strokes as possible; be careful not to overmix.

Pour the batter into the prepared baking pan. Bake for 45 to 50 minutes, until the cornbread is golden brown and a cake tester inserted in the center comes out clean.

Cut the cornbread into squares and serve warm.

Savory Spoonbread

This savory spoonbread, which some folks call cornbread soufflé, is a welcome addition to the table at breakfast, lunch, or dinner. Stiffly whipped egg whites are folded into the batter, giving the spoonbread a light, almost pudding-like texture. The finely ground cornmeal and sharp cheddar cheese make this simple old-fashioned comfort food. Spoonbread is meant to be enjoyed the day it is made.

SERVES 8

2½ cups (592 ml) whole milk

½ teaspoon fine sea salt

½ cup (64 g) cornmeal

4 tablespoons (57 g) unsalted butter, cut into ½-inch (1.5 cm) cubes, plus butter for serving

6 large (300 g) eggs, separated

1 cup (4 ounces/113 g) shredded sharp cheddar cheese

Position a rack in the middle of the oven and preheat the oven to 350°F (175°C). Lightly butter a 1½-quart (1.4 L) baking dish.

In a medium saucepan, combine the milk and salt and heat over medium heat until the milk starts to steam and small bubbles appear around the edges. Whisking constantly, add the cornmeal, then reduce the heat to medium-low and cook, whisking, until the mixture thickens, about 4 minutes. Add the butter and stir to melt and combine. Remove from the heat, transfer to a large bowl, and let cool slightly, about 10 minutes.

(Continued)

In the bowl of a stand mixer fitted with the whisk attachment (or in a large mixing bowl, using a handheld mixer), beat the egg whites on medium-high speed until stiff peaks form.

One at a time, whisk the egg yolks into the cornmeal mixture, mixing well. Add the cheese and stir to combine. Using a rubber spatula, gently fold in one-third of the egg whites to lighten the batter. Fold in the rest of the egg whites, working quickly but being careful not to deflate the whites.

Pour the batter into the prepared baking dish and smooth the top. Bake for 45 minutes, or until the top is golden brown. Spoon onto plates and serve with butter.

Roasted Jalapeño Corn Sticks

In the South, collard greens are often served with hot peppers in vinegar and a side of cornbread. The cornbread is for dipping in the pot likker, the liquid gold left in the pot after slow-stewing the greens. This recipe adds roasted jalapeño peppers to the batter to riff on the hot pepper vinegar that is a staple on most Southern family tables. The corn sticks are crispy and perfect for eating on their own or dipping.

MAKES 12 CORN STICKS

1 jalapeño

A splash of olive oil

1 cup (128 g) cornmeal

½ cup (63 g) unbleached all-purpose flour

1 tablespoon light brown sugar

2 teaspoons (9 g) baking powder, preferably
    aluminum-free

½ teaspoon (3 g) baking soda

1¼ teaspoons fine sea salt

½ teaspoon freshly ground black pepper

1¼ cups (296 ml) buttermilk

4 tablespoons (57 g) unsalted butter, melted

2 large (100 g) eggs

SPECIAL EQUIPMENT

Two cast-iron corn stick pans (see Tip)

Position a rack in the middle of the oven and preheat the oven to 400°F (205°C). Line a pie pan or small baking sheet with parchment.

Slice the jalapeño lengthwise in half. Carefully remove and discard the seeds and membranes. Lightly coat the jalapeño with olive oil. Roast for 8 to 10 minutes, until the edges start to char. Set aside to cool, then finely mince the jalapeño. (Leave the oven on.)

Grease two cast-iron corn stick pans (see Tip) and put them in the oven to preheat for at least 15 minutes while you mix the batter.

In a large mixing bowl, whisk together the cornmeal, flour, sugar, baking powder, baking soda, salt, and black pepper. Stir in the jalapeño.

In a medium bowl, whisk together the buttermilk, melted butter, and eggs. Make a well in the center of the dry ingredients and pour in the liquid ingredients, mixing until just combined.

Remove the hot pans from the oven and fill each well two-thirds full. Return the pans to the oven and bake the corn sticks for about 15 minutes, until golden. Serve hot.

Tip: If you have only one corn stick pan, you can bake the corn sticks in two batches. Don't forget to reheat the pan for the second batch.

Buttermilk Crackers

These peppery crackers go with everything from a cheese plate to bowls of hot soup. This recipe makes a lot of crackers, but they disappear quickly.

MAKES ABOUT 100 CRACKERS

2 cups (250 g) self-rising flour

1 teaspoon fine sea salt

½ teaspoon freshly ground black pepper

4 tablespoons (57 g) unsalted butter, cut into
    ½-inch (1.5 cm) cubes

½ cup (118 ml) buttermilk

Flaky sea salt, such as Maldon, for sprinkling

In the bowl of a stand mixer fitted with the paddle attachment (or in a large mixing bowl, using a handheld mixer), combine the flour, fine sea salt, and pepper and mix on low speed until well blended. With the mixer running, add the butter a few pieces at a time, mixing until the mixture looks crumbly. Drizzle in the buttermilk, mixing until the dough just comes together.

Scrape the dough out, divide it into 2 equal pieces, and shape each piece into a disk. Wrap in plastic and chill for at least 1 hour. (*The dough can be frozen, well wrapped, for up to 3 months.*)

Position the racks in the middle and lower third of the oven and preheat the oven to 350°F (175°C). Line two baking sheets with parchment.

Working with one disk of dough at a time, on a lightly floured surface, using a lightly floured rolling pin, roll the dough into a very thin rectangle, about 1⁄16 inch (1.5 mm) thick. With a sharp knife or a pizza wheel, cut the dough into 2-inch (5 cm) squares. Arrange about 1 inch (3 cm) apart on the baking sheets. Prick the tops of the crackers with a fork and sprinkle with flaky sea salt.

Bake the crackers for 16 to 18 minutes, until puffed and lightly golden. Let cool completely on wire racks.

Stored in an airtight container, the crackers will keep for up to 1 week.

Benne Crackers

PICTURED ON PAGE 56

Southern legend has it that benne is a good-luck plant. The seeds were brought to America by enslaved Africans and then planted near their quarters on the grounds of cotton and rice plantations. The seeds, which have a savory, nutty flavor, were a treasured, tangible connection to their African heritage. Benne seeds are increasingly easy to find, but you can make these crackers with ordinary sesame seeds too.

MAKES 36 CRACKERS

½ pound (2 sticks/227 g) unsalted butter, at room
    temperature

1 pound (454 g) sharp cheddar cheese, grated

2 cups (250 g) unbleached all-purpose flour

½ teaspoon fine sea salt

1 teaspoon freshly ground black pepper

¼ cup (36 g) benne or sesame seeds, toasted

In the bowl of a stand mixer fitted with the paddle attachment (or in a large mixing bowl, using a handheld mixer), beat the butter and cheese until thoroughly combined. Add the flour, salt, pepper, and benne seeds, mixing until completely incorporated.

(Continued)

Turn the dough out onto a large piece of plastic wrap. Fold the plastic wrap over so it covers the dough and, using your hands, shape and roll the dough into a log about 2 inches (5 cm) in diameter. Chill until firm, about 1 hour. (*The dough can be frozen, well wrapped, for up to 2 months. Thaw overnight in the refrigerator before slicing and baking.*)

Position the racks in the middle and lower third of the oven and preheat the oven to 350° (175°C). Line two baking sheets with parchment.

Remove the dough from the refrigerator, unwrap it, and place on a cutting board. Using a sharp knife, cut the log into slices about ¼ inch (6 mm) thick. Carefully transfer to the prepared baking sheets, leaving about 1 inch (3 cm) between the crackers.

Bake the crackers for 16 to 18 minutes, until golden brown. Let cool completely on wire racks.

Stored in an airtight container, the crackers will keep for up to 1 week; they can also be frozen for up to 1 month.

Sea Salt Crackers

PICTURED ON PAGE 56

Crackers are something you might take for granted. After all, you can pick them up at any grocery store. But they are easy to make at home, so forget the store-bought versions. This recipe, a straightforward introduction to the process of cracker-making, is for a homemade version of the familiar salty ones that come in a box. These have good sea salt sprinkled on top.

If you like, rather than cutting the dough into squares, you can use cookie cutters to cut out crackers of various shapes.

MAKES ABOUT 100 CRACKERS

4 cups (500 g) unbleached all-purpose flour

1 teaspoon (4 g) baking powder, preferably aluminum-free

¾ teaspoon fine sea salt

12 tablespoons (1½ sticks/170 g) unsalted butter, cut into ½-inch (1.5 cm) cubes and chilled

1¼ cups (296 ml) whole milk

Flaky sea salt, such as Maldon, for sprinkling

In the bowl of a stand mixer fitted with the paddle attachment, mix the flour, baking powder, and salt on low speed to combine, 30 seconds. Add the cubed butter and mix until you have a sandy mixture with pieces of butter in various sizes. With the mixer running, gradually pour in the milk, mixing until combined.

Turn the dough out onto a lightly floured surface and shape into an 8-by-6-inch (20 by 15 cm) rectangle. Wrap in plastic wrap and refrigerate for 30 minutes.

Position the racks in the middle and lower third of the oven and preheat the oven to 350°F (175°C). Line two baking sheets with parchment.

Cut the dough into 3 equal strips. Working with one piece of dough at a time (leave the rest of the dough in the refrigerator), on a lightly floured surface, using a lightly floured rolling pin, roll the dough into a very thin square about 14 by 14 inches (36 cm by 36 cm) and ⅛ inch (3 mm) thick. With a sharp knife or a pizza wheel, cut the dough into 2-inch (5 cm) squares and arrange about 1 inch (3 cm) apart on the baking sheets. Gather any scraps together and reroll to make more crackers. Prick the tops of the crackers with a fork and sprinkle with flaky sea salt.

Bake the crackers for 16 to 18 minutes, until golden. Let cool completely on wire racks.

Stored in an airtight container, the crackers will keep for up to 1 week.

Parmesan-Rosemary-Pecan Shortbread

PICTURED ON THE FOLLOWING PAGE

These savory shortbread rounds are a perfect buttery and delicate bite. Eat them on their own, or serve with a soft cheese, and pair with your favorite spirits or wine.

MAKES ABOUT 30 CRACKERS

8 tablespoons (1 stick/113 g) unsalted butter, at room temperature

½ cup (50 g) grated Parmesan cheese

1 cup (125 g) unbleached all-purpose flour

½ cup (57 g) toasted pecans, coarsely chopped

1 tablespoon finely chopped fresh rosemary

½ teaspoon fine sea salt

¼ teaspoon freshly ground black pepper

Pinch of cayenne pepper

In the bowl of a stand mixer fitted with the paddle attachment (or in a large mixing bowl, using a handheld mixer), cream the butter and Parmesan together until well combined. Add the flour, pecans, rosemary, salt, black pepper, and cayenne and mix until completely incorporated.

Turn the dough out onto a large piece of plastic wrap. Fold the plastic wrap over so it covers the dough and, using your hands, shape and roll the dough into a log about 2 inches (5 cm) in diameter. Chill until firm, about 1 hour. (*The dough can be frozen, well wrapped, for up to 2 months. Thaw overnight in the refrigerator before slicing and baking.*)

Position the racks in the middle and lower third of the oven and preheat the oven to 350°F (175°C). Line two baking sheets with parchment.

Remove the dough from the refrigerator, unwrap it, and place on a cutting board. Using a sharp knife, cut the log into slices about ¼ inch (6 mm) thick. Carefully transfer to the prepared baking sheets, leaving about 1 inch (3 cm) between the rounds.

Bake the shortbread for 16 to 18 minutes, until lightly golden. Let cool completely on wire racks.

Stored in an airtight container, the shortbread will keep for up to 1 week; it can also be frozen for up to 1 month.

Cheese Straws

PICTURED ON THE FOLLOWING PAGE

Learning how to make cheese straws is a rite of passage for Southern bakers. Southern folks expect to see them at any party, no matter how casual or fancy. You don't want to skimp on the cheese, and do take the time to grate the cheese by hand rather than using pre-grated.

You can keep cheese straws in the freezer for up to 3 months, so you'll always have some on hand to serve to drop-in guests. Because this recipe makes a lot, you can slice and bake just half of the dough if you prefer and freeze the rest for another time.

MAKES ABOUT 100 CHEESE STRAWS

1½ cups plus 2 tablespoons (203 g) unbleached all-purpose flour

1½ tablespoons fine sea salt

½ teaspoon cayenne pepper

¼ teaspoon smoked paprika

(Continued)

CLOCKWISE FROM TOP LEFT: BENNE CRACKERS (PAGE 53), SEA SALT CRACKERS (PAGE 54), CHEESE STRAWS (PAGE 55), PARMESAN-ROSEMARY-PECAN SHORTBREAD (PAGE 55)

2 ounces (57 g) Parmesan cheese, very finely grated

6 ounces (170 g) sharp cheddar cheese, grated

8 tablespoons (1 stick/113 g) butter, at room temperature

½ teaspoon Worcestershire sauce

Flaky sea salt, such as Maldon, for sprinkling

In a large bowl, whisk together the flour, fine sea salt, cayenne, and paprika. Set aside.

In the bowl of a stand mixer fitted with the paddle attachment (or in a large mixing bowl, using a handheld mixer), combine both cheeses, the butter, and Worcestershire. Mix on low speed until the ingredients come together, then increase the speed to medium-high and mix until smooth and well blended, 4 to 5 minutes.

With the mixer on low, add the flour mixture in thirds, scraping down the sides and bottom of the bowl with a rubber spatula as necessary. Increase the speed to medium-high and mix for about 1 minute, until a soft dough forms.

Scrape out the dough, divide it into 2 equal pieces, and shape each piece into a disk. Wrap in plastic and chill for at least 1 hour. (*The dough can also be frozen, well wrapped, for up to 3 months. Thaw overnight in the refrigerator.*)

Position the racks in the middle and lower third of the oven and preheat the oven to 375°F (190°C). Line two baking sheets with parchment.

If the dough has been chilled for longer than an hour, it may need to sit at room temperature for 10 to 15 minutes before you roll it out. Working with one piece of dough at a time, on a lightly floured surface, using a lightly floured rolling pin, roll the dough into a 14-inch (36 cm) square that is ¼ inch (6 mm) thick. With a sharp knife or a pizza wheel, cut the dough into 4-by-¾-inch (10 by 2 cm) strips. Arrange 1 inch (3 cm) apart on the prepared baking sheets. Sprinkle the cheese straws with flaky sea salt, lightly pressing the salt into the dough. Bake the cheese straws, rotating the pans halfway through for even baking, for 12 to 15 minutes, or until lightly browned. Let cool completely on wire racks.

Stored in an airtight container, the crackers will keep for up to 1 week.

Crispy Cheese Crackers

Crisped rice cereal is the unexpected ingredient in these cheesy crackers. They make an addictive party snack, and your guests will be clamoring for the recipe. If you like, keep some of the dough in the freezer so you can bake off crackers when the urge for a quick snack hits.

MAKES ABOUT 100 CRACKERS

1½ cups (188 g) unbleached all-purpose flour

¼ teaspoon cayenne pepper

1 teaspoon smoked paprika

1 teaspoon fine sea salt

2½ cups (12 ounces/340 g) shredded sharp cheddar cheese

10 ounces (2½ sticks/284 g) unsalted butter, at room temperature

2 cups (56 g) Rice Krispies cereal

In a medium bowl, whisk together the flour, cayenne, paprika, and salt. Set aside.

In the bowl of a stand mixer fitted with the paddle attachment (or in a large mixing bowl, using a handheld mixer), cream the cheese and butter together on medium speed until thoroughly blended.

Turn the mixer down to low and add the flour mixture in thirds, mixing until just combined and scraping down the sides and bottom of the bowl with a rubber spatula as necessary. Gradually add the Rice Krispies, being careful not to crush them too much. Remove the bowl and finish mixing by hand to make sure all the ingredients are completely incorporated.

Turn the dough out onto a large piece of plastic wrap. Fold the plastic wrap over so it covers the dough and, using your hands, shape and roll the dough into a log about 2 inches (5 cm) in diameter. Chill until firm, about 1 hour. (*The dough can be frozen for up to 2 months. Thaw overnight in the refrigerator before slicing and baking the crackers.*)

Position the racks in the middle and lower third of the oven and preheat the oven to 350°F (175°C). Line two baking sheets with parchment.

Remove the dough from the refrigerator, unwrap it, and place on a cutting board. Using a sharp knife, cut the log into slices about ¼ inch (6 mm) thick. Carefully transfer to the prepared baking sheets, leaving about 1 inch (3 cm) between the crackers.

Bake the crackers for 12 to 15 minutes, until lightly golden. Let cool completely on wire racks.

Stored in an airtight container, the crackers will keep for up to 1 week; they can also be frozen, well wrapped, for up to 1 month.

Southern Party Mix

This satisfying party snack comes together easily, especially when you've saved some of your leftover biscuits to make it.

MAKES ABOUT 12 CUPS (1 KG)

6 cups (440 g) cubed (½-inch/1.5 cm) Flaky Butter
    Biscuits (page 33)
3 cups (93 g) Chex cereal (corn, rice, or wheat,
    or a combination)
2 cups (80 g) bite-sized pretzels
1 cup (114 g) pecans, coarsely chopped
½ cup (75 g) white sesame seeds
12 tablespoons (1½ sticks/170 g) unsalted butter
¼ cup (59 ml) Worcestershire sauce
2 teaspoons honey
1 tablespoon fine sea salt
1½ teaspoons garlic powder
1 teaspoon onion powder
1 teaspoon cayenne pepper (optional)

Position the racks in the middle and lower third of the oven and preheat the oven to 350°F (175°C). Line two baking sheets with parchment.

Divide the cubed buttermilk biscuits between the prepared pans. Bake for 8 to 12 minutes, tossing the cubes halfway through for even toasting, until golden brown. Let the biscuits cool to room temperature. Reduce the oven temperature to 250°F (120°C).

In a large bowl, combine the cooled biscuit cubes (set the baking sheets aside), Chex, pretzels, pecans, and sesame seeds and stir gently to mix.

In a small saucepan, combine the butter, Worcestershire, honey, salt, garlic powder, onion powder, and cayenne, if using, and heat over medium-low heat until the butter melts, stirring occasionally to blend. Pour the butter mixture over the party mix and stir until evenly coated.

Divide the mixture between the parchment-lined baking sheets. Bake for about 1 hour, stirring the mixture every 15 minutes, until golden brown. Let cool completely.

Stored in an airtight container, the party mix will keep for up to 2 weeks.

CREATING SOUTHERN COMFORT

Creating a warm, welcoming, and gracious atmosphere is a hallmark of hospitality in the South, whether the occasion is an afternoon tea or an impromptu potluck supper with friends. It is a generosity of spirit that makes for a memorable experience. Careful planning and organization will ensure that everything goes smoothly, and that both you and your guests have a good time. Here are a few ideas to make your next gathering convivial.

- Send out handwritten invitations via snail mail. These days, it is truly special to receive a sweet note in your mailbox.

- Decorate your home with flowers and herbs in abundance to add beauty and a welcoming scent. Small cuttings from your yard can add to the effortless feel of the table setting if you arrange them in old milk bottles, sugar bowls, pitchers, and/ or vintage teacups. Add candles to create a warm ambience.

- Cloth napkins are easy to make. Pick up about 3 yards (3 m) of an inexpensive cotton fabric and cut into 4- to 5-inch (10 to 13 cm) squares with pinking shears, which will create a zigzag design and prevent the edges from fraying. Or hunt for vintage white linens and dye them pretty colors to complement your decor.

- If you don't have matching linens or tableware, don't let that stop you. Mixing and matching what you have will add character and charm to your table.

- Print out a menu, or handwrite one.

- A serving board can set the tone for a special occasion. It can become an edible centerpiece that sparks conversation. Fill yours with a gorgeous assortment of cured meats, cheeses, crudités, pickles, homemade crackers, spreads, and jams to showcase the best of the season.

- For a large casual party, set up multiple food and drink stations to keep your guests on the move. Be sure to include Southern Party Mix (opposite) as one of the offerings.

Coffee Cakes, Loaf Cakes, and Bundt Cakes

COFFEE CAKES AND LOAF CAKES are an expression of the joy and simplicity of baking, and they are foundational recipes in the South. Southern bakers pride themselves on the time-tested methods of gently mixing and folding ingredients to create easy cakes that have always been the heart of the home. Coffee cakes and loaf cakes allow you to bake a quick sweet treat for your family, and they can also be a generous gift of neighborly kindness to your friends or coworkers.

These recipes are the perfect segue to the more advanced recipes in this book, but because they are so simple, they could easily transform you into a weekday baker too. Turn on your oven and begin your own story with the Sweet Bread, Cinnamon Streusel Coffee Cake, 7-Up Cake, Very Chocolate Bundt Cake, Lemon Blueberry Cake, Cold-Oven Pound Cake, or Orange Date Cake. Many of the recipes include buttermilk, sour cream, and fruit, and some include drizzles of warm syrup, which means the cakes and loaves will keep well for several days.

Sweet Bread

This recipe has been handed down from mother to daughter for generations. It's a modest cake, a reminder of simpler times when many ingredients were scarce or unaffordable for many folks, true to the Southern spirit of making do with what you have on hand. It's one of those weekday cakes that you can whip up whenever you're craving just a little something sweet. The cake is never frosted, but you can dust the top with confectioners' sugar, if you like.

SERVES 12

2 cups (250 g) unbleached all-purpose flour

2½ teaspoons (11 g) baking powder, preferably aluminum-free

¼ teaspoon fine sea salt

½ cup (118 ml) whole milk

1 tablespoon pure vanilla extract

8 tablespoons (1 stick/113 g) unsalted butter, at room temperature

1⅓ cups (267 g) granulated sugar

3 large (150 g) eggs, at room temperature

Position a rack in the middle of the oven and preheat the oven to 350°F (175°C). Butter a 9-by-3-inch (23 by 8 cm) round cake pan or a 9-by-5-by-3-inch (23 by 13 by 8 cm) loaf pan, then line the bottom with parchment and butter it as well. Lightly dust the pan with flour, tapping the pan on the counter to shake out the excess.

Sift together the flour, baking powder, and salt into a medium bowl. Set aside.

In a large measuring cup or small bowl, stir together the milk and vanilla. Set aside.

In the bowl of a stand mixer fitted with the paddle attachment (or in a large mixing bowl, using a handheld mixer), cream the butter and sugar together on medium-high speed for 3 to 5 minutes, until light and fluffy. Turn the speed down to low and add the eggs one (50 g) at a time, mixing well after each addition and scraping down the sides and bottom of the bowl with a rubber spatula as necessary.

With the mixer still on low speed, add the flour mixture in thirds, alternating with the milk mixture and beginning and ending with the flour, mixing until just combined. Scrape down the sides and bottom of the bowl as necessary.

Scrape the batter into the prepared pan and smooth the top with a spatula. Tap the pan firmly on the countertop to remove any air bubbles from the batter. Bake for 35 to 40 minutes, until a cake tester inserted in the center of the cake comes out clean.

Let the cake cool slightly before slicing into wedges. Serve warm or cold; it's delicious either way.

The cake can be stored in an airtight container at room temperature for up to 3 days.

Blueberry Buckle

A wonderfully tender cake sits beneath a thick layer of crumb topping. As it bakes, the topping craters with deep crevices, or "buckles," to reveal plump berries bursting with flavor. Make this cake when fresh blueberries are in season, of course, but it's also good made with frozen berries; do not thaw before folding them into the batter.

SERVES 8 TO 10

FOR THE CRUMB TOPPING

½ cup (100 g) granulated sugar

⅓ cup (67 g) packed light brown sugar

1 teaspoon ground cinnamon

⅛ teaspoon freshly grated nutmeg

1⅓ cups (167 g) unbleached all-purpose flour

8 tablespoons (1 stick/113 g) cold unsalted butter, cut into ½-inch (1.5 cm) cubes

FOR THE BUCKLE

1¼ cups (156 g) unbleached all-purpose flour

1 teaspoon (4 g) baking powder, preferably aluminum-free

¼ teaspoon (1 g) baking soda

½ teaspoon fine sea salt

¼ teaspoon ground cardamom

6 tablespoons (85 g) unsalted butter, at room temperature

¾ cup (150 g) granulated sugar

2 large (100 g) eggs, at room temperature

1 teaspoon pure vanilla extract

½ teaspoon grated lemon zest

⅔ cup (160 g) sour cream

2 cups (340 g) fresh or frozen blueberries

Confectioners' sugar for dusting

Position a rack in the lower third of the oven and preheat the oven to 350°F (175°C). Butter the sides of a 9-inch (23 cm) round cake pan and line the bottom with parchment.

To make the crumb topping: In a medium bowl, combine both sugars, the cinnamon, nutmeg, and flour and stir until well blended. Cut in the butter with a pastry blender until the crumbs are the size of peas. Transfer the topping to a covered container and set in the freezer to chill while you mix the cake batter.

To make the buckle: Sift together the flour, baking powder, baking soda, salt, and cardamom into a medium bowl. Set aside.

In the bowl of a stand mixer fitted with the paddle attachment (or in a large mixing bowl, using a handheld mixer), cream the butter and granulated sugar together on high speed for 5 to 7 minutes, until light and fluffy. Reduce the speed to low and add the eggs one (50 g) at a time, mixing well after each addition; scrape down the sides and bottom of the bowl with a rubber spatula as necessary. Mix in the vanilla, lemon zest, and sour cream.

With the mixer still on low speed, add the dry ingredients, mixing until just incorporated. Remove the bowl from the mixer stand (if using) and gently fold in the blueberries.

Scrape the batter into the prepared pan and spread it evenly with a spatula. Sprinkle the crumb topping evenly over the top. Bake for 40 to 50 minutes, until the top is golden brown and firm to the touch.

Serve warm or at room temperature, right out of the baking dish. Sprinkle the top of the buckle lightly with confectioners' sugar just before serving.

The buckle can be stored, tightly covered, in the refrigerator for up to 3 days.

Cinnamon Streusel Coffee Cake

This classic coffee cake is spiced with cinnamon and cardamom—two ingredients you should always have in your pantry. Topping it with a brown sugar–cinnamon streusel and a drizzle of simple vanilla glaze makes the cake a real crowd-pleaser.

SERVES 12

FOR THE STREUSEL

½ cup (100 g) packed light brown sugar

½ cup (63 g) unbleached all-purpose flour

1½ teaspoons ground cinnamon

½ teaspoon fine sea salt

6 tablespoons (85 g) cold unsalted butter, cut into 1-inch (3 cm) cubes

1½ cups (180 g) chopped pecans

FOR THE CAKE

2½ cups (313 g) unbleached all-purpose flour

2 teaspoons (9 g) baking powder, preferably aluminum-free

1 teaspoon (6 g) baking soda

1 teaspoon fine sea salt

¼ teaspoon ground cardamom

½ pound (2 sticks/227 g) unsalted butter, at room temperature

1½ cups (300 g) granulated sugar

3 large (150 g) eggs, at room temperature

1 tablespoon pure vanilla extract

1¼ cups (300 g) sour cream, at room temperature

FOR THE VANILLA SUGAR GLAZE

1 cup (125 g) confectioners' sugar

2 tablespoons whole milk

½ teaspoon pure vanilla extract

Position a rack in the middle of the oven and preheat the oven to 350°F (175°C). Butter a 9-by-13-inch (23 by 33 cm) baking pan and line the bottom with parchment.

To make the streusel: In a small bowl, combine the brown sugar, flour, cinnamon, and salt. Cut in the butter with a pastry blender until the crumbs are the size of small peas. Add the pecans and toss to combine. Transfer the streusel to a covered container and set in the freezer to chill while you mix the cake batter.

To make the cake: Sift together the flour, baking powder, baking soda, salt, and cardamom into a medium bowl. Set aside.

In the bowl of a stand mixer fitted with the paddle attachment (or in a large mixing bowl, using a handheld mixer), cream the butter and sugar together for 4 to 5 minutes, until light and fluffy. Add the eggs one (50 g) at a time, mixing well after each addition. Add the vanilla and sour cream and mix until just blended.

With the mixer on low, add the flour mixture in thirds, mixing until just combined and no streaks of flour are visible; scrape down the sides and bottom of the bowl with a rubber spatula as necessary.

Scrape the batter into the prepared pan and spread evenly with a spatula. Sprinkle the top evenly with the streusel.

Bake for 45 to 50 minutes, until a cake tester inserted in the center of the cake comes out clean. Let the cake cool in the pan on a wire rack for 20 minutes.

While the cake cools, make the glaze: In a small bowl, mix the confectioners' sugar, milk, and vanilla together until smooth. Set aside.

Turn the cooled cake out onto another wire rack, remove the parchment, and invert onto a serving plate, streusel side up. Use a fork to drizzle the glaze over the top of the cake. Let stand until the glaze has set before serving.

The cake can be stored in an airtight container at room temperature for up to 3 days.

Applesauce Cake with Butterscotch Icing

This delicious old-timey recipe combines a variety of spices, along with some cocoa powder (surprise!), to make a cake that is absolutely delicious; applesauce gives the cake its moistness. The cake is finished with a butterscotch icing.

SERVES 12

4 cups (500 g) unbleached all-purpose flour

¼ cup (20 g) Dutch-processed cocoa powder

1 tablespoon (17 g) baking soda

1½ teaspoons fine sea salt

1 teaspoon ground cinnamon

1 teaspoon ground cloves

1 teaspoon freshly grated nutmeg

1 teaspoon ground allspice

½ pound (2 sticks/227 g) unsalted butter, at room temperature

3 cups (600 g) granulated sugar

4 large (200 g) eggs, at room temperature

3 cups (765 g) applesauce

1½ cups (143 g) walnuts

1½ cups (195 g) dried apricots, coarsely chopped

1 recipe Butterscotch Icing (recipe follows)

Position a rack in the middle of the oven and preheat the oven to 350°F (175°C). Spray a 10-inch (25 cm) Bundt pan with nonstick spray, making sure to get into all the crevices.

Sift together the flour, cocoa powder, baking soda, salt, cinnamon, cloves, nutmeg, and allspice into a medium bowl. Set aside.

In the bowl of a stand mixer fitted with the paddle attachment (or in a large mixing bowl, using a handheld mixer), cream the butter and sugar together on medium-high speed for 4 to 5 minutes, until light and fluffy. Add the eggs one (50 g) at a time, mixing well after each addition and scraping down the sides and bottom of the bowl with a rubber spatula as necessary.

With the mixer on low speed, add the sifted dry ingredients in thirds, alternating with the applesauce, beginning and ending with the dry ingredients. Remove the bowl from the mixer stand (if using) and gently fold in the walnuts and apricots. Scrape the batter into the prepared pan and spread it evenly with a spatula.

Bake for 50 to 60 minutes, until a cake tester inserted in the center of the cake comes out clean. Let the cake cool in the pan on a wire rack for 20 minutes, then invert it onto another rack and let cool completely.

Transfer the cake to a serving plate. Spread the icing over the top of the cake, letting it drip down the sides too so that everyone gets plenty of icing in every bite.

The cake can be stored in an airtight container at room temperature for up to 5 days. It will get better every day as the flavors of the spices continue to marry.

BUTTERSCOTCH ICING

MAKES 2½ CUPS (592 ML)

8 tablespoons (1 stick/113 g) unsalted butter

⅔ cup (133 g) packed dark brown sugar

½ cup (118 ml) heavy cream

3 cups (375 g) confectioners' sugar

1 teaspoon pure vanilla extract

In a medium saucepan, melt the butter over medium heat. Add the brown sugar and cook, whisking frequently, until the sugar has completely dissolved, about 3 minutes. Gradually add the cream, then continue whisking until smooth, 2 to 3 minutes.

Transfer the mixture to the bowl of a stand mixer fitted with the paddle attachment (or transfer to a large mixing bowl and use a handheld mixer) and beat the mixture on low speed for about 1 minute to cool it down. With the mixer running, gradually add the confectioners' sugar and vanilla, then continue beating until the icing turns lighter in color and texture and looks creamy. Use immediately.

Sock-It-to-Me Cake

PICTURED ON PAGE 70

This cake, with its clever name, became popular in the 1970s, and it was usually made with a box of yellow cake mix. It's even better, of course, if you make it from scratch and update it with the addition of browned butter in the batter, as in this version.

SERVES 12

FOR THE STREUSEL

2 tablespoons unbleached all-purpose flour

¼ cup (50 g) packed light brown sugar

2 teaspoons ground cinnamon

¼ teaspoon fine sea salt

2 tablespoons unsalted butter, melted and cooled slightly

¾ cup (86 g) toasted pecans, finely chopped

FOR THE CAKE

9 ounces (2¼ sticks/255 g) unsalted butter

2½ cups (313 g) unbleached all-purpose flour

1 teaspoon (4 g) baking powder, preferably aluminum-free

½ teaspoon (3 g) baking soda

1 teaspoon fine sea salt

2 cups (400 g) granulated sugar

4 large (200 g) eggs, at room temperature

1 cup (240 g) sour cream, at room temperature

1 teaspoon pure vanilla extract

FOR THE VANILLA GLAZE

1 cup (125 g) confectioners' sugar

2 tablespoons whole milk

½ teaspoon pure vanilla extract

Position a rack in the middle of the oven and preheat the oven to 325°F (165°C). Butter and flour a nonstick 10-inch (25 cm) Bundt pan, making sure to get into all the crevices.

To make the streusel: In a small bowl, combine the flour, brown sugar, cinnamon, and salt. Gradually drizzle in the melted butter and toss with your hands or a fork until the mixture is crumbly. Stir in the pecans. Set aside.

To make the cake: In a medium saucepan, brown the butter: Melt the butter over medium heat, then continue to cook until the butter has turned a golden-brown color and smells fragrant. Remove from the heat and set aside to cool slightly. (For more details, see Brown Butter, page 387.)

In a medium bowl, whisk together the flour, baking powder, baking soda, and salt. Set aside.

In the bowl of a stand mixer fitted with the paddle attachment (or in a large mixing bowl, using a handheld mixer), beat the sugar, eggs, sour cream, and vanilla on medium-low speed for about 1 minute, until completely combined. With the mixture running on low, slowly pour in the melted brown butter, mixing until incorporated. Add the flour mixture in thirds, mixing until just combined and no streaks of flour are visible; scrape down the sides and bottom of the bowl with a rubber spatula as necessary.

Remove the bowl from the mixer stand (if using) and use the rubber spatula to incorporate any ingredients hiding at the bottom of the bowl, making sure the batter is completely mixed. Scrape half of the batter into the prepared pan and spread it evenly with a spatula. Sprinkle the streusel evenly on top. Spoon the rest of the batter into the pan, spreading it evenly. Tap the pan firmly on the countertop to remove any air bubbles from the batter.

Bake for 50 to 60 minutes, until a cake tester inserted in the center of the cake comes out clean. Let the cake cool in the pan on a wire rack for 20 minutes, then invert it onto a serving platter and let cool completely.

To make the glaze: In a small bowl, mix the confectioners' sugar, milk, and vanilla together until smooth.

Drizzle the glaze over the top of the cooled cake. Let the glaze set before serving the cake.

The cake can be stored in an airtight container at room temperature for up to 3 days.

Fresh Berry Crumb Cake

PICTURED ON PAGE 70

Adding fruit is a great way to increase the appeal of a simple cake. Blueberries and raspberries mingle well together and give this cake a sweet and tangy flavor. The cornmeal in the batter is a Southern touch, lending texture and dimension to the delicate cake.

SERVES 8

FOR THE CRUMB TOPPING

½ cup (63 g) unbleached all-purpose flour

6 tablespoons (75 g) light brown sugar

½ teaspoon fine sea salt

3 tablespoons cold unsalted butter, cut into ½-inch (1.5 cm) cubes

¼ cup (29 g) pecans, chopped

FOR THE CAKE

¾ cup plus 3 tablespoons (188 g) granulated sugar

1 teaspoon ground cinnamon

1½ cups (188 g) unbleached all-purpose flour

1 tablespoon cornmeal

½ teaspoon (2 g) baking powder, preferably aluminum-free

½ teaspoon (3 g) baking soda

½ teaspoon fine sea salt

6 tablespoons (85 g) unsalted butter, at room temperature

1 teaspoon pure vanilla extract

2 large (100 g) eggs

2 cups (473 ml) buttermilk

1 cup (120 g) fresh raspberries

1 cup (145 g) fresh blueberries

Position a rack in the middle of the oven and preheat the oven to 350°F (175°C). Butter an 8-by-2-inch (20 by 5 cm) square baking pan, then line the bottom with parchment and butter it as well. Lightly dust the pan with flour, tapping it on the counter to shake out the excess.

To make the crumb topping: In a medium bowl, whisk together the flour, sugar, and salt. Toss in the butter and, using your fingertips, work the butter into the dry ingredients until large crumbs form. Add the pecans. Cover and refrigerate.

To make the cake: In a small bowl, mix 3 tablespoons of the sugar and the cinnamon together. Set aside.

Sift together the flour, cornmeal, baking powder, baking soda, and salt into a large bowl.

In the bowl of a stand mixer fitted with the paddle attachment (or in a large mixing bowl, using a handheld mixer), cream the remaining ¾ cup (150 g) sugar and the butter together for 3 to 5 minutes, until light and fluffy. Add the vanilla, mixing until just combined. Add the eggs one (50 g) at a time, mixing well after each addition, then mix for 3 to 5 minutes, until the mixture is light and fluffy. On low speed, add the flour mixture in thirds, alternating with the buttermilk and starting and ending with the flour; scrape down the sides and bottom of the bowl with a rubber spatula as necessary.

Scrape half of the batter into the prepared pan and smooth the top with a spatula. Sprinkle the cinnamon sugar evenly over the batter. Gently scrape the remaining batter on top and smooth with a spatula. Scatter the berries evenly over the batter. Sprinkle the crumb topping evenly over the berries.

Bake for 55 to 65 minutes, until a cake tester inserted in the center of the cake comes out clean. Let cool completely in the pan on a wire rack.

The cake can be stored in an airtight container at room temperature for up to 3 days.

7-Up Cake

Soda-pop cakes are popular all over the South. The carbonation is said to make the cakes light and moist, and this one certainly is. To give it even more lemon-lime flavor, I add lemon and lime zest to the batter and fresh juice to the cake in the form of a soaking syrup.

SERVES 12

FOR THE CAKE

3 cups (375 g) unbleached all-purpose flour

1 teaspoon fine sea salt

½ teaspoon (2 g) baking powder, preferably aluminum-free

½ teaspoon (3 g) baking soda

¾ cup (177 ml) 7-Up or other lemon-lime soda

¼ cup (59 ml) buttermilk

1 tablespoon pure vanilla extract

½ pound (2 sticks/227 g) unsalted butter, at room temperature

2 cups (400 g) granulated sugar

2 tablespoons grated lemon zest

2 tablespoons grated lime zest

4 large (200 g) eggs, at room temperature

FOR THE SOAKING SYRUP

1 cup (200 g) granulated sugar

¼ cup (59 ml) fresh lemon juice

¼ cup (59 ml) fresh lime juice

FOR THE GLAZE

2 cups (250 g) sifted confectioners' sugar

⅓ cup (79 ml) 7-Up or other lemon-lime soda

Grated lemon and lime zest for sprinkling (optional)

To make the cake: Position a rack in the middle of the oven and preheat the oven to 325°F (165°C). Butter a 10-inch (25 cm) Bundt pan, making sure to get into all the crevices. Lightly dust the pan with flour, tapping the pan on the counter to shake out the excess.

Sift together the flour, salt, baking powder, and baking soda into a large bowl. Set aside.

In a small bowl, mix together the 7-Up, buttermilk, and vanilla. Set aside.

In the bowl of a stand mixer fitted with the paddle attachment (or in a large mixing bowl, using a handheld mixer), cream the butter, sugar, and lemon and lime zests together on medium speed until light and fluffy, 3 to 5 minutes. Add the eggs one (50 g) at a time, mixing well after each addition and scraping down the sides and bottom of the bowl with a rubber spatula as necessary. With the mixer on low speed, add the flour mixture in thirds, alternating with the 7-Up soda mixture and beginning and ending with the flour; scrape down the sides and bottom of the bowl as necessary.

Scrape the batter into the prepared pan and spread it evenly with a spatula. Bake for 50 to 55 minutes, until a cake tester inserted in the center of the cake comes out clean. Remove from the oven and let the cake cool in the pan on a wire rack for about 10 minutes.

Meanwhile, make the soaking syrup: In a small nonreactive saucepan, combine the sugar and lemon and lime juices and cook over low heat, stirring frequently, until the sugar completely dissolves,

CLOCKWISE FROM TOP LEFT: SOCK-IT-TO-ME CAKE (PAGE 67), FRESH BERRY CRUMB CAKE (PAGE 68), VERY CHOCOLATE BUNDT CAKE WITH DARK CHOCOLATE GANACHE FROSTING (PAGE 72), ALMOND BUTTER CAKE (OPPOSITE)

then continue cooking until the syrup turns golden, about 5 minutes. Remove from the heat.

While the cake is still warm, use a skewer to poke holes all over the top of it. Gradually pour the soaking syrup over the cake in a few additions, waiting until it is absorbed each time before adding more.

Let the cake cool in the pan on a wire rack for 20 minutes more, then invert it onto another rack and let cool completely.

To make the glaze: In a medium bowl, whisk the confectioners' sugar and 7-Up together until smooth.

Pour the glaze over the top of the cake, letting it run down the sides. Sprinkle with lemon and lime zest, if desired.

The cake can be stored in an airtight container at room temperature for up to 3 days.

Almond Butter Cake

PICTURED OPPOSITE

Almonds have a warm, buttery taste, but it's their texture that is so appealing when the nuts are used in baked goods. This cake is deliciously rich and ultra-moist inside, with just the right amount of crunch on the outside from toasted almonds. I add a little bit of almond extract to amplify the almond flavor.

SERVES 12

1 cup (96 g) sliced unblanched almonds

2 cups (250 g) unbleached all-purpose flour

2 cups (400 g) granulated sugar

1 teaspoon (4 g) baking powder, preferably aluminum-free

½ teaspoon (3 g) baking soda

1 teaspoon fine sea salt

12 tablespoons (1½ sticks/170 g) unsalted butter, melted

2 large (100 g) eggs, at room temperature

1 cup (237 ml) buttermilk

1 teaspoon pure vanilla extract

½ teaspoon pure almond extract

Position a rack in the middle of the oven and preheat the oven to 350°F (175°C). Butter a 9-by-2-inch (23 by 5 cm) round cake pan, then line the bottom with parchment and butter it as well. Lightly dust the pan with flour, tapping the pan on the counter to shake out the excess.

Spread the almonds in a single layer on a baking sheet and bake for about 5 minutes, until lightly toasted. Set aside to cool completely.

In a large bowl, whisk together the flour, sugar, baking powder, baking soda, and salt. Stir in ½ cup (48 g) of the toasted almonds.

In a medium bowl, combine the butter, eggs, buttermilk, vanilla extract, and almond extract and stir to blend. Fold this mixture into the dry ingredients with a rubber spatula.

Pour the batter into the prepared pan and smooth the top. Sprinkle the remaining ½ cup (48 g) toasted almonds on top of the batter. Bake for 45 to 50 minutes, or until a cake tester inserted in the center of the cake comes out clean.

Let the cake cool in the pan on a wire rack for 20 minutes, then invert it onto another rack, peel off the parchment, turn right side up, and let cool completely.

The cake can be stored in an airtight container at room temperature for up to 3 days.

Very Chocolate Bundt Cake with Dark Chocolate Ganache Frosting

PICTURED ON PAGE 70

Moist and decadent, this cake is guaranteed to satisfy all of your chocolate cravings. Choose your favorite coffee blend for this recipe. Coffee elevates the flavor of chocolate, giving it more complexity. Depending on the coffee you select, the cake may have a hint of fruit, honey, caramel, or floral notes.

SERVES 12

FOR THE CAKE PAN

1 tablespoon unsalted butter, melted

1 tablespoon Dutch-processed cocoa powder

FOR THE CAKE

1¾ cups (219 g) unbleached all-purpose flour

¾ cup (60 g) Dutch-processed cocoa powder

2 cups (400 g) granulated sugar

1½ teaspoons (7 g) baking powder, preferably aluminum-free

1½ teaspoons (8 g) baking soda

1 teaspoon fine sea salt

1 cup (237 ml) hot strong brewed coffee

3 large (150 g) eggs

½ cup (118 ml) vegetable oil

1 cup (237 ml) buttermilk

2 teaspoons pure vanilla extract

FOR THE DARK CHOCOLATE GANACHE FROSTING

½ cup (118 ml) heavy cream

4 tablespoons (57 g) unsalted butter, cut into 1-inch (3 cm) cubes

3 tablespoons granulated sugar

Pinch of fine sea salt

½ pound (227 g) dark chocolate, chopped

2 tablespoons hot strong brewed coffee

½ teaspoon pure vanilla extract

A splash or two of whole milk, if needed

Position a rack in the middle of the oven and preheat the oven to 350°F (175°C).

To prepare the cake pan: In a small bowl, stir together the melted butter and cocoa to make a thick paste. Using a pastry brush, coat the inside of a 10-inch (25 cm) Bundt pan, making sure to get into all the crevices. If the paste starts to thicken too much as you work, warm it in the microwave for about 10 seconds and then continue. Set aside. (The coating will set while you mix your batter.)

To make the cake: In a large bowl, whisk together the flour, cocoa, sugar, baking powder, baking soda, and salt. Add the hot coffee and whisk until completely combined. Add the eggs, oil, buttermilk, and vanilla and whisk until completely incorporated.

Pour the batter into the prepared pan. Bake for about 40 minutes, until a cake tester inserted in the center of the cake comes out clean. Let the cake cool in the pan on a wire rack for 20 minutes, then invert it onto another rack and let cool completely.

To make the ganache: Combine the cream, butter, sugar, and salt in a heatproof bowl set over a saucepan of simmering water (do not let the bottom of the bowl touch the water) and stir frequently until the butter is melted. Add the chocolate and stir until it is about 80 percent melted.

Remove the bowl from the heat and stir until the chocolate is completely melted and the mixture is smooth. Add the coffee and vanilla, stirring until the ganache is smooth and shiny. (If you have overheated the chocolate, the ganache may have separated or broken and will be dull and lumpy, and this is not what you want to serve to your guests. If that happens, return the bowl to the heat, add a splash or two of whole milk, and whisk briskly to return the ganache to its shining glory.) Then stir occasionally as the ganache cools and thickens enough to frost your cake. Making the perfect ganache cannot be rushed; resist the urge to refrigerate it or whisk it faster to cool it.

To frost the cake: Pile the ganache frosting onto the center of the cake and spread it evenly over the top, letting it drip down the sides. The cake can be stored in an airtight container at room temperature for up to 3 days.

Banana Chocolate Cake

Banana and chocolate is such a happy pairing of flavors. Here they come together in a Bundt cake that is easy to make and serves a lot of folks. Bundt cakes are also pretty enough to display on a table for guests for any occasion or holiday.

SERVES 12

3 cups (375 g) unbleached all-purpose flour

2½ teaspoons (11 g) baking powder, preferably aluminum-free

1 teaspoon (6 g) baking soda

¾ teaspoon fine sea salt

½ teaspoon ground cardamom

2 cups (450 g) mashed very ripe bananas (about 5 bananas)

½ cup (120 g) sour cream

½ cup (118 ml) whole milk

1 tablespoon pure vanilla extract

12 tablespoons (1½ sticks/170 g) unsalted butter

1 cup (200 g) granulated sugar

¾ cup (150 g) packed light brown sugar

3 large (150 g) eggs, at room temperature

½ cup (85 g) semisweet chocolate chunks

Position a rack in the lower third of the oven and preheat the oven to 350°F (175°C). Butter a 10-inch (25 cm) tube pan, then line the bottom with a ring of parchment and butter it as well. Lightly dust the pan with flour, tapping the pan on the counter to shake out the excess.

In a large bowl, whisk together the flour, baking powder, baking soda, salt, and cardamom. Set aside.

In a medium bowl, mash the bananas, sour cream, milk, and vanilla together. Set aside.

In the bowl of a stand mixer fitted with the paddle attachment (or in a large mixing bowl, using a handheld mixer), beat the butter and both sugars until light and fluffy, 3 to 5 minutes. Add the eggs one (50 g) at a time, beating well after each addition, then mix for 2 minutes, until light and fluffy again. Add the banana mixture, mixing until just combined.

On low speed, add the flour mixture in thirds, beating until combined and scraping down the sides and bottom of the bowl with a rubber spatula as necessary. Remove the bowl from the mixer stand (if using) and fold in the chocolate chunks.

Pour the batter into the prepared pan and smooth the top with a spatula. Tap the pan firmly on the countertop to remove any air bubbles from the batter. Bake for 50 to 65 minutes, until a cake tester inserted in the center of the cake comes out clean.

Let the cake cool in the pan on a wire rack for 20 minutes, then invert it onto another rack, remove the parchment, and let cool completely.

The cake can be stored in an airtight container at room temperature for up to 3 days.

Lemon Poppy Seed Cake with Lemon Buttermilk Frosting

This cake is light and fluffy, thanks to the whipped egg whites folded into the batter. The sour cream makes it super moist, and the poppy seeds add great texture. Top it off with a lemon buttermilk frosting for an irresistible finish.

SERVES 12

FOR THE CAKE

2 cups (250 g) unbleached all-purpose flour

1 teaspoon (4 g) baking powder, preferably aluminum-free

1 teaspoon (6 g) baking soda

½ teaspoon fine sea salt

½ pound (2 sticks/227 g) unsalted butter, at room temperature

1 cup (200 g) granulated sugar

1 tablespoon grated lemon zest (from 1 medium lemon)

3 large (150 g) eggs, separated

1 teaspoon pure vanilla extract

1 tablespoon poppy seeds

1 cup (240 g) sour cream

¼ cup (59 ml) fresh lemon juice

FOR THE LEMON BUTTERMILK FROSTING

½ pound (2 sticks/227 g) unsalted butter, at room temperature

½ teaspoon pure vanilla extract

1 teaspoon grated lemon zest

½ teaspoon fine sea salt

3 cups (375 g) confectioners' sugar

¼ cup (59 ml) buttermilk

To make the cake: Position a rack in the lower third of the oven and preheat the oven to 350°F (175°C). Butter a 10-inch (25 cm) Bundt or tube pan, making sure to get into all the crevices. Lightly dust the pan with flour, tapping the pan on the counter to shake out the excess.

Sift together the flour, baking powder, baking soda, and salt into a medium bowl. Set aside.

In the bowl of a stand mixer fitted with the paddle attachment (or in a large mixing bowl, using a handheld mixer), cream the butter, sugar, and zest together until light and fluffy, 3 to 5 minutes. Add the egg yolks and vanilla and mix until combined. Turn the speed down to low, add one-third of the flour mixture, and mix until just combined. Add the poppy seeds and sour cream and mix until combined. Gradually add the remaining flour mixture in two additions, alternating with the lemon juice and beginning and ending with the flour; scrape down the sides and bottom of the bowl with a rubber spatula as necessary. If using a stand mixer, transfer the batter to another large bowl (unless you have a second mixer bowl), thoroughly wash and dry the mixer bowl, and reattach to the mixer stand; switch the paddle attachment for the whisk attachment.

In the bowl of the stand mixer (or in a large mixing bowl, using the handheld mixer with clean beaters), whip the egg whites until they hold stiff peaks, about 2 minutes. Gently fold about one-quarter of the egg whites into the batter to lighten it, then fold in the remaining whites until they are incorporated and no white streaks are visible.

Scrape the batter into the prepared pan and spread it evenly with a spatula. Bake for 45 to 50 minutes, until a cake tester inserted in the center of the cake comes out clean. Let the cake cool in the pan on a wire rack for 20 minutes, then invert it onto another rack and let cool completely.

Meanwhile, make the frosting: In the bowl of the stand mixer fitted with the paddle attachment (or in a large mixing bowl, using the handheld mixer), cream the butter, vanilla, lemon zest, and salt together on medium speed for 2 to 3 minutes, until light and fluffy. Turn the speed down to low and gradually add the confectioners' sugar, mixing until combined. Gradually add the buttermilk, mixing

until incorporated, then continue beating until the frosting has thickened and is light and creamy.

Transfer the cake to a serving plate and frost with the frosting.

The cake can be stored in an airtight container at room temperature for up to 2 days.

Lemon Blueberry Cake

Southerners have a long blueberry growing season that lasts from spring to late summer, and fresh berries make all the difference in this cake. Studded with the sweet berries, it is topped with a piquant lemon glaze.

SERVES 12

FOR THE CAKE

2½ cups (313 g) unbleached all-purpose flour

2 teaspoons (9 g) baking powder, preferably aluminum-free

½ teaspoon (3 g) baking soda

½ teaspoon fine sea salt

1 tablespoon Citrus Paste (page 383), made with lemons

¼ cup (59 ml) buttermilk

2 teaspoons pure vanilla extract

½ pound (2 sticks/227 g) unsalted butter, at room temperature

2 cups (400 g) granulated sugar

3 large (150 g) eggs, at room temperature

1 cup (240 g) sour cream, at room temperature

1½ cups (218 g) fresh blueberries

FOR THE LEMON GLAZE

2 cups (250 g) confectioners' sugar

Juice of 1 lemon

1 tablespoon unsalted butter, at room temperature

To make the cake: Position a rack in the middle of the oven and preheat the oven to 350°F (175°C). Spray a 10-inch (25 cm) Bundt pan with nonstick spray, making sure to get into all the crevices.

Sift together the flour, baking powder, baking soda, salt, and citrus paste into a large bowl. Set aside.

In a large measuring cup or small bowl, mix together the buttermilk and vanilla.

In the bowl of a stand mixer fitted with the paddle attachment (or in a large mixing bowl, using a handheld mixer), cream the butter and sugar together on medium-high speed for 4 to 5 minutes, until light and fluffy. Add the eggs one (50 g) at a time, mixing well after each addition and scraping down the sides and bottom of the bowl with a rubber spatula as necessary. Add the sour cream and mix until just blended, about 1 minute.

With the mixer on low speed, add the flour mixture in thirds, alternating with the buttermilk mixture and beginning and ending with the flour. Gently fold in the blueberries.

Scrape the batter into the prepared pan and spread it evenly with a spatula. Bake for 50 to 60 minutes, until a cake tester inserted in the center of the cake comes out clean. Let the cake cool in the pan on a wire rack for 20 minutes, then invert it onto another rack and let cool completely.

To make the glaze: In a small bowl, whisk the confectioners' sugar, lemon juice, and butter together until smooth.

Spread the glaze evenly over the top of the cooled cake.

The cake can be stored in an airtight container at room temperature for up to 3 days.

Three-Citrus Cake

PICTURED ON PAGE 79

The South is blessed during the winter months with many different varieties of citrus, which come into season just when you need a little boost from the cold weather. Neighbors happily share their bounty from satsuma, Meyer lemon, and lime trees, and if yours do so, you can return the favor with this cake. You can be creative, using whatever citrus you have available. The almond paste gives the cake a delicious texture and adds a sweet floral quality.

SERVES 12

FOR THE CAKE

2¼ cups (281 g) cake flour (not self-rising)

1½ teaspoons (7 g) baking powder, preferably
   aluminum-free

¼ teaspoon fine sea salt

½ cup (118 ml) whole milk

1 teaspoon pure vanilla extract

⅔ cup (155 g) almond paste

1 cup (200 g) granulated sugar

2 teaspoons grated orange zest

1 teaspoon grated lemon zest

½ teaspoon grated lime zest

½ pound (2 sticks/(227 g) unsalted butter, cut into
   1-inch (3 cm) cubes, at room temperature

4 large (200 g) eggs

FOR THE CITRUS GLAZE

¾ cup (94 g) confectioners' sugar

1 tablespoon unsalted butter, melted and cooled

½ teaspoon grated orange zest

½ teaspoon grated lemon zest

¼ teaspoon grated lime zest

1 tablespoon fresh orange juice

To make the cake: Position a rack in the lower third of the oven and preheat the oven to 350°F (175°C). Butter a 10-inch (25 cm) Bundt or tube pan, making sure to get into all the crevices. Lightly dust the pan with flour, tapping the pan on the counter to shake out the excess.

In a large bowl, whisk together the flour, baking powder, and salt. Set aside.

In a large measuring cup or small bowl, combine the milk and vanilla. Set aside.

In the bowl of a stand mixer fitted with the paddle attachment (or in a large mixing bowl, using a handheld mixer), beat the almond paste on low speed for about 1 minute, just to break it up. With the mixer on low speed, gradually add the sugar and orange, lemon, and lime zests, mixing until completely incorporated.

With the mixer still on low speed, gradually add the pieces of butter, mixing until incorporated and scraping down the sides and bottom of the bowl with a rubber spatula as necessary. Increase the speed to medium-high and mix for about 4 minutes, until the butter mixture is light and fluffy. Add the eggs one (50 g) at a time, beating well after each addition and scraping down the sides and bottom of the bowl as necessary. With the mixer on low speed, add the flour mixture in two additions, alternating with the milk mixture, and scraping down the sides and bottom of the bowl. Mix for another 30 seconds or so, until the batter is thoroughly mixed.

Scrape the batter into the prepared pan and spread it evenly with a spatula. Bake for 55 minutes, or until a cake tester inserted in the center of the cake comes out clean. Let the cake cool in the pan on a wire rack for 20 minutes, then invert it onto another rack and let cool completely.

To make the glaze: In a small bowl, whisk the confectioners' sugar, butter, orange, lemon, and lime zests, and orange juice together until smooth.

Transfer the cake to a serving plate. Using a pastry brush, generously coat the top and sides with the glaze. The cake can be stored in an airtight container at room temperature for up to 3 days.

Brown Sugar Spice Cake with Butterscotch Glaze

This cake could not be any simpler to make or more delicious to eat. It is rich and moist with a tender, delicate crumb. The aroma as it bakes will fill your kitchen with the scent of autumn.

SERVES 12

FOR THE CAKE

2¼ cups (281 g) unbleached all-purpose flour

½ teaspoon (3 g) baking soda

½ teaspoon fine sea salt

½ teaspoon ground cardamom

¼ teaspoon ground mace

½ pound (2 sticks/227 g) unsalted butter, at room temperature

2 cups (400 g) packed light brown sugar

1 teaspoon pure vanilla extract

3 large (150 g) eggs, at room temperature

1 cup (240 g) sour cream

FOR THE BUTTERSCOTCH GLAZE

7 tablespoons (99 g) unsalted butter

1 cup (200 g) packed light brown sugar

1 cup (237 ml) heavy cream

To make the cake: Position a rack in the lower third of the oven and preheat the oven to 325°F (165°C). Butter a 10-inch (25 cm) Bundt pan, making sure to get into all the crevices. Lightly dust the pan with flour, tapping the pan on the counter to shake out the excess.

Sift together the flour, baking soda, salt, cardamom, and mace into a medium bowl. Set aside.

In the bowl of a stand mixer fitted with the paddle attachment (or in a large mixing bowl, using a handheld mixer), cream the butter and brown sugar together on medium-low speed for 3 to 5 minutes, until light and fluffy. Add the vanilla and mix to combine. Add the eggs one (50 g) at a time, beating well after each addition. Add the flour mixture in thirds, alternating with the sour cream, beginning and ending with the flour and scraping down the sides and bottom of the bowl with a rubber spatula as necessary, then mix for about 1 minute, or until well blended.

Remove the bowl from the mixer stand (if using) and, using the spatula, incorporate any ingredients hiding at the bottom of the bowl, making sure the batter is completely mixed.

Pour the batter into the prepared pan. Tap the pan firmly on the countertop to remove any air bubbles from the batter. Bake for 60 to 75 minutes, until a cake tester inserted in the center of the cake comes out clean. Let the cake cool in the pan on a wire rack for 15 minutes, then invert it onto another rack, turn right side up, and cool completely.

To make the glaze: In a medium saucepan, combine the butter, brown sugar, and cream and cook over medium heat, stirring, until the sugar has completely dissolved. Then bring to a boil and cook until the glaze has thickened, about 5 minutes. Remove from the heat and let cool slightly.

Set the cake, still on the rack, on a baking sheet, and pour the glaze over the cake, letting it run down the sides.

The cake can be stored in an airtight container at room temperature for up to 3 days.

OPPOSITE: THREE-CITRUS CAKE (PAGE 76)

Cold-Oven Pound Cake

PICTURED ON PAGE 84

Recipes for pound cakes started in a cold oven first appeared in advertising campaigns designed to entice homemakers into replacing their wood-fired ovens with the gas stoves that were being introduced to the American market in the early twentieth century. (Imagine having to stoke a fire just to bake a cake and wait for the temperature to be just right! It's no wonder Southern bakers had baking prowess.) The thought of a cooler kitchen in the hot summers was appealing to bakers. You simply mixed the batter and placed the cake pan in a cold oven, then turned the oven on; pound cakes are so dense, they don't need the usual initial blast of high heat.

This cake bakes slowly as the temperature of the oven rises, which allows more time for the leavening agents to lift the cake. It has a fine delicate crumb and develops a thin golden crust that is unlike that of any other cake.

SERVES 12 TO 16

3½ cups (438 g) unbleached all-purpose flour
1 teaspoon (4 g) baking powder, preferably
    aluminum-free
1 teaspoon fine sea salt
1½ cups (355 ml) whole milk
2 teaspoons pure vanilla extract
3 sticks (340 g) unsalted butter, at room temperature
3 cups (600 g) granulated sugar
6 large (300 g) eggs, at room temperature
Confectioners' sugar for dusting (optional)

Butter a 10-inch (25 cm) Bundt pan, making sure to get into all the crevices. Lightly dust the pan with flour, tapping the pan on the counter to shake out the excess.

In a large bowl, whisk together the flour, baking powder, and salt. Set aside.

In a large measuring cup or small bowl, mix together the milk and vanilla.

In the bowl of a stand mixer fitted with the paddle attachment (or in a large mixing bowl, using a handheld mixer), cream the butter on medium-high speed until very light and fluffy, about 3 minutes. Turn the speed down to low and gradually add the sugar. Then increase the speed to medium-high and continue beating for 2 to 3 minutes, until the mixture is very light and fluffy. Reduce the speed to low again and add the eggs one (50 g) at a time, beating well after each addition and scraping down the sides and bottom of the bowl with a rubber spatula as necessary. Add the flour mixture in thirds, alternating with the milk mixture, beginning and ending with the flour and scraping down the sides and bottom of the bowl as necessary.

Remove the bowl from the mixer stand (if using) and, using the rubber spatula, incorporate any ingredients hiding at the bottom of the bowl, making sure the batter is completely mixed.

Pour the batter into the prepared pan and spread evenly with a spatula. Place the pan on the middle rack of the cold oven and set the oven temperature to 325°F (165°C).

Bake for 60 to 70 minutes, until the cake is golden on top; a cake tester inserted in the center should come out clean. Let the cake cool in the pan on a wire rack for 20 minutes, then invert it onto another rack, turn right side up, and let cool completely.

Dust the cooled cake generously with confectioners' sugar, if desired.

The cake can be stored in an airtight container at room temperature for up to 5 days.

Chocolate Pound Cake

This cake includes some of the most popular ingredients in the Southern pantry—buttermilk, coffee, and chocolate—which means you can easily whip it up on a whim. The pleasing tang of buttermilk balances the rich dark flavor of the chocolate. This cake travels well, and it is even better the next day.

SERVES 12

¾ cup (94 g) cake flour (not self-rising)

6 tablespoons (47 g) unbleached all-purpose flour

6 tablespoons (30 g) Dutch-processed cocoa powder

1 teaspoon (4 g) baking powder, preferably aluminum-free

¾ teaspoon (4 g) baking soda

½ teaspoon fine sea salt

½ cup (118 ml) buttermilk

½ cup (118 ml) strong brewed coffee, cooled

1½ teaspoons pure vanilla extract

11½ ounces (326 g) dark chocolate (64 to 70% cacao), coarsely chopped (about 1¾ cups)

10 tablespoons (1¼ sticks/142 g) unsalted butter, at room temperature

1 cup plus 2 tablespoons (225 g) granulated sugar

3 large (150 g) eggs, at room temperature

Position a rack in the middle of the oven and preheat the oven to 350°F (175°C). Lightly spray a 9-by-5-inch (23 by 13 cm) loaf pan with nonstick spray. Line the pan with parchment, leaving an overhang on two opposite sides.

In a large bowl, whisk together both flours, the cocoa powder, baking powder, baking soda, and salt. Set aside.

In a large measuring cup or small bowl, combine the buttermilk, coffee, and vanilla. Set aside.

In a heatproof bowl set over a saucepan of simmering water (do not let the bottom of the bowl touch the water), melt ¾ cup (140 g) of the chocolate, stirring until smooth and glossy. Remove from the heat and set aside.

In the bowl of a stand mixer fitted with the paddle attachment (or in a large mixing bowl, using a handheld mixer), cream the butter and sugar together on medium-high speed for 3 to 5 minutes, until light and fluffy. Add the eggs one (50 g) at a time, beating well after each addition and scraping down the sides and bottom of the bowl with a rubber spatula as necessary. With the mixer on low speed, add the flour mixture in thirds, mixing until just combined.

Gradually add the buttermilk-coffee mixture to the egg mixture, mixing until just combined; scrape down the sides and bottom of the bowl as necessary. With the mixer on low, add the melted chocolate. Remove the bowl from the mixer stand (if using) and fold in the remaining chopped chocolate.

Scrape the batter into the prepared pan and gently smooth the top with a spatula. Tap the pan firmly on the counter to remove any air bubbles. Bake for 25 to 28 minutes, until a cake tester inserted in the center of the cake comes out clean.

Using the parchment "handles," remove the loaf from the pan and set it on a wire rack to cool slightly before slicing into wedges. Serve warm or cold; it's delicious either way.

The cake can be stored in an airtight container at room temperature for up to 3 days.

Angel Food Cake with Whipped Cream and Berries

This cake is light and airy and as delicate as can be. Taking the time to whip the egg whites just right (in a very clean bowl) is the key to success when making an angel food cake. Serve with fresh berries and big dollops of sweetened whipped cream.

SERVES 12 TO 16

1⅓ cups (167 g) cake flour (not self-rising)

2 cups (400 g) granulated sugar

½ teaspoon fine sea salt

1½ cups (355 ml) large egg whites, at room temperature

1 teaspoon cream of tartar

2 teaspoons pure vanilla extract

1 recipe Chantilly Cream (page 373) for serving

Fresh berries for serving

Position a rack in the lower third of the oven and preheat the oven to 350°F (175°C). Have an ungreased 10-inch (25 cm) tube pan ready.

Sift together the flour, ½ cup (100 g) of the sugar, and the salt into a small bowl, then repeat two more times. Set aside.

In the *impeccably* clean bowl of a stand mixer fitted with the whisk attachment (or in a large clean mixing bowl, using a handheld mixer), beat the egg whites and cream of tartar on medium speed until frothy, about 2 minutes. Beating on high speed, add the remaining 1½ cups (300 g) sugar 1 tablespoon at a time, then beat until the egg whites are stiff and shiny. Beat in the vanilla. Remove the bowl from the mixer stand (if using).

Gently but thoroughly fold the flour mixture about one-quarter at a time into the egg whites. Spoon the batter into the tube pan. (Don't be tempted to smack the pan against the kitchen counter to level the batter; you want to retain all of that air you just incorporated into your egg whites.)

Bake for 35 to 40 minutes, until the top is golden brown and a cake tester inserted in the center of the cake comes out clean. Invert the cake pan onto its feet on the counter. (If the pan does not have feet, invert it over a long-necked bottle, such as a wine bottle.) Cooling the cake upside down prevents it from deflating. Let cool completely, about 1 hour.

Run a knife around the edges of the pan and the center tube to release the cake with ease and invert it onto a wire rack, then place top side up on a serving platter. Serve with the Chantilly cream and berries.

The cake can be stored in an airtight container at room temperature for up to 3 days.

Sweet Potato Cake

PICTURED ON PAGE 85

Roasting sweet potatoes brings out their natural sugars, which give this sweet loaf cake caramel undertones. Spiced with the warm aromatic flavors of cinnamon, nutmeg, and cloves, along with the citrus note of orange zest, and topped with chocolate ganache, this loaf cake is perfect for an afternoon snack.

SERVES 12

1 pound (454 g) sweet potatoes (1 large or 2 small
    potatoes), peeled and cut into 1-inch (3 cm) cubes

2½ cups (313 g) unbleached all-purpose flour

1 teaspoon (4 g) baking powder, preferably
    aluminum-free

½ teaspoon (3 g) baking soda

1½ teaspoons fine sea salt

2 teaspoons ground cinnamon

½ teaspoon freshly grated nutmeg

¼ teaspoon ground cloves

2 large (100 g) eggs, at room temperature

Grated zest of 1 orange

1 teaspoon pure vanilla extract

1½ cups plus 1 tablespoon (313 g) granulated sugar

1 cup (237 ml) vegetable oil

1 recipe Dark Chocolate Ganache (page 175)

Position a rack in the middle of the oven and preheat the oven to 400°F (205°C). Line a baking sheet with parchment.

Spread the sweet potato cubes on the prepared baking sheet and cover with aluminum foil. Roast the sweet potatoes for about 50 minutes, until fork-tender. Set the baking sheet on a wire rack to cool. Turn the oven down to 325°F (165°C).

Transfer the sweet potatoes to a bowl and mash them with a potato masher or a fork until smooth. Measure out 2 cups (250 g) for this loaf. (*The sweet potatoes can be prepared up to 3 days in advance and stored in an airtight container in the refrigerator.*)

Lightly spray a 9-by-5-inch (23 by 13 cm) loaf pan with nonstick spray. Line the pan with parchment, leaving an overhang on two opposite sides.

In a medium bowl, whisk together the flour, baking powder, baking soda, salt, cinnamon, nutmeg, and cloves. Set aside.

In a large bowl, whisk the mashed sweet potatoes, eggs, orange zest, vanilla, and sugar together until smooth. Gradually add the oil, whisking until completely combined.

Add half of the dry ingredients and fold gently until just combined. Repeat with the rest of the flour mixture, using as few strokes as possible; do not overmix, but make sure there is no longer any flour visible.

Pour the batter into the prepared pan and smooth the top with a spatula. Bake for 70 to 80 minutes, until the top of the cake is golden and a cake tester inserted in the center comes out clean.

Using the parchment "handles," remove the loaf from the pan and set it on a wire rack. Let cool completely before piling the ganache onto the center of the cake and spreading it evenly over the top, letting it drip down the sides.

The cake can be stored in an airtight container at room temperature for up to 3 days.

OPPOSITE: COLD-OVEN POUND CAKE (PAGE 80)
ABOVE: SWEET POTATO CAKE (PAGE 83)

Orange Date Cake with Orange Glaze

Dates have been a staple ingredient in Middle Eastern cooking for thousands of years, but date palm trees are also cultivated in South Florida. This cake combines the golden caramel sweetness of dates with the bright flavor of juicy oranges for an old-fashioned Southern-style dessert.

SERVES 12

FOR THE CAKE

2 cups (250 g) unbleached all-purpose flour

½ teaspoon (3 g) baking soda

½ teaspoon fine sea salt

½ teaspoon ground cinnamon

8 tablespoons (1 stick/113 g) unsalted butter, at room temperature

1 cup (200 g) granulated sugar

2 large (150 g) eggs

1 tablespoon grated orange zest (from 1 large orange)

1 teaspoon pure vanilla extract

⅔ cup (158 ml) buttermilk

1 cup (145 g) chopped pitted dates

½ cup (57 g) pecans, coarsely chopped

FOR THE ORANGE GLAZE

1 cup (125 g) confectioners' sugar

1 tablespoon grated orange zest (from 1 large orange)

¼ cup (59 ml) fresh orange juice

To make the cake: Position a rack in the middle of the oven and preheat the oven to 350°F (175°C). Butter a 10-inch (25 cm) Bundt pan, making sure to get into all the crevices. Lightly dust the pan with flour, tapping the pan on the counter to shake out the excess.

Sift together the flour, baking soda, salt, and cinnamon into a medium bowl. Set aside.

In the bowl of a stand mixer fitted with the paddle attachment (or in a large mixing bowl, using a handheld mixer), cream the butter and sugar together for 3 to 5 minutes, until light and fluffy. Add the eggs one (50 g) at a time, mixing well after each addition. Add the orange zest and vanilla and mix just to combine. With the mixer on low speed, add the flour mixture in thirds, alternating with the buttermilk and beginning and ending with the flour, mixing until just combined; scrape down the sides and bottom of the bowl with a rubber spatula as necessary.

Remove the bowl from the mixer stand (if using) and, using the rubber spatula, incorporate any ingredients hiding at the bottom of the bowl, making sure the batter is completely mixed. Gently fold in the dates and pecans.

Scrape the batter into the prepared pan. Tap the pan firmly on the countertop to remove any air bubbles from the batter.

Bake for 40 to 45 minutes, until a cake tester inserted in the center of the cake comes out clean. Let the cake cool in the pan on a wire rack for 15 minutes, then invert it onto another rack and let cool completely.

To make the glaze: In a small bowl, whisk the confectioners' sugar, orange zest, and orange juice together until smooth and silky.

Let the glaze cool slightly, then pour over the cooled cake, letting it drip down the sides.

The cake can be stored in an airtight container at room temperature for up to 3 days.

Rum-Raisin Milk Punch Cake

Milk punch is an old-fashioned drink that is popular at Christmastime in the South. Like eggnog, milk punch is spiked with a spirit like brandy, bourbon, or rum and sprinkled with freshly grated nutmeg. This cake, which plays on those flavors and includes some boozy golden raisins as well as eggnog, is a great addition to any holiday sideboard.

SERVES 12

½ cup (73 g) golden raisins

3 tablespoons dark rum

1 teaspoon pure vanilla extract

3 cups (375 g) unbleached all-purpose flour

2 teaspoons (9 g) baking powder, preferably
    aluminum-free

¼ teaspoon fine sea salt

¼ teaspoon ground cardamom

¼ teaspoon freshly grated nutmeg

½ pound (2 sticks/227 g) unsalted butter, at room
    temperature

2 cups (400 g) granulated sugar

3 large (150 g) eggs

1 cup (237 ml) eggnog

In a small bowl, combine the raisins with the rum and vanilla. Set aside to soak for at least 30 minutes.

Position a rack in the middle of the oven and preheat the oven to 350°F (175°C). Butter a 10-inch (25 cm) Bundt pan, then lightly dust the pan with flour, tapping the pan on the counter to shake out the excess.

In a large bowl, whisk together the flour, baking powder, salt, cardamom, and nutmeg. Set aside.

In the bowl of a stand mixer fitted with the paddle attachment (or in a large mixing bowl, using a handheld mixer), cream the butter and sugar together on medium-high speed for about 5 minutes, until light and fluffy. Add the eggs one (50 g) at a time, beating well after each addition and scraping down the sides and bottom of the bowl with a rubber spatula as necessary.

With the mixer on low speed, add the flour mixture in thirds, alternating with the eggnog and beginning and ending with the flour, mixing until just combined; scrape down the sides and bottom of the bowl as necessary. Fold in the rum raisins, along with any remaining liquid.

Remove the bowl from the mixer stand (if using) and, using the rubber spatula, incorporate any ingredients hiding at the bottom of the bowl, making sure the batter is completely mixed. Pour the batter into the prepared pan. Tap the pan firmly on the countertop to remove any air bubbles from the batter.

Bake for 50 to 60 minutes, until a cake tester inserted in the center of the cake comes out clean. Let the cake cool in the pan on a wire rack for 15 minutes, then invert it onto another rack and let cool completely.

The cake can be stored in an airtight container at room temperature for up to 3 days.

Muffins and Scones

MUFFINS AND SCONES are found in various baking cultures; what turns them into Southern fare are the ingredients typically used: cornmeal, pecans, sorghum, cane syrup, apples, peaches, citrus, and seasonal fresh berries. And nutmeg, mace, and cardamom—spices that are always in a Southern pantry—can be incorporated into muffin and scone batters to turn the prosaic into something extraordinary.

Thanks to quick-acting leavenings like baking powder and baking soda, it's easy to make a batch of muffins or scones and serve them hot. Mixing muffins calls for a light touch, and learning not to overmix the batter is the key to the perfect delicate bite. Bake the muffins right away, or refrigerate the batter overnight and then bake them fresh the next morning.

If you've traveled anywhere in the South, you've likely picked up some of our best ingredients, from stone-ground grits to pecans to sorghum syrup. And all can be put to good use in your own muffins or scones. Try your hand at Spiced Apple Crisp Muffins; Red, White, and Blue Muffins; and Lemon Poppy Seed Muffins. Then make a batch of Cinnamon Swirl Buns or one of the scones, whether Bacon Cheddar or Lemon Coriander (or both).

Spiced Apple Crisp Muffins

PICTURED ON PAGE 88

Rome, Cameo, Honeycrisp, and Granny Smith apples are all excellent choices for this recipe. Or try an apple local to your region. Feel free to mix and match varieties, just like you would when making an apple pie. The apples are tossed with Angostura bitters and with black pepper, which accentuates the warm spices in the crisp topping. The brown sugar–oat mix adds crunch to these fall-season muffins.

MAKES 12 MUFFINS

FOR THE CRISP TOPPING

1 cup (90 g) old-fashioned rolled oats

¾ cup (94 g) unbleached all-purpose flour

¼ cup (50 g) packed light brown sugar

¼ teaspoon ground cinnamon

¼ teaspoon ground cardamom

¼ teaspoon fine sea salt

6 tablespoons (85 g) unsalted butter,
   melted and cooled slightly

FOR THE MUFFINS

3 apples (see headnote), peeled, cored, and diced
   (about 3 cups/480 g)

1 teaspoon fresh lemon juice

½ teaspoon Angostura bitters

¼ teaspoon coarsely ground black pepper

2 cups (250 g) unbleached all-purpose flour

1 cup (200 g) granulated sugar

1 tablespoon (13 g) baking powder, preferably
   aluminum-free

1 teaspoon fine sea salt

8 tablespoons (1 stick/113 g) unsalted butter, melted

¼ cup (59 ml) vegetable oil

2 large (100 g) eggs

¾ cup (177 ml) whole milk

1 teaspoon pure vanilla extract

Position a rack in the middle of the oven and preheat the oven to 375°F (190°C). Line 12 standard muffin cups with paper liners.

To make the crisp topping: In a medium bowl, combine the oats, flour, brown sugar, cinnamon, cardamom, and salt. Drizzle the butter over the top and toss together with a big spoon until incorporated. Now get in there with your hands and mix together until there are no dry ingredients remaining in the bottom of the bowl. The mixture should hold together in clumps of various sizes, from almond- to pea-sized bits. Set aside, uncovered, while you make the batter (this will help the topping dry out a bit so it will hold its shape better during baking).

To make the muffins: In a medium bowl, toss the apples with the lemon juice, Angostura bitters, and pepper; set aside. In a large mixing bowl, whisk together the flour, sugar, baking powder, and salt until thoroughly combined; set aside.

In a medium bowl, whisk the butter, vegetable oil, and eggs together until thoroughly blended and light in color. Whisk in the milk and vanilla.

Make a well in the center of the dry ingredients and gradually pour in the liquid ingredients, folding gently with a rubber spatula until just combined; use as few strokes as possible and don't overmix, or the muffins will be tough.

With a large ice cream scoop or spoon, scoop the batter into the prepared muffin cups, filling them approximately two-thirds full. Sprinkle the tops generously with the crisp topping.

Bake for 20 to 25 minutes, rotating the pan halfway through for even baking, until the muffins are golden brown. The tops should be firm to the touch and a toothpick inserted in the center of a muffin should come out clean. Remove from the oven and let cool in the pan on a wire rack for about 10 minutes.

Turn the muffins out of the pan and enjoy warm or at room temperature.

The muffins can be stored in an airtight container for up to 2 days.

Sweet Honey Corn Muffins

Corn muffins are delicious topped with honey butter that melts down the sides, but you can make them even sweeter by adding honey to the batter.

MAKES 12 MUFFINS

3½ cups (438 g) unbleached all-purpose flour

1½ cups (192 g) yellow cornmeal, plus more for sprinkling

2 tablespoons baking powder (26 g), preferably aluminum-free

¼ teaspoon (1 g) baking soda

¾ teaspoons fine sea salt

12 tablespoons (1½ sticks/170 g) unsalted butter, melted

3 cups (710 ml) buttermilk

3 large (150 g) eggs

¼ cup (59 ml) honey

2 cups (90 g) fresh corn kernels (from 3 to 4 ears) or two 15-ounce (425 g) cans corn kernels, drained

Position a rack in the middle of the oven and preheat the oven to 375°F (190°C). Generously grease 12 standard muffin cups or line with paper liners.

In a large mixing bowl, whisk the flour, cornmeal, baking powder, baking soda, and salt together until thoroughly combined.

In a medium bowl, whisk the melted butter, buttermilk, eggs, and honey together until thoroughly blended. Make a well in the center of the dry ingredients, pour in the liquid ingredients, and mix just until combined. Gently fold in the corn kernels, using as few strokes as possible; be careful not to overmix.

With a large ice cream scoop or spoon, scoop the batter into the prepared muffin cups, filling them approximately two-thirds full. Sprinkle the top of each one with about ½ teaspoon cornmeal.

Bake for 15 to 20 minutes, rotating the pan halfway through for even baking, until the muffins are golden brown. The tops of the muffins should be firm to the touch and a toothpick inserted in the center of a muffin should come out clean. Remove from the oven and let cool in the pan on a wire rack for about 10 minutes.

Turn the muffins out of the pan and enjoy warm or at room temperature.

The muffins can be stored in an airtight container for up to 2 days.

Peach Streusel Muffins

When the hottest summer months bring you peaches, you'll want to pick as many crates of them as you can. Then incorporate them into ice cream, cobbler, or these streusel muffins, or just eat them out of hand—over the sink. Here a batter filled with sweet chunky pieces of fruit is topped with a cinnamon–brown sugar streusel that really makes the muffins shine.

MAKES 12 LARGE MUFFINS

FOR THE STREUSEL

1½ cups (188 g) unbleached all-purpose flour

⅔ cup (133 g) packed light brown sugar

1½ teaspoons ground cinnamon

¼ teaspoon fine sea salt

4 tablespoons (57 g) cold unsalted butter, cut into ½-inch (1.5 cm) cubes

FOR THE MUFFINS

4 cups (500 g) unbleached all-purpose flour

1½ teaspoons (7 g) baking powder, preferably aluminum-free

2 teaspoons (11 g) baking soda

2 teaspoons fine sea salt

1 teaspoon ground cinnamon

1½ cups (300 g) granulated sugar

2 cups (472 ml) buttermilk

½ cup (118 ml) vegetable oil

2 large (100 g) eggs, at room temperature

1½ teaspoons pure vanilla extract

3 cups cubed (½-inch/1.5 cm) peeled fresh peaches (see sidebar) or cubed unthawed frozen peaches

Position a rack in the middle of the oven and preheat the oven to 375°F (190°C). Lightly spray 12 jumbo muffin cups with nonstick spray or line with paper liners.

(Continued on page 96)

HOW TO PEEL A PEACH

Peeling peaches can be a messy task, and sometimes you may choose not to peel them at all. Peach skins can actually be delicious, especially in pies that bake for a long time. But if you don't like the skins, here are a few tips.

The best way to remove the skin while preserving all the fruit is to blanch the peaches. Using a paring knife, cut a small X in the bottom of each peach. Fill a bowl with ice-cold water and set it next to the stove. Bring a pot of water to a rolling boil.

Carefully add the peaches a few at a time to the boiling water and blanch for 30 to 45 seconds. Remove the peaches with a slotted spoon and immediately dunk them into the ice bath for 10 to 20 seconds to stop the cooking, then remove from the ice water. Using the back of a paring knife, gently pull the skin at the X on each peach; the skin should easily peel away. If not, repeat the process, blanching the peaches for only 20 seconds this time.

To make the streusel: In a small bowl, combine the flour, brown sugar, cinnamon, and salt. Cut in the butter with a pastry blender until the crumbs are the size of peas. Set aside.

To make the muffins: In a large mixing bowl, whisk together the flour, baking powder, baking soda, salt, cinnamon, and sugar.

In a medium bowl, whisk together the buttermilk, oil, eggs, and vanilla.

Make a well in the center of the dry ingredients and gradually add the liquid ingredients, mixing with a rubber spatula until just combined. Gently fold in the peaches, using as few strokes as possible; be careful not to overmix.

With a large ice cream scoop or spoon, scoop the batter into the prepared muffin cups, filling them approximately two-thirds full. Sprinkle the tops with the streusel.

Bake for 25 to 30 minutes, rotating the pan halfway through the baking, until the muffins are golden brown. The tops should be firm to the touch and a toothpick inserted in the center of a muffin should come out clean. Remove from the oven and let cool in the pan on a wire rack for 10 minutes.

Turn the muffins out of the pan and enjoy warm or at room temperature.

The muffins can be stored in an airtight container for up to 2 days.

Strawberry and Cream Muffins

Strawberries are now available year-round, but April to June is their peak season. Pairing a strawberry batter with a cream cheese glaze makes these muffins reminiscent of strawberry shortcake.

MAKES 12 MUFFINS

FOR THE MUFFINS

2 cups (250 g) unbleached all-purpose flour

1 cup (200 g) granulated sugar

2 teaspoons (9 g) baking powder, preferably
    aluminum-free

1 teaspoon fine sea salt

2 large (100 g) eggs, at room temperature

⅔ cup (160 g) sour cream, at room temperature

½ cup (118 ml) vegetable oil

2 teaspoons pure vanilla extract

2 cups (300 g) strawberries, hulled and
    quartered if large, halved if smaller

FOR THE CREAM CHEESE GLAZE

¼ pound (113 g) cream cheese

1 cup (125 g) confectioners' sugar

1 teaspoon pure vanilla extract

3 to 4 tablespoons whole milk

To make the muffins: Position a rack in the middle of the oven and preheat the oven to 375°F (190°C). Line 12 standard muffin cups with paper liners.

In a large bowl, whisk together the flour, sugar, baking powder, and salt until thoroughly combined. Set aside.

In a medium bowl, whisk together the eggs, sour cream, oil, and vanilla.

Make a well in the center of the dry ingredients and gradually pour in the liquid ingredients, mixing with a rubber spatula until just combined. Gently fold in the strawberries, using as few strokes as possible; be careful not to overmix.

With a large ice cream scoop or spoon, scoop the batter into the prepared muffin cups, filling them approximately two-thirds full.

Bake for 25 to 30 minutes, rotating the pan halfway through the baking, until the muffins are golden brown. The tops should be firm to the touch

and a toothpick inserted in the center of a muffin should come out clean. Remove from the oven and let cool in the pan on a wire rack for about 10 minutes.

Turn the muffins onto the rack and let cool completely.

To make the glaze: In the bowl of a stand mixer fitted with the whisk attachment (or in a large mixing bowl, using a handheld mixer), beat the cream cheese until very smooth. Gradually add the confectioners' sugar, vanilla, and 3 tablespoons of the milk until combined. Add more milk to make a thinner glaze.

Drizzle the glaze over the tops of the muffins.

The muffins can be stored in an airtight container for up to 1 day.

Red, White, and Blue Muffins

PICTURED ON PAGE 102

The quintessential bakery muffins you dream of, bursting with berries and a crackled sugary top, are yours with this recipe. You could use just one type of berry, or a variety of any berries you like, especially when local berries are at their peak. Make these, and your house will be filled with the smells of summer. Out of season, you can use good-quality frozen berries (see sidebar), but don't thaw them before adding them to the batter. If you like, sprinkle the muffins with one of the flavored sugars on page 376 rather than regular sugar before baking.

MAKES 12 MUFFINS

2 cups (250 g) unbleached all-purpose flour

1 cup (200 g) granulated sugar, plus more for sprinkling

1 tablespoon (13 g) baking powder, preferably aluminum-free

½ teaspoon fine sea salt

¼ teaspoon ground cardamom

¼ cup (59 ml) vegetable oil

4 tablespoons (57 g) unsalted butter, melted

2 large (100 g) eggs

¾ cup (177 ml) whole milk

½ teaspoon pure vanilla extract

½ cup (85 g) fresh or frozen blueberries

½ cup (60 g) fresh or frozen raspberries

FREEZING SEASONAL FRUITS

Jams, preserves, and baked goods made with frozen fruit can taste just as good as those made with fresh fruit. If the fruit is picked at the height of the season and quickly frozen, it will keep well for 4 to 6 months, which means you can enjoy seasonal fruit all year long.

To freeze blueberries or blackberries that you pick yourself or buy in season at the farmers' market, first rinse them in a colander and then spread them out on paper towels to dry thoroughly. When they are dry, line a baking sheet with parchment and spread the berries out on the pan, leaving space between them, then place the pan in the freezer for about 30 minutes, until frozen. Then transfer the berries to ziplock freezer bags, mark with the date, and store in the freezer until ready to use.

Strawberries are also easy to freeze. You don't even have to wash them before freezing—just leave them in their little basket and put the whole thing in a ziplock freezer bag. It might seem counterintuitive, but if you don't wash them, you don't add any extra moisture, and they will keep longer. When you are ready to use them, defrost the strawberries in the fridge and clean and hull them. Stone fruits like cherries, peaches, plums, and apricots should be pitted before freezing. But don't worry about the skins; they will fall away after you defrost the fruit, a bonus for peaches especially, which otherwise can be difficult to peel. Freeze the fruits on baking sheets until solid, then put in large ziplock bags and seal, carefully releasing all the air, and mark with the weight as well as the date. Use still frozen for baking and for jams or preserves.

Position a rack in the middle of the oven and preheat the oven to 375°F (190°C). Line 12 standard muffin cups with paper liners.

In a large mixing bowl, whisk the flour, sugar, baking powder, salt, and cardamom together until thoroughly combined.

In a medium bowl, whisk together the vegetable oil, butter, eggs, milk, and vanilla. Make a well in the center of the dry ingredients, pour in the liquid ingredients, and mix until combined. Gently fold in the berries, using as few strokes as possible; be careful not to overmix.

With a large ice cream scoop or spoon, scoop the batter into the prepared muffin cups, filling them approximately two-thirds full. Sprinkle the tops with sugar.

Bake for 25 to 30 minutes, rotating the pan halfway through for even baking, until the muffins are golden brown. The tops should be firm to the touch and a toothpick inserted in the center of a muffin should come out clean. Remove from the oven and let cool in the pan on a wire rack for 10 minutes.

Turn the muffins out of the pan and enjoy warm or at room temperature.

The muffins can be stored in an airtight container for up to 2 days.

Chocolate Orange Muffins

Chocolate and orange is a classic flavor combination. Here chocolate chunks melt into an orange-zested batter as the muffins bake. Topping the muffins with an orange glaze makes them an extra-sweet treat.

MAKES 12 MUFFINS

FOR THE MUFFINS

3 cups (375 g) unbleached all-purpose flour

1½ teaspoons (7 g) baking powder, preferably
    aluminum-free

1½ teaspoons (8 g) baking soda

½ teaspoon fine sea salt

12 tablespoons (1½ sticks/170 g) unsalted butter, at room
    temperature

1½ cups (300 g) granulated sugar

3 large (150 g) eggs

2 teaspoons pure vanilla extract

Grated zest of 1 orange or 1 teaspoon Citrus Paste
    (page 383), made with oranges

1½ cups (360 g) sour cream, at room temperature

1 cup (6 ounces/170 g) dark chocolate chunks

FOR THE GLAZE

2 cups (250 g) confectioners' sugar

3 to 4 tablespoons fresh orange juice

To make the muffins: Position a rack in the middle of the oven and preheat the oven to 375°F (190°C). Line 12 standard muffin cups with paper liners.

In a large mixing bowl, whisk together the flour, baking powder, baking soda, and salt. Set aside.

In the bowl of a stand mixer fitted with the paddle attachment (or in a large mixing bowl, using a handheld mixer), cream the butter and sugar together on medium-high speed for 3 to 5 minutes, until light and fluffy. Turn the mixer speed down to low and add the eggs one (50 g) at a time, beating well after each addition and scraping down the sides and bottom of the bowl with a rubber spatula as necessary. Add the vanilla and orange zest and mix until just blended. Add the flour mixture in thirds, mixing until just combined and there are no visible streaks of flour; scrape down the sides and bottom of the bowl as necessary. Add the sour cream and mix until combined, about 1 minute. Add the chocolate chunks, beating until just incorporated.

With a large ice cream scoop or spoon, scoop the batter into the prepared muffin cups, filling them approximately two-thirds full.

Bake for 20 to 25 minutes, rotating the pan halfway through for even baking, until the muffins are golden brown. The tops should be firm to the touch and a toothpick inserted in the center of a muffin should come out clean. Remove from the oven and let cool in the pan on a wire rack for about 10 minutes.

Turn the muffins out onto the rack and let cool completely.

To make the glaze: In a small bowl, mix the confectioners' sugar and juice together until smooth.

Drizzle the glaze over the tops of the muffins.

The muffins can be stored in an airtight container for up to 2 days.

Lemon Poppy Seed Muffins

Citrus fruits sustain us during the winter months in the South, with so many lovely varieties to pick from. With a burst of bright lemon flavor in every bite, these muffins are moist and delicate thanks to good old-fashioned buttermilk. You can make the muffins with any type of citrus you like, from limes to oranges.

MAKES 12 MUFFINS

2 cups (250 g) unbleached all-purpose flour

½ cup (100 g) granulated sugar, plus more for sprinkling

¼ cup (50 g) packed light brown sugar

1 teaspoon (4 g) baking powder, preferably aluminum-free

1 teaspoon (6 g) baking soda

½ teaspoon fine sea salt

¼ cup (36 g) poppy seeds

3 large (150 g) eggs

½ cup (118 ml) buttermilk

1 tablespoon pure vanilla extract

8 tablespoons (1 stick/113 g) unsalted butter, melted

¼ cup (59 ml) Citrus Paste (page 383), made with lemons or 2 tablespoons lemon zest

Position a rack in the middle of the oven and preheat the oven to 375°F (190°C). Line 12 standard muffin cups with paper liners.

In a large mixing bowl, whisk together the flour, both sugars, the baking powder, baking soda, salt, and poppy seeds.

In the bowl of a stand mixer fitted with the whisk attachment (or in a large mixing bowl, using a handheld mixer), beat the eggs, buttermilk, and vanilla on low speed until completely blended. Gradually add the melted butter, mixing until completely incorporated; scrape down the sides and bottom of the bowl with a rubber spatula as necessary. Add the citrus paste and mix until incorporated. Add the flour mixture, mixing until just combined.

With a large ice cream scoop or spoon, scoop the batter into the prepared muffin cups, filling them approximately two-thirds full. Sprinkle the tops with sugar.

Bake for 22 to 28 minutes, rotating the pan halfway through for even baking, until the muffins are golden brown. The tops should be firm to the touch and a toothpick inserted in the center of a muffin should come out clean. Remove from the oven and let cool in the pan on a wire rack for 10 minutes.

Turn the muffins out of the pan and enjoy warm or at room temperature.

The muffins can be stored in an airtight container for up to 2 days.

Bacon Cheddar Scones

PICTURED ON THE FOLLOWING PAGE

To get the delicate texture of a Southern buttermilk biscuit in a rich, buttery English scone, use this one-bowl, no-roll technique. It saves time, and, more important, the result is tender, flaky pastry—what you might call a biscone. You can't go wrong with the bacon cheddar combination, but I've also provided a few variations; or use your imagination and what you have on hand to come up with other versions.

MAKES 12 SCONES

1½ cups (188 g) unbleached all-purpose flour

1½ cups (188 g) cake flour (not self-rising)

2 tablespoons (26 g) baking powder, preferably aluminum-free

½ teaspoon (3 g) baking soda

1 teaspoon fine sea salt

½ teaspoon granulated sugar

2 teaspoons freshly ground black pepper

½ pound (2 sticks/227 g) cold unsalted butter, cut into ½-inch (1.5 cm) cubes

10 slices bacon, cooked and roughly chopped

¾ pound (340 g) extra-sharp cheddar cheese, grated (1½ cups)

1½ cups (355 ml) buttermilk, plus more if needed

1 large (50 g) egg, beaten with a pinch of fine sea salt, for egg wash

Position a rack in the middle of the oven and preheat the oven to 375°F (190°C). Line a baking sheet with parchment.

In a large mixing bowl, combine both flours, the baking powder, baking soda, salt, sugar, and pepper and whisk until completely blended. Add the butter and, working quickly, cut it in with a pastry blender. You should have various-sized pieces of butter ranging from coarse sandy patches to flat shaggy pieces to pea-sized chunks, with some larger bits as well. Add the bacon and cheese and toss to distribute evenly.

Gradually pour in the buttermilk and gently fold the ingredients together until you have a soft dough with no bits of flour on the bottom of the bowl. If the dough seems dry, you may need to add a little more buttermilk. You should still see bits of butter in the dough; these will give you light and flaky scones. The dough will be moist and slightly sticky.

Turn the dough out onto a lightly floured surface and roll or pat it into a 12-inch (30 cm) square about 1½ inches (4 cm) thick. Cut into 12 squares and arrange about 1 inch (3 cm) apart on the prepared baking sheet, so the scones have room to puff up and rise. Brush the tops of the scones liberally with the egg wash.

Bake for 30 to 35 minutes, rotating the baking sheet halfway through for even baking, until the scones are lightly golden brown. Cool the scones on a wire rack for about 10 minutes, then serve warm or at room temperature.

The scones are best eaten the day they are made.

VARIATIONS

SUN-DRIED TOMATO–PARMESAN SCONES

Omit the bacon and cheddar cheese. After cutting in the butter, add ½ cup (65 g) pine nuts, ½ cup (30 g) chopped sun-dried tomatoes, and 1 cup (8 ounces/100 g) grated Parmesan cheese and mix gently to incorporate.

STRAWBERRY VANILLA SCONES

Omit the black pepper, bacon, and cheddar cheese. Add ¼ cup (50 g) granulated sugar and ¼ teaspoon ground cardamom to the dry ingredients. After cutting in the butter, add ¾ cup (110 g) fresh strawberries, hulled and cut into quarters if large or in half if smaller.

(Continued)

CLOCKWISE FROM TOP LEFT: PEACH STREUSEL MUFFINS (PAGE 93), RED, WHITE, AND BLUE MUFFINS (PAGE 98), LEMON CORIANDER SCONES (OPPOSITE), BACON CHEDDAR SCONES (PAGE 101)

Brush the tops of the scones liberally with milk or the egg wash before baking. While they are baking, whisk ¾ cup (94 g) confectioners' sugar, 2 tablespoons whole milk, and 1 teaspoon pure vanilla extract together in a small bowl until smooth. Let the scones cool for about 10 minutes, then drizzle the glaze over them.

BLUEBERRY LEMON SCONES

Omit the black pepper, bacon, and cheddar cheese. Add ¼ cup (50 g) granulated sugar and the grated zest of 1 lemon to the dry ingredients. After cutting in the butter, add ½ cup (75 g) blueberries. Use fresh berries if in season; if using frozen berries, don't thaw them. Brush the tops of the unbaked scones liberally with the egg wash and sprinkle with turbinado or sanding sugar.

Lemon Coriander Scones

PICTURED OPPOSITE

Scones are one of those pastries that are like a blank canvas. You can stick to traditional flavors or get creative. Here lemon, with its lovely blend of citrusy and floral notes, meets coriander's warm, woodsy nuttiness. The poppy seeds add a delicate crunch.

MAKES 12 SCONES

FOR THE SCONES

3½ cups (438 g) unbleached all-purpose flour

5 tablespoons (67 g) granulated sugar

4 teaspoons (18 g) baking powder, preferably
    aluminum-free

½ teaspoon (3 g) baking soda

2½ teaspoons fine sea salt

1 teaspoon ground coriander

¼ cup (36 g) poppy seeds

1¼ cups (295 ml) buttermilk, plus more if needed

Grated zest of 2 lemons, preferably Meyer lemons

9 ounces (2¼ sticks/255 g) cold unsalted butter,
    cut into ½-inch (1.5 cm) cubes

1 large (50 g) egg, beaten, for egg wash

FOR THE GLAZE

2 cups (250 g) confectioners' sugar

Grated zest and juice of 1 lemon, preferably
    a Meyer lemon

To make the scones: Position a rack in the middle of the oven and preheat the oven to 375°F (190°C). Line a baking sheet with parchment.

In a large bowl, whisk together the flour, sugar, baking powder, baking soda, salt, coriander, and poppy seeds. In a large measuring cup or small bowl, stir together the buttermilk and lemon zest.

Add the butter to the flour mixture and, working quickly, cut it in with a pastry blender. You should have various-sized pieces of butter ranging from coarse sandy patches to flat shaggy pieces to pea-sized chunks, with some larger bits as well. Gradually pour in the buttermilk and gently fold the ingredients together until you have a soft dough with no bits of flour in the bottom of the bowl. If the dough seems dry, you may need to add a little more buttermilk. You should still see bits of butter in the dough; these will give you light and flaky scones.

Turn the dough out onto a lightly floured surface and divide it in half. One at a time, roll or pat each piece into a 5-inch (13 cm) round, about 1½ inches (4 cm) thick. Cut each round in half, then cut each half into 3 triangles and arrange about 1 inch (3 cm) apart on the baking sheet, so the scones have room to puff up and rise. Brush the tops of the scones liberally with the egg wash.

(Continued)

Bake for 27 to 30 minutes, rotating the baking sheet halfway through for even baking, until the scones are golden brown. Let cool completely on a wire rack.

To make the glaze: In a medium bowl, whisk together the confectioners' sugar and lemon zest and juice until smooth.

Spread the glaze over the tops of the scones.

The scones are best eaten the day they are made.

Cinnamon Swirl Buns

A brown sugar and cinnamon filling is swirled between buttery layers of pastry dough flavored with five-spice powder, and then the buns are coated with a delicate vanilla glaze to finish them.

MAKES 12 BUNS

FOR THE CINNAMON SUGAR FILLING

1 cup plus 2 tablespoons (225 g) packed light brown sugar

1 tablespoon ground cinnamon

¼ teaspoon fine sea salt

4 tablespoons (57 g) unsalted butter, melted and still warm

FOR THE BUNS

6½ cups (813 g) unbleached all-purpose flour

3 tablespoons granulated sugar

2 tablespoons plus 2 teaspoons (35 g) baking powder, preferably aluminum-free

1½ teaspoons (8 g) baking soda

1 teaspoon five-spice powder

1 tablespoon fine sea salt

¾ pound (3 sticks/340 g) cold unsalted butter, cut into ½-inch (1.5 cm) cubes

3 cups (710 ml) cold buttermilk

2 tablespoons unsalted butter, melted

FOR THE GLAZE

3 ounces (85 g) cream cheese, at room temperature

4 tablespoons (57 g) unsalted butter, at room temperature

1½ cups (188 g) confectioners' sugar

½ teaspoon fine sea salt

½ teaspoon pure vanilla extract

Position a rack in the middle of the oven and preheat the oven to 425°F (220°C). Line a baking sheet with parchment.

To make the filling: In a large bowl, stir together the brown sugar, cinnamon, salt, and melted butter. Set aside.

To make the buns: In the bowl of a stand mixer fitted with the paddle attachment (or in a large mixing bowl, using a handheld mixer), combine the flour, sugar, baking powder, baking soda, five-spice powder, and salt and mix on low speed until well blended. With the mixer running, gradually add the cold butter cubes and mix until you have various-sized pieces of butter ranging from coarse sandy patches to flat shaggy shards to pea-sized chunks. Slowly add the buttermilk, mixing until completely incorporated. The dough will look shaggy, and there will still be bits of dry ingredients at the bottom of the bowl, which is exactly what you want.

Turn the dough, with all the dry bits, out onto a lightly floured surface and bring the dough together with your hands, kneading it gently, until there are no more dry bits remaining. Flour a rolling pin and lightly dust your work surface with flour. Roll the dough into an 18-by-12-inch (46 by 30 cm) rectangle that is ½ inch (1.5 cm) thick.

Brush the dough with the melted butter, going all the way to the edges. Sprinkle the cinnamon sugar mixture over the dough. Beginning with a long side, roll the dough up like a jelly roll, keeping the roll as tight and uniform as possible. Pinch the seam together to seal and turn the dough seam side down.

Using a bench cutter or a sharp knife, trim off the ragged ends of the roll (about ½ inch/ 1.5 cm) and discard. Cut the roll into 12 equal pieces. Arrange the buns cut side down on the prepared baking sheet.

Slide the baking sheet into the oven and reduce the oven temperature to 400°F (205°C). Bake the buns for 22 to 24 minutes, rotating the baking sheet halfway through, until golden brown. Let the buns cool on a wire rack for about 10 minutes.

Meanwhile, make the glaze: In the bowl of the stand mixer fitted with the paddle attachment (or in a large mixing bowl, using a handheld mixer), beat the cream cheese and butter on medium-low speed until thoroughly combined, 2 to 3 minutes. Increase the speed to medium-high and gradually add the confectioners' sugar, mixing until combined, then add the salt and vanilla and continue beating until very light and fluffy, 2 to 3 minutes.

Spread the glaze over the tops of the buns.

The buns can be stored in an airtight container for up to 1 day.

Slow Breads

(BREADS THAT NEED TIME TO RISE)

*Southern is a great yeast roll, the dough put down overnight
to rise and the next morning, shaped into rolls and baked.
Served hot from the oven, they are as light as a dandelion in a
high wind.*

—EDNA LEWIS

SLOW BREADS CAN BE EITHER SWEET OR SAVORY. Made with yeast as
the leavening agent and enriched with eggs, the doughs need a rest and a rise
before baking. These are the breads that will leave your kitchen smelling like
your local bakeshop, and they'll give you a greater appreciation for the craft
of making bread. It's not very difficult to make any of these recipes, but you
do need time and patience. The reward is knowing that what you baked will
taste better than anything store-bought.

When mixing bread dough, you need to understand the science behind it. So
many variables can affect the result. Take the time to learn about each dough,
the way it feels and how the weather and temperature can affect it. Shaping
and folding is an important part of the process of making bread. Be gentle
but confident when following the directions that tell you how to shape, fold,
and rest each dough. Pay attention to how slowly or how fast the bread rises
because of ambient temperature. As the dough rises, the yeast helps break
down the sugars in the flour and develop the complex flavor that you expect
in a good homemade loaf of bread.

Get your hands in the dough and build your bread-making skills with
Wildflower Honey–Caramel Buns, sweet buns with a honey filling; Chocolate
Pull-Apart Bread, an easy, sweet loaf; Brioche, a classic enriched bread; and,
yes, Raised Yeast Doughnuts.

Brioche

PICTURED ON PAGE 122

French cuisine was a major influence in the South all the way from Charleston down to New Orleans. The local cuisines blended the refinement of Southern ingredients with the flavors and techniques of France. Brioche, the enriched bread made with butter and eggs, is the welcome accompaniment to many Southern dishes. Any leftovers can be transformed into Pain Perdu with Jam (page 48).

The dough must be refrigerated overnight before baking, so plan accordingly.

MAKES 1 LOAF

FOR THE DOUGH

1¾ cups (219 g) unbleached all-purpose flour

1¾ cups (223 g) bread flour

¼ cup plus 1 tablespoon (64 g) sugar

5 teaspoons (16 g) instant yeast

1½ teaspoons fine sea salt

3 tablespoons whole milk

5 large (250 g) eggs plus 1 large (19 g) yolk, lightly beaten

½ pound (2 sticks/227 g) unsalted butter, cut into
   1-inch (3 cm) cubes, at room temperature

FOR THE EGG WASH

2 large (38 g) egg yolks

2 tablespoons heavy cream

Generous pinch of fine sea salt

To make the dough: In the bowl of a stand mixer fitted with the dough hook, combine both flours, the sugar, yeast, salt, milk, and eggs and yolk and mix on low speed until blended, 1 to 2 minutes. Increase the speed to medium and mix for 5 minutes; stop the mixer to push the dough off the hook as necessary and then continue mixing.

Reduce the mixer speed to low and add the cubed butter one piece at a time. Then continue to mix until the butter is thoroughly incorporated.

Stop the mixer and scrape down the sides and bottom of the bowl with a rubber spatula, pushing the dough toward the dough hook. Increase the speed to medium and mix for 5 to 7 minutes. The dough will start out very loose but will eventually come together; it will still be sticky and elastic.

Turn the dough out onto a well-floured work surface and shape into a rough rectangle. Fold the dough in half, then rotate it a quarter turn and fold in half again; rotate a quarter turn again and fold in half once more.

Divide the dough into 2 equal pieces (about 11 ounces/312 g) each). Shape each one into a rough round and place both pieces of dough on a greased baking sheet. Cover with plastic wrap and refrigerate overnight.

The next day, grease a 9-by-5-inch (23 by 13 cm) loaf pan.

Working with one piece of dough at a time, gently flatten the dough into a round. Then lift the edges of the dough, working your way all around it, and press them into the center to create a ball. Invert the ball of dough and, with cupped hands, begin massaging the edges of the ball of dough and rotating the dough on the work surface to create tension while sealing the bottom of the dough with your fingers. Place both balls of dough in the prepared loaf pan, loosely cover the pan with plastic wrap, and allow to rise for 3 to 4 hours, or until the dough has risen above the edges of the pan.

Meanwhile, an hour before you are ready to bake, preheat the oven to 350°F (175°C).

To make the egg wash: In a small bowl, stir together the egg yolks, cream, and salt.

Lightly but evenly brush the top of the dough with the egg wash. Bake for 30 to 35 minutes, until the crust is dark golden brown and an instant-read thermometer inserted in the center of the loaf reaches 190°F (90°C).

(Continued)

Allow the bread to cool in the pan on a wire rack for 15 minutes. Then remove from the pan and cool completely on the rack.

This bread is best eaten the same day it's baked, but you can wrap it well and freeze for up to 1 month.

Wildflower Honey–Caramel Buns

All yeasted doughs will require a portion of your day to prepare and bake. On average, you'll need to allow up to four hours to mix and proof your dough. You can bake these buns the same day you make them or refrigerate the unbaked buns overnight and bake them first thing the next day—the scent of cinnamon buns baking in the morning is as comforting as it gets. Covered with a honey caramel goo and then a light cream cheese icing, they are tender and decadent. Decorate them with edible wildflowers, if you like.

MAKES 12 BUNS

FOR THE DOUGH

2¾ cups (344 g) unbleached all-purpose flour

¾ cup (94 g) cake flour (not self-rising)

6 tablespoons plus 2 teaspoons (83 g) granulated sugar

2½ teaspoons (8 g) instant yeast

1 teaspoon fine sea salt

¼ teaspoon ground cardamom

1 large (50 g) egg

¾ cup (177 ml) water

¼ cup (59 ml) buttermilk

1 teaspoon pure vanilla extract

6 tablespoons (85 g) unsalted butter, at room temperature

FOR THE CARAMEL TOPPING

8 tablespoons (1 stick/113 g) unsalted butter

1 cup (200 g) packed light brown sugar

¼ cup (59 ml) wildflower honey (or substitute tupelo or orange blossom honey)

3 tablespoons water

½ teaspoon pure vanilla extract

FOR THE FILLING

1¼ cups (250 g) packed light brown sugar

1 tablespoon ground cinnamon

6 tablespoons (85 g) unsalted butter

FOR THE CREAM CHEESE ICING

6 ounces (170 g) cream cheese, at room temperature

8 tablespoons (1 stick/113 g) unsalted butter, at room temperature

3 cups (375 g) confectioners' sugar

½ teaspoon pure vanilla extract

¼ teaspoon fine sea salt

SPECIAL EQUIPMENT

Candy thermometer

To make the dough: In the bowl of a stand mixer fitted with the dough hook, combine both flours, the sugar, yeast, salt, and cardamom and mix on low speed for 2 minutes, or until thoroughly blended. Add the egg, water, buttermilk, vanilla, and butter and beat until the dough begins to pull away from the sides of the bowl and is only slightly sticky. Increase the speed to medium and mix for 7 minutes, or until the dough is silky and supple.

Lightly oil a large bowl. Transfer the dough to the bowl and turn the dough gently to coat it with oil. Cover the bowl with plastic wrap and let the dough rise in a warm, draft-free place for 1 hour, or until doubled in size.

Meanwhile, make the caramel topping: In a medium saucepan, stir together the butter, brown sugar, honey, water, and vanilla and cook over medium heat, stirring, until the sugar is dissolved. Clip a candy thermometer to the side of the pan, bring the mixture to a boil, and cook until it registers 220°F (105°C) on the thermometer. Pour the caramel into a 9-by-13-by-2-inch (23 by 33 by 5 cm) baking dish, spreading it evenly with a heatproof spatula. Set aside to cool to room temperature.

To prepare the filling: In a small bowl, mix together the brown sugar and cinnamon; set aside. Melt the butter in the microwave or on the stovetop over low heat; remove from the heat.

To assemble the buns: Remove the risen dough from the bowl and place on a lightly floured surface. Lightly dust the top of the dough with flour and, using a rolling pin, gently roll the dough into an 18-by-9-inch (46 by 23 cm) rectangle, about ¾ inch (2 cm) thick. Don't overwork the dough, or it will become tough.

Using a pastry brush, brush the dough evenly from edge to edge with the melted butter. Sprinkle the brown sugar mixture evenly over the dough and press it lightly into the melted butter.

Beginning with a long side, roll the dough up like a jelly roll, keeping the roll as tight and uniform as possible. Pinch the seam to seal the dough and turn the dough seam side down.

Using a bench cutter or a sharp knife, trim off the ragged ends of the roll (about ½ inch/1.5 cm) and discard. Cut the roll into 12 equal pieces and arrange the buns in the caramel-coated baking dish in four rows of 3 buns each.

Cover the baking dish loosely with plastic wrap and allow the buns to rise in a warm, draft-free place until they have doubled in size and are touching one another, about 1 hour. (*At this point, you can cover the rolls with plastic wrap and place in the refrigerator overnight before baking.*)

Position a rack in the middle of the oven and preheat the oven to 350°F (175°C). Slip a foil-lined baking sheet onto the lower oven rack to catch any drips.

Remove the plastic wrap and bake the buns for 20 to 25 minutes, rotating the baking dish halfway through for even baking, until they are a deep golden brown and the caramel is bubbling. Remove from the oven and let the buns cool in the pan for 5 to 10 minutes. (Caution: Do not serve the buns straight out of the oven—the caramel will be dangerously hot.)

Invert the buns onto a large serving platter. Let cool for 15 minutes.

Meanwhile, prepare the icing: In the bowl of the stand mixer fitted with the paddle attachment (or in a large mixing bowl, using a handheld mixer), combine the cream cheese and butter and beat on medium-low speed until smooth, 2 to 3 minutes. With the mixer on low, add the confectioners' sugar, vanilla, and salt, mixing until combined. Increase the speed to medium-high and beat until the icing is superlight and fluffy, 3 to 4 minutes.

Smear the icing over the tops of the buns. Serve warm.

The buns can be stored in an airtight container for up to 1 day.

Chocolate Pull-Apart Bread

PICTURED ON PAGE 122

This sweet breakfast bread is one to enjoy any day of the week. Pulling apart the still-warm bread reveals intricate layers, nooks, and crannies of caramelized sugar and chocolatey goodness. It's a delicious pleasure to pair with a cup of your favorite coffee or tea.

MAKES 1 LOAF

FOR THE DOUGH

2¾ cups (344 g) unbleached all-purpose flour

¼ cup (50 g) granulated sugar

1½ teaspoons (5 g) instant yeast

¾ teaspoon fine sea salt

4 tablespoons (57 g) unsalted butter, at room temperature

1 large (19 g) egg yolk

¾ cup (177 ml) whole milk, at room temperature

FOR THE CHOCOLATE FILLING

6 ounces (170 g) semisweet chocolate, finely chopped (about 1 cup)

½ cup (57 g) pecans, chopped

½ cup (100 g) granulated sugar

2 tablespoons unsalted butter, melted

2 teaspoons Dutch-processed cocoa powder

FOR THE LEMON GLAZE

1 cup (125 g) confectioners' sugar

1 tablespoon grated lemon zest

2 to 3 tablespoons fresh lemon juice

SPECIAL EQUIPMENT

Instant-read thermometer

To make the dough: In the bowl of a stand mixer fitted with the dough hook, combine the flour, sugar, yeast, and salt and mix on low speed to blend. Add the butter, egg yolk, and milk, mixing until incorporated. Then mix on medium speed for 8 to 10 minutes, or until a smooth dough forms.

Scrape the dough out onto a lightly floured work surface. Knead it a few times and form it into a ball.

Lightly oil a large bowl. Transfer the dough to the bowl and turn the dough gently to coat it with oil. Cover the bowl with plastic wrap and let the dough rise in a warm, draft-free place for 2 hours, or until doubled in size.

To make the filling: In a small bowl, mix together the chocolate, pecans, sugar, melted butter, and cocoa powder.

Lightly spray a 9-by-5-inch (23 by 13 cm) loaf pan with nonstick spray.

Remove the risen dough from the bowl and gently shape it into an 8-inch (20 cm) square. Cut the dough into 16 equal pieces. Form each piece into a ball.

Arrange 8 dough balls in the bottom of the prepared loaf pan. Scatter half of the chocolate filling over the dough. Arrange the remaining dough balls on top and scatter the remaining chocolate filling over them.

Cover the pan loosely with plastic wrap and allow the dough to rise in a warm, draft-free place for about 1 hour, until doubled in size; it should crest the sides of the pan by about 1 inch (3 cm).

Position a rack in the middle of the oven and preheat the oven to 325°F (165°C).

Put the loaf in the oven and bake for 20 minutes. Rotate the pan and bake for another 10 to 15 minutes, until an instant-read thermometer inserted in the center of the bread reaches 190°F (90°C). Put the pan on a wire rack and cool for 10 minutes.

Meanwhile, make the glaze: In a small bowl, stir together the confectioners' sugar, lemon zest, and 2 tablespoons lemon juice until smooth; if necessary, thin the glaze with up to 1 tablespoon more lemon juice.

Invert the loaf onto a serving dish and turn right side up. Drizzle the lemon glaze over the loaf and serve warm.

The bread can be stored in an airtight container for up to 3 days. To freeze, wrap in plastic wrap and then aluminum foil; it'll keep for up to 1 month.

Raised Yeast Doughnuts

It's fun to make a batch of fresh doughnuts right in your own kitchen. There are endless possibilities for fillings and glazes to make your doughnuts unique; see the following pages for a few ideas for the filling and many more for the glaze. When planned, making doughnuts can be a fun weekend activity, and the results will be worth it. If you prefer, you can refrigerate the dough overnight and make the doughnuts the next day.

MAKES 12 DOUGHNUTS

FOR THE DOUGH

2¾ cups (344 g) unbleached all-purpose flour

¾ cup (94 g) cake flour (not self-rising)

6 tablespoons plus 2 teaspoons (83 g) granulated sugar

2½ teaspoons (8 g) instant yeast

1 teaspoon fine sea salt

1 large (50 g) egg

¾ cup (177 ml) water

¼ cup (59 ml) buttermilk

1 teaspoon pure vanilla extract

6 tablespoons (85 g) unsalted butter, at room temperature

1 to 2 quarts (1 to 2 L) vegetable oil for deep-frying

Sugar for rolling (see the following page for suggestions), preserves or another filling (see Variations), and/or one of the Glazes (see page 117)

SPECIAL EQUIPMENT

3-inch (8 cm) round or square cutter; 1-inch (3 cm) round cutter if not making filled doughnuts

Spider skimmer

To make the dough: In the bowl of a stand mixer fitted with the dough hook, combine the flours, sugar, yeast, and salt and mix on low speed for 2 minutes, or until thoroughly blended. Still on low speed, add the egg, water, buttermilk, and vanilla and mix until combined. Add the butter, still beating on low speed; the dough will fall apart as the butter is integrated into it, but do not be tempted to add more flour—you want a medium-loose dough. Continue to mix until the dough begins to pull away slightly from the sides of the bowl, 4 to 5 minutes. Stop the mixer and scrape down the sides and bottom of the bowl with a rubber spatula, pushing the dough toward the dough hook. Then increase the speed to medium and mix for another 10 minutes; the dough will still be of medium consistency and slightly sticky.

Turn the dough out onto a floured work surface and shape into a rough rectangle. Fold it into thirds, as if you were folding a business letter, then shape into a rectangle again, adding just enough flour so it doesn't stick to the work surface. Repeat the folding three more times. Finally, with the dough seam side down, use your hands to gently rotate and tuck the edges under to shape the dough into a tight ball.

Lightly oil a large bowl and transfer the dough to the bowl, turning it gently to coat it with oil. Cover the bowl with plastic wrap and let the dough rise in a warm, draft-free place for 1 hour, or until doubled in size.

Transfer the dough to a floured work surface, folding the dough in thirds, then shaping it into a ball and placing it back in the bowl to rise. With the dough seam side down, use your hands to gently rotate and tuck the edges under to shape the dough into a tight ball.

At this point, you can let the dough rise for another 45 to 60 minutes, until doubled in size, or you can refrigerate it overnight, or for up to 16 hours, before making the doughnuts.

To make the doughnuts: If you refrigerated the dough overnight, turn it out onto a lightly floured work surface, cover with a kitchen towel, and let rest for 20 minutes before proceeding. If you didn't refrigerate the dough, transfer it to a floured work surface and proceed.

This is the time to have fun with the doughnut shapes. You can make them square or round. Cut the centers out to make doughnut holes, or leave them whole if you want to make filled doughnuts.

Gently roll the dough out to a ½-inch (1.5 cm) thickness. Using a 3-inch (8 cm) round or square cutter, cut 9 to 12 doughnuts and transfer them to a parchment-lined baking sheet, arranging them about 1½ inches (4 cm) apart. If you are not going to make filled doughnuts, using a 1-inch (3 cm) round cutter, cut a small hole in the middle of each doughnut, if desired, and place the doughnut holes on the pan as well. You can wrap and refrigerate the scraps, then reroll them to make more doughnuts after chilling for 1 hour. Because you always want more doughnuts, right?

Cover the doughnuts with plastic wrap and allow to rise at room temperature until almost doubled in size, about 30 minutes.

Line a baking sheet with paper towels and set a wire rack on it. In a Dutch oven or other large heavy-bottomed pot or a countertop fryer, heat about 3 inches (8 cm) of oil to 370°F (185°C). You can test the oil by dropping in a tiny piece of dough: The oil should sizzle and the dough should brown within 10 seconds. Once the oil reaches the correct temperature, one at a time, remove the doughnuts from the baking sheet, being careful not to deflate them, place on a spider skimmer, and carefully lower into the oil. Work in batches of 2 to 3 doughnuts at a time so that the temperature of the oil does not drop too much; you don't want it to go below 340°F (170°C). Cook the doughnuts for 1½ to 2 minutes on each side, until lightly golden, using the skimmer to flip the doughnuts and then to remove them from the oil. When you remove the doughnuts, let the excess oil drip back into the pot, then transfer them to the wire rack. Make sure the oil is at the correct temperature before you add the next batch of doughnuts. If the oil gets too hot, the doughnuts may color too much before they are cooked through; if it's too cool, the doughnuts will absorb oil and be greasy.

Let the doughnuts cool before sugaring, filling, and/or glazing them. You can simply roll the doughnuts in confectioners' sugar, granulated sugar, or one of the flavored sugars on page 376. Or you can fill them with your favorite preserves or custard; see below for suggestions. See opposite for glaze recipes.

VARIATIONS

For filled doughnuts, make a ½-inch (1.5 cm) slit in the side of each doughnut with a chopstick, skewer, or paring knife and create a pocket in the doughnut. Fill a pastry bag with your favorite preserves, Milk Jam (page 386), Pastry Cream (page 386), or Lemon Curd (page 384) and pipe into the doughnuts, filling them generously (using about 2 tablespoons for each) and allowing some of the filling to peek out. Place each doughnut in a muffin liner and line the doughnuts up on a tray for serving.

DOUGHNUT GLAZES

To make glazed doughnuts, once the doughnuts are cooled, mix the glaze of your choice and dip the top half of each doughnut in the glaze. Transfer to a wire rack and let stand for at least 10 minutes, until the glaze is set.

VANILLA BEAN GLAZE

2 cups (250 g) confectioners' sugar

½ vanilla bean, split lengthwise, seeds scraped out and reserved

2 tablespoons plus 2 teaspoons water

In a medium mixing bowl, combine the confectioners' sugar and vanilla seeds. Slowly whisk in the water until smooth.

CAFÉ AU LAIT GLAZE

2 cups (250 g) confectioners' sugar

¼ teaspoon coffee or espresso powder

¼ cup (59 ml) hot strong brewed coffee or espresso

In a medium mixing bowl, combine the confectioners' sugar and coffee powder. Slowly whisk in the coffee until smooth.

LEMON GLAZE

2 cups (250 g) confectioners' sugar

Grated zest of 1 lemon

2 tablespoons plus 2 teaspoons fresh lemon juice

In a medium mixing bowl, combine the confectioners' sugar and lemon zest. Slowly whisk in the lemon juice until smooth.

BUTTERMILK GLAZE

2 cups (250 g) confectioners' sugar

¼ teaspoon fine sea salt

3 tablespoons buttermilk

In a medium mixing bowl, combine the confectioners' sugar and salt. Slowly whisk in the buttermilk until smooth and creamy.

STRAWBERRY GLAZE

3 tablespoons freeze-dried strawberry powder

2 cups (250 g) confectioners' sugar

2 to 3 tablespoons water

In a medium mixing bowl, whisk together the strawberry powder and confectioners' sugar. Gradually whisk in the water and mix until smooth.

DULCE DE LECHE GLAZE

¾ cup (150 g) packed light brown sugar

6 tablespoons (85 g) unsalted butter, cut into 1-inch (3 cm) cubes

¼ cup (59 ml) sweetened condensed milk

¼ cup (59 ml) whole milk

1 tablespoon light corn syrup

1 teaspoon pure vanilla extract

½ teaspoon fine sea salt

1 cup (125 g) confectioners' sugar

In a medium saucepan, combine the brown sugar and butter and heat over low heat, stirring, until the sugar is completely dissolved. Add the condensed milk, whole milk, corn syrup, vanilla, and salt, stirring until completely combined. Bring the mixture to a boil, then gradually add the confectioners' sugar, stirring until completely smooth. Let cool slightly before using.

CHOCOLATE GLAZE

¼ cup (50 g) sugar

3 to 4 tablespoons heavy cream

1 tablespoon unsalted butter, diced

6 ounces (170 g) dark chocolate (60 to 70% cacao), chopped (about 1 cup)

¼ teaspoon fine sea salt

Set a large heatproof bowl over a saucepan of simmering water (make sure the bowl does not touch the water), add the sugar and 3 tablespoons of the cream, and whisk until combined. Add the butter, chocolate, and salt and heat, stirring frequently, until the butter and chocolate are completely melted and the glaze is smooth; stir in up to 1 tablespoon more cream if necessary. Set aside to cool slightly.

Lemon Sweet Potato Bread

PICTURED ON PAGE 122

Sweet potatoes are a staple in Southern households. This sweet potato bread flavored with lemon makes a great turkey club sandwich. Roasting sweet potatoes brings out their natural sugars and adds a caramel flavor to the loaf. The crust has a deep golden hue, and the crumb is fluffy and tender.

MAKES 2 LOAVES

2 sweet potatoes

5½ cups (688 g) unbleached all-purpose flour

½ cup (100 g) packed light brown sugar

½ cup (90 g) fine yellow cornmeal

1 tablespoon fine sea salt

2 teaspoons grated lemon zest

1½ teaspoons (5 g) instant yeast

2 large (100 g) eggs

1¼ cups (296 ml) room-temperature water

1 large (50 g) egg, lightly beaten with a pinch of fine sea salt, for egg wash

OPTIONAL SPECIAL EQUIPMENT

Instant-read thermometer

To roast the sweet potatoes: Position a rack in the middle of the oven and preheat the oven to 400°F (205°C). Line a baking sheet with parchment and spray the parchment with nonstick spray.

Peel the sweet potatoes and cut into 1-inch (3 cm) cubes. Place the cubes on the prepared baking sheet and bake for about 1 hour, until fork-tender.

Mash the sweet potatoes and set aside to cool, then measure out 1 cup (250 g) for this recipe (any leftovers are yours for snacking).

In the bowl of a stand mixer fitted with the dough hook, combine the flour, brown sugar, cornmeal, salt, lemon zest, and yeast and mix to blend.

In a medium bowl, whisk the sweet potatoes and eggs to combine. Add to the flour mixture, then

turn the mixer on to low speed, add the water, and mix for 3 to 5 minutes, scraping down the sides and bottom of the bowl with a rubber spatula as necessary, until the dough comes together. Increase the mixer speed to medium and mix for 7 minutes, or until you have a smooth dough.

Transfer the dough to a lightly floured work surface and knead for about 1 minute, until smooth and elastic. Shape the dough into a ball.

Lightly butter a large bowl and put the dough in the bowl, turning it to coat with butter. Cover the bowl with plastic wrap and let the dough rise in a warm, draft-free place for 2 hours, or until doubled in size.

Grease two 9-by-5-inch (23 by 13 cm) loaf pans with butter. Divide the dough into 2 equal pieces. One at a time, using a rolling pin, roll each piece into an 8-by-10-inch (20 by 25 cm) rectangle. Starting from a short end, roll each piece up into a log and place seam side down in one of the loaf pans.

Loosely cover each pan with plastic wrap and allow the dough to rise until doubled in size, about 1 hour.

Position a rack in the middle of the oven and preheat the oven to 350°F (175°C).

Lightly brush the tops of the loaves with the egg wash. Bake the bread for 30 to 40 minutes, until the crust is the color of dark honey; an instant-read thermometer inserted in the center of a loaf should read 190°F (90°C).

Remove the pans from the oven and let cool on a wire rack for 10 minutes. Remove the bread from the pans and let cool completely.

The bread can be stored in an airtight container for up to 5 days. To freeze, wrap each loaf in plastic wrap and then aluminum foil; they will keep for up to 1 month.

120   CHERYL DAY'S TREASURY OF SOUTHERN BAKING

Buttermilk Rolls

Buttermilk adds a tremendous amount of flavor and tenderness to these rolls. What makes them different is the technique of first combining some of the flour with water and buttermilk and cooking the mixture over low heat to gelatinize the flour and make a pudding-like buttermilk roux. The roux, which is then added to the dough, helps retain moisture and creates a light and tender dinner roll like no other.

MAKES 12 ROLLS

FOR THE ROUX

3 tablespoons water

3 tablespoons buttermilk

2 tablespoons unbleached all-purpose flour

FOR THE DOUGH

2½ cups (313 g) unbleached all-purpose flour

2 tablespoons milk powder

¼ cup (50 g) granulated sugar

1 teaspoon fine sea salt

1 tablespoon (10 g) instant yeast

½ cup (118 ml) whole milk, at room temperature

1 large (50 g) egg

4 tablespoons (57 g) unsalted butter, melted

FOR THE EGG WASH

1 large (19 g) egg yolk

1 tablespoon heavy cream or milk

1 tablespoon unsalted butter, melted

OPTIONAL SPECIAL EQUIPMENT

Instant-read thermometer

To make the roux: In a small saucepan, combine the water and buttermilk, then gradually add the flour, whisking briskly until smooth, without any lumps. Place the saucepan over low heat and cook, stirring constantly with a heatproof spatula, until the mixture has thickened and reaches 148°F (65°C) on an instant-read thermometer.

Transfer the roux to a small bowl. Cover with plastic wrap placed directly on the surface and let it cool to room temperature. (You can put the roux in the fridge to speed up the cooling process.)

To make the dough: In the bowl of a stand mixer fitted with the dough hook, combine the flour, milk powder, sugar, salt, and yeast and mix on low speed to combine.

In a large measuring cup or medium bowl, whisk the milk, egg, melted butter, and cooled roux together until well combined. Add the milk mixture to the flour mixture and mix on low speed until the dough comes together around the dough hook. The dough will be very sticky at first, but resist the urge to add more flour; once it comes together during mixing, the dough will be loose and still slightly tacky. Increase the speed to medium-low and continue mixing until the dough is smooth and elastic; it will take 15 to 20 minutes to develop a dough that is soft but still feels tacky.

Transfer the dough to a well-floured surface. Sprinkle the top of the dough with flour and do a final kneading of the dough, shaping it into a ball and tucking the edges of the dough to the bottom center, creating a smooth, taut ball.

Lightly oil a large bowl. Transfer the dough to the bowl and turn gently to coat it with oil. Cover the bowl with plastic wrap and let the dough rise in a warm, draft-free place for 45 minutes to 1 hour, until doubled in size.

Lightly spray a baking sheet with nonstick spray. Transfer the dough to a clean work surface. Gently shape into an 8-inch (20 cm) square. Cut the dough into 12 equal pieces.

Shape each piece of dough into a smooth, firm ball. Place the balls on the prepared baking sheet, spaced about 2 inches (5 cm) apart. Cover loosely

CLOCKWISE FROM TOP LEFT: BRIOCHE (PAGE 109), CHOCOLATE PULL-APART BREAD (PAGE 114), LEMON SWEET POTATO BREAD (PAGE 120), QUEEN'S FAMOUS ICEBOX ROLLS (OPPOSITE)

with plastic wrap and allow the rolls to rise for 45 to 60 minutes, until doubled in size.

Preheat the oven to 350°F (175°C).

To make the egg wash: In a small bowl, whisk together the egg yolk and cream.

When you are ready to bake, remove the plastic wrap from the rolls and lightly brush the tops with the egg wash. Bake the rolls for 30 minutes, or until golden brown; an instant-read thermometer inserted in a roll should reach 190°F (90°C).

Remove the rolls from the oven and immediately brush with the melted butter. (Yes, more butter!) Serve warm or at room temperature.

The rolls can be stored in an airtight container for up to 2 days.

Queen's Famous Icebox Rolls

PICTURED OPPOSITE

Sunday in the South is often baking day. With this recipe, you can shape the rolls and bake some of them for Sunday dinner, then refrigerate the rest for the days that follow (this recipe makes a lot of rolls!). Leftover mashed potatoes were my grandmother Queen's secret ingredient for these tender icebox rolls. The potassium and starch molecules in the potatoes allow the yeast to rise quickly and also condition the dough, which makes for a soft, delicate crumb.

MAKES ABOUT 48 ROLLS

7 cups (875 g) unbleached all-purpose flour

1 tablespoon (10 g) instant yeast

1 cup (237 ml) whole milk

12 tablespoons (1½ sticks/170 g) unsalted butter, at room temperature

¾ cup (150 g) granulated sugar

2 teaspoons fine sea salt

½ cup (118 ml) water

2 cups (500 g) mashed potatoes (about 4 medium russet potatoes, boiled until tender, peeled, mashed, and cooled to room temperature)

2 large (100 g) eggs, beaten

FOR THE EGG WASH

1 large (19 g) egg yolk

2 teaspoons heavy cream

In a large bowl, combine the flour and yeast, stirring to blend. Set aside.

In a medium saucepan, heat the milk and butter over low heat, stirring frequently, until the butter melts. Add the sugar and salt and stir until they dissolve. Remove from the heat and let cool to room temperature.

Add the cooled milk mixture to the bowl of a stand mixer fitted with the dough hook. Add the flour mixture, water, potatoes, and eggs and mix on low speed for 3 minutes. Increase the speed to medium and mix for another 7 minutes, or until you have a smooth dough.

Transfer the dough to a lightly floured surface. Sprinkle the top of the dough with flour and do a final kneading of the dough, shaping it into a ball and tucking the edges of the dough to the bottom center, creating a smooth, taut ball.

Lightly spray a large bowl with nonstick spray. Add the dough and turn to coat with oil, then turn seam side down, cover with a tea towel or plastic wrap, and let rise in a warm, draft-free place for 1 hour, or until doubled in size.

Lightly butter a 12-by-17-inch (30 by 43 cm) baking sheet.

Turn the dough out onto a lightly floured surface and divide into 48 (about 1½-ounce/44 g) pieces. Shape into balls and place in the prepared pan, 8 rows by 6, arranging them on the baking pan so they just barely kiss each other. *(You also have the option to cover and refrigerate the rolls in the pan until ready to bake, up to 1 day.)*

(Continued)

Allow the rolls to rise in a warm, draft-free place for 1 hour, or until doubled in size.

When you are ready to bake, preheat the oven to 400°F (205°C).

To make the egg wash: In a small bowl, beat the egg yolk and cream together. Lightly brush the tops of the rolls with the egg wash.

Bake the rolls for 14 to 16 minutes, until golden brown. Remove from the oven and serve warm with butter alongside.

Although these rolls reheat well, they are best served the day they are baked. To reheat them before serving, warm in a preheated 350°F (175°C) oven for 6 to 8 minutes.

Concha Buns

The South is a melting pot of many cultures. New immigrants to our region bring their cherished food traditions and recipes with them, and those recipes become a part of the shared culture. Concha Buns are a Southern spin on one of the best-known pan dulce, or sweet rolls, served in panaderias (bakeries) all across Mexico City. Made with the same dough as my Buttermilk Rolls, each of these lightly sweetened buns has a cap of crumbly crust on top that looks like a *concha*, or shell. If you like, you can fill the buns jelly doughnut–style with jam or pastry cream (see page 386). These are perfect for dunking in hot chocolate or coffee.

MAKES 12 BUNS

1 recipe dough for Buttermilk Rolls (page 121),
    risen and ready to shape

FOR THE CONCHA TOPPING

¾ cup (94 g) unbleached all-purpose flour

½ teaspoon (2 g) baking powder, preferably
    aluminum-free

¼ teaspoon fine sea salt

8 tablespoons (1 stick/113 g) cold unsalted butter,
    cut into ½-inch (1.5 cm) cubes

½ teaspoon pure vanilla extract

SPECIAL EQUIPMENT

2¼-inch (6 cm) biscuit cutter

Lightly spray a baking sheet with nonstick spray. Transfer the risen dough to a clean work surface. Gently shape into an 8-inch (20 cm) square. Cut the dough into 12 equal pieces.

Shape each piece of dough into a smooth, firm ball. Place the balls on the prepared baking sheet about 2 inches (5 cm) apart. Cover loosely with plastic wrap and allow the rolls to rise for 45 to 60 minutes, until doubled in size.

While the buns rise, make the concha topping: In the bowl of a stand mixer fitted with the paddle attachment (or in a large mixing bowl, using a handheld mixer), combine the flour, baking powder, and salt and mix on low speed for about 1 minute, until thoroughly combined. With the mixer still on low speed, add the cubed butter and the vanilla and mix for 3 to 5 minutes, until the mixture resembles soft cookie dough.

Lay a large sheet of parchment on a clean work surface. Turn the dough out onto the parchment. Top with another piece of parchment, and roll out to a ⅛-inch (3 mm) thickness. Transfer the dough, with the parchment, to a baking sheet and place in the refrigerator to chill for 15 to 20 minutes. This will make it easier to cut out the concha tops.

Remove the top piece of parchment and, using a 2¼-inch (6 cm) biscuit cutter, punch out 12 circles. Using a paring knife, score each circle of dough to mimic the ridges of a seashell. Carefully lay a circle on top of each risen roll.

Cover the rolls with a tea towel and set aside in a warm place to rise for 30 minutes, or until they have doubled in size again.

Preheat the oven to 375°F (190°C).

Bake the conchas for 25 to 30 minutes, until golden brown. Let cool completely on a wire rack.

Sorghum Whole Wheat Bread

Sorghum syrup is known as liquid gold in the South. Sometimes confused with cane syrup, sorghum is processed in a similar fashion as sugarcane but has its own unique sweetness, along with a bit of sourness that is unmatched by any other sweetener. In this recipe, it lends a deep caramelized and nutty flavor to a hearty whole wheat loaf.

MAKES 1 LOAF

3½ cups (438 g) whole wheat flour

1 tablespoon (10 g) instant yeast

1 tablespoon fine sea salt

¼ cup (59 ml) sorghum syrup

¼ cup (59 ml) vegetable oil

½ cup (118 ml) whole milk

¾ cup (177 ml) room-temperature water

1 large (50 g) egg, lightly beaten with a pinch of
    fine sea salt, for egg wash

OPTIONAL SPECIAL EQUIPMENT
Instant-read thermometer

In the bowl of a stand mixer fitted with the dough hook, combine the flour, yeast, and salt and mix on low speed to blend. Add the sorghum syrup, oil, milk, and water and mix for 3 minutes. Increase the speed to medium and mix for 8 minutes, or until a dough forms; it should be somewhat loose yet firm to the touch. Transfer the dough to a lightly floured work surface and knead until smooth, then shape into a ball.

Lightly oil a large bowl. Transfer the dough to the bowl and turn the dough gently to coat it with oil. Cover the bowl with plastic wrap and let the dough rise in a warm, draft-free place for 2 hours, or until almost doubled in size.

Lightly spray a 9-by-5-inch (23 by 13 cm) loaf pan with nonstick spray. Transfer the dough to a lightly floured work surface and shape it into a rectangle about 8 inches by 6 inches (20 by 15 cm) wide. Starting with a long side, gently roll the dough up into a cylinder. Place the dough seam side down in the prepared pan, cover with plastic wrap, and allow to rise for 1 hour, or until the dough has risen about 1 inch (3 cm) above the edges of the pan.

Position an oven rack in the middle of the oven and preheat the oven to 350°F (175°C).

Brush the top of the dough with the egg wash. Place the loaf pan in the oven and bake for 30 to 35 minutes, until the bread is nicely browned; an instant-read thermometer inserted in the center of the loaf should read 190°F (90°C).

Remove the bread from the oven and let cool in the pan on a wire rack for 5 minutes, then remove the bread from the pan and cool completely on the rack.

The bread can be stored in an airtight container for up to 2 days. To freeze, wrap in plastic wrap and then aluminum foil; it'll keep for up to 1 month.

Sally Lunn Bread

There are many legends surrounding the name of this bread. One attributes it to the appearance of the bread, theorizing that perhaps "Sally Lunn" is a mispronunciation of the French "soleil et lune": The top bakes as gold as the sun (*soleil* in French), and the bottom as light as the moon (*lune*). Another charming story claims that a tea shop proprietress found the recipe hidden in a secret panel above a fireplace with a note from a French baker named Solange Luyon, who had fled to England as a refugee late in the seventeenth century. She baked and sold the bread on the streets of Bath, where she became known as Sally Lunn.

No matter the origin, this recipe was carried over the pond with the colonists as a remembrance of England; it later became the daily bread of the American South. It is based on an enriched dough made with milk, butter, eggs, and a bit of sugar. And because bakers love to share, this recipe makes two loaves.

MAKES 2 LOAVES

5½ cups (688 g) unbleached all-purpose flour

1 tablespoon fine sea salt

1½ teaspoons (5 g) instant yeast

1 teaspoon granulated sugar

8 tablespoons (1 stick/113 g) unsalted butter, melted and cooled

2 large (100 g) eggs, lightly beaten

1 cup (237 ml) whole milk, at room temperature

1½ tablespoons honey

¾ cup (177 ml) water, at room temperature

1 large (50 g) egg, lightly beaten with a pinch of fine sea salt, for egg wash

In the bowl of a stand mixer fitted with the dough hook, combine the flour, salt, yeast, and sugar and mix on low speed to blend. Add the melted butter, eggs, milk, honey, and water and mix for 3 to 5 minutes, scraping down the sides and bottom of the bowl with a rubber spatula occasionally, until the dough comes together in a shaggy mass. Increase the speed to medium and mix for a full 7 minutes; the dough will begin to rise up on the dough hook.

Transfer the dough to a lightly floured work surface and knead for 30 to 60 seconds, until smooth and elastic. Shape the dough into a ball.

Butter a large bowl and put the dough in the bowl, turning to coat it with butter. Cover the bowl with plastic wrap and let the dough rise in a warm, draft-free place for 1 hour, or until doubled in size.

Grease two 9-by-5-inch (23 by 13 cm) loaf pans with butter.

Divide the dough in half. Using a rolling pin, roll each piece into an 8-by-10-inch (20 by 25 cm) rectangle. Starting from a short side, roll each piece up into a log. Pinch the seams to seal and place seam side down in the prepared loaf pans. Loosely cover each pan with plastic wrap and allow the dough to rise for about 1 hour, or until doubled in size.

Position a rack in the middle of the oven and preheat the oven to 350°F (175°C).

Brush the tops of the loaves with the egg wash. Bake for 40 to 45 minutes; the crust should look like dark honey and an instant-read thermometer inserted in the center of a loaf should read 190°F (90°C).

Place the pans on a wire rack and let cool for 5 minutes. Loosen the bread from the sides of the pans, turn out the loaves, and then turn right side up on the rack to cool completely.

The bread can be stored in an airtight container for up to 2 days.

Gathering Cakes

Food builds bridges.
If you can eat with someone,
you can learn from them,
and when you learn from someone,
you can make big changes.

—LEAH CHASE

WHENEVER FOLKS GET TOGETHER IN THE SOUTH, you can count on there being cake. But it's not only fancy layer cakes; there are also gathering cakes, which are plain cakes that travel well and are enjoyed as a part of everyday life. Gathering cakes make appearances at both joyful and solemn occasions. You'll find them displayed on long tables at casual get-togethers such as cookbook club meetings, covered-dish parties, neighborhood picnics, tailgates, and church dinners. They're great for simple entertaining too. Have one on hand for when friends stop over. These cakes are made in rectangular baking pans, sheet pans, or Bundt pans, and they are easier to whip up than showy layer cakes.

Gathering cakes can demonstrate Southern hospitality at its best. Deliver a Lemon Buttermilk Cake to a friend to celebrate a new baby or a Salted Caramel Pecan Cake to provide a loved one with a dose of comfort. The Coca-Cola Cake is perfect for a church picnic. Take the 'Nana Pudding Poke Cake or German Chocolate Cake to your next potluck. If the party is adults-only, wow them with the Grown Folks' Rum Cake; it may become your favorite recipe to bring and to share.

Sunday Snack Cake

PICTURED ON PAGE 141

This rich yellow cake with a delicate crumb and delightfully colored frosting is super cheery and quick to make. It is perfect for a Sunday brunch or family dinner, but it's also an easy weeknight dessert if you crave something to soothe your sweet tooth. The buttercream frosting can be tinted in vibrant or pastel colors; try pink, and decorate the cake with sprinkles.

SERVES 12 TO 16

3¼ cups (406 g) cake flour (not self-rising)
2 teaspoons (9 g) baking powder, preferably aluminum-free
1½ teaspoons (8 g) baking soda
1½ teaspoons fine sea salt
1½ cups (355 ml) buttermilk
¾ cup (177 ml) vegetable oil
2 teaspoons pure vanilla extract
½ pound (2 sticks/227 g) unsalted butter, at room temperature
2 cups (400 g) granulated sugar
½ cup (100 g) packed light brown sugar
5 large (250 g) eggs, at room temperature
3 large (57 g) egg yolks, at room temperature
1 recipe American Buttercream Frosting (recipe follows)
Colored sprinkles (optional)

Position a rack in the middle of the oven and preheat the oven to 350°F (175°C). Butter an 11-by-17-by-2-inch (28 by 43 by 5 cm) baking pan or coat with nonstick spray. Line the pan with parchment, leaving an overhang on two opposite sides.

Sift together the flour, baking powder, baking soda, and salt into a medium bowl. Set aside.

In a large measuring cup or small bowl, mix together the buttermilk, oil, and vanilla. Set aside.

In the bowl of a stand mixer fitted with the paddle attachment (or in a large mixing bowl, using a handheld mixer), cream the butter and both sugars together on medium-high speed for 3 to 5 minutes, until light and fluffy. Turn the speed down to low and add the eggs and yolks one (50 g/19 g) at a time, beating well after each addition and scraping down the sides and bottom of the bowl with a rubber spatula as necessary.

With the mixer still on low speed, add the flour mixture in thirds, alternating with the buttermilk mixture and beginning and ending with the flour, mixing until just combined. Remove the bowl from the mixer stand (if using) and, using the rubber spatula, incorporate any ingredients hiding at the bottom of the bowl, making sure the batter is completely mixed.

Scrape the batter into the prepared pan and gently smooth the top with a spatula. Tap the pan firmly on the countertop to remove any air bubbles from the batter.

Bake for 25 to 30 minutes, until a cake tester inserted in the center of the cake comes out clean.

Let the cake cool in the pan on a wire rack for 20 minutes, then use the parchment "handles" to lift the cake out of the pan and set it on the rack to cool completely. (*The cake can be made ahead and stored in the refrigerator for up to 3 days. Bring to room temperature before frosting.*)

To assemble the cake: Cut the cake crosswise in half. Place one piece on a serving plate (you can keep the edges of the plate clean while you frost the cake by sliding strips of parchment underneath the cake). Using an offset spatula, spread the layer with a big dollop of buttercream, going all the way to the edges. Place the second layer right side up on top and frost the top and down the sides of the cake with a thin layer of frosting to create a crumb coat. Place the cake in the refrigerator for about 20 minutes to set the crumb coat; the frosting should still feel a bit tacky, so that the final layer of frosting will adhere properly.

(Continued)

Frost the top and sides of the cake with the remaining frosting, using the back of the spatula or a spoon to create big, luscious swirls. Sprinkle with colored sprinkles after the frosting has set, if you like.

The cake can be stored, loosely covered, at room temperature for up to 3 days.

AMERICAN BUTTERCREAM FROSTING

MAKES ABOUT 3 CUPS (710 ML)

8 tablespoons (1 stick/113 g) unsalted butter,
    at room temperature
About 4 cups (500 g) confectioners' sugar
½ teaspoon fine sea salt
¼ cup (59 ml) whole milk
½ teaspoon pure vanilla extract
½ teaspoon white vinegar
Liquid gel food coloring (optional)

In the bowl of a stand mixer fitted with the paddle attachment (or in a large mixing bowl, using a handheld mixer), cream the butter on medium speed until light and fluffy, about 2 minutes. With the mixer on low speed, gradually add 3 cups (375 g) confectioners' sugar, then add the salt, milk, vanilla, and vinegar and mix until smooth and creamy, 1 to 2 minutes. If necessary, gradually add up to 1 more cup (125 g) confectioners' sugar, mixing on low speed, until the frosting is light and fluffy.

If desired, to tint the frosting, add a drop or two of food coloring to the frosting, mixing well; add more coloring if necessary until you reach the desired shade.

The frosting can be used immediately or stored in an airtight container at room temperature for up to 2 days. You can also refrigerate it for up to 5 days; bring to room temperature before using.

Chocolate Chip Snack Cake

This wonderfully tender vanilla cake is dotted with just the right amount of chocolate chips and topped with chocolate buttercream, for a dessert most anyone will love.

SERVES 12 TO 16

1 cup (237 ml) whole milk
1 teaspoon pure vanilla extract
1¾ cups (219 g) cake flour (not self-rising)
1¼ cups (156 g) unbleached all-purpose flour
1 tablespoon (13 g) baking powder, preferably
    aluminum-free
¾ teaspoon fine sea salt
½ pound (2 sticks/227 g) unsalted butter, at room
    temperature
1½ cups (300 g) granulated sugar
½ cup (100 g) packed light brown sugar
4 large (200 g) eggs, at room temperature
1 cup (175 g) semisweet chocolate chips
1 recipe Chocolate Buttercream (recipe follows)

Position a rack in the middle of the oven and preheat the oven to 350°F (175°C). Butter a 9-by-13-by-2-inch (23 by 33 by 5 cm) baking pan or coat with nonstick spray. Line the pan with parchment, leaving an overhang on two opposite sides.

In a large measuring cup or small bowl, mix together the milk and vanilla. Set aside.

Sift together both flours, the baking powder, and salt into a medium bowl. Set aside.

In the bowl of a stand mixer fitted with the paddle attachment (or in a large mixing bowl, using a handheld mixer), cream the butter and both sugars together on medium-high speed for 3 to 5 minutes, until light and fluffy. Turn the mixer speed down to low and add the eggs one (50 g) at a time, beating well after each addition and scraping down the sides and bottom of the bowl with a rubber spatula as necessary. With the mixer on low speed, add the flour mixture in thirds, alternating with the milk and beginning and ending with the flour, scraping down the sides and bottom of the bowl as necessary.

Remove the bowl from the mixer stand (if using) and gently fold in the chocolate chips. Using the rubber spatula, incorporate any ingredients hiding at the bottom of the bowl, making sure the batter is completely mixed.

Scrape the batter into the prepared pan and gently smooth the top with a spatula. Tap the pan firmly on the countertop to remove any air bubbles from the batter.

Bake for 35 to 40 minutes, until a cake tester inserted in the center of the cake comes out clean. Let the cake cool in the pan on a wire rack for 20 minutes, then use the parchment "handles" to lift the cake out of the pan and set it on the rack to cool completely.

Invert the cake onto a platter and frost the top and sides with the buttercream frosting.

The cake can be stored, loosely covered, in the refrigerator for up to 3 days. Bring to room temperature before serving.

CHOCOLATE BUTTERCREAM

MAKES ABOUT 3 CUPS (710 ML)

⅔ cup (113 g) semisweet chocolate chips or ¼ pound (113 g) semisweet chocolate, chopped
12 tablespoons (1½ sticks/170 g) unsalted butter, at room temperature
1 tablespoon whole milk
½ teaspoon pure vanilla extract
1½ cups (188 g) confectioners' sugar, sifted

Put the chocolate in a heatproof bowl set over a saucepan of simmering water (do not let the bottom of the bowl touch the water) and stir occasionally until the chocolate is completely melted. Set the chocolate aside to cool to room temperature.

In the bowl of a stand mixer fitted with the paddle attachment (or in a medium mixing bowl, using a handheld mixer), beat the butter on medium speed until smooth and creamy. Add the milk, mixing until blended. Add the cooled chocolate and mix until completely incorporated, 2 to 3 minutes, scraping down the sides and bottom of the bowl with a rubber spatula as necessary. Beat in the vanilla. With the mixer on low speed, gradually add the confectioners' sugar and continue beating until the frosting is creamy and silky smooth.

The frosting can be made ahead and stored in an airtight container at room temperature for up to 2 days; rewhip it slightly until it is smooth and creamy again.

Salted Caramel Pecan Cake

This delicate butter cake has a double dose of caramel, in the cake itself and in the quick caramel frosting. There is just enough flaky sea salt on top to keep it from being cloyingly sweet. Be sure to make the Salted Caramel Sauce in advance, so it's ready when you need it.

SERVES 12 TO 16

2½ cups (313 g) unbleached all-purpose flour

2½ teaspoons (11 g) baking powder, preferably aluminum-free

1 teaspoon fine sea salt

1 cup (237 ml) Salted Caramel Sauce (page 380), at room temperature

½ cup (118 ml) water

8 tablespoons (1 stick/113 g) unsalted butter, at room temperature

1⅓ cups (267 g) granulated sugar

3 large (150 g) eggs, at room temperature

Salted Caramel Frosting (recipe follows)

1 cup (114 g) pecans, toasted and chopped

Flaky sea salt, such as Maldon, for sprinkling

Position a rack in the lower third of the oven and preheat the oven to 350°F (175°C). Butter a 9-by-13-by-2-inch (23 by 33 by 5 cm) baking pan or coat with nonstick spray. Line the pan with parchment, leaving an overhang on two opposite sides.

Sift together the flour, baking powder, and fine sea salt into a medium bowl. Set aside.

In a small bowl, combine the caramel sauce and water and stir until completely smooth. Set aside.

In the bowl of a stand mixer fitted with the paddle attachment (or in a large mixing bowl, using a handheld mixer), cream the butter and sugar together on medium-high speed for 3 to 5 minutes, until light and fluffy. Add the eggs one (50 g) at a time, beating well after each addition and scraping down the sides and bottom of the bowl with a rubber spatula as necessary.

With the mixer on low speed, add the flour mixture in thirds, alternating with the caramel mixture and beginning and ending with the flour, mixing until just combined. Scrape down the sides and bottom of the bowl as necessary.

Pour the batter into the prepared pan. Bake for 20 to 25 minutes, until a cake tester inserted in the center of the cake comes out clean. Let the cake cool in the pan on a wire rack for about 20 minutes, then use the parchment "handles" to lift the cake out of the pan and set it on the rack to cool completely.

To finish the cake: Place the cake on a serving plate (you can keep the edges of the plate clean while you frost the cake by sliding strips of parchment underneath the cake). Using an offset spatula, frost the top and sides of the cake with a thin layer of frosting to create a crumb coat. Place the cake in the refrigerator for about 20 minutes to set the crumb coat; the frosting should still feel a bit tacky, so that the final layer of frosting will adhere properly.

Frost the cake with the remaining frosting, using the back of the spatula or a spoon to create big, luscious swirls. Decorate the top with the pecans and sprinkle with flaky sea salt, and you are ready to go!

The cake can be stored, loosely covered, at room temperature or in the refrigerator for up to 3 days. If it's been refrigerated, bring to room temperature before serving.

SALTED CARAMEL FROSTING

MAKES ABOUT 4 CUPS (946 ML)

2 cups (400 g) packed dark brown sugar

12 tablespoons (1½ sticks/170 g) unsalted butter, cut into tablespoon-sized pieces

½ teaspoon fine sea salt

½ cup (118 ml) heavy cream

1½ teaspoons pure vanilla extract

2 cups (250 g) confectioners' sugar, sifted

In a medium heavy-bottomed saucepan, combine the brown sugar, 8 tablespoons (1 stick/113 g) of the butter, and the salt and cook over medium heat, stirring constantly to dissolve the sugar, until the mixture comes to a gentle boil, 5 to 8 minutes. Whisk in the cream and bring back to a boil. Remove from the heat and add the vanilla.

Pour the mixture into the bowl of a stand mixer fitted with the paddle attachment (or use a large mixing bowl and a handheld mixer) and, with the mixer on low speed, gradually add the confectioners' sugar, beating until incorporated. Increase the speed to medium and beat until the frosting lightens in color and has cooled to warm, 3 to 5 minutes. Add the remaining 4 tablespoons (57 g) butter one piece at a time and continue to mix until the frosting is light and fluffy. Use immediately.

German Chocolate Cake

Researching a recipe's history is especially interesting when the dessert's name references its origins. In 1852, Sam German, an employee of Baker Chocolate Company, created a sweet baking chocolate that was used to make German's Chocolate Cake. It became famous a century later when it was featured as a "Recipe of the Day" in the *Dallas Morning News* in 1957. The original frosting was made with evaporated milk, sugar, butter, and coconut; I use sweetened cream of coconut instead of evaporated milk for more flavor. The pecans were added later, and the name was shortened to German chocolate cake.

SERVES 12

5 ounces (142 g) unsweetened chocolate, finely chopped (about ¾ cup)

1 cup (237 ml) hot brewed coffee

2 teaspoons pure vanilla extract

1½ cups (188 g) cake flour (not self-rising)

2 cups (400 g) granulated sugar

¾ teaspoon (4 g) baking soda

½ teaspoon fine sea salt

2 large (100 g) eggs, at room temperature

½ cup (118 ml) vegetable oil

½ cup (120 g) sour cream, at room temperature

1 recipe German Chocolate Frosting (recipe follows)

Position a rack in the lower third of the oven and preheat the oven to 350°F (175°C). Butter a 9-by-13-by-2-inch (23 by 33 by 5 cm) baking pan or coat with nonstick spray. Line the pan with parchment, leaving an overhang on two opposite sides.

Put the chocolate in a medium bowl and pour in the hot coffee and vanilla. Let stand for about 2 minutes to melt the chocolate, then stir until smooth.

While the chocolate is melting, in the bowl of a stand mixer fitted with the paddle attachment (or in a large mixing bowl, using a handheld mixer), combine the flour, sugar, baking soda, and salt. Let the mixer run on low speed for 2 to 3 minutes to aerate the flour.

(Continued on page 138)

In a medium bowl, whisk the eggs and oil together until thick, satiny, and light in color. Whisk in the sour cream, being careful not to overmix; leave some visible streaks of white. Pour in the melted chocolate mixture and mix until just combined.

With the mixer on medium speed, add the chocolate–sour cream mixture to the dry ingredients in thirds, mixing until well blended. Remove the bowl from the mixer stand (if using) and, using a rubber spatula, incorporate any ingredients hiding at the bottom of the bowl, making sure the batter is completely mixed.

Scrape the batter into the prepared pan and smooth the top with a spatula. Tap the pans firmly on the countertop to remove any air bubbles from the batter.

Bake for 35 to 40 minutes, until a cake tester inserted in the center of the cake comes out clean. Let the cake cool in the pan on a wire rack for about 20 minutes, then use the parchment "handles" to lift the cake out of the pan and set it on the rack to cool completely.

Transfer the cake to a serving platter (you can keep the edges of the platter clean while you frost the cake by sliding strips of parchment underneath the cake). Frost the top and sides of the cake with the frosting.

The cake can be stored, loosely covered, in the refrigerator for up to 3 days. Bring to room temperature before serving.

GERMAN CHOCOLATE FROSTING

MAKES 2 CUPS (473 ML)

1 cup (114 g) pecans
½ cup (118 ml) whole milk
1 cup (237 ml) cream of coconut, such as Coco López
4 tablespoons (57 g) unsalted butter
1 teaspoon pure vanilla extract
3 large (57 g) egg yolks
½ cup (100 g) granulated sugar
2 tablespoons cornstarch
½ teaspoon fine sea salt
1 cup (85 g) sweetened shredded coconut

Preheat the oven to 350°F (175°C). Line a baking sheet with parchment.

Scatter the pecans evenly over the baking sheet and toast in the oven for about 5 minutes, until lightly toasted and fragrant. Cool the nuts completely and chop.

In a medium saucepan, combine the milk, cream of coconut, and butter and cook over medium heat, stirring, until the butter is completely melted. Remove from the heat and stir in the vanilla.

In a medium bowl, whisk the egg yolks, sugar, cornstarch, and salt together until smooth. Slowly pour in about ¼ cup (59 ml) of the hot milk mixture to temper the eggs, so they won't curdle, and then, whisking constantly, add the remainder of the milk in a steady stream. Continue to whisk until the mixture thickens, 10 to 12 minutes. Stir in the coconut and pecans. Let cool completely before frosting the cake.

The frosting can be made ahead and stored in an airtight container in the refrigerator for up to 1 week.

Pineapple Upside-Down Cake

PICTURED ON PAGE 141

Upside-down cakes are such a joy to bake; it's the surprise when you unmold them that makes them so satisfying. You can make this cake with just about any fruit, but pineapple is the true retro classic. You can add a little rum or bourbon to the glaze if you're serving grown folks.

SERVES 12

FOR THE CARAMEL PINEAPPLE TOPPING

1 ripe pineapple or one 15-ounce (425 g) can
    pineapple slices, drained
6 tablespoons (85 g) unsalted butter
1 cup (200 g) packed light brown sugar
1 tablespoon pure vanilla extract
½ teaspoon fine sea salt
8 maraschino cherries, preferably Luxardo

FOR THE CAKE

2½ cups (313 g) cake flour (not self-rising)
1 tablespoon (13 g) baking powder, preferably
    aluminum-free
1½ teaspoons fine sea salt
¼ teaspoon ground mace
3 large (150 g) eggs, at room temperature
1 tablespoon pure vanilla extract
12 tablespoons (1½ sticks/170 g) unsalted butter,
    at room temperature
1½ cups (300 g) granulated sugar
1½ cups (360 g) sour cream

Preheat the oven to 350°F (175°C). Have a 9-by-13-inch (23 by 33 cm) baking pan at hand.

To prepare the pineapple: If using a fresh pineapple, slice off the top and bottom. Stand the pineapple up and remove the peel by slicing it away in long strips following the contours of the fruit, making sure to remove all the "eyes" as well. Put the peeled pineapple on its side and cut into ½-inch-thick (1.5 cm) rounds; you want 8 slices. Using a 1-inch (3 cm) cookie cutter, remove the core from each slice. Set the pineapple aside on paper towels to drain. If using canned pineapple, place 8 slices on paper towels to drain thoroughly.

To make the caramel pineapple topping: In a small saucepan, melt the butter over medium heat. Add the brown sugar, vanilla, and salt and cook, stirring occasionally, until the sugar dissolves and the butter is melted, 3 to 4 minutes. Remove from the heat.

Pour the butter mixture into the baking pan and swirl the pan to evenly coat the bottom. Arrange the fresh pineapple slices or canned pineapple rings on top of the caramel mixture, without overlapping. Place a cherry in the middle of each pineapple ring.

To make the cake: In a medium bowl, whisk together the flour, baking powder, salt, and mace. Set aside.

In a small bowl, whisk together the eggs and vanilla. Set aside.

In the bowl of a stand mixer fitted with the paddle attachment (or in a large mixing bowl, using a handheld mixer), cream the butter and sugar together on medium-high speed until light and fluffy, 3 to 5 minutes. Add the egg mixture a little at a time, beating well after each addition and scraping down the sides and bottom of the bowl with a rubber spatula as necessary.

Turn the speed down to low and add the flour mixture in thirds, alternating with the sour cream, beginning and ending with the flour and scraping down the sides and bottom of the bowl as necessary. Remove the bowl from the mixer stand (if using) and use the rubber spatula to incorporate any ingredients hiding at the bottom of the bowl, making sure the batter is completely mixed. Pour the batter over the pineapple slices and smooth it with a spatula.

Bake for 40 to 45 minutes, until a cake tester inserted in the center of the cake comes out clean.

(Continued)

Let the cake cool in the pan on a wire rack for about 15 minutes.

Run a small knife around the edges of the pan, then place a large serving plate upside down on top and invert the pan to release the cake onto the plate. Serve warm or at room temperature.

The cake can be stored in an airtight container at room temperature for up to 3 days.

Boozy Fruitcake

PICTURED OPPOSITE

Every Southern community has at least one "cake lady" known for her fruitcake. She likely starts preparations in October, and if you're lucky, you've made the list to be gifted one wrapped in cheesecloth and stored in a Christmas tin each December. A true Southern fruitcake is made with good-quality dried fruit, not the artificially colored fruit you see in the grocery store. After the cake is baked, it is brushed with brandy once a week over the course of several months, which softens the fruit and builds the delicious flavor that comes only with time. Plan on baking the cake at least a month ahead.

To gild the lily, serve the fruitcake with Chantilly Cream (page 373) spiked with brandy.

SERVES 12 TO 16

2 cups (250 g) unbleached all-purpose flour

1 tablespoon (17 g) baking soda

½ teaspoon fine sea salt

12 tablespoons (1½ sticks/170 g) unsalted butter, at room temperature

1 cup (200 g) granulated sugar

3 large (150 g) eggs, at room temperature

1 teaspoon pure vanilla extract

1 Granny Smith apple, peeled, cored, and diced

2 cups (228 g) pecans, coarsely chopped

1 cup (149 g) chopped dried figs

1 cup (120 g) mixed dried fruit, such as cranberries, cherries, chopped apricots, and raisins

¾ cup (177 ml) fruit preserves, such as peach, apricot, or fig

About 1 cup (237 ml) brandy for brushing

Position a rack in the lower third of the oven and preheat the oven to 275°F (135°C). Butter a 9-by-5-by-3-inch (23 by 13 by 5 cm) loaf pan. Lightly dust the pan with flour, tapping the pan on the counter to shake out the excess.

Sift together the flour, baking soda, and salt into a medium bowl. Set aside.

In the bowl of a stand mixer fitted with the paddle attachment (or in a large mixing bowl, using a handheld mixer), cream the butter and sugar together on medium-high speed until light and fluffy, 3 to 5 minutes. Add the eggs one (50 g) at a time, beating well after each addition and scraping down the sides and bottom of the bowl with a rubber spatula as necessary. Beat in the vanilla. Turn the speed down to low and add the flour mixture in thirds, beating until just combined. Add the apples, pecans, dried fruit, and preserves, mixing well.

Pour the batter into the prepared pan. Bake for 1½ hours, or until a cake tester inserted in the center of the cake comes out clean. Let cool in the pan on a wire rack for about 20 minutes, then remove the cake from the pan and turn right side up on the rack to cool completely.

Brush the cake liberally all over with the brandy. Wrap it in cheesecloth or parchment and then in aluminum foil. Place in a cake keeper and refrigerate for at least 4 weeks, and up to 2 months, brushing it liberally with brandy once a week.

CLOCKWISE FROM TOP LEFT: SUNDAY SNACK CAKE (PAGE 131), FRESH FRUIT DUMP CAKE (PAGE 143),
BOOZY FRUITCAKE (OPPOSITE), PINEAPPLE UPSIDE-DOWN CAKE (PAGE 139)

Grown Folks' Rum Cake

Rich tipsy cakes infused with rum get better with age, as the flavor develops over time. The rum gives this Bundt cake a mature flavor that warms you all over. Make it for a dinner party with good friends.

SERVES 12 TO 16

FOR THE CAKE

1 cup (114 g) pecans, coarsely chopped

3 cups (375 g) unbleached all-purpose flour

1 teaspoon (4 g) baking powder, preferably
    aluminum-free

½ teaspoon fine sea salt

⅔ cup (160 g) sour cream

½ cup (118 ml) dark rum

1 tablespoon pure vanilla extract

½ pound (2 sticks/227 g) unsalted butter,
    at room temperature

2½ cups (500 g) granulated sugar

5 large (250 g) eggs, at room temperature

FOR THE RUM GLAZE

½ cup (100 g) granulated sugar

4 tablespoons (57 g) unsalted butter

⅛ teaspoon fine sea salt

¼ cup (59 ml) dark rum

¼ cup (59 ml) water

¼ teaspoon pure vanilla extract

To make the cake: Position a rack in the middle of the oven and preheat the oven to 350°F (175°C). Line a baking sheet with parchment. Butter a 10-inch (25 cm) Bundt pan, making sure to get into all the crevices. Lightly dust the pan with flour, tapping the pan on the counter to shake out the excess.

Scatter the pecans over the prepared baking sheet and bake for about 5 minutes, until lightly toasted and fragrant. Let cool completely, then sprinkle the pecans evenly over the bottom of the prepared pan.

Sift together the flour, baking powder, and salt into a medium bowl. Set aside.

In a large measuring cup or small bowl, mix together the sour cream, rum, and vanilla. Set aside.

In the bowl of a stand mixer fitted with the paddle attachment (or in a large mixing bowl, using a handheld mixer), cream the butter and sugar together on medium-high speed until light and fluffy, 3 to 5 minutes. Add the eggs one (50 g) at a time, beating well after each addition and scraping down the sides and bottom of the bowl with a rubber spatula as necessary. Turn the speed down to low and add the flour mixture in thirds, alternating with the sour cream mixture, beginning and ending with the flour and scraping down the sides and bottom of the bowl as necessary.

Scrape the batter into the prepared pan and smooth the top with a spatula. Bake for about 1 hour and 20 minutes, until the cake is lightly golden on top and a cake tester inserted in the center comes out clean. Remove the cake from the oven and let cool in the pan on a wire rack for 20 minutes, then turn the cake out onto a serving plate.

To make the glaze: In a small saucepan, combine the sugar, butter, salt, rum, and water and cook over medium heat, stirring, until the sugar has dissolved. Then cook the glaze until it comes to a gentle boil. Remove from the heat and stir in the vanilla. Let the glaze cool slightly.

Pour the glaze over the warm cake, letting it run down the sides. Let the glaze set before serving.

The cake can be stored, covered with plastic wrap, in the refrigerator for up to 1 week.

Fresh Fruit Dump Cake

PICTURED ON PAGE 141

What a descriptive name for this easy-peasy dessert. It's a nod to an old recipe from the side of a cake box mix that became famous. The recipe usually starts with cans of fruit, but this one uses fresh fruit. It is the cake to make when you have an abundance of seasonal fruit. You can choose one favorite type or include a mix.

SERVES 12

3 pounds (1.4 kg) fresh fruit, such as berries, sliced peaches, apples, and/or plums

1¾ cups (350 g) granulated sugar

2½ tablespoons cornstarch

½ teaspoon fine sea salt

1¼ cups (156 g) unbleached all-purpose flour

1 teaspoon (4 g) baking powder, preferably aluminum-free

¼ teaspoon ground cardamom

12 tablespoons (1½ sticks/170 g) unsalted butter, melted

Preheat the oven to 350°F (175°C). Butter a 9-by-13-inch (23 by 33 cm) baking dish.

In a large bowl, combine the fruit, ½ cup (100 g) of the sugar, the cornstarch, and ¼ teaspoon of the salt and toss until completely combined.

In a medium bowl, whisk together the flour, the remaining 1¼ cups (250 g) sugar, the baking powder, cardamom, and the remaining ¼ teaspoon salt.

Sprinkle the flour mixture evenly over the fruit. Drizzle the melted butter all over the top. Pour into the prepared pan.

Bake for 35 to 45 minutes, or until the fruit juices are bubbling up through the center of the topping and the top is golden brown. Let the cake cool slightly on a wire rack, or let cool completely.

Serve big scoops of the cake, warm or at room temperature.

The cake can be stored, covered, in the refrigerator for up to 3 days.

Lemon Buttermilk Cake

This zesty lemon cake is a refreshing way to end a good home-cooked meal. It's a sheet cake that is frosted right in the pan with a lemony buttermilk buttercream. You might offer your guests a scoop of vanilla ice cream or lemon sherbet on top of each slice.

SERVES 12 TO 16

3 cups (375 g) unbleached all-purpose flour

1 teaspoon (4 g) baking powder, preferably aluminum-free

½ teaspoon (3 g) baking soda

½ teaspoon fine sea salt

1 cup (237 ml) buttermilk

2 tablespoons grated lemon zest (from 1 medium lemon)

¾ pound (3 sticks/340 g) unsalted butter, at room temperature

3 cups (600 g) granulated sugar

6 large (300 g) eggs, at room temperature

1 recipe Buttermilk Buttercream Frosting (recipe follows)

Position a rack in the lower third of the oven and preheat the oven to 350°F (175°C). Butter an 11-by-17-by-1-inch (28 by 43 by 3 cm) baking sheet.

Sift together the flour, baking powder, baking soda, and salt into a large bowl. Set aside.

(Continued)

In a large measuring cup or small bowl, combine the buttermilk and lemon zest. Set aside.

In the bowl of a stand mixer fitted with the paddle attachment (or in a large mixing bowl, using a handheld mixer), cream the butter and sugar together until light and fluffy, 3 to 5 minutes. Add the eggs one (50 g) at a time, beating well after each addition and scraping down the sides and bottom of the bowl with a rubber spatula as necessary.

On low speed, add the flour mixture in thirds, alternating with the buttermilk mixture and beginning and ending with the flour, mixing until just combined. Remove the bowl from the mixer stand (if using) and, using the rubber spatula, incorporate any ingredients hiding at the bottom of the bowl, making sure the batter is completely mixed.

Pour the batter into the prepared pan and gently smooth the top with a spatula. Tap the pan firmly on the counter to remove any air bubbles from the batter.

Bake for 20 to 25 minutes, until a cake tester inserted in the center of the cake comes out clean. Let cool completely in the pan on a wire rack.

Frost the cooled cake right in the pan, and you are ready to go!

The cake can be stored, loosely covered, in the refrigerator for up to 3 days. Bring to room temperature before serving.

BUTTERMILK BUTTERCREAM FROSTING

MAKES 3 CUPS (710 ML)

½ pound (2 sticks/227 g) unsalted butter, at room
    temperature
½ teaspoon fine sea salt
3 to 4 cups (375 to 500 g) confectioners' sugar
¼ cup (59 ml) buttermilk
2 tablespoons grated lemon zest (from 1 medium lemon)

In the bowl of a stand mixer fitted with the paddle attachment (or in a large mixing bowl, using a handheld mixer), cream the butter and salt on medium speed until light and fluffy, 2 to 3 minutes. With the mixer on low speed, gradually add 3 cups (375 g) confectioners' sugar, the buttermilk, and lemon zest, mixing until smooth and creamy, 2 to 3 minutes. Gradually add 1 cup (125 g) more sugar, mixing until the frosting is light and fluffy, about 2 minutes. The frosting can be used immediately or stored in an airtight container at room temperature for up to 2 days. It can also be refrigerated for up to 5 days; bring to room temperature before using.

Ginger Cake Squares with Chantilly Cream

If you're looking for a simple dessert for the Christmas holiday table, this ginger cake is just the thing (but it's good any time of year, really). This recipe has been passed down in my family for at least four generations. Made with two types of ginger, both ground and candied, as well as blackstrap molasses and plenty of warm spices, it has an unforgettable rich ginger flavor.

MAKES 12 TO 16 SQUARES

1 cup (200 g) granulated sugar

½ pound (2 sticks/227 g) unsalted butter, melted

2 cups (473 ml) blackstrap molasses

2 large (100 g) eggs, at room temperature

4 cups (500 g) unbleached all-purpose flour

1 tablespoon (17 g) baking soda

1 teaspoon fine sea salt

2 tablespoons ground ginger

1 tablespoon ground cinnamon

1 teaspoon ground cloves

1 teaspoon freshly grated nutmeg

1 teaspoon ground allspice

2 cups (473 ml) boiling water

½ cup (85 g) finely chopped candied ginger

1 recipe Chantilly Cream (page 373) for serving

Position a rack in the lower third of the oven and preheat the oven to 350°F (175°C). Butter a 9-by-13-by-2-inch (23 by 33 by 5 cm) baking pan or coat with nonstick spray. Line the pan with parchment, leaving an overhang on two opposite sides.

In a large bowl, whisk together the sugar, butter, molasses, and eggs. Set aside.

Sift together the flour, baking soda, and salt into a medium bowl. Whisk in the ground ginger, cinnamon, cloves, nutmeg, and allspice. Stir the dry ingredients into the molasses-egg mixture, then add the boiling water, whisking until well blended. Fold in the candied ginger.

Pour the batter into the prepared pan and bake for 35 to 40 minutes, until a cake tester inserted in the center of the cake comes out clean. Let the cake cool in the pan on a wire rack for 15 minutes.

Cut the ginger cake into 12 to 16 squares, transfer to plates, and serve warm, with the Chantilly cream.

The cake is even better the next day, and it can be stored, loosely covered, at room temperature for up to 3 days.

'Nana Pudding Poke Cake

Poke cakes are poked with holes after the cake has baked, and the holes are filled with pudding or jam, or another sweet filling, to infuse more flavor (and moisture) into every bite. Poke cakes became popular in the 1970s, after they appeared in print advertisements designed to increase Jell-O pudding sales. This version is a light and airy cake filled with homemade vanilla pudding, then topped with sliced bananas and whipped topping, and finished off with a layer of vanilla wafers. Eat with either a fork or a spoon.

SERVES 12 TO 16

FOR THE CAKE

1¾ cups (219 g) cake flour (not self-rising)

1 teaspoon (4 g) baking powder, preferably aluminum-free

½ teaspoon fine sea salt

8 tablespoons (1 stick/113 g) unsalted butter, melted and cooled

¼ cup (59 ml) vegetable oil

1 teaspoon fresh lemon juice

10 large (300 g) egg whites, at room temperature (save 2 [38 g] of the yolks for the filling; see page 23 for info on storing extra egg yolks)

1½ cups (300 g) granulated sugar

1 teaspoon pure vanilla extract

FOR THE VANILLA PUDDING

2½ cups (592 ml) whole milk

1 cup (237 ml) heavy cream

6 tablespoons (50 g) cornstarch

2 large (100 g) eggs, at room temperature

2 large (38 g) egg yolks, at room temperature

½ cup (100 g) granulated sugar

4 teaspoons pure vanilla extract

½ teaspoon fine sea salt

3 tablespoons unsalted butter, cut into cubes. at room temperature

5 ripe bananas, peeled and sliced

1 recipe Whipped Topping (page 372)

Vanilla wafers, homemade (see page 251) or store-bought

To make the cake: Position a rack in the middle of the oven and preheat the oven to 350°F (175°C). Butter a 9-by-13-by-2-inch (23 by 33 by 5 cm) baking pan.

Sift together the flour, baking powder, and salt into a medium bowl. Set aside.

In a small bowl, whisk the butter and oil together until combined. Set aside.

Add the lemon juice to the bowl of a stand mixer (or a large mixing bowl) and then wipe it clean with a paper towel; pour out any excess juice. Do not skip this step: It really makes a difference when whipping egg whites to get their fullest potential. Attach the mixer bowl (if using) to the mixer stand and fit it with the whisk attachment.

Now, in the impeccably clean mixer bowl (or large mixing bowl, using a handheld mixer), beat the egg whites on medium speed until frothy, about 2 minutes. Gradually add the sugar, about 1 tablespoon at a time, beating on high speed, then beat until the egg whites are stiff and shiny. Add the vanilla and whip until just combined. Remove the bowl from the mixer stand (if using).

Gently but thoroughly fold the flour mixture, about one-quarter at a time, into the egg whites. Once the flour is almost fully incorporated, fold in the butter and oil mixture until incorporated.

Spoon the batter into the prepared baking pan and carefully smooth the top to level. (Don't be tempted to smack the pan against the kitchen counter to level the batter; you want to retain all of that air you just incorporated into your egg whites.)

Bake for 25 to 30 minutes, until the cake is golden brown and a cake tester inserted in the center comes out clean. Set the pan on a wire rack to cool completely.

Meanwhile, make the pudding: In a large heavy-bottomed saucepan, whisk the milk, cream, cornstarch, eggs, yolks, sugar, vanilla, and salt together until well combined. Place the saucepan over medium heat and whisk the mixture constantly until it is thick and glossy and a few air bubbles have started to rise to the surface, 5 to 7 minutes.

Remove from the heat and transfer the pudding to a heatproof bowl. Whisk in the butter; the pudding should be smooth and silky. Place a piece of plastic wrap directly on the surface of the pudding so that a skin does not form and let cool for 30 minutes, or until it reaches room temperature, then place in the refrigerator to chill for at least 1 hour. (*The pudding can be made in advance and refrigerated for up to 2 days.*)

To assemble the cake: Use the end of a big wooden spoon to poke holes all over the top of the cake. Spread the vanilla pudding over the cake, allowing it to settle into the holes you just made. Arrange a layer of the sliced bananas on top. Spread the whipped topping on top of the bananas. Finish the cake with a layer of the vanilla wafers. Cover with plastic wrap and refrigerate for at least 1 hour before serving.

The cake can be stored, covered, in the refrigerator for up to 3 days.

Coca-Cola Cake

The love for an ice-cold Coca-Cola seems to cross all social, ethnic, and economic boundaries. In the 1960s, this iconic beverage found its way into a cake, and it became one of the most popular cakes on the community table. It's a chocolate-marshmallow cake with a poured chocolate icing.

SERVES 12 TO 16

FOR THE CAKE
2 cups (250 g) unbleached all-purpose flour
¼ cup (20 g) Dutch-processed cocoa powder
1 teaspoon (6 g) baking soda
1 cup (237 ml) Coca-Cola
½ cup (118 ml) buttermilk
2 tablespoons pure vanilla extract
½ pound (2 sticks/227 g) unsalted butter,
    at room temperature
1¾ cups (350 g) granulated sugar
2 large (100 g) eggs, at room temperature
1½ cups (68 g) mini marshmallows

FOR THE CHOCOLATE ICING
8 tablespoons (1 stick/113 g) unsalted butter, melted
5 tablespoons (25 g) Dutch-processed cocoa powder
⅓ cup (79 ml) Coca-Cola
1 teaspoon pure vanilla extract
3¾ cups (454 g) confectioners' sugar (one 16-ounce box)
1 cup (114 g) pecans, chopped

To make the cake: Position a rack in the middle of the oven and preheat the oven to 350°F (175°C). Butter a 9-by-13-by-2-inch (23 by 33 by 5 cm) baking pan.

Sift together the flour, cocoa, and baking soda into a medium bowl. Set aside.

In a small bowl, mix together the cola, buttermilk, and vanilla. Set aside.

In the bowl of a stand mixer fitted with the paddle attachment (or in a large mixing bowl, using a handheld mixer), cream the butter and sugar together on medium-high speed for 4 to 5 minutes, until light and fluffy. Add the eggs one (50 g) at a time, mixing well after each addition and scraping down the sides and bottom of the bowl with a rubber spatula as necessary. Turn the speed down to low and add the flour mixture in thirds, alternating with the Coca-Cola mixture and beginning and ending with the flour. Remove the bowl from the mixer and, using the rubber spatula, incorporate any ingredients hiding at the bottom of the bowl, making sure the batter is completely mixed.

Scrape the batter into the prepared pan and spread it evenly with a spatula. Bake for 30 to 35 minutes, until a cake tester inserted in the center of the cake comes out clean.

Scatter the marshmallows over the top of the hot cake and return it to the oven for about 2 minutes, until they are melted.

Meanwhile, make the icing: In a medium bowl, combine the melted butter, cocoa, Coca-Cola, and vanilla and stir until smooth and creamy. Gradually add the confectioners' sugar, mixing until the icing is completely smooth. Fold in the pecans.

When the cake is done, remove from the oven and let cool in the pan on a wire rack for 10 minutes.

Using an offset spatula, spread the frosting over the warm cake. It will firm up as the cake cools.

The cake can be stored, loosely covered, at room temperature or in the refrigerator for up to 3 days. If it's been refrigerated, bring to room temperature before serving.

Layer Cakes and Cupcakes

BAKING A LAYER CAKE for a special occasion is an integral part of Southern culture. And for this reason, layer cakes evoke many happy memories. Proudly displayed on a beautiful glass pedestal or cake plate, layer cakes are worthy of becoming the focal point of every celebration. In this chapter, you'll find endless variations on the theme. And if you can make a two- or three-layer cake, why not really wow with a twelve-layer cake? Stack cakes (see page 176) are distinctly Southern.

An old Southern tradition that bears reviving is the passing down of handwritten recipes. It was often a new bride who received such a collection of cherished recipes—not just from her mother, but from her wedding guests as well. Receiving the gift of a detailed handwritten recipe from an excellent baker is an honor, setting a path forward to preserve the craft of Southern baking.

Many of the layer cakes in this chapter have a long history in the South, while some are updated creations with a nod to the past. All are frosted and filled; many can be dressed up with buttercream flowers or fresh roses from the garden to make them extra-special. There are also cupcake recipes for the child in all of us.

Any way you slice it, these cakes are a delight to look at and to eat, from the Old-Fashioned Caramel Cake, which is a birthday party favorite, to the Hummingbird Cake, with its roots in Jamaica. The Vanilla Jam Cake can be customized with your favorite flavors; the Little Layer Chocolate Cake is for the chocolate lover in your life. Before you make any of the cakes in this chapter, consult the tips on pages 189–194 to set yourself up for success.

Coconut Cake

PICTURED ON PAGE 167

Back in the day, fresh coconuts were available in the South only during the cold winter months. So this elegant snowy beauty of a cake became a favorite dessert-table centerpiece at Christmastime. The billowy creamy coconut milk buttercream frosting, covered with flaked coconut, is the perfect complement to the cardamom-flecked vanilla cake.

SERVES 12 TO 16

3 cups (375 g) unbleached all-purpose flour

1 teaspoon (4 g) baking powder, preferably
     aluminum-free

½ teaspoon (3 g) baking soda

¼ teaspoon ground cardamom

½ teaspoon fine sea salt

¾ cup (177 ml) cream of coconut, such as Coco López

¼ cup (59 ml) water

2 teaspoons pure vanilla extract

¾ pound (3 sticks/340 g) unsalted butter,
     at room temperature

2 cups (400 g) granulated sugar

6 large (300 g) eggs, at room temperature

1 recipe Coconut Milk Soak (see page 190)

1 recipe Coconut Filling (recipe follows)

1 recipe Coconut Milk Buttercream Frosting
     (recipe follows)

2 cups (170 g) sweetened flaked coconut

Position a rack in the lower third of the oven and preheat the oven to 350°F (175°C). Butter two 9-by-2-inch (23 by 5 cm) round cake pans and dust with flour, tapping the pans on the counter to shake out the excess.

Sift together the flour, baking powder, baking soda, cardamom, and salt into a large bowl. Set aside.

In a large measuring cup or small bowl, stir together the cream of coconut, water, and vanilla.

In the bowl of a stand mixer fitted with the paddle attachment (or in a large mixing bowl, using a handheld mixer), cream the butter and sugar together on medium-high speed until light and fluffy, 3 to 5 minutes. Add the eggs one (50 g) at a time, beating well after each addition and scraping down the sides and bottom of the bowl with a rubber spatula as necessary. With the mixer on low speed, add the flour mixture in thirds, alternating with the cream of coconut mixture and beginning and ending with the flour, mixing until just combined; scrape down the sides and bottom of the bowl as necessary.

Divide the batter evenly between the prepared pans and smooth the tops with a spatula. Tap the pans firmly on the counter to remove any air bubbles from the batter.

Bake for 45 to 50 minutes, until a cake tester inserted in the center of a cake comes out clean. Let the cakes cool in the pans on a wire rack for 20 minutes, then invert them onto another rack, turn right side up, and let cool completely.

(You can make the Coconut Milk Soak, Coconut Filling, and Coconut Milk Buttercream Frosting while the layers are cooling.)

To assemble the cake: Level the top of one of the layers with a serrated knife so it is flat. Place it cut side up on a serving plate (you can keep the edges of the plate clean by sliding strips of parchment under the cake while you frost it). Brush the top of the layer with the coconut milk soak (see page 189). Spread the coconut filling over the top of the layer. Place the second layer, right side up, on top of the filling and frost the top and sides of the cake with the frosting, making swirls with the spatula.

Sprinkle some of the flaked coconut on top of the cake and press the rest into the sides. Cover the entire cake with the remaining flaked coconut.

The cake can be stored, loosely covered, at room temperature or in the refrigerator for up to 3 days. Bring to room temperature before serving.

(Continued)

COCONUT FILLING

MAKES ABOUT 3 CUPS (710 ML)

2 cups (170 g) sweetened flaked coconut
½ cup (118 ml) heavy cream
½ cup (118 ml) Coconut Milk Buttercream Frosting
(recipe follows)

In a medium bowl, stir together the coconut and heavy cream. Let stand for about 10 minutes, then stir in the frosting. Use immediately.

COCONUT MILK BUTTERCREAM FROSTING

MAKES ABOUT 4 CUPS (946 ML)

¼ cup (59 ml) coconut milk
2 teaspoons pure vanilla extract
½ pound (2 sticks/227 g) unsalted butter, at room
temperature
5 to 5½ cups (625 to 688 g) confectioners' sugar
Pinch of fine sea salt

In a large measuring cup or small bowl, stir together the coconut milk and vanilla.

In the bowl of a stand mixer fitted with the paddle attachment (or in a large mixing bowl, using a handheld mixer), cream the butter on medium speed until light and fluffy, about 2 minutes. Gradually add 3 cups (375 g) of the confectioners' sugar and the salt, then add the coconut milk mixture and mix on low until smooth and creamy, 1 to 2 minutes. Gradually add 2 to 2½ cups (250 to 313 g) more confectioners' sugar, mixing until the frosting is light and fluffy, about 2 minutes.

The frosting can be stored in an airtight container at room temperature for up to 2 days. You can also refrigerate it for up to 5 days; bring to room temperature before using.

Old-Fashioned Caramel Cake

This buttery yellow cake is covered with a slow-cooked caramel icing that is poured over the top of it and allowed to drip down the sides. The icing recipe is a common one passed down through generations of Southerners, and some consider it a rite of passage to master it. The recipe may seem simple, since it's made in one pan and stirred by hand, but you need to take your time. It simply can't be rushed.

SERVES 12 TO 16

2 cups (250 g) unbleached all-purpose flour
1 tablespoon (13 g) baking powder, preferably
aluminum-free
1 teaspoon fine sea salt
¾ cup (177 ml) whole milk
1 teaspoon pure vanilla extract
8 tablespoons (1 stick/113 g) unsalted butter, at room
temperature
1¼ cups (250 g) granulated sugar
2 large (100 g) eggs, at room temperature
1 recipe Slow-Cooked Caramel Icing (recipe follows)
1 recipe Vanilla Milk Soak (see page 190)

Position a rack in the lower third of the oven and preheat the oven to 350°F (175°C). Butter two 9-by-2-inch (23 by 5 cm) cake pans.

Sift together the flour, baking powder, and salt into a medium bowl. Set aside.

In a large measuring cup or small bowl, combine the milk and vanilla. Set aside.

In the bowl of a stand mixer fitted with the paddle attachment (or in a large mixing bowl, using a handheld mixer), cream the butter and sugar together on medium-high speed until light and fluffy, 3 to 5 minutes. Add the eggs one (50 g) at a time, beating well after each addition and scraping down the sides and bottom of the bowl with a rubber spatula as necessary. With the mixer on low speed, add the flour mixture in thirds, alternating with the milk mixture and beginning and ending with flour, mixing until just combined; scrape down the sides and bottom of the bowl as necessary.

Divide the batter between the prepared pans. Bake for 25 to 30 minutes, until a cake tester inserted in the center of a cake comes out clean. Let the cakes cool in the pans on a wire rack for 20 minutes, then invert them onto another rack, turn right side up, and let cool completely.

To assemble the cake: Level the top of one of the layers with a serrated knife so it is flat. Place a small dollop of the icing on a serving plate and place the layer on top (you can keep the edges of the plate clean by sliding strips of parchment under the cake while you frost it). Brush the top of the layer with the vanilla milk soak (see page 189). Spread some of the icing over the top of the layer. (If the icing gets too cool and begins to harden, rewarm it over low heat before continuing.) Place the second layer on top and pour the remaining icing over the top of the cake. It will drip down the sides, and that is exactly what you want. Use an offset spatula to smooth the icing around the sides of the cake.

Let the cake stand for at least 1 hour to allow the icing to set before serving at your celebration.

The cake can be stored, loosely covered, in the refrigerator for up to 3 days. Bring to room temperature before serving.

SLOW-COOKED CARAMEL ICING

MAKES 3½ CUPS (830 ML)

12 tablespoons (1½ sticks/170 g) unsalted butter, cut into 1-inch (3 cm) cubes
Two 12-ounce (355 ml) cans evaporated milk
2 cups (400 g) granulated sugar
½ teaspoon fine sea salt
1 tablespoon pure vanilla extract

In a large (at least 3-quart/2.8 L) heavy-bottomed saucepan, combine the butter, evaporated milk, sugar, and salt and cook over medium-low heat, stirring occasionally with a heatproof spatula, until the sugar has completely dissolved and the butter is melted and incorporated. Bring the mixture to a boil, reduce the heat to low, and cook, stirring frequently, until the icing thickens and turns a golden-brown color, 1½ to 2 hours; watch carefully, as the mixture will foam and rise in the pan, and turn down the heat as necessary. Start to check the consistency of the icing after 1½ hours: Dip a spoon in the icing, pull it out quickly, and let it cool slightly, then run your finger down the back of the spoon. If the line you made with your finger remains, it's ready; if it is still runny, it needs more time. Continue to check every 5 to 10 minutes. Timing is the secret ingredient in this recipe.

Remove the pan from the heat and stir in the vanilla. Let the icing cool for about 20 minutes, stirring occasionally, before frosting the cake. You need to use the icing while it is still warm, as it will set as it cools.

You can make the icing ahead and store it in the refrigerator for up to 1 week. Rewarm it over low heat until it has loosened and is smooth and shiny again.

Lemon Cheese Layer Cake

PICTURED ON PAGE 167

Don't be fooled by the name—there is no cheese in this cake. But there was a time when Southern folks called lemon curd "lemon cheese." This is an old-fashioned yellow layer cake filled and frosted with lemon curd, but here it gets a modern update with the addition of coconut oil to the batter in place of the traditional vegetable shortening, which will keep the cake moist for days. The whipped egg whites make the cake light and airy. Decorate the frosted cake with fresh lemon slices, if you like.

SERVES 12 TO 16

3 cups (375 g) unbleached all-purpose flour

2 teaspoons (9 g) baking powder, preferably
    aluminum-free

½ teaspoon fine sea salt

½ cup (118 ml) whole milk, at room temperature

½ cup (118 ml) buttermilk

¼ cup (59 ml) heavy cream, at room temperature

1 tablespoon pure vanilla extract

8 tablespoons (1 stick/113 g) unsalted butter, at room
    temperature

½ cup (118 ml) virgin coconut oil

2 cups (400 g) granulated sugar

4 large (200 g) eggs, separated, at room temperature

A few drops of fresh lemon juice

½ cup (118 ml) Vanilla Simple Syrup (see page 189)

2 recipes American Buttercream (page 132)

1 recipe Lemon Curd (page 384)

Lemon slices for decoration (optional)

Position a rack in the lower third of the oven and preheat the oven to 350°F (175°C). Butter three 9-by-2-inch (23 by 5 cm) round cake pans, then line the bottoms with parchment and butter it as well. Lightly dust the pans with flour, tapping the pans on the counter to shake out the excess.

Sift together the flour, baking powder, and salt into a large bowl. Set aside.

In a large measuring cup or small bowl, combine the milk, buttermilk, heavy cream, and vanilla. Set aside.

In the bowl of a stand mixer fitted with the paddle attachment (or in a large mixing bowl, using a handheld mixer), cream the butter, coconut oil, and sugar together on medium-high speed until light and fluffy, 3 to 5 minutes. Add the egg yolks one (19 g) at a time, beating well after each addition and scraping down the sides and bottom of the bowl with a rubber spatula as necessary. Then continue to beat until light in color and texture, 2 to 3 minutes.

On low speed, add the flour mixture in thirds, alternating with the milk mixture and beginning and ending with the flour, mixing until just combined; scrape down the sides and bottom of the bowl as necessary. If using a stand mixer, transfer the batter to another large bowl (if you don't have a second mixer bowl).

Wash and dry the mixer bowl and wipe the inside of the bowl (or another large mixing bowl) with the lemon juice to make sure the bowl is squeaky clean. Attach the bowl to the mixer stand (if using) and fit it with the whisk attachment. Put the egg whites in the mixer bowl (or large mixing bowl) and beat with the whisk attachment or a handheld mixer (with clean beaters if using a handheld mixer) until stiff peaks form, about 3 minutes.

Scoop up a little of the egg whites with a rubber spatula and gently stir them into the batter to lighten it and make it easier to fold in the rest of the egg whites. Gently fold in the remaining egg whites until thoroughly incorporated, about 1 minute.

Gently scrape the batter into the prepared pans, dividing it evenly. Smooth the tops with a spatula. Bake for 22 to 28 minutes, until the cake is lightly golden on top and a cake tester inserted in the center of a cake comes out clean.

Let the cakes cool in the pans on a large wire rack for 20 minutes, then invert them onto another rack, peel off the parchment, turn right side up, and let cool completely.

To assemble the cake: Level the tops of two of the layers with a serrated knife to make them flat. Place one layer cut side up on a serving plate (you can keep the edges of the plate clean while you frost the cake by sliding strips of parchment underneath the cake). Brush the top of the layer with the simple syrup.

Fit a pastry bag with a large plain tip (or use a large ziplock bag with a bottom corner snipped off) and fill the bag halfway with the frosting. Pipe a circle of frosting around the border of the cake to create a dam. Fill the center with about 3 tablespoons lemon curd. Pipe a few long stripes of frosting over the lemon curd.

Place the second cake layer right side up on top and repeat. Place the final cake layer right side up on top and, using an offset spatula or a butter knife, frost the tops and sides of the cake with the frosting. Pipe a thin layer of frosting around the border of the cake to create a 1-inch (3 cm) border and fill the center of the cake with about ¼ cup (59 ml) lemon curd. Return the cake to the refrigerator until ready to serve.

If desired, decorate the cake with lemon slices just before serving.

The cake can be stored, loosely covered, in the refrigerator for up to 3 days. Remove from the refrigerator about 1 hour before serving.

Hummingbird Cake

In 1968, the Jamaican Tourist Board created a marketing plan to attract American travelers to the island. Press kits included local Jamaican recipes, among them one for "Doctor Bird Cake," named after the island's national bird—the hummingbird. Soon thereafter, this cake was *Southern Living*'s most requested recipe, becoming a new Southern classic.

SERVES 12 TO 16

3 cups (375 g) unbleached all-purpose flour

1 teaspoon (6 g) baking soda

1 teaspoon ground cinnamon

1 teaspoon fine sea salt

2 cups (400 g) granulated sugar

1¼ cups (296 ml) vegetable oil

3 large (150 g) eggs, at room temperature

2 teaspoons pure vanilla extract

2 cups (450 g) mashed very ripe bananas
    (about 5 large bananas)

1 cup (165 g) finely chopped fresh pineapple or one
    8-ounce (227 g) can crushed pineapple, drained

1 cup (120 g) chopped pecans, toasted

1 recipe Vanilla Milk Soak (see page 190)

1 recipe Cream Cheese Frosting (page 176)

Position a rack in the lower third of the oven and preheat the oven to 350°F (175°C). Butter two 9-by-2-inch (23 by 5 cm) round cake pans, then line the bottoms with parchment and butter it as well. Lightly dust the pans with flour, tapping the pans on the counter to shake out the excess.

Sift together the flour, baking soda, cinnamon, and salt into a large mixing bowl. Set aside.

In the bowl of a stand mixer fitted with the paddle attachment (or in a large mixing bowl, using a handheld mixer), beat the sugar and oil until smooth, 2 to 3 minutes. Add the eggs one (50 g) at a time, beating well after each addition, then mix until light and fluffy, about 2 minutes. Add the vanilla, bananas, and pineapple, mixing until just incorporated. On low speed, add the flour mixture in thirds, beating until just combined and scraping down the sides

and bottom of the bowl with a rubber spatula as necessary. Fold in ½ cup (60 g) of the pecans.

Divide the batter evenly between the prepared pans and smooth the tops with a spatula. Tap the pans firmly on the countertop to remove any air bubbles from the batter.

Bake for 30 to 40 minutes, until a cake tester inserted in the center of a cake comes out clean. Let the cakes cool in the pans on a wire rack for 20 minutes, then invert them onto another rack, peel off the parchment, turn right side up, and let cool completely.

To assemble the cake: Level the top of one of the layers with a serrated knife so it is flat. Place it cut side up on a serving plate (you can keep the edges of the plate clean by sliding strips of parchment under the cake while you frost it). Brush the top of the layer with the vanilla milk soak (see page 189). Using an offset spatula or a butter knife, spread the layer with a large dollop of the frosting.

Place the second cake layer on top, right side up, and frost the top and sides of the cake with the remaining frosting. Decorate the sides of the cake with the remaining ½ cup (60 g) pecans.

The cake can be stored, covered, in the refrigerator for up to 3 days. Bring to room temperature before serving.

Italian Cream Cake

There is some mystique surrounding this cake. How did such a popular Southern cake get the word "Italian" in its name? Some folks say an Italian baker working for a wealthy family in the South created the recipe using local ingredients instead of Italian ingredients like ricotta or mascarpone. The delicate white cake layers are brushed with a coconut milk soak and finished off with a sweet and tangy cream cheese frosting, coconut, and toasted pecans.

SERVES 12 TO 16

2 cups (250 g) unbleached all-purpose flour

1 teaspoon (6 g) baking soda

½ teaspoon fine sea salt

1 cup (237 ml) buttermilk

1 tablespoon pure vanilla extract

8 tablespoons (1 stick/113 g) unsalted butter, at room temperature

½ cup (118 ml) refined coconut oil

2 cups (400 g) granulated sugar

5 large (250 g) eggs, separated, at room temperature

1 cup (80 g) unsweetened flaked coconut, plus 1 cup (80 g) for finishing the cake

A few drops of fresh lemon juice

1 recipe Coconut Milk Soak (see page 190)

1 recipe Cream Cheese Frosting (page 176)

1½ cups (180 g) chopped pecans, toasted

Position a rack in the middle of the oven and preheat the oven to 350°F (175°C). Butter three 9-by-2-inch (23 by 5 cm) round cake pans, then line the bottoms with parchment and butter it as well. Lightly dust the pans with flour, tapping the pans on the counter to shake out the excess.

Sift together the flour, baking soda, and salt into a medium bowl. Set aside.

In a large measuring cup or small bowl, combine the buttermilk and vanilla. Set aside.

In the bowl of a stand mixer fitted with the paddle attachment (or in a large mixing bowl, using a handheld mixer), cream the butter, coconut oil, and sugar together on medium-high speed until light and fluffy, 3 to 5 minutes. Add the egg yolks one (19 g) at a time, beating well after each addition and scraping down the sides and bottom of the bowl with a rubber spatula as necessary. Then continue to beat until light in color and texture, 2 to 3 minutes.

Turn the mixer speed down to low and add the flour mixture in thirds, alternating with the buttermilk mixture and beginning and ending with the flour, mixing until just combined. Gradually add the 1 cup (80 g) coconut. If using a stand mixer, transfer the batter to another large bowl (if you don't have a second mixer bowl).

Wash and dry the mixer bowl and wipe the inside of the bowl (or another large mixing bowl)

with the lemon juice to make sure the bowl is squeaky clean. Attach the bowl to the mixer stand (if using) and fit it with the whisk attachment. Put the egg whites in the mixer bowl (or large mixing bowl) and beat (with clean beaters if using a handheld mixer) until stiff peaks form, 3 to 5 minutes.

Scoop up a little of the egg whites with a rubber spatula and gently stir them into the cake batter to lighten it and make it easier to fold in the rest of the egg whites. Then gently fold in the remaining egg whites until thoroughly incorporated, about 1 minute.

Gently scrape the batter into the prepared pans, dividing it evenly. Smooth the tops with a spatula.

Bake for 20 to 25 minutes, until a cake tester inserted in the center of a cake comes out clean and the cake is lightly golden. Let the cakes cool in the pans on a large wire rack for 20 minutes, then invert them onto another rack, peel off the parchment, and let cool completely.

To assemble the cake: Level the tops of two of the layers with a serrated knife to make them flat. Place one layer cut side up on a serving plate (you can keep the edges of the plate clean while you frost the cake by sliding strips of parchment underneath the cake). Brush the top of the layer with half of the coconut milk soak (see page 189). Using an offset spatula or a butter knife, spread the layer with a big dollop of the frosting. Place the second leveled layer on top and brush with the remaining milk soak, then spread with another big dollop of frosting. Place the final cake layer right side up and frost the top and sides with a thin layer of the remaining frosting.

Place the cake in the refrigerator for at least 30 minutes to set the frosting.

To finish the cake: Fold 1 cup (114 g) of the pecans into the remaining cream cheese frosting. Using an offset spatula or a butter knife, frost the top and sides of the cake. Sprinkle the top of the cake with the 1 cup (80 g) coconut and the remaining pecans.

The cake can be stored, covered, in the refrigerator for up to 5 days. Bring to room temperature before serving.

Chocolate Church Cake

This sumptuous layer cake is everything you want a chocolate cake to be: three rich, dark layers infused with coffee and frosted with a decadent Chocolate Butter Roux Frosting—an old-fashioned cooked buttercream that is silky and as light as a cloud.

SERVES 12 TO 16

9 ounces (255 g) unsweetened chocolate, finely chopped (about 1½ cups)

2 cups (473 ml) hot strong brewed coffee

1 tablespoon pure vanilla extract

3 cups (375 g) cake flour (not self-rising)

3½ cups (700 g) granulated sugar

1½ teaspoons (8 g) baking soda

1 teaspoon fine sea salt

4 large (200 g) eggs, at room temperature

1 cup (237 ml) vegetable oil

1 cup (240 g) sour cream, at room temperature

1 recipe Chocolate Milk Soak (see page 190)

1 recipe Chocolate Butter Roux Frosting
    (recipe follows)

Position a rack in the lower third of the oven and preheat the oven to 350°F (175°C). Butter three 9-by-2-inch (23 by 5 cm) round cake pans, then line the bottoms with parchment and butter it as well. Lightly dust the pans with flour, tapping the pans on the counter to shake out the excess.

Put the chocolate in a medium bowl and pour in the hot coffee and vanilla. Let stand for about 2 minutes to melt the chocolate, then stir until smooth.

Meanwhile, in the bowl of a stand mixer fitted with the paddle attachment (or in a large mixing bowl, using a handheld mixer), combine the flour, sugar, baking soda, and salt. Let the mixer run on low speed for 2 to 3 minutes to aerate the flour.

In a medium bowl, whisk the eggs and oil together until thick, satiny, and light in color. Whisk in the sour cream, being careful not to overmix; leave some visible streaks of white. Pour in the melted chocolate mixture and mix until just combined.

With the mixer on medium speed, add the chocolate–sour cream mixture to the dry ingredients in thirds, mixing until well blended. Remove the bowl from the mixer stand (if using) and, using a rubber spatula, incorporate any ingredients hiding at the bottom of the bowl, making sure the batter is completely mixed.

Divide the batter evenly among the prepared pans and smooth the tops with a spatula. Tap the pans firmly on the countertop to remove any air bubbles from the batter.

Bake for 40 to 50 minutes, until the center of a cake springs back a little when touched and a cake tester inserted in the center of a cake comes out clean. The cakes will be a deep, dark chocolate brown with slight cracks on top. Let the cakes cool in the pans on a large wire rack for 20 minutes, then invert them onto another rack, peel off the parchment, turn right side up, and let cool completely.

To assemble the cake: Level the tops of two of the layers with a serrated knife to make them flat. Place one layer cut side up on a serving plate (you can keep the edges of the plate clean by sliding strips of parchment under the cake while you frost it). Brush the top of the layer with half of the chocolate milk soak (see page 189). Using an offset spatula, spread the top with a big dollop of the frosting.

Place the second leveled layer cut side up on top and brush with the remaining milk soak. Spread the top with another big dollop of frosting. Place the final layer on top, right side up, and frost the top and sides of the cake with the remaining frosting, making big, luscious swirls with the spatula.

The cake can be stored in an airtight container at room temperature for up to 3 days.

CHOCOLATE BUTTER ROUX FROSTING

MAKES ABOUT 4 CUPS (946 ML)

½ cup (63 g) unbleached all-purpose flour
2 cups (473 ml) whole milk
1 pound (454 g) unsalted butter, at room temperature
1 tablespoon pure vanilla extract
2 cups (400 g) granulated sugar
1 teaspoon fine sea salt
14 ounces (397 g) semisweet chocolate, melted and slightly cooled
3 tablespoons hot strong brewed coffee

In a small heavy-bottomed saucepan, combine the flour and ½ cup (118 ml) of the milk and whisk until blended. Set the pan over medium heat and gradually add the remaining 1½ cups (355 ml) milk, whisking constantly, then cook, whisking, until the mixture comes to a low boil. Reduce the heat to low and whisk until the mixture begins to thicken and starts to "burp," 2 to 3 minutes.

Transfer the mixture to a small heatproof bowl and stir occasionally as it cools to keep it lump-free. (You can put the mixture in the refrigerator for 10 minutes to speed up the cooling process.)

In the bowl of a stand mixer fitted with the whisk attachment (or in a large mixing bowl, using a handheld mixer), beat the butter and vanilla on medium speed until soft and creamy, 2 to

3 minutes. Gradually add the sugar and salt, then beat on high speed until the mixture is light and fluffy, 5 to 7 minutes.

Reduce the speed to low and gradually add the milk mixture, then increase the speed to medium-high and whip until the frosting is light and fluffy, scraping down the sides and bottom of the bowl with a rubber spatula as necessary. Add the melted chocolate and coffee and mix until completely combined.

You can use the frosting immediately, or store in an airtight container in the refrigerator for up to 2 days. To use buttercream that has been chilled, see the Lemon Meringue Buttercream recipe (page 174).

Pig-Pickin' Cake

The South is particularly famous for two things: hot sticky summers and hot sticky barbecue. This cake is a great way to enjoy both. Don't worry; there is no pig in this cake, but it is a dessert that shows up on tables at barbecues, picnics, and other communal gatherings—especially in North Carolina, and especially when a whole hog is on the pit waiting to be "picked." Traditionally the sweet mandarin orange cake starts with a box of yellow cake mix, but this one is made from scratch and finished with homemade whipped topping sweetened with pineapple.

SERVES 12 TO 16

2½ cups (313 g) cake flour (not self-rising)

2½ teaspoons (11 g) baking powder, preferably aluminum-free

1 teaspoon fine sea salt

½ cup (118 ml) whole milk

1 teaspoon pure vanilla extract

½ pound (2 sticks/227 g) unsalted butter, at room temperature

1½ cups (300 g) granulated sugar

2 tablespoons grated orange zest (from 2 oranges)

4 large (200 g) eggs, at room temperature

Two 11-ounce (312 g) cans mandarin oranges in light syrup

1 recipe Whipped Topping (page 372)

1 cup (165 g) chopped fresh pineapple, or one 8-ounce (227 g) can crushed pineapple, drained

Position a rack in the middle of the oven and preheat the oven to 350°F (175°C). Butter two 9-by-2-inch (23 by 5 cm) round cake pans, then line the bottoms with parchment and butter it as well. Lightly dust the pans with flour, tapping the pans on the counter to shake out the excess.

Sift together the flour, baking powder, and salt into a large mixing bowl. Set aside.

In a large measuring cup or small bowl, stir together the milk and vanilla. Set aside.

In the bowl of a stand mixer fitted with the paddle attachment (or in a large mixing bowl, using a handheld mixer), cream the butter, sugar, and orange zest together on medium-high speed until light and fluffy, 3 to 5 minutes. Add the eggs one (50 g) at a time, beating well after each addition and scraping down the sides and bottom of the bowl with a rubber spatula as necessary. On low speed, add the flour mixture in thirds, alternating with the milk mixture and beginning and ending with the flour, mixing until just combined.

Remove the bowl from the mixer stand (if using) and, using the rubber spatula, incorporate any ingredients hiding at the bottom of the bowl, making sure the batter is completely mixed. Fold in one can (312 g) of the mandarin oranges, with their juice.

Divide the batter evenly between the prepared pans and gently smooth the tops with a spatula.

Tap the pans firmly on the counter to remove any air bubbles from the batter.

Bake for 25 to 35 minutes, until a cake tester inserted in the center of a cake comes out clean. Let the cakes cool in the pans on a wire rack for 15 minutes, then remove from the pans, peel off the parchment, and let cool completely on the rack.

Meanwhile, transfer the whipped topping to a bowl and fold in the pineapple. Cover and refrigerate until ready to frost the cake.

To assemble the cake: Level the top of one of the layers with a serrated knife so it is flat. Place it cut side down on a serving plate (you can keep the edges of the plate clean by sliding strips of parchment under the cake while you frost it). Using an offset spatula or a butter knife, spread a large dollop of the whipped topping over the top of the layer. Place the second cake layer on top, right side up, and frost the top and sides with the remaining whipped topping.

Drain the remaining can (312 g) of mandarin oranges and decorate the top of the cake with orange slices. Refrigerate until ready to serve.

The cake can be stored, loosely covered, in the refrigerator for up to 3 days.

Strawberries and Cream Cake PICTURED ON PAGE 167

This cake is a celebration of summer. The light and airy chiffon cake layers are filled with strawberry jam, whipped cream, and sliced strawberries and then topped with whipped cream. (You can use other berries or any sliced summer fruit you like.)

SERVES 12 TO 16

½ cup (118 ml) vegetable oil

¾ cup (177 ml) water

6 large (300 g) eggs, separated, at room
   temperature

1½ teaspoons pure vanilla extract

Grated zest of 1 lemon, plus a few drops of fresh
   lemon juice

2¼ cups (281 g) unbleached all-purpose flour

1 tablespoon (13 g) baking powder, preferably
   aluminum-free

1½ cups (300 g) granulated sugar

¾ teaspoon fine sea salt

3 tablespoons Strawberry Chamomile Jam (page 350)
   or your favorite jam

1 recipe Chantilly Cream (page 373)

2 cups (300 g) strawberries, hulled and sliced

Confectioners' sugar for sprinkling

Position a rack in the middle of the oven and preheat the oven to 350°F (175°C). Butter the bottoms of two 9-by-2-inch (23 by 5 cm) round cake pans, then line the bottoms with parchment and butter it as well. (Do not butter the sides of the pans, or the cake will not rise to its full potential.)

In a medium bowl, whisk together the oil, water, egg yolks, vanilla, and lemon zest. Set aside.

Sift together the flour and baking powder into a large bowl. Add 1 cup (200 g) of the granulated sugar and the salt and whisk to combine. Make a well in the center of the flour mixture, add the egg yolk mixture, and whisk briskly until very smooth, about 1 minute.

Add the lemon juice to the bowl of a stand mixer (or a large mixing bowl) and wipe it clean with a paper towel. Do not skip this step: It really makes a difference when whipping egg whites to get their fullest potential. Attach the impeccably clean bowl to the mixer stand and fit it with the whisk attachment (or use the large mixing bowl and a handheld mixer), then beat the egg whites on medium speed until they become a white frothy foam. With the mixer on high speed, gradually add the remaining ½ cup (100 g) granulated sugar, 1 tablespoon at a time, then beat until the whites hold firm, shiny peaks, 3 to 5 minutes.

Using a rubber spatula, scoop about one-third of the whites onto the yolk mixture and gently fold in to lighten the batter. Then gently but thoroughly fold in the remaining whites.

Divide the batter between the prepared pans, smoothing the tops with a spatula. (Don't be tempted to smack the pans against the counter to level the batter; you want to retain all of that air you just incorporated into your egg whites.)

Bake for 25 to 30 minutes, until the cake is golden brown on top and a cake tester inserted in the center comes out clean. Let the cake cool in the pans on a wire rack for 20 minutes, then run a small knife around the sides of each pan to loosen the cake, invert onto another rack, remove the parchment, and let cool completely on the rack.

To assemble the cake: Place one of the cake layers right side up on a serving plate (you can keep the edges of the plate clean by sliding strips of parchment under the cake while you decorate it). Spread the top of the layer with the jam. Using an offset spatula or a butter knife, spread a big dollop of the Chantilly cream over the jam. Smooth the surface of the cream with the spatula and scatter about half of the strawberries over it. Place the second cake layer on top, right side up. Top with big dollops of the remaining Chantilly cream and then arrange the remaining strawberries on top. Dust the top generously with confectioners' sugar. Refrigerate until ready to serve.

The cake can be stored, loosely covered, in the refrigerator for up to 3 days

Vanilla Jam Cake

PICTURED OPPOSITE

Buying local jam is a lovely way to celebrate the seasons or to commemorate a place you visited and remember fondly. Try one of those jams made of berries, rhubarb, or stone fruit in this cake. The rich, buttery yellow cake is filled with jam and then filled and iced with a good old-fashioned Butter Roux Frosting. When you take a bite, all the flavors mingle and complement one another in the best way.

SERVES 8 TO 12

1 cup (237 ml) whole milk

1 teaspoon pure vanilla extract

1¾ cups (219 g) cake flour (not self-rising)

1¼ cups (156 g) unbleached all-purpose flour

2 cups (400 g) granulated sugar

1 tablespoon (13 g) baking powder, preferably
  aluminum-free

¾ teaspoon fine sea salt

½ pound (2 sticks/227 g) unsalted butter, cut into
  ½-inch (1.5 cm) cubes, at room temperature

4 large (200 g) eggs, at room temperature

1 recipe Vanilla Milk Soak (see page 190)

3 tablespoons Strawberry Chamomile Jam (page 350)
  or your favorite jam

1 recipe Butter Roux Frosting (recipe follows)

Position a rack in the middle of the oven and preheat the oven to 350°F (175°C). Butter three 8-inch (20 cm) round cake pans, then line the bottoms with parchment and butter it as well. Lightly dust the pans with flour, tapping the pans on the counter to shake out the excess.

In a large measuring cup or small bowl, mix together the milk and vanilla. Set aside.

In the bowl of a stand mixer fitted with the paddle attachment (or in a large mixing bowl, using a handheld mixer), combine both flours, the sugar, baking powder, and salt and mix on low speed until thoroughly combined. Add the cubed butter a few pieces at a time, beating until the

CLOCKWISE FROM TOP LEFT: LEMON CHEESE LAYER CAKE (PAGE 156), VANILLA JAM CAKE (OPPOSITE), STRAWBERRIES AND CREAM CAKE (PAGE 165), COCONUT CAKE (PAGE 153)

mixture resembles coarse sand, about 2 minutes. With the mixer on medium speed, add the eggs one (50 g) at a time, mixing well after each addition and scraping down the sides and bottom of the bowl with a rubber spatula as necessary. Turn the speed down to low and gradually add the milk mixture, then mix for another 1 to 2 minutes.

Remove the bowl from the mixer stand (if using) and, using the rubber spatula, incorporate any ingredients hiding at the bottom of the bowl, making sure the batter is completely mixed.

Divide the batter evenly between the prepared pans and smooth the tops with a spatula. Tap the pans firmly on the countertop to remove any air bubbles from the batter.

Bake for 20 to 25 minutes, until a cake tester inserted in the center of a cake comes out clean. Let the cakes cool in the pans on a wire rack for 20 minutes, then invert them onto another rack, peel off the parchment, turn right side up, and let cool completely.

To assemble the cake: Level the tops of two of the layers with a serrated knife to make them flat. Place one layer cut side up on a serving plate (you can keep the edges of the plate clean while you frost the cake by sliding strips of parchment underneath the cake). Brush the top of the layer with the milk soak (see page 189).

Fit a pastry bag with a large plain tip (or use a large ziplock bag with a bottom corner snipped off) and fill the bag halfway with the frosting. Pipe a circle of frosting around the border of the cake to create a dam. Fill the center with the jam. Pipe a few long stripes of frosting over the jam.

Place the second cake layer right side up on top and repeat the process above.

Place the third cake layer right side up on top and, using an offset spatula or a butter knife, frost the tops and sides of the cake with the remaining frosting, making big swirls with the spatula or knife.

The cake can be stored, loosely covered, for up to 3 days in the refrigerator.

BUTTER ROUX FROSTING

MAKES 4 CUPS (496 ML)

¼ cup (32 g) unbleached all-purpose flour
1 cup (237 ml) whole milk
½ pound (2 sticks/227 g) unsalted butter, at room temperature
1 teaspoon pure vanilla extract
1 cup (125 g) confectioners' sugar

In a small heavy-bottomed saucepan, combine the flour and ¼ cup (59 ml) of the milk and whisk until blended. Set the pan over medium heat and gradually add the remaining ¾ cup (177 ml) milk, whisking constantly, then cook, whisking, until the mixture comes to a low boil. Reduce the heat to low and whisk until the mixture begins to thicken and starts to "burp," 2 to 3 minutes.

Transfer the mixture to a small heatproof bowl and stir occasionally as it cools to keep it lump-free. If you do get a few lumps, don't worry—you can whisk the mixture briskly to dissolve them. (You can put the mixture in the refrigerator for 10 minutes to speed up the cooling process.)

In the bowl of a stand mixer fitted with the whisk attachment (or in a large mixing bowl, using a handheld mixer), whip the butter and vanilla on medium speed until soft and creamy, 2 to 3 minutes. Gradually add the confectioners' sugar and then beat on high speed until the mixture is light and fluffy, 5 to 7 minutes.

Reduce the speed to low and gradually add the milk mixture, then increase the speed to medium-high and whip until the frosting is light and fluffy, scraping down the sides and bottom of the bowl with a rubber spatula as necessary.

Use the frosting immediately, or store in an airtight container in the refrigerator for up to 2 days. To use buttercream that has been chilled, see the Lemon Meringue Buttercream recipe (page 174).

Little Layer Chocolate Cake

This cake is a childhood memory for many Southerners; it's also as showy as it can get, with twelve delicate layers of yellow butter cake so thin they almost melt in your mouth. The layers are sandwiched with a warm boiled chocolate icing, and then the entire cake is covered in more chocolate icing. The recipe calls for baking the layers individually, rather than slicing bigger cakes into layers, to ensure that all the layers are the same thickness. Do yourself a favor and buy twelve disposable aluminum foil pans to save time and stress, then bake three to four layers at a time.

SERVES 12 TO 16

FOR THE CAKE

2½ cups (313 g) cake flour (not self-rising)

2 cups (250 g) unbleached all-purpose flour

2 tablespoons (26 g) baking powder, preferably aluminum-free

1 teaspoon fine sea salt

2 cups (473 ml) whole milk

1½ teaspoons pure vanilla extract

¾ pound (3 sticks/340 g) unsalted butter, cut into ½-inch (1.5 cm) cubes, at room temperature

3 cups (600 g) granulated sugar

6 large (300 g) eggs, at room temperature

FOR THE BOILED CHOCOLATE ICING

3 cups (710 ml) evaporated milk

3 cups (600 g) granulated sugar

1 cup (80 g) Dutch-processed cocoa powder

3 tablespoons light corn syrup

½ teaspoon fine sea salt

½ pound (2 sticks/227 g) unsalted butter, at room temperature, cut into ½-inch (1.5 cm) cubes

2 teaspoons pure vanilla extract

SPECIAL EQUIPMENT

Twelve 8-inch (20 cm) aluminum foil cake pans (optional)

Candy thermometer

To make the cake: Position the racks in the middle and lower third of the oven and preheat the oven to 375°F (190°C). You need to bake 12 cake layers. Butter the bottoms and sides of twelve 8-inch (20 cm) aluminum foil cake pans or as many 8-inch (20 cm) round cake pans as you have, then line the bottoms with parchment and butter it as well. (Do not even think about cutting layers in half to make this cake.) Lightly dust the pans with flour, tapping the pans on the counter to shake out the excess.

Sift together both flours, the baking powder, and salt into a large bowl. Set aside.

In a large measuring cup or small bowl, combine the milk and vanilla.

In the bowl of a stand mixer fitted with the paddle attachment (or in a large mixing bowl, using a handheld mixer), cream the butter and sugar together on medium-high speed until light and fluffy, 3 to 5 minutes. Add the eggs one (50 g) at a time, beating well after each addition and scraping down the sides and bottom of the bowl with a rubber spatula as necessary. With the mixer on low speed, add the flour mixture in thirds, alternating with the milk mixture and beginning and ending with the flour, mixing until just combined; scrape down the sides and bottom of the bowl as necessary.

Spread ¾ cup (177 ml) of the batter in each prepared pan and smooth the tops with a spatula. Cover the batter in the bowl and refrigerate until you are ready to bake the next layers. Bake the cakes for 8 to 10 minutes, rotating the pans halfway through and switching their positions, until the tops are lightly browned and a cake tester inserted in the center of a cake comes out clean.

Let the cakes cool in the pans on wire racks for 10 minutes, then invert them onto other racks, peel off the parchment, turn right side up, and let cool completely.

(Continued)

While the cakes are cooling, make the icing: In a large heavy-bottomed saucepan, whisk together the evaporated milk, sugar, cocoa powder, corn syrup, and salt and cook over medium heat, stirring, until the sugar dissolves. Clip a candy thermometer to the side of the pot and cook until the mixture reaches 248°F (120°C), the "soft ball stage," about 15 minutes.

Once the icing reaches the soft ball stage, reduce the heat to a simmer, add the butter, and stir until the butter is melted and thoroughly incorporated. Remove from the heat and stir in the vanilla. Let cool, stirring occasionally, until the icing has thickened but is still glossy and pourable.

To assemble the cake: Place a small dollop of icing on a serving plate and place one cake layer on top (you can keep the edges of the plate clean by sliding strips of parchment under the cake while you frost it). Spread ¼ cup (59 ml) of the icing evenly over the top. Place a second layer on top of the icing, and press down lightly to secure it. Spread another ¼ cup (59 ml) of icing over that layer. Some of the icing will drip down the sides, and that is exactly what you want. Repeat the process with 9 more layers of cake. At this point, the icing will start to cool down and become thicker, making it easier for you to finish decorating the cake. (If the icing cools too much, just warm it up over low heat until pourable again.)

Set the final layer on top and press down lightly. Pour the remaining icing over the top, letting it drip down the sides, then use an offset spatula to spread the icing evenly over the sides of the cake.

Let the cake stand until the icing sets, at least 1 hour, before serving at your celebration.

The cake can be stored, loosely covered, in the refrigerator for up to 5 days. Bring to room temperature before serving.

Lane Cake

This old-timey cake, which is also known as Prize Cake, was created by Emma Rylander Lane of Alabama. She won first prize with this cake at the county fair in Columbus, Georgia, at the turn of the twentieth century. Lane Cake is mentioned in the Southern classic novel *To Kill a Mockingbird*; it stirs up a rivalry between two of the neighborhood cake ladies. It's a moist white cake filled and frosted with a thick cooked whiskey-laced custard.

SERVES 12 TO 16

FOR THE CAKE

3½ cups (438 g) cake flour (not self-rising)

1 tablespoon (13 g) baking powder, preferably aluminum-free

½ teaspoon fine sea salt

1 cup (237 ml) whole milk

1½ teaspoons pure vanilla extract

½ pound (2 sticks/227 g) unsalted butter, at room temperature

2 cups (400 g) granulated sugar

A few drops of fresh lemon juice

8 large (240 g) egg whites

1 recipe Vanilla Milk Soak (see page 190)

FOR THE FROSTING

1½ cups (171 g) pecans

12 tablespoons (1½ sticks/170 g) unsalted butter

1½ cups (300 g) granulated sugar

12 large (228 g) egg yolks

1½ cups (128 g) sweetened flaked coconut

1½ cups (218 g) golden raisins, finely chopped

½ cup (118 ml) bourbon or brandy

OPTIONAL SPECIAL EQUIPMENT

Instant-read thermometer

To make the cake: Position a rack in the middle of the oven and preheat the oven to 350°F (175°C). Butter three 9-by-2-inch (23 by 5 cm) round cake pans, then line the bottoms with parchment and butter it as well. Lightly dust the pans with flour, tapping the pans on the counter to shake out the excess.

Sift together the flour, baking powder, and salt into a large bowl. Set aside.

In a large measuring cup or small bowl, combine the milk and vanilla. Set aside.

In the bowl of a stand mixer fitted with the paddle attachment (or in a large mixing bowl, using a handheld mixer), cream the butter and sugar together on medium-high speed until light and fluffy, 3 to 5 minutes. Turn the speed down to low and add the flour mixture in thirds, alternating with the milk mixture and beginning and ending with the flour, mixing until just combined; scrape down the sides and bottom of the bowl with a rubber spatula as necessary. If using a stand mixer, transfer the mixture to another large bowl (unless you have a second mixer bowl).

Wash and dry the mixer bowl and wipe the inside of the bowl (or another large mixing bowl) with the lemon juice to make sure the bowl is squeaky clean. Attach the bowl to the mixer stand (if using) and fit it with the whisk attachment. Put the egg whites in the mixer bowl (or large mixing bowl) and beat (with clean beaters if using a handheld mixer) until the whites hold soft peaks, about 3 minutes. Fold one-quarter of the egg whites into the cake batter to lighten it, then gently fold in the remaining egg whites until incorporated.

Divide the batter evenly among the prepared pans and smooth the tops with a spatula.

Bake for 25 to 30 minutes, until a cake tester inserted in the center of a cake comes out clean. Let the cakes cool in the pans on a large wire rack for 15 minutes, then invert onto another rack, peel off the parchment, and turn right side up to cool completely. Leave the oven on.

While the cake is cooling, make the frosting: Spread the pecans on a baking sheet and toast in the oven for about 5 minutes, until lightly toasted and fragrant. Let cool, then chop into ¼-inch (6 mm) pieces.

In a medium saucepan, melt the butter over medium heat. Remove from the heat and let cool to tepid, then whisk in the sugar and egg yolks until smooth.

Return the pan to medium heat and cook, stirring constantly with a wooden spoon, until the frosting has thickened enough to coat the back of the spoon; it should read 180°F (80°C) on an instant-read thermometer. Be careful not to let the mixture come to a boil.

Remove from the heat and add the toasted pecans, coconut, golden raisins, and bourbon, stirring well. Transfer the frosting to a heatproof bowl to cool; it will continue to thicken as it cools. It will be gooey, and that is exactly what you want.

To assemble the cake: Level the tops of two of the layers with a serrated knife to make them flat. Place one layer cut side up on a serving plate (you can keep the edges of the plate clean while you frost the cake by sliding strips of parchment underneath the cake). Brush the top of the layer with half of the vanilla milk soak (see page 189). Using an offset spatula or a butter knife, spread the layer with one-third of the frosting. Place the second cake layer cut side up and brush with the remaining vanilla milk soak, then spread with another third of the frosting. Place the final layer right side up on top and frost the top with the remaining frosting, leaving the sides of the cake naked.

The cake can be stored, loosely covered, at room temperature for up to 1 day or refrigerated for 5 days. If it has been refrigerated, bring to room temperature before serving.

Doberge Cake

First, you need to learn how to pronounce the name of this legendary cake: It's *doe*-bash. As the story goes, in the 1930s, New Orleans bakery owner Beulah Ledner, inspired by the Hungarian Dobos torte, created the legendary cake, and it soon became a local favorite for special occasions. She replaced the original chocolate buttercream with a custard filling and covered the chocolate icing with a thin layer of fondant to withstand the heat and humidity of New Orleans. Many variations—chocolate, caramel, strawberry, and lemon—can be found, and some bakeries in New Orleans make "half and half cakes," pairing two flavors. This one is six layers of lemon cake filled alternately with lemon curd and lemon meringue buttercream, then finished with a glossy triumph of chocolate ganache.

SERVES 12 TO 16

3 cups (375 g) unbleached all-purpose flour

1 teaspoon (4 g) baking powder, preferably aluminum-free

½ teaspoon (3 g) baking soda

½ teaspoon salt

1 cup (237 ml) buttermilk

2 tablespoons grated lemon zest (from 1 medium lemon)

¾ pound (3 sticks/340 g) unsalted butter, at room temperature

3 cups (600 g) granulated sugar

6 large (300 g) eggs, at room temperature

1 recipe Lemon Meringue Buttercream (recipe follows)

1 recipe Lemon Curd (page 384)

1 recipe Dark Chocolate Ganache (recipe follows)

Position a rack in the lower third of the oven and preheat the oven to 350°F (175°C). Butter three 8-by-2-inch (20 by 5 cm) round pans, then line the bottoms with parchment and butter it as well. Lightly dust the pans with flour, tapping the pans on the counter to shake out the excess.

Sift together the flour, baking powder, baking soda, and salt into a large bowl. Set aside.

In a large measuring cup or small bowl, combine the buttermilk and lemon zest. Set aside.

In the bowl of a stand mixer fitted with the paddle attachment (or in a large mixing bowl, using a handheld mixer), cream the butter and sugar together until light and fluffy, 3 to 5 minutes. Turn the speed down to low and add the eggs one (50 g) at a time, beating well after each addition and scraping down the sides and bottom of the bowl with a rubber spatula as necessary.

On low speed, add the flour mixture in thirds, alternating with the buttermilk mixture and beginning and ending with the flour, mixing until just combined; scrape down the sides and bottom of the bowl as necessary. Remove the bowl from the mixer stand (if using) and, using the rubber spatula, incorporate any ingredients hiding at the bottom of the bowl, making sure the batter is completely mixed.

Divide the cake batter among the prepared cake pans and spread it evenly, using an offset spatula.

Bake for 20 to 22 minutes, until a cake tester inserted in the center of a cake comes out clean. Let the cakes cool in the pans on a wire rack for 20 minutes, then invert them onto another rack, peel off the parchment, turn right side up, and let cool completely on the rack.

To assemble the cake: You have 3 cakes, but you need 6 cake layers. Run a small knife around the sides of each pan to loosen the cake. Using a long serrated knife, carefully split each layer in half: Make 4 evenly spaced horizontal marks around each layer, halfway up the side. Slice a few inches (8 cm) in toward the center from one mark, turn the layer 90 degrees and slice in at the next mark, then continue all around the cake; the cuts should meet at the center. Once you have sliced through the center, lift off the top layer and set it aside.

(Continued)

Place one cake layer cut side up on a serving plate (you can keep the edges of the plate clean while you frost the cake by sliding strips of parchment underneath the cake). Fit a pastry bag with a large plain tip, or use a large ziplock bag with a bottom corner snipped off, and fill the bag halfway with the buttercream. Pipe a circle of buttercream around the border of the cake to create a dam. Using an offset spatula or a butter knife, spread a big dollop of lemon curd in the middle of the frosting dam. Place another layer on top and cover with more buttercream and curd, then repeat with 3 more cake layers. Place the final cake layer right side up on top and frost the top and sides of the cake with a thin layer of the remaining frosting. Place the cake in the refrigerator for at least 1 hour, or, loosely covered, overnight, to set the frosting.

(Make the ganache while the cake is in the refrigerator.)

Using an offset spatula or a butter knife, frost the top and sides of the cake with the ganache.

The cake can be stored, loosely covered, in the refrigerator for up to 3 days. Bring to room temperature before serving.

LEMON MERINGUE BUTTERCREAM

MAKES ABOUT 4 CUPS (496 ML)

6 large (180 g) egg whites

1½ cups (300 g) granulated sugar

¼ teaspoon fine sea salt

1¼ pounds (5 sticks/567 g) unsalted butter, cut into
    ½-inch (1.5 cm) chunks, at room temperature

1½ tablespoons grated lemon zest (from 1 medium lemon)

2 tablespoons fresh lemon juice

SPECIAL EQUIPMENT

Instant-read thermometer

In the bowl of a stand mixer (or in a large heatproof metal bowl), whisk together the egg whites, sugar, and salt. Set the bowl over a saucepan of simmering water (do not let the bottom of the bowl touch the water) and cook, whisking constantly, until the sugar is dissolved. Rub the mixture between your fingers to make sure the sugar has dissolved; the mixture should be warm to the touch and register 140°F (60°C) on an instant-read thermometer.

Remove the bowl from the heat, attach it to the mixer stand (if using), and fit with the whisk attachment (or use a handheld mixer). Beat on high speed until stiff peaks form and the meringue has cooled to room temperature, 3 to 5 minutes.

Once the mixture has cooled to room temperature, replace the whisk with the paddle attachment (if using a stand mixer). Beat in the butter chunks a few at a time, waiting for the butter to be incorporated each time before adding more and scraping down the sides and bottom of the bowl with a rubber spatula as necessary. If the mixture begins to look curdled, slow down and make sure you completely incorporate each addition of butter before adding more.

When all the butter has been added, add the lemon zest and juice and beat for another 1 to 2 minutes. The frosting should be smooth, thick, and glossy.

You can use the buttercream immediately or transfer it to an airtight container and store it at room temperature or in the refrigerator.

When you're ready to use it, if the buttercream has been chilled, remove it from the refrigerator and bring to room temperature. Then transfer to the bowl of a stand mixer fitted with the paddle attachment and beat on medium speed (or use a handheld mixer) until soft and spreadable, 2 to 3 minutes, before using.

DARK CHOCOLATE GANACHE

MAKES ABOUT 3 CUPS (710 ML)

1 cup (237 ml) heavy cream

8 tablespoons (1 stick/113 g) unsalted butter,
    cut into 1-inch (3 cm) pieces

⅓ cup (67 g) granulated sugar

¼ teaspoon fine sea salt

1 pound (454 g) dark chocolate (at least 64% cacao),
    finely chopped

¼ cup (59 ml) hot brewed coffee

1 teaspoon pure vanilla extract

Combine the cream, butter, sugar, and salt in a heatproof bowl set over a saucepan of simmering water (do not let the bottom of the bowl touch the water), and stir occasionally until the butter is melted. Add the chocolate and stir until it is completely melted and smooth.

Remove from the heat, add the coffee and vanilla, and stir until smooth. Then let cool, stirring occasionally, until the ganache thickens to a spreadable consistency. Making the perfect ganache cannot be rushed; resist the urge to refrigerate it or to whisk it to cool it faster. Once it is thickened and glistening, you are ready to decorate your cake.

Carrot Cake

Carrot cake reached its peak popularity in the 1970s, but it remains beloved today. This version is chock-full of grated carrots, spices, and pineapple and frosted with a sweet and tangy cream cheese frosting. It's a cake that gets even better with time, but it usually disappears quickly.

SERVES 12 TO 16

2½ cups (313 g) unbleached all-purpose flour

2 teaspoons (9 g) baking powder, preferably
    aluminum-free

¾ teaspoon (4 g) baking soda

2 teaspoons ground cinnamon

1 teaspoon ground cardamom

1½ teaspoons fine sea salt

1 pound (454 g) carrots, peeled and coarsely grated

1 cup (165 g) finely chopped fresh pineapple or one
    8-ounce (227 g) can crushed pineapple, drained

1 cup (237 ml) buttermilk

¾ cup (150 g) granulated sugar

1 cup (200 g) packed light brown sugar

4 large (200 g) eggs, at room temperature

2 teaspoons pure vanilla extract

¾ cup (177 ml) vegetable oil

1 recipe Vanilla Milk Soak (see page 190)

1 recipe Cream Cheese Frosting (recipe follows)

Position a rack in the lower third of the oven and preheat the oven to 350°F (175°C). Butter two 9-by-2-inch (23 by 5 cm) round cake pans, then line the bottoms with parchment and butter it as well. Lightly dust the pans with flour, tapping the pans on the counter to shake out the excess.

Sift together the flour, baking powder, baking soda, cinnamon, cardamom, and salt into a medium bowl. Set aside.

In another medium bowl, combine the carrots, pineapple, and buttermilk. Set aside.

In the bowl of a stand mixer fitted with the paddle attachment (or in a large mixing bowl, using a handheld mixer), beat both sugars and the eggs on medium-high speed until light and fluffy, 3 to 5 minutes. Beat in the vanilla, then reduce the speed to low and gradually stream in the oil, beating until thoroughly blended. On low speed, add the flour mixture in two additions, alternating with the carrot mixture, mixing until just combined.

Divide the batter evenly between the prepared pans and smooth the tops with a spatula. Tap the pans on the countertop to remove any air bubbles.

Bake for 35 to 40 minutes, until a cake tester inserted in the center of a cake comes out clean.

Let the cakes cool in the pans on a wire rack for 20 minutes, then invert them onto another rack, peel off the parchment, turn right side up, and let cool completely.

To assemble the cake: Level the top of one of the layers with a serrated knife so it is flat. Place it cut side up on a serving plate (you can keep the edges of the plate clean by sliding strips of parchment under the cake while you frost it). Brush the top of the layer with the vanilla milk soak (see page 189). Using an offset spatula or a butter knife, spread the top of the layer with a big dollop of the frosting. Place the second cake layer on top, right side up, and frost the top and sides of the cake with the remaining frosting.

The cake can be stored, loosely covered, in the refrigerator for up to 3 days. Bring to room temperature before serving.

CREAM CHEESE FROSTING

MAKES ABOUT 5 CUPS (1.2 L)

10 tablespoons (1¼ sticks/142 g) unsalted butter, cut into chunks, at room temperature

Two 8-ounce (227 g) packages cream cheese, cut into chunks, at room temperature

1 tablespoon pure vanilla extract

¼ teaspoon fine sea salt

5 to 6 cups (625 to 750 g) confectioners' sugar

In the bowl of a stand mixer fitted with the paddle attachment (or in a large mixing bowl, using a handheld mixer), beat the butter, cream cheese, vanilla, and salt on medium speed until smooth and creamy, 3 to 5 minutes. Gradually add 5 cups (625 g) confectioners' sugar, beating until thoroughly incorporated. Then continue to beat, adding up to 1 cup (125 g) more confectioners' sugar if needed, until the frosting is light and fluffy, 4 to 6 minutes.

The frosting can be made ahead and refrigerated in an airtight container for up to 5 days. Bring to room temperature before using.

Apple Stack Cake

The apple stack cake has deep roots in Appalachian culture. Making one of these multilayered cakes is a time-honored tradition—and a labor of love. Thin layers of spice cake made using modest pantry staples are layered with a thick apple butter that traditionally included dried apples put up from the fall harvest. The cake is finished with a whiskey glaze. This recipe was inspired by my friend Sean Brock's grandmother Audrey's recipe, which is a treasured family heirloom. Go ahead and buy twelve

disposable aluminum foil pans to save time and stress, and then you can bake three to four layers at a time.

SERVES 12 TO 16

FOR THE CAKE

9 cups (1.1 kg) self-rising flour, preferably White Lily

4 teaspoons ground ginger

2 teaspoons ground allspice

2 teaspoons ground cinnamon

1 teaspoon freshly ground black pepper

2 cups (473 ml) sorghum syrup or molasses

1½ cups (355 ml) refined coconut oil

2 cups (400 g) granulated sugar

6 large (300 g) eggs, at room temperature

2 cups (473 ml) buttermilk

5½ cups (1.3 L) Apple Butter (page 361)

FOR THE GLAZE

2 cups (400 g) packed light brown sugar

½ cup (118 ml) bourbon or rye whiskey

One 14-ounce (300 ml) can sweetened condensed milk

8 tablespoons (1 stick/113 g) unsalted butter,
    cut into ½-inch (1.5 cm) cubes

½ cup (118 ml) whole milk

1 teaspoon pure vanilla extract

OPTIONAL SPECIAL EQUIPMENT

Twelve 9-inch (23 cm) aluminum foil cake pans

To make the cake: Position the racks in the middle and lower third of the oven and preheat the oven to 350°F (175°C). You need to bake 12 cake layers. Butter the bottoms and sides of twelve 9-inch (23 cm) aluminum foil cake pans or as many 9-inch (23 cm) round cake pans as you have, then line the bottoms with parchment and butter it as well. Lightly dust the pans with flour, tapping the pans on the counter to shake out the excess.

Sift together the flour, ginger, allspice, cinnamon, and pepper into a large bowl. Set aside.

In the bowl of a stand mixer fitted with the paddle attachment (or in a large mixing bowl, using a handheld mixer), beat the sorghum, coconut oil, and sugar on medium-high speed until smooth and creamy. Add the eggs one (50 g) at a time, mixing well after each addition and scraping down the sides and bottom of the bowl with a rubber spatula as necessary.

Reduce the speed to low and add the flour mixture in thirds, alternating with the buttermilk and beginning and ending with the flour, mixing

until just combined; scrape down the sides and bottom of the bowl as necessary. Remove the bowl from the mixer stand (if using) and, using the rubber spatula, incorporate any ingredients hiding at the bottom of the bowl, making sure the batter is completely mixed.

Pour 1 cup (237 ml) of batter into each prepared pan and smooth the tops with an offset spatula. Cover the batter in the bowl and refrigerate until you are ready to bake the next cake layers.

Bake the cakes for 14 to 16 minutes, rotating the pans halfway through and switching their positions, until the tops are lightly browned and a cake tester inserted in the center of a cake comes out clean. Allow the cake layers to cool in the pans on wire racks for at least 20 minutes, then invert onto other racks, remove the parchment, turn right side up, and cool completely on the racks. Repeat with the remaining layers.

Wrap the layers individually in plastic wrap and refrigerate for at least 1 hour, or overnight, if time allows. This step will make it easier to assemble the cake.

To assemble the cake: Place one layer on a cake plate. Spread a heaping ½ cup (118 ml) of apple butter evenly over the top. Place a second layer on top of the apple butter and spread another ½ cup (118 ml) of apple butter over it. Continue the process with the remaining layers, but leave the last layer plain.

To make the glaze: In a medium saucepan, combine the brown sugar, bourbon, and condensed milk and cook over medium heat, stirring constantly, until the sugar dissolves. Remove from the heat and stir in the butter until it is melted. Stir in the milk and vanilla. Set aside to cool completely.

Pour the glaze over the cake, allowing it to run down the sides. Let the cake stand for at least 1 hour, or, preferably, overnight, until the glaze sets before serving at your celebration.

The cake can be stored, loosely covered, in the refrigerator for up to 1 week. It gets even better with time. Bring to room temperature before serving.

Ultimate Celebration Cake

When you want a truly spectacular celebration cake, this is it. Make a three-layer cake for your next birthday party, baby shower, or any other special occasion. Or double the recipe and turn it into a multitiered cake (as pictured here) for your best friend's wedding. Customize your cake by using different simple syrups (see pages 189–190) or milk soaks (see page 190) and frostings. See Tips and Tricks for Creating Delicious Cakes, page 189, for decorating ideas and instructions for assembling a multitiered cake.

SERVES 12 TO 16

3 cups (375 g) cake flour (not self-rising)

1½ teaspoons (7 g) baking powder, preferably
    aluminum-free

¾ teaspoon (4 g) baking soda

¾ teaspoon fine sea salt

¾ pound (3 sticks/340 g) unsalted butter,
    at room temperature

2⅓ cups (467 g) granulated sugar

3 large (90 g) egg whites

2 teaspoons pure vanilla extract

1½ cups (355 ml) buttermilk

1 recipe Vanilla Milk Soak (see page 190)

10 cups (2.4 L) Italian Meringue Buttercream
    (recipe follows)

Position a rack in the middle of the oven and preheat the oven to 350°F (175°C). Butter three 9-by-2-inch (23 by 5 cm) round cake pans, then line the bottoms with parchment and butter it as well. Lightly dust the pans with flour, tapping the pans on the counter to shake out the excess.

Sift together the flour, baking powder, baking soda, and salt into a medium bowl. Set aside.

In the bowl of a stand mixer fitted with the paddle attachment (or in a large mixing bowl, using a handheld mixer), cream the butter and sugar together on medium-high speed until light and fluffy, 3 to 5 minutes. Scrape down the sides and bottom of the bowl with a rubber spatula as necessary. Add the egg whites and vanilla and mix until completely incorporated.

With the mixer on low speed, add the flour mixture in thirds, alternating with the buttermilk and beginning and ending with the flour, mixing until just combined; scrape down the sides and bottom of the bowl as necessary. Remove the bowl from the mixer stand (if using) and, using the rubber spatula, incorporate any ingredients hiding at the bottom of the bowl, making sure the batter is completely mixed.

Pour the batter into the prepared pans and gently smooth the tops with a spatula. Tap the pans firmly on the counter to remove any air bubbles from the batter.

Bake for 20 to 25 minutes, until the tops of the cakes are lightly golden and a cake tester inserted in the center of a cake comes out clean. Let the cakes cool in the pans on a large wire rack for 15 minutes, then invert them onto another rack, peel off the parchment, turn right side up, and let cool completely.

To assemble the cake: Level the tops of two of the layers with a serrated knife to make them flat. Place one layer cut side up on a serving plate (you can keep the edges of the plate clean by sliding strips of parchment under the cake while you frost it). Brush the top of the layer with half of the milk soak (see page 189). Using an offset spatula, spread the top with a big dollop of the buttercream. Place the second leveled layer on top and brush with the remaining milk soak. Spread the top with another big dollop of buttercream. Place the final layer on top, right side up, and frost the top and sides of the cake with the remaining buttercream.

The cake can be stored, loosely covered, in the refrigerator for up to 3 days.

(Continued)

ITALIAN MERINGUE BUTTERCREAM

MAKES 10 CUPS (2.4 L)

2 cups (400 g) granulated sugar

½ cup (118 ml) water

10 large (300 g) egg whites, at room temperature

¼ teaspoon cream of tartar

2 pounds (907 g) unsalted butter, cut into ½-inch
(1.5 cm) cubes, at room temperature

1 tablespoon pure vanilla extract

SPECIAL EQUIPMENT

Pastry brush

Candy thermometer

In a small saucepan, combine 1½ cups (300 g) of the sugar and the water and cook over medium heat, stirring occasionally, until the sugar has dissolved. Brush down the sides of the saucepan with a pastry brush dipped in warm water to remove any crystals; do not stir again. Clip a candy thermometer to the side of the saucepan and cook until the syrup reaches 248°F/120°C (the "soft ball stage"), 8 to 10 minutes.

Meanwhile, combine the egg whites and cream of tartar in the bowl of a stand mixer fitted with the whisk attachment and beat until the whites are foamy and barely hold soft peaks, about 3 minutes. Gradually add the remaining ½ cup (100 g) sugar and beat for another 1 to 2 minutes, until the meringue holds soft peaks. Turn the mixer off.

As soon as the sugar syrup reaches 248°F (120°C), carefully remove the hot pan from the heat and, with the mixer running on low, pour the hot syrup into the egg white mixture in a slow, steady stream, avoiding the spinning whisk. Be careful: The syrup is very hot, and you don't want it to splash. Once all the syrup is added, increase the speed to high and beat until the meringue has cooled to room temperature, 8 to 12 minutes. It will have greatly expanded and will look like marshmallow cream.

Once the mixture has cooled to room temperature, begin adding the butter: Switch to the paddle attachment and, beating on medium speed, drop in the butter a few cubes at a time (the mixture will deflate), waiting for it to be incorporated each time before adding more and scraping down the sides and bottom of the bowl with a rubber spatula as necessary. If the mixture begins to look curdled, slow down and make sure you are completely incorporating the butter each time before adding more. When all the butter has been incorporated, add the vanilla, increase the speed to high, and whip for 1 to 2 minutes. The buttercream should be smooth, thick, and glossy.

You can use the buttercream immediately, or store it in an airtight container in the refrigerator for up to 1 week. To use buttercream that has been chilled, see the Lemon Meringue Buttercream recipe (page 174).

VARIATIONS

You can add different flavors to customize the buttercream. For each 1 cup (237 ml) buttercream, add 3 tablespoons Lemon Curd (page 384) or Raspberry–Vanilla Bean Jam (page 354) or 1 tablespoon of your favorite liqueur, such as Grand Marnier, amaretto, or Chambord. You can replace the vanilla with 1 tablespoon almond, mint, or coconut extract.

Happy Birthday Cupcakes

Here's your go-to recipe for the quintessential vanilla-vanilla birthday cupcake. The buttery vanilla cake is light, fluffy, and delicate. Frost the cupcakes with American Buttercream Frosting tinted in assorted pastel colors and decorate with lots of sprinkles.

MAKES 24 CUPCAKES

1 cup (237 ml) whole milk

1 teaspoon pure vanilla extract

1¾ cups (219 g) cake flour (not self-rising)

1¼ cups (156 g) unbleached all-purpose flour

2 cups (400 g) granulated sugar

1 tablespoon (13 g) baking powder, preferably
    aluminum-free

¾ teaspoon fine sea salt

½ pound (2 sticks/227 g) unsalted butter, cut into
    ½-inch (1.5 cm) cubes, at room temperature

4 large (200 g) eggs, at room temperature

1 recipe American Buttercream Frosting (page 132),
    tinted as desired with liquid gel food coloring

Colored sprinkles (optional)

Position a rack in the lower third of the oven and preheat the oven to 350°F (175°C). Line 24 cupcake cups with paper liners.

In a large measuring cup or small bowl, mix together the milk and vanilla. Set aside.

In the bowl of a stand mixer fitted with the paddle attachment (or in a large mixing bowl, using a handheld mixer), combine both flours, the sugar, baking powder, and salt and mix on low speed until thoroughly combined, 2 to 3 minutes. With the mixer still on low speed, add the cubed butter a few pieces at a time, beating until the mixture resembles coarse sand. Increase the speed to medium and add the eggs one (50 g) at a time, mixing well after each addition and scraping down the sides and bottom of the bowl with a rubber spatula as necessary. Turn the speed to low and gradually add the milk mixture, then mix for another 1 to 2 minutes, until thoroughly incorporated.

Remove the bowl from the mixer stand (if using) and, using the rubber spatula, incorporate any ingredients hiding at the bottom of the bowl, making sure the batter is completely mixed.

With a large ice cream scoop or spoon, scoop the batter into the prepared cupcake cups, filling them about two-thirds full. Bake for 20 to 25 minutes, until a cake tester inserted in the center of a cupcake comes out clean. Let the cupcakes cool for 20 minutes in the pans on a wire rack, then remove from the pans and cool completely on the rack.

To frost the cupcakes: Using a spatula or a butter knife, spread the tops of the cupcakes with swirls of the buttercream frosting. Top with sprinkles, if desired.

The cupcakes can be stored in an airtight container at room temperature for up to 2 days.

Red Velvet Cupcakes

In 1905, John Adams moved his company, the Adams Extract Company, from Battle Creek, Michigan, to Beeville, Texas. He was one of the first to sell food coloring and flavor extracts in the United States. With the encouragement of his wife, Betty, who was an avid baker, he created food colorings and flavorings that would not bake or freeze out, like the ones she had been using. She whipped up a cake using his vanilla extract and red food coloring and proclaimed them to be the best she had ever tried. Soon afterward, her Red Velvet Cake was found in kitchens all across the South, as the company began using point-of-sale posters and tear-off recipe cards to promote their new food colorings. The crimson-colored buttermilk cake, as soft as velvet with a hint of cocoa, was one of Betty's own original recipes. The cake was traditionally frosted with a butter roux icing (see page 168), but sweet and tangy cream cheese frosting became the more popular choice over time.

MAKES 24 CUPCAKES

3 cups (375 g) cake flour (not self-rising)

1 teaspoon fine sea salt

1 teaspoon (6 g) baking soda

3 tablespoons Dutch-processed cocoa powder, sifted

8 tablespoons (1 stick/113 g) unsalted butter, at room temperature

1 cup (237 ml) vegetable oil

2 cups (400 g) granulated sugar

4 large (200 g) eggs, at room temperature

One 1-ounce (30 ml) bottle red food coloring

1 tablespoon apple cider vinegar

1½ teaspoons pure vanilla extract

1 cup (237 ml) buttermilk

1 recipe Cream Cheese Frosting (page 176)

Colored sprinkles (optional)

Position a rack in the lower third of the oven and preheat the oven to 350°F (175°C). Line 24 cupcake cups with paper liners.

Sift together the cake flour, salt, baking soda, and cocoa into a medium bowl. Set aside.

In the bowl of a stand mixer fitted with the paddle attachment (or in a large mixing bowl, using a handheld mixer), cream the butter, oil, and sugar together on medium-low to medium speed for 5 to 7 minutes, until very pale and thick. Add the eggs one (50 g) at a time, beating well after each addition and scraping down the sides and bottom of the bowl with a rubber spatula as necessary. Add the food coloring, vinegar, and vanilla and mix for 1 minute. With the mixer on low speed, add the flour mixture in thirds, alternating with the buttermilk, beginning and ending with the flour, scraping down the sides and bottom of the bowl as necessary. Mix for another minute.

Remove the bowl from the mixer stand (if using) and, using the rubber spatula, incorporate any ingredients hiding at the bottom of the bowl, making sure the batter is completely mixed.

With a large ice cream scoop or spoon, scoop the batter into the prepared cupcake cups, filling them about two-thirds full. Bake for 20 to 25 minutes, until a cake tester inserted in the center of a cupcake comes out clean. Let the cupcakes cool for 20 minutes in the pans on a wire rack, then remove from the pans and cool completely on a wire rack.

To frost the cupcakes: Use a spatula or a butter knife to spread the tops of the cupcakes with big swirls of the cream cheese frosting. Sprinkles are always a lovely touch.

The cupcakes can be stored in an airtight container in the refrigerator for up to 3 days. Bring to room temperature before serving.

Coconut Cupcakes

Ground coriander adds a floral citrusy note to these cupcakes, and it is a lovely complement to the sweet coconut and the Lemon Buttermilk Frosting. If you don't have coriander in your spice cabinet, try cardamom or a teaspoon of grated lemon zest instead.

MAKES 24 CUPCAKES

3 cups (375 g) unbleached all-purpose flour

1 teaspoon (4 g) baking powder, preferably aluminum-free

½ teaspoon (3 g) baking soda

1½ teaspoons fine sea salt

½ teaspoon ground coriander

¾ pound (3 sticks/340 g) unsalted butter, at room temperature

2 cups (400 g) granulated sugar

5 large (250 g) eggs, at room temperature

1 teaspoon pure vanilla extract

1 cup (237 ml) buttermilk

2¾ cups (234 g) sweetened flaked coconut

1 recipe Lemon Buttermilk Frosting (see page 74)

Position a rack in the middle of the oven and preheat the oven to 350°F (175°C). Line 24 cupcake cups with paper liners.

Sift together the flour, baking powder, baking soda, salt, and coriander into a medium bowl. Set aside.

In the bowl of a stand mixer fitted with the paddle attachment (or in a large mixing bowl, using a handheld mixer), cream the butter and sugar together on medium-high speed until light and fluffy, 3 to 5 minutes. Turn the speed down to low and add the eggs one (50 g) at a time, beating well after each addition and scraping down the sides and bottom of the bowl with a rubber spatula as necessary. Add the vanilla and mix until combined.

On low speed, add the flour mixture in thirds, alternating with the buttermilk and beginning and ending with the flour, mixing until just incorporated; scrape down the sides and bottom of the bowl as necessary. Remove the bowl from the mixer stand (if using) and, using the rubber spatula, incorporate any ingredients hiding at the bottom of the bowl, making sure the batter is completely mixed. Fold in ¾ cup (64 g) of the coconut.

With a large ice cream scoop or spoon, scoop the batter into the prepared cupcake cups, filling them about two-thirds full. Bake for 20 to 25 minutes, until a cake tester inserted in the center of a cupcake comes out clean. Let the cupcakes cool for 20 minutes in the pans on a wire rack, then remove from the pans and cool completely on the rack.

To frost and finish the cupcakes: Use a spatula or a butter knife to spread the tops of the cupcakes generously with the frosting. Put the remaining 2 cups (170 g) coconut in a medium bowl and dunk the tops in coconut to cover.

The cupcakes can be stored in an airtight container at room temperature for up to 2 days.

Strawberry Cupcakes

The South is blessed with a long growing season for strawberries that stretches from December to May; you can pick them wild then in Georgia, Florida, the Carolinas, and Louisiana. These cupcakes are packed with strawberries, in both the batter and the frosting. If you want to make these cupcakes all year long, be sure to "put up" strawberries in the freezer when they are in season (see page 98). If using frozen berries, no need to thaw them before using.

MAKES 24 CUPCAKES

3 cups (375 g) unbleached all-purpose flour

2 teaspoons (9 g) baking powder, preferably
    aluminum-free

½ teaspoon fine sea salt

1⅓ cups (300 g) pureed fresh strawberries (about
    2 cups/300 g whole strawberries, hulled)

½ cup (118 ml) whole milk, at room temperature

2 teaspoons pure vanilla extract

2 teaspoons grated lemon zest

½ pound (2 sticks/227 g) unsalted butter,
    at room temperature

2 cups (400 g) granulated sugar

2 large (100 g) eggs, at room temperature

4 large (120 g) egg whites, at room temperature

1 recipe Strawberry Cream Cheese Frosting (recipe follows)

Position a rack in the lower third of the oven and preheat the oven to 350°F (175°C). Line 24 cupcake cups with paper liners.

Sift together the flour, baking powder, and salt into a medium bowl.

In a small bowl, whisk together the pureed strawberries, milk, vanilla, and lemon zest.

In the bowl of a stand mixer fitted with the paddle attachment (or in a large mixing bowl, using a handheld mixer), cream the butter on medium-high speed until superlight in color, 3 to 5 minutes. Turn the speed down to low and gradually add the sugar, then continue to beat until it is completely incorporated and the mixture is fluffy, 2 to 3 minutes. Add the eggs and egg whites one (50 g/30 g) at a time, mixing well after each addition and scraping down the sides and bottom of the bowl with a rubber spatula as necessary. Add the flour mixture in thirds, alternating with the strawberry mixture and beginning and ending with the flour. Scrape down the sides and bottom of the bowl and mix for another 1 to 2 minutes.

Remove the bowl from the mixer stand (if using) and, using the rubber spatula, incorporate any ingredients hiding at the bottom of the bowl, making sure the batter is completely mixed.

With a large ice cream scoop or spoon, scoop the batter into the prepared cupcake cups, filling them about two-thirds full. Bake for 20 to 25 minutes, until a cake tester inserted in the center of a cupcake comes out clean. Let the cupcakes cool for 20 minutes in the pans on a wire rack, then remove from the pans and cool completely on the rack.

To frost the cupcakes: Using a spatula or a butter knife, spread the tops of the cupcakes with swirls of the cream cheese frosting.

The cupcakes can be stored in an airtight container in the refrigerator for up to 3 days. Bring to room temperature before serving.

STRAWBERRY CREAM CHEESE FROSTING

MAKES ABOUT 5 CUPS (1.2 L)

Two 8-ounce (227 g) packages cream cheese,
    cut into chunks, at room temperature
8 tablespoons (1 stick/113 g) unsalted butter, cut into
    1-inch (3 cm) cubes, at room temperature
¼ teaspoon fine sea salt
½ teaspoon fresh lemon juice
¼ cup (5 g) freeze-dried strawberries
About 4½ cups (563 g) confectioners' sugar

In the bowl of a stand mixer fitted with the paddle attachment (or in a medium mixing bowl, using a handheld mixer), combine the cream cheese, butter, and salt and beat on medium speed until combined, about 3 minutes. Add the lemon juice and strawberries and mix until incorporated. Gradually add 2½ cups (313 g) of the confectioners' sugar and beat until smooth and creamy, about 3 minutes. Gradually add 2 more cups (250 g) confectioners' sugar, or as needed, beating until the frosting is smooth and creamy.

TIPS AND TRICKS FOR CREATING DELICIOUS CAKES

❧

CAKE DECORATING DOESN'T HAVE TO BE INTIMIDATING. You want to see the handwork in every stroke of your spatula; it shows the love and care you poured into the cake. There is a special art to old-fashioned layer cakes that sets these homemade cakes apart. Here are some guidelines for decorating a stunning layer cake, but use them as a starting point. Your personal style will develop as you explore your creativity through cake design.

First and foremost, your cake should be freshly made. Once the layers are baked, you want to keep them fresh so that you can deliver something that tastes as good as it looks. You can frost your cake the same day you bake it, or you can wrap your cake layers securely in plastic wrap and store at room temperature for up to 1 day or in the refrigerator for up to 3 days; you can also freeze them for up to 1 month. If you choose to freeze your cake layers, be sure to pull them out several hours before you plan to decorate the cake, so they have time to thaw completely. Don't forget to label and date each layer that goes into your freezer.

When you're ready to assemble the cake, unwrap each cake layer and gently poke holes in the top of each one with the tines of a fork. This will allow a flavored simple syrup or milk soak to be absorbed by the cake, keeping it moist and elevating the flavor. Brush the syrup or milk soak onto the layers with a pastry brush.

Try a plain or flavored simple syrup. These are so easy, but they can make all the difference in your finished cake.

To make simple syrup, in a small saucepan, combine 1 cup (237 ml) water and 1 cup (200 g) sugar and heat over medium heat, stirring, until the sugar completely dissolves. Set aside to cool before using. Simple syrup can be refrigerated in an airtight container for up to 1 month. To make flavored syrups, try these variations, adding the flavoring to the cooled syrup:

Vanilla Simple Syrup: Add 1 teaspoon pure vanilla extract, coconut extract, or pure almond extract

Coffee Simple Syrup: Add 1 tablespoon strong hot coffee or espresso

Floral Simple Syrup: Add ½ teaspoon rose, strawberry, lavender, or orange blossom water

Citrus Simple Syrup: Add 1 tablespoon fresh lemon juice or other citrus juices

Boozy Simple Syrup: Add 1 tablespoon liquor or spirits, such as Grand Marnier, amaretto, Chambord, tequila, Marsala, gin, brandy, or bourbon

Or, for something different and less sweet, try a milk soak. A milk soak can add flavor and moisture to cakes without the sweetness of simple syrups. You can add extracts or substitute other milks, such as almond, to flavor a milk soak. These can be stored in the refrigerator for up to 1 week.

Chocolate Milk Soak: In a small saucepan, combine 1 cup (237 ml) whole milk and 1½ ounces (43 g) finely chopped chocolate (at least 64% cacao) and heat over medium heat, stirring, until the chocolate is completely melted.

Vanilla Milk Soak: In a measuring cup, combine ¼ cup (59 ml) whole milk and 1 teaspoon pure vanilla extract.

Coconut Milk Soak: In a measuring cup, combine ¼ cup (59 ml) coconut milk and 1 teaspoon pure vanilla extract.

After you've brushed your cake layers with a simple syrup or milk soak, the next step is to fill and frost the cake. A good buttercream frosting will provide the perfect canvas for decorating a cake.

The American Buttercream Frosting (page 132) is a versatile frosting recipe. You can also use the Italian Meringue Buttercream (page 180) and its variations to frost your cake as well as to decorate it with your signature look (see page 194 for ideas).

Start with room-temperature frosting. If you've made your buttercream in advance, remove it from the refrigerator and allow it to come to room temperature before you use it. Then transfer the buttercream to the bowl of a stand mixer fitted with the paddle attachment (or use a large mixing bowl and a handheld mixer) and beat on medium speed until smooth, about 2 minutes.

You can also add a filling like jam, fresh fruit, caramel, or lemon curd. Fit a pastry bag with a large plain tip (or use a large ziplock bag with a bottom corner snipped off). Fill the bag halfway with your buttercream. Pipe a circle of buttercream around the edge of the first layer to create a dam. Using an offset spatula or a butter knife, spread a big dollop of your choice of filling inside the buttercream dam. Repeat with a second layer if you're making a three-tiered cake, then top with the third layer, or place the second layer on top to finish a two-layer cake.

Create a crumb coat. Frost the top and sides of the cake with a thin layer of the buttercream frosting. This thin layer is called a crumb coat, because it seals in any stray crumbs before the second layer of frosting is applied. You should still be able to see the cake layers through the frosting at this point. A crumb coat also fills in any gaps between the layers, giving your cake a more finished look. Be sure to work from a small separate bowl of frosting when applying a crumb coat so that you don't introduce any crumbs into the frosting you will be using for the final coat. The crumb coat is just setting the foundation, so it doesn't have to be perfect, but it does create a smooth base for your frosting. After applying your crumb coat, chill the cake for about 20 minutes before applying the final layer of frosting. The frosting should still feel a bit tacky, so that the final layer will adhere properly. To finish, use an offset spatula or a butter knife to spread a big dollop of frosting over the top of the cake, going all the way to the edges, and then frost the sides with the remaining frosting, making big, luscious swirls with the back of the spatula or a spoon.

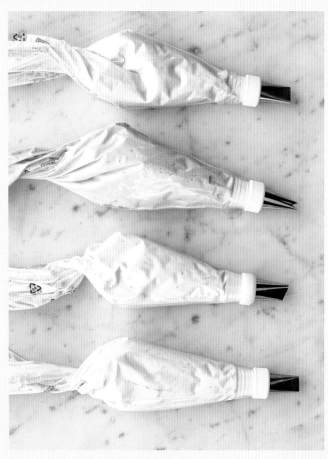

To assemble two- or three-layer cakes: The cake layers should be completely cooled (or thawed) before assembling. For a two-layer cake, level the top of one of the layers with a serrated knife so it is flat; for a three-layer cake, level the tops of two layers. Place the first layer cut side up on a serving plate (you can keep the edges of the plate clean by sliding strips of parchment under the cake while you frost it). Brush the top of the layer with plain or flavored simple syrup (see pages 189–190) or milk soak (see page 190). Using an offset spatula, spread the top with a big dollop of frosting. For a three-layer cake, place the second leveled layer on top and repeat. For either cake, place the final layer flat side up on top.

To build a multitiered cake: Prepare all the cake layers in advance. Double-wrap the cooled layers in plastic wrap, then double-wrap (yes, double-wrap them twice) in foil and label with the date. You can store the wrapped layers in the refrigerator for up to 3 days or freeze for up to 1 month. Pull frozen layers out the night before, leaving them in the wrapping until they are completely thawed.

Here are the tools you'll need to assemble your cake:

One 8- or 9-inch (20 or 23 cm) and one 6-inch (15 cm) cardboard cake round
  for the base of each tier of the cake (see Resources, page 389)
A decorating turntable
A 10- to 12-inch (25 to 30 cm) cake stand or plate
4 plastic drinking straws

To prepare and assemble the cake tiers: Level the tops of all the cake layers with a serrated knife (discard the excess, or baker's treat!). Put a dab of frosting on the cardboard cake round (to anchor the cake) and put one of the cake layers, cut side down, on the round, then put it on the decorating turntable. Brush the layer generously with simple syrup or milk soak (about 2 tablespoons). Using an offset spatula or a butter knife, spread the layer with a big dollop of frosting. Place another cake layer upside down on top and brush with the syrup or milk soak. Frost the top and sides of the cake with a thin layer of frosting (the crumb coat). Refrigerate it for at least 10 minutes (so the frosting takes hold), then repeat with the final layer. Repeat the same process with the next size of cake layers. Once the frosting is set, refrigerate until ready to stack the cake.

To stack the cake: Remove the larger cake tier from the refrigerator, unwrap it, and put it on the cake stand or plate. Insert a plastic straw vertically through the center of the tier, mark the straw with kitchen shears at the point where it is level with the top of the cake, and remove the straw. Using the shears, cut the straw at the marked point. Using the straw as a guide, cut 3 more straws to this length. Press the 6-inch (15 cm) cardboard round gently down on the cake to make an outline of where the top tier should go. Insert the 4 straws at regular intervals just inside the circle outline to support the top tier (and keep it level), spacing them evenly. Position the 6-inch (15 cm) tier on top of the straws. To gild the lily, you can add a tiny (4-inch/10 cm) layer on top without using straws for support. Simply secure the cake with a big dollop of frosting and press down to level it.

Decorate the cake to give it your signature finish.

Top the cake with fresh or dried flowers. You can use fresh edible flowers like nasturtiums, borage starflowers, strawberry blossoms, or feverfew. These don't have to be perfect whole flowers; try pulling off petals and scattering them all over your cake. You can also use dried organic flowers. You can dry them yourself just when they are starting to turn by simply tying the stems together with twine and leaving enough string so you can suspend them upside down in a cool, dry place for 2 to 3 weeks. Or purchase organic dried flowers online (see Resources, page 389). Store them in an airtight container lined with paper towels.

Or use pressed flowers for decoration. You can forage or purchase pansies, violets, snapdragons, or flowering herbs (make sure they have not been sprayed). Lay your blooms on a small sheet of parchment. Top with a second sheet and press down gently. Place the sheets between the pages of a large book and stack several heavy books on top. Leave in a dry spot for 1 to 2 weeks, until completely dried. Carefully remove the blooms to decorate your cake.

Add a special touch with sugared petals or fruit. Brush delicate rose and marigold petals or fresh culinary herbs like lemon verbena, mint, citrus leaves, lavender, or rosemary with an egg-white wash (made of 1 egg white, beaten with 1 tablespoon water) and sprinkle with granulated sugar. Place on a parchment-lined tray and set aside to dry and crystallize. Stored in an airtight container, these will keep for up to 3 months.

Or coat fresh berries with simple syrup (see page 189) and roll in granulated sugar. Allow to dry on a parchment-lined tray.

Or keep it fresh. Sliced fresh fruit like peaches, plums, champagne grapes, kumquats, apricots, cherries, and even cocktail cherries, like Luxardo, would be delicious too.

Pipe on buttercream blossoms and other designs. Real buttercream blossoms and piped designs will create a stunning presentation for a celebration cake. Use the Italian Meringue Buttercream (page 180).

Learn to cut clean slices of cake like a pro. When it's time to cut the cake, have a sharp knife and a bowl of hot water at hand. Before each slice, dip the blade of the knife into the water for a few seconds, then wipe it dry. Use the hot blade to cut straight down to slice the cake into wedges.

Pies

PIE AND THE AMERICAN SOUTH are inextricably connected because some of the most well-known and beloved creations originated here. Mastering the craft of making a pie is a rite of passage and an important part of Southern culture. And that is not limited to fruit pies and custard pies. Savory pies are also a treasured tradition. The perfect delicate flaky piecrust can be filled with everything from in-season fruit, chocolate, and nuts to chicken, pork, oysters, and fresh vegetables.

Even during hard times when sugar was scarce, Southern folks would find a way to bake up a humble pie using whatever ingredients they had in the pantry, substituting sorghum, cane syrup, or honey for sugar and cornmeal for flour. Pies were also a great way to preserve the bounty of the season, as they still are, of course. And while a meal wouldn't be complete without something sweet as the finish, sometimes the meal *is* the pie, when it's, for example, filled with oysters and cream or garden-fresh tomatoes and Fontina cheese.

In this chapter, you will find all the storied, classic pies and contemporary creations too. If you like your pies with a pucker, try Lemon Meringue Pie, Key Lime Pie, or Bill Smith's Famous Atlantic Beach Pie. Golden Buttermilk Chess Pie, Salted Honey Peanut Pie, and Bourbon Peach Hand Pies will all satisfy your sweet tooth. And don't overlook the savory pies, whether it's a Chicken Potpie or a Deep-Dish Spinach Quiche.

Razzleberry Pie

The filling for this double-crust berry pie combines different textures and flavors. Make it when all the berries are in season, or mix and match, using some fresh and some frozen berries. If you use frozen, add them straight from the freezer.

SERVES 8

1 recipe dough for Extra-Flaky All-Butter Piecrust (page 237), chilled

FOR THE FILLING

1½ cups (225 g) fresh strawberries, hulled and quartered

1 cup (120 g) fresh raspberries

1 cup (140 g) fresh blackberries

1 cup (145 g) fresh blueberries

¾ cup (150 g) granulated sugar

3 tablespoons cornstarch

1 tablespoon grated lemon zest

½ teaspoon fresh lemon juice

¼ teaspoon fine sea salt

2 tablespoons unsalted butter, at room temperature

1 large (50 g) egg, lightly beaten with a pinch of fine sea salt, for egg wash

Turbinado sugar for sprinkling

Lightly flour your work surface. Roll out one disk of dough into a 12-inch (30 cm) round. Transfer the dough to a 9-inch (23 cm) pie dish, using your fingertips to gently ease the dough into the dish, leaving a 1½-inch (4 cm) overhang all around.

Roll out the second disk of dough into a 10-inch (25 cm) round and transfer it to a parchment-lined baking sheet. Cover both crusts with plastic wrap and refrigerate for 25 to 30 minutes.

Meanwhile, make the filling: In a large bowl, combine the strawberries, raspberries, blackberries, blueberries, sugar, cornstarch, lemon zest and juice, and salt and gently toss until combined. Using your hands, mash up about a cup (140 g) of the berries to break them open, releasing some juices and pectin that will help thicken the filling as it bakes.

Transfer the filling to the chilled piecrust. Dot the fruit with the butter.

Remove the top crust from the refrigerator and let stand at room temperature for a few minutes, then drape the crust over the filling. Press the edges of the pie shell together to seal, then fold the edge of the dough under itself and crimp the edge of the crust with your thumb and forefinger, pressing gently against the pie dish as you go. Brush the top crust with the egg wash and sprinkle with turbinado sugar. Cut a few slits in the top crust for steam vents.

Place the pie in the freezer for 15 minutes to allow the crust to set.

Position a rack in the middle of the oven and preheat the oven to 400°F (205°C).

Place the chilled pie on a parchment-lined baking sheet and bake for 30 minutes, then lower the temperature to 375°F (190°C) and bake until the crust is a deep golden brown and the juices are bubbling, about 30 minutes longer.

Cool the pie completely on a wire rack, 2 to 3 hours.

The pie can be stored, covered, in the refrigerator for up to 1 week. Reheat in a preheated 350°F (175°C) oven for about 10 minutes to refresh the crust before serving.

Scuppernong Grape Pie

Just the mention of scuppernongs (or muscadines) is nostalgic for many Southerners, with memories of childhood summers spent slurping out the juicy grape flesh and spitting out the seeds and skins. This pie is a bit of a song and dance, but it is well worth the effort: The process starts with squeezing the muscadine grapes to separate the thick skins from the pulp. The pie is another great example of Southerners' resourcefulness and no-waste approach, because the entire grape is used.

SERVES 8

1 recipe dough for Extra-Flaky All-Butter Piecrust (page 237), chilled

FOR THE FILLING

1 cup (200 g) granulated sugar

¼ cup (32 g) unbleached all-purpose flour

1 teaspoon fine sea salt

¼ teaspoon ground allspice

5 cups (750 g) scuppernong or muscadine grapes

1 tablespoon fresh lemon juice

3 tablespoons unsalted butter, cut into cubes

Heavy cream for brushing

Remove the dough from the refrigerator. If it has been chilled overnight, let it sit at room temperature for 10 to 15 minutes before you roll it out.

Lightly flour your work surface and roll out one disk of dough into a 12-inch (30 cm) round. Transfer the dough to a 9-inch (23 cm) pie dish, using your fingertips to ease the dough into the dish, leaving a 1½-inch (4 cm) overhang all around.

Roll out the second disk of dough into a 10-inch (25 cm) round and transfer it to a parchment-lined baking sheet. Chill both crusts in the refrigerator for 25 to 30 minutes.

Meanwhile, make the filling: In a small mixing bowl, whisk together the sugar, flour, salt, and allspice. Set aside.

To prepare the grapes, set out two medium bowls. One at a time, squeeze the grapes to split the skins, separating the skins from the pulp, and put the skins in one bowl and the pulp in the other. Don't worry about the seeds for now.

Transfer the pulp to a medium saucepan and cook over medium heat, stirring occasionally, until the pulp starts to break down, then softens and turns translucent, about 10 minutes. Transfer the pulp to a strainer and set it over the bowl of grape skins. Press the pulp through the strainer into the bowl, using the back of a large spoon to push through as much of it as possible; discard the seeds.

Return the mixture of pulp and skins to the saucepan and cook over medium heat to soften the skins, 8 to 10 minutes. Add the lemon juice and stir well to combine. Add the flour mixture and stir until completely combined, then cook until the mixture starts to bubble and thicken, about 5 minutes. Set aside to cool slightly.

Transfer the filling to the chilled piecrust and dot the top of it with the butter. Drape the top crust over the fruit. Press the edges of the crusts together to seal. Fold the edges of the dough under and crimp the edge of the crust with your thumb and forefinger, pressing gently against the pie dish as you go. Brush the top crust with heavy cream. Cut a few slits in the top crust for steam vents.

Place the pie in the freezer for 15 minutes.

Position a rack in the middle of the oven and preheat the oven to 400°F (205°C).

Place the pie on a parchment-lined baking sheet and bake for 20 minutes, then lower the temperature to 375°F (190°C) and bake until the crust is a deep golden brown and the juices are bubbling, 30 to 40 minutes.

Remove the pie from the oven and let cool completely on a wire rack, 2 to 3 hours.

The pie can be stored, covered, in the refrigerator for up to 3 days.

Blackberry Pie

Make this pie with fresh blackberries when you can, but the recipe also works well if you have summer berries put up in your freezer (do not defrost them before making the filling). The cardamom in the crumb topping adds a floral note, and the coriander in the filling contributes a bright citrus flavor. Together the spices add a delicious sweet surprise to the pie.

SERVES 8

½ recipe dough for Extra-Flaky All-Butter Piecrust
    (page 237), chilled

FOR THE CRUMB TOPPING

1 cup (125 g) unbleached all-purpose flour

½ cup (45 g) old-fashioned rolled oats

¼ cup (50 g) packed light brown sugar

1 teaspoon fine sea salt

¼ teaspoon ground cardamom

8 tablespoons (1 stick/113 g) unsalted butter, melted

2 tablespoons whole milk

FOR THE FILLING

6 cups (840 g) fresh blackberries

¾ cup (150 g) granulated sugar

3 tablespoons unbleached all-purpose flour

½ teaspoon fine sea salt

¼ teaspoon ground coriander

2 tablespoons fresh lemon juice

Remove the dough from the refrigerator. If it has been chilled overnight, let it sit at room temperature for 10 to 15 minutes before rolling.

Lightly flour your work surface and roll the dough into a 12-inch (30 cm) round. Transfer the dough to a 9-inch (23 cm) pie dish, using your fingertips to ease the dough into the dish, leaving a 1½-inch (4 cm) overhang all around. Chill the crust in the refrigerator for 25 to 30 minutes.

To make the crumb topping: In a medium mixing bowl, stir together the flour, oats, brown sugar, salt, and cardamom with a fork until completely blended.

In a large measuring cup or small bowl, mix together the melted butter and milk. Pour the melted butter mixture over the oat mixture and toss with your hands until completely incorporated. Once the mixture will hold clumps in your hand, it's ready!

Position a rack in the middle of the oven and preheat the oven to 400°F (205°C). Place the piecrust on a parchment-lined baking sheet.

To make the filling: Put the blackberries in a large bowl, add the sugar, flour, salt, coriander, and lemon juice, and gently toss until combined. Using your hands, mash up about a cup (140 g) of the blackberries to release some juices and pectin, which will help thicken the filling as it bakes.

Pour the filling into the chilled piecrust. Top the pie with the crumb topping, making sure you have various-sized chunks on top to create texture.

Place the pie in the oven, reduce the temperature to 375°F (190°C), and bake for about 1 hour, until the crust is a deep golden brown and the juices are bubbling. Cool completely on a wire rack, 2 to 3 hours.

The pie can be stored, covered, in the refrigerator for up to 3 days. Reheat in a preheated 350°F (175°C) oven for about 5 minutes to refresh the crust before serving.

Apple Rose Pie

PICTURED ON PAGE 213

Before vanilla extract was widely available, the most popular flavoring in America was rose water. A dash of it was called for in recipes from cakes and cookies to, most famously, the all-American apple pie. Making rose water was as simple as boiling rose petals from the garden in a pot of water and then straining the flavored water. Both the very first American cookbook, *American Cookery* by Amelia Simmons, published in 1796, and *The Carolina Housewife* by Sarah Rutledge, which first appeared in 1847, featured recipes for puddings, pound cakes, cookies, and pies using rose water.

This recipe brings the lovely taste of rose water back to apple pie. The traditional pie spices cinnamon and nutmeg marry well with the less-traditional cardamom, and serving this pie with a rose water–scented Chantilly cream makes it special enough for any occasion.

Note that the apples for the filling must be macerated for at least 4 hours, or, preferably, overnight.

SERVES 8

6 large apples, such as Granny Smith, Pink Lady, Rome, or Cameo, or a combination, cored, peeled, and thinly sliced

¼ cup (50 g) granulated sugar

¼ cup (50 g) packed light brown sugar

2 tablespoons unsalted butter, cut into ½-inch (1.5 cm) cubes

1 tablespoon fresh lemon juice

1 teaspoon rose water (see Resources, page 389)

2 tablespoons unbleached all-purpose flour

2 teaspoons ground cinnamon

¼ teaspoon ground cardamom

¼ teaspoon freshly grated nutmeg

½ teaspoon fine sea salt

1 recipe dough for Extra-Flaky All-Butter Piecrust (page 237), chilled

2 tablespoons heavy cream, for brushing

1 recipe Chantilly Cream (page 373), flavored with rose water, for serving (optional)

In a large bowl, toss the apples with both sugars, the butter, lemon juice, and rose water.

In a small bowl, whisk together the flour, cinnamon, cardamom, nutmeg, and salt. Add to the apples and toss until evenly distributed. Cover the bowl with plastic wrap and refrigerate for at least 4 hours, or, preferably, overnight to release the juices from the apples.

When you are ready to assemble the pie, drain the apples in a sieve set over a bowl and return them to the large bowl. Pour the liquid into a saucepan, bring to a simmer, and cook, stirring frequently, until it has reduced by half and become a thin gooey caramel, about 4 minutes.

Pour the liquid over the apples and toss to combine.

Remove the chilled disks of dough from the refrigerator. If the dough has been chilled overnight, let it sit at room temperature for 10 to 15 minutes before you roll it out.

Lightly flour your work surface and roll out one disk of dough into a 12-inch (30 cm) round. Transfer the dough to a 9-inch (23 cm) pie dish, using your fingertips to gently ease the dough into the dish, leaving a 1½-inch (4 cm) overhang all around.

Roll out the second disk of dough into a 10-inch (25 cm) round and transfer it to a parchment-lined baking sheet. Cover both crusts with plastic wrap and refrigerate for about 15 minutes.

To assemble the pie: Pour the apple mixture into the prepared piecrust.

Remove the top crust from the refrigerator, place on a work surface, and cut 4 to 8 vent holes in the center with a mini cookie cutter of whatever shape you like. Drape the crust over the filling and crimp the edges to seal. Decorate with the cutout pieces.

Put the pie in the freezer for 15 minutes to set the crust.

Position a rack in the lower third of the oven and preheat the oven to 400°F (205°C).

Remove the pie from the freezer and place on a parchment-lined baking sheet. Brush the entire crust with the heavy cream.

Bake the pie for 20 minutes, then turn the oven down to 375°F (190°C) and bake for an additional 45 to 60 minutes, until the juices are bubbling and the crust is golden brown. Remove the pie from the oven and let it cool for at least 3 hours on a wire rack before serving.

The pie can be stored, covered, in the refrigerator for 2 to 3 days.

Tip: Freezing a Whole Pie

You can freeze whole fruit-filled pies or galettes to bake whenever you are ready. Cut small steam vents in the top crust of a pie before you freeze it, but wait until you are ready to bake it before you brush the pie—or galette—with the egg wash. Be sure to use a metal pie dish that can go from the freezer to the hot oven. Glass pie dishes are great in general, but glass, or porcelain, is not a good choice in this situation. It will likely crack in the oven unless you let it warm up on the counter before baking.

Plum Pie

This pie requires sweet-tart plums that are in season and good enough to eat out of hand. The grape jelly intensifies the flavor of the plums.

SERVES 8

1 recipe dough for Extra-Flaky All-Butter Piecrust
    (page 237), chilled

FOR THE FILLING
3 tablespoons cornstarch
1 tablespoon water
2 teaspoons fresh lemon juice
¼ cup (85 g) grape jelly
3 tablespoons turbinado sugar, plus more
    for sprinkling
¼ teaspoon fine sea salt

10 ripe plums, halved, pitted, and sliced
1 large (50 g) egg, beaten, for egg wash

Remove the dough from the refrigerator. If it has been chilled overnight, let it sit at room temperature for 10 to 15 minutes before you roll it out.

Lightly flour your work surface and roll out one disk of dough into a 12-inch (30 cm) round. Transfer the dough to a 9-inch (23 cm) pie dish, using your fingertips to ease the dough into the dish, leaving a 1½-inch (4 cm) overhang all around.

Roll out the second disk of dough into a 10-inch (25 cm) round and transfer it to a parchment-lined baking sheet. Chill both crusts in the refrigerator for 25 to 30 minutes.

(Continued)

Meanwhile, *make the filling:* In a large bowl, whisk the cornstarch, water, and lemon juice together until smooth. Add the jelly, sugar, and salt, whisking until smooth. Add the plums and stir gently to combine.

Transfer the filling to the chilled piecrust. Drape the top crust over the fruit. Press the edges of the crusts together to seal. Fold the edges of the dough under and crimp the edge of the crust, pressing gently against the pie dish as you go. Brush the top crust with the egg wash. Cut a few slits in the top crust for steam vents.

Place the pie in the freezer for 15 minutes.

Position a rack in the middle of the oven and preheat the oven to 400°F (205°C).

Place the pie on a parchment-lined baking sheet and bake for 30 minutes, then lower the temperature to 375°F (190°C) and bake until the crust is a deep golden brown and the juices are bubbling, about 30 minutes.

Let the pie cool completely on a wire rack, 2 to 3 hours.

The pie can be stored, covered, in the refrigerator for up to 1 week. Reheat in a preheated 350°F (175°C) oven for about 10 minutes to refresh the crust before serving.

Peach Lattice Pie

PICTURED ON PAGE 213

The peaches caramelize under the lattice top as this juicy filling, spiced with freshly grated nutmeg, bakes. You don't even have to peel the peaches for this pie. Top slices with Vanilla Bean Ice Cream (page 344) for the ultimate celebration of summer.

SERVES 8

1 recipe dough for Extra-Flaky All-Butter Piecrust
    (page 237), chilled
3 pounds (1.4 kg) ripe but firm peaches, halved, pitted,
    and cut into ¼-inch (6 mm) slices
2 teaspoons grated lemon zest
1½ tablespoons fresh lemon juice
¼ cup (50 g) granulated sugar
½ cup (100 g) packed light brown sugar
¼ cup (32 g) unbleached all-purpose flour
½ teaspoon fine sea salt
½ teaspoon freshly grated nutmeg
2 tablespoons unsalted butter, cut into cubes,
    at room temperature
3 tablespoons heavy cream
1 tablespoon coarse sanding sugar or turbinado sugar
    for sprinkling

Remove the dough from the refrigerator. If the dough has been chilled overnight, let it sit at room temperature for 10 to 15 minutes before you roll it out.

Lightly flour your work surface and roll out one disk of dough into a 12-inch (30 cm) round. Transfer the dough to a 9-inch (23 cm) pie dish, using your fingertips to ease the dough into the pie dish, leaving a 1½-inch (4 cm)

overhang all around. Refrigerate until ready to fill the crust.

For the lattice crust, roll out the second disk of dough into a circle approximately 12 inches (30 cm) in diameter. Using a pastry wheel, pizza cutter, or sharp knife, cut off a 1-inch-wide (3 cm) strip from two opposite sides of the circle. Cut the remaining dough into eight 1-inch-wide (3 cm) strips. Transfer the strips to a parchment-lined baking sheet and refrigerate until you are ready to use.

Put the peaches in a large bowl, add the lemon zest and juice, and toss gently.

In a small bowl, mix together both sugars, the flour, salt, and nutmeg. Gently toss the peaches with this mixture to coat. Pour the filling into the chilled piecrust. Dot the top of the fruit with the butter.

To make the lattice: Starting with the longest strips, lay one strip across the center of the filled pie. Lay another strip across the middle of that strip (like a plus sign), then lay another strip perpendicular to that strip, about ½ inch (1.5 cm) away. Gently pull back one end of the bottom strip, lay another strip down perpendicular to it, and then put the strip back in place—it's like weaving. Repeat until you have used all the strips and covered your pie.

Roll the edges of the bottom and top crusts inward all around the pie, creating a rolled edge. Make sure the crust is resting on the edge of the pie plate. Then crimp the crust all around, using both thumbs and an index finger to create a letter C for a ruffle effect.

Place the pie in the freezer for 15 to 20 minutes to set the crust.

(Continued)

Position a rack in the middle of the oven and preheat the oven to 400°F (205°C). Remove the pie from the freezer and place it on a parchment-lined baking sheet. Brush the crust with the heavy cream. Sprinkle with the coarse sugar.

Place the pie in the oven and bake for 30 minutes, then reduce the temperature to 375°F (190°C), rotate the pie, and bake until the crust is a deep golden brown and the juices are bubbling, 25 to 30 more minutes.

Let the pie cool completely on a wire rack, about 2 hours.

The pie can be stored, covered, in the refrigerator for up to 1 week. Reheat in a preheated 350°F (175°C) oven for about 10 minutes to refresh the crust before serving.

Strawberry Rhubarb Slab Pie

A slab pie can feed a crowd. As with other fruit pies, you can make it in advance and freeze it, then pop it in the oven on the day you plan to serve it (see Freezing a Whole Pie, page 205).

SERVES 12 TO 16

1 recipe dough for Slab Pie Crust (page 240), chilled
5 cups (750 g) fresh strawberries, hulled
4 cups (488 g) 1-inch (3 cm) pieces peeled rhubarb
1 cup (200 g) granulated sugar
3 tablespoons unbleached all-purpose flour
1 tablespoon cornstarch
½ teaspoon fine sea salt
1 tablespoon grated lemon zest
1 tablespoon fresh lemon juice
1 large (50 g) egg, lightly beaten with a pinch of
      fine sea salt, for egg wash
Turbinado sugar for sprinkling

On a lightly floured work surface, with a lightly floured rolling pin, roll the larger piece of dough out to a 19-by-14-inch (48 by 36 cm) rectangle. Fit it into a 15-by-10-inch (38 by 25 cm) jelly roll pan, pressing it into the corners. The crust will hang over the edges of the pan. Chill the crust in the refrigerator while you put the filling together.

In a large bowl, combine the strawberries and rhubarb. Add the sugar, flour, cornstarch, salt, and lemon zest and juice and toss with the fruit until thoroughly mixed. Pour the filling into the prepared piecrust.

On a lightly floured work surface, with a lightly floured rolling pin, roll the smaller piece of dough out to a 15-by-10-inch (38 by 25 cm) rectangle. Place it over the filling. Fold the edges of the bottom crust up over the edges of the top crust and pinch the edges to seal. Cut out shapes from the trimmings with mini cookie cutters, if desired, and use them to decorate the top of the pie. Chill the pie for 15 minutes in the freezer or 30 minutes in the refrigerator to set the crust.

Position a rack in the lower third of the oven and preheat the oven to 375°F (190°C). Place a parchment-lined baking sheet on the lower rack to catch any juices that spill out when the pie bakes.

Remove the pie from the freezer or refrigerator and cut a few slits in the top for steam vents. Brush the crust with the egg wash and sprinkle with the turbinado sugar. Bake for 40 to 55 minutes, until the crust is golden brown and the juices are bubbling.

Let the pie cool completely on a wire rack before slicing.

The pie can be stored, covered, in the refrigerator for up to 3 days.

Key Lime Pie

The first written mention of this pie, a true American creation, has been traced back to Key West's first millionaire, William Curry. His beloved cook, "Aunt Sally," made the pie for him using condensed milk that magically thickened when combined with lime juice. Don't fret if you can't find key limes; you can use regular limes for this recipe.

SERVES 8

1 baked Graham Cracker Piecrust (page 239), cooled

One 14-ounce (300 ml) can sweetened condensed milk

1 cup (237 ml) heavy cream

4 large (76 g) egg yolks

½ teaspoon pure vanilla extract

2 teaspoons grated lime zest, plus more for
    finishing the pie

1 cup (237 ml) fresh key lime juice (8 to 10 limes)

1 recipe Buttermilk Whipped Cream (page 372)
    for serving

Position a rack in the lower third of the oven and preheat the oven to 325°F (165°C). Place the baked piecrust on a baking sheet.

In a large bowl, whisk the condensed milk, heavy cream, egg yolks, and vanilla together until smooth. Add the lime zest and juice and whisk until combined.

Pour the filling into the crust. Bake for 15 to 18 minutes, until the filling is puffed up at the edges and the center no longer looks wet but still wobbles slightly when jiggled; it will continue to set as it cools.

Cool the pie on a wire rack for 1 hour, then refrigerate until cold, at least 3 hours, or overnight.

Serve the pie chilled with the whipped cream.

The pie can be refrigerated, loosely covered, for up to 3 days.

Coconut Cream Pie

An icebox pie like this one should be your go-to dessert during the hot summer months. An easy-to-make graham cracker crust is filled with a delicate coconut custard. Vanilla and cardamom add brightness to the tropical coconut flavors of this Southern favorite.

SERVES 8

6 tablespoons (75 g) granulated sugar

3 tablespoons cornstarch

¼ teaspoon salt

5 large (95 g) egg yolks

1 cup (237 ml) coconut milk

1 cup (237 ml) whole milk

¼ teaspoon ground cardamom

2½ teaspoons unsalted butter, at room temperature

1 teaspoon pure vanilla extract

1¾ cups (149 g) sweetened flaked coconut

1 baked Graham Cracker Piecrust (page 239), cooled

1 recipe Chantilly Cream (page 373) for serving

In a medium heatproof bowl, combine the sugar, cornstarch, salt, and egg yolks and whisk until well blended. Set aside.

In a medium heavy-bottomed saucepan, combine the coconut milk, milk, and cardamom and heat to just under the boiling point.

Whisk about 1 cup (237 ml) of the hot milk mixture into the egg yolk mixture to temper the yolks, so they won't curdle, and then, continuing to whisk, add the remainder of the milk mixture in a steady stream, whisking constantly. Transfer the mixture to the saucepan and cook over medium heat, stirring with a heatproof spatula and scraping the bottom of the pan, until the custard has thickened and bubbles appear in the center, 4 to 6 minutes.

Remove from the heat and add the butter, whisking until it is melted and incorporated. Stir in the vanilla, then fold in 1 cup (85 g) of the coconut.

Pour the filling into a bowl and cover with plastic wrap, pressing the plastic directly onto the surface so that a skin does not form. Let cool for about 30 minutes, or until the filling reaches room temperature.

Spread the filling evenly in the baked piecrust. Scatter the remaining ¾ cup (64 g) coconut over the top and refrigerate until thoroughly chilled, at least 3 hours.

Serve the pie chilled with the Chantilly cream.

The pie is best served the same day it's made, but it can be refrigerated, loosely covered, for up to 3 days.

Bill Smith's Famous Atlantic Beach Pie

PICTURED ON PAGE 213

Bill Smith was the chef at the iconic Crook's Corner in Chapel Hill, North Carolina, for nearly three decades, and he is one of the foremost experts on Southern food. He is famous for reinterpreting heirloom recipes from savory to sweet, including this pie, which is based on his childhood memories of enjoying big slices of it after a day of eating oysters on the Outer Banks. The tangy lemon custard is balanced by the crisp salty cracker crust. Top off the lemon custard with a cloud of Buttermilk Whipped Cream.

SERVES 8

1 baked Saltine Cracker Piecrust (page 239), cooled

One 14-ounce (300 ml) can sweetened condensed milk

4 large (76 g) egg yolks, lightly beaten

1 tablespoon grated lemon zest

½ cup (118 ml) fresh lemon juice

1 recipe Buttermilk Whipped Cream (page 372)

Position a rack in the lower third of the oven and preheat the oven to 325°F (165°C). Place the baked piecrust on a parchment-lined baking sheet.

In a large bowl, whisk the condensed milk and egg yolks together until smooth. Add the lemon zest and juice, whisking until combined.

Pour the filling into the crust. Bake for 16 to 18 minutes, until the filling is puffed up at the edges and the center no longer looks wet but still wobbles slightly when jiggled; it will continue to set as it cools.

Cool the pie on a wire rack for 1 hour, then refrigerate until cold, at least 3 hours, or overnight.

Serve the pie chilled with the whipped cream.

The pie can be refrigerated, loosely covered, for up to 3 days.

Blueberry Icebox Pie

PICTURED OPPOSITE

There are so many variations of this nostalgic Southern favorite, which is also known as "Yum Yum Pie" (for obvious reasons). The light and creamy lemon filling is topped with blueberries and a homemade whipped cream for an easy-peasy no-bake dessert to whip up when it's so hot you just can't bear to turn on the oven.

SERVES 8

FOR THE FILLING

½ cup (118 ml) heavy cream

½ pound (227 g) cream cheese, cut into chunks, at room temperature

¾ cup (180 g) sour cream

¾ cup (94 g) confectioners' sugar

1 tablespoon grated lemon zest

1 tablespoon fresh lemon juice

½ teaspoon fine sea salt

1 teaspoon pure vanilla extract

1 baked Graham Cracker Piecrust (page 239), cooled

FOR THE BLUEBERRY TOPPING

2 tablespoons cornstarch

¼ cup (59 ml) water

2 cups (290 g) fresh blueberries

½ cup (100 g) granulated sugar

1 teaspoon pure vanilla extract

1 recipe Chantilly Cream (page 373) for serving

To make the filling: In the bowl of a stand mixer fitted with the whisk attachment (or in a large mixing bowl, using a handheld mixer), whip the cream on medium speed until it holds stiff peaks.

Cover and refrigerate while you make the rest of the filling.

In the clean bowl of the stand mixer fitted with the paddle attachment (or in a large mixing bowl, using a handheld mixer), beat the cream cheese and sour cream until smooth and creamy, 3 to 5 minutes. Gradually add the confectioners' sugar and mix until light and fluffy. Add the lemon zest and juice, salt, and vanilla and mix to combine.

Gently fold in the chilled whipped cream until just combined, being careful not to overmix.

Pour the filling into the baked piecrust and refrigerate until completely chilled, at least 3 hours, or overnight.

To make the blueberry topping: In a large measuring cup or small bowl, whisk the cornstarch and water together until smooth. Set aside.

In a medium saucepan, combine the blueberries and sugar and bring to a boil over medium-high heat, stirring occasionally. Then cook, stirring for 3 to 5 minutes, until the sugar is dissolved and the blueberries are soft. Pour the cornstarch mixture into the blueberry mixture, bring to a gentle boil, and cook, stirring frequently, until the mixture thickens, about 1 minute. Remove from the heat and stir in the vanilla.

Pour the topping into a bowl and set aside to cool to room temperature, then cover with plastic wrap and refrigerate until completely chilled.

Just before serving, spoon the blueberry topping on top of the filling. Serve with the Chantilly cream.

The pie can be refrigerated, loosely covered, for up to 3 days.

CLOCKWISE FROM TOP LEFT: APPLE ROSE PIE (PAGE 204), PEACH LATTICE PIE (PAGE 207),
BLUEBERRY ICEBOX PIE (OPPOSITE), BILL SMITH'S FAMOUS ATLANTIC BEACH PIE (PAGE 211)

Lemon Meringue Pie

This lovely super-tart lemon custard pie is a Southern classic with timeless appeal. When other fruits are scarce during the winter months, you can always look forward to a citrus pie. A couple of tips to keep in mind when making the billowy mile-high meringue for this delightful showstopper: Allow the egg whites to come to room temperature before whipping them, and make sure to whip the whites thoroughly after each addition of sugar so the sugar completely dissolves (if it doesn't, beads of moisture will form on the meringue after it is baked).

SERVES 8

1 prebaked Extra-Flaky All-Butter Piecrust (page 237), cooled

6 large (114 g) egg yolks

1½ cups (300 g) granulated sugar

⅓ cup (45 g) cornstarch

½ teaspoon fine sea salt

1¼ cups (296 ml) water

¼ cup (59 ml) whole milk

1 tablespoon grated lemon zest (from 1 medium lemon)

½ cup (118 ml) fresh lemon juice

3 tablespoons unsalted butter, cut into pieces

1 recipe Billowy Meringue (recipe follows)

Position a rack in the lower third of the oven and preheat the oven to 375°F (190°C). Place the prebaked piecrust on a parchment-lined baking sheet.

In a medium bowl, lightly whisk the egg yolks. Set aside.

In a medium heavy nonreactive saucepan, whisk together the sugar, cornstarch, and salt. Set the pan over medium heat and gradually add the water and milk, whisking until smooth. Continue to whisk until the mixture comes to a boil, 4 to 5 minutes, then whisk constantly until the mixture begins to thicken, 1 to 2 minutes longer. Remove from the heat.

To temper the egg yolks, add about 1 cup (237 ml) of the hot milk mixture to them, whisking vigorously so the yolks do not curdle, then pour the warmed egg yolk mixture into the rest of the milk mixture and set over low heat. Whisk in the lemon zest and juice, bring to a simmer, whisking, and simmer until the custard is thick and glossy, 4 to 6 minutes. Be careful not to overheat the custard; it will scorch if the heat is too high. Remove from the heat and stir in the butter until melted and fully incorporated.

Pour the custard into the crust and set aside while you make the meringue.

Pile the meringue all over the surface of the pie, making sure it touches the crust all around. Use a spatula or the back of a spoon to make big, luscious swirls.

Bake for 8 to 10 minutes, until the meringue is lightly golden brown. Remove the pie from the oven and cool on a wire rack for at least 1 hour before serving.

The pie is best served the same day it's baked, but it can be covered with plastic wrap and refrigerated for up to 3 days.

BILLOWY MERINGUE

MAKES ABOUT 2 CUPS (473 ML)

6 large (180 g) egg whites, at room temperature

½ teaspoon cream of tartar

⅛ teaspoon fine sea salt

½ cup (100 g) granulated sugar

¼ cup (31 g) confectioners' sugar

In the impeccably clean bowl of a stand mixer fitted with the whisk attachment (or in a large mixing bowl, using a handheld mixer), beat the egg whites, cream of tartar, and salt on low speed for 1 minute, or until the egg whites begin to thicken and look frothy. Slowly add the granulated sugar, then continue beating until soft peaks form.

Add the confectioners' sugar and whip on medium speed until the meringue is stiff and glossy; it should form stiff peaks that hold their shape when you lift the whisk out of the bowl. Use immediately.

Black Bottom Chocolate Cream Pie

PICTURED ON PAGE 230

This is also known as Mississippi Mud Pie, since some folks say its color is reminiscent of the muddy waters of the Mississippi River. It is the ultimate treat for chocolate lovers: a chocolate cookie crust filled with a chilled rich chocolate pastry cream and topped with fresh whipped cream.

SERVES 8

6 tablespoons (75 g) granulated sugar

3 tablespoons cornstarch

¼ teaspoon fine sea salt

5 large (95 g) egg yolks

2 cups (473 ml) whole milk

2½ tablespoons unsalted butter, cut into cubes, at room temperature

1 teaspoon pure vanilla extract

6 ounces (170 g) dark chocolate (60 to 70% cacao), melted

1 baked Black Bottom Piecrust (page 238), cooled

1 recipe Chantilly Cream (page 373)

In a medium heatproof bowl, combine the sugar, cornstarch, salt, and egg yolks and whisk until well blended. Set aside.

In a medium heavy-bottomed saucepan, heat the milk to just under the boiling point. Gradually whisk about 1 cup (237 ml) of the hot milk into the egg yolk mixture to temper the yolks, so they won't curdle, then add the remainder of the milk in a steady stream, whisking constantly. Transfer the mixture to the saucepan and cook over medium heat, stirring with a heatproof spatula and scraping the bottom of the pan, until the custard has thickened and bubbles appear in the center, 4 to 6 minutes.

Remove from the heat and add the butter one piece at a time, whisking until melted and incorporated. Stir in the vanilla, then whisk in the melted chocolate.

Pour the chocolate filling into a bowl and cover with plastic wrap, pressing the plastic directly onto the surface so that a skin does not form. Let cool for about 30 minutes, until the filling reaches room temperature.

Spread the filling evenly in the baked piecrust. Refrigerate until completely chilled, at least 3 hours.

Just before serving, spread the Chantilly cream over the top of the pie.

The pie is best served the same day it's made, but it can be stored, loosely covered, in the refrigerator for up to 3 days.

Golden Buttermilk Chess Pie

This pie has a history of more than two hundred years. Legend has it that when a freed slave who made a living selling her pies to her neighbors was asked what smelled so good, she replied: "Oh, it's jes' pie," which, delivered in a Southern drawl, was heard as "chess pie." All Southern families have at least one recipe for this pie in their keepsake box. The pure and silky custard filling is made from humble ingredients: sugar, butter, eggs, and buttermilk. Vanilla and lemon zest make this version of it even more delicious.

SERVES 8

1 parbaked Extra-Flaky All-Butter Piecrust (page 237), cooled

8 tablespoons (1 stick/113 g) unsalted butter, at room temperature

1½ cups (300 g) granulated sugar

4 large (200 g) eggs, at room temperature

3 tablespoons cornmeal

½ teaspoon grated lemon zest

1 tablespoon fresh lemon juice

1 teaspoon pure vanilla extract

¼ teaspoon fine sea salt

½ cup (118 ml) buttermilk

Position a rack in the lower third of the oven and preheat the oven to 350°F (175°C). Place the parbaked piecrust on a parchment-lined baking sheet.

In the bowl of a stand mixer fitted with the paddle attachment (or in a large mixing bowl, using a handheld mixer), cream the butter and sugar together until light and creamy, 3 to 5 minutes. Add the eggs one (50 g) at a time, beating well after each addition and scraping down the sides and bottom of the bowl with a rubber spatula as necessary. Add the cornmeal, lemon zest and juice, vanilla, and salt and mix until well blended. With the mixer on low, slowly add the buttermilk, scraping down the sides and bottom of the bowl as necessary.

Pour the filling into the crust. Bake for 45 to 50 minutes, until the filling is golden and puffed up at the edges and the center no longer looks wet but still wobbles slightly when jiggled; it will continue to set as it cools.

Remove the pie from the oven and let cool completely. Serve at room temperature or chilled.

The pie can be stored, loosely covered, in the refrigerator for up to 3 days.

Chocolate Chess Pie

PICTURED ON PAGE 230

Use the best-quality chocolate you can find in this variation on the classic chess pie; it will really make a difference. Acalli Chocolate from New Orleans is a great chocolate for baking and for eating out of hand; try it, or use your favorite dark chocolate. The coriander adds just a whisper of citrus and floral flavors.

SERVES 8

1 parbaked Extra-Flaky All-Butter Piecrust (page 237), cooled

8 tablespoons (1 stick/113 g) unsalted butter

2 ounces (57 g) dark chocolate (65 to 70% cacao), coarsely chopped

1½ cups (300 g) granulated sugar

2 tablespoons plus 1 teaspoon unbleached all-purpose flour

(Continued)

2 tablespoons Dutch-processed cocoa powder

¼ teaspoon ground coriander

¼ teaspoon fine sea salt

¾ cup (177 ml) buttermilk

3 large (150 g) eggs, at room temperature

½ teaspoon pure vanilla extract

Position a rack in the middle of the oven and preheat the oven to 350°F (175°C). Place the parbaked piecrust on a parchment-lined baking sheet.

In a heatproof bowl set over a saucepan of simmering water (do not let the bottom of the bowl touch the water), combine the butter and chocolate and heat, stirring, until the chocolate and butter are melted and smooth. Remove from the heat and let cool slightly.

In a large bowl, whisk together the sugar, flour, cocoa powder, coriander, and salt.

In a medium bowl, whisk together the buttermilk, eggs, and vanilla. Gently whisk in the melted chocolate mixture.

Add the chocolate mixture to the sugar mixture and whisk until smooth.

Pour the filling into the crust and bake for 40 to 50 minutes, or until the filling is puffed up at the edges and the center no longer looks wet but still wobbles slightly when jiggled; it will continue to set as it cools.

Remove the pie from the oven and let cool on a wire rack before serving.

Store, covered, at room temperature for up to 1 day or refrigerated for up to 3 days.

Chocolate Honey Pie

A rich dark chocolate custard is sweetened with just enough honey to satisfy your sweet tooth and accented with a finishing touch of flaky sea salt.

SERVES 8

1 parbaked Shortcut Piecrust (page 236) or Extra-Flaky
    All-Butter Piecrust (page 237), cooled

1½ cups (355 ml) honey

4½ tablespoons (23 g) Dutch-processed cocoa powder

6 tablespoons (85 g) unsalted butter

¾ cup (177 ml) heavy cream

3 large (150 g) eggs, at room temperature

Flaky sea salt, such as Maldon, for sprinkling

Position a rack in the lower third of the oven and preheat the oven to 325°F (165°C). Place the parbaked piecrust on a parchment-lined baking sheet.

In a medium heavy-bottomed saucepan, combine the honey, cocoa, butter, and cream and cook over medium heat, stirring occasionally, until the butter is melted and the mixture is just starting to simmer. Remove from the heat.

In a medium heatproof bowl, whisk the eggs to blend. Whisking constantly, slowly pour about ½ cup (118 ml) of the honey mixture into the eggs to temper them, so they won't curdle, and then add the remainder of the honey mixture in a steady stream, whisking constantly until smooth.

Pour the filling into the crust. Bake for 45 minutes to 1 hour, until the filling is puffed up at the edges and the center no longer looks wet but still wobbles slightly when jiggled; it will continue to set as it cools.

Remove the pie from the oven and let cool completely on a wire rack. Serve at room temperature or chilled; sprinkle with flaky sea salt just before serving.

The pie can be stored, covered, at room temperature for up to 1 day or refrigerated for up to 3 days.

Transparent Pie

This historic sugar pie dates back to frontier days, but it was Magee's Bakery in Maysville, Kentucky, which opened in the 1930s, that made it famous in the region. Made with the simple ingredients that were available on every farm (and now in every modern kitchen), it has a silky-smooth transparent custard filling hiding beneath a crunchy top. The filling is rich, so a small sliver of this pie is a satisfying treat.

SERVES 8

1 parbaked Shortcut Piecrust (page 236) or Extra-Flaky
    All-Butter Piecrust (page 237), cooled
8 tablespoons (1 stick/113 g) unsalted butter, at room
    temperature
2 cups (400 g) granulated sugar
1 cup (237 ml) heavy cream
4 large (200 g) eggs, at room temperature
2 tablespoons unbleached all-purpose flour
1 teaspoon pure vanilla extract

Position a rack in the lower third of the oven and preheat the oven to 375°F (190°C). Place the parbaked piecrust on a parchment-lined baking sheet.

In the bowl of a stand mixer fitted with the paddle attachment (or in a large mixing bowl, using a handheld mixer), mix the butter and sugar until light and fluffy, 2 to 4 minutes. Add the cream and mix on high speed until the mixture is slightly thickened, about 2 minutes. Add the eggs, flour, and vanilla and mix until incorporated.

Pour the filling into the crust. Bake for about 45 minutes, until the filling is puffed up at the edges and the center no longer looks wet but still wobbles slightly when jiggled; it will continue to set as it cools.

Remove the pie from the oven and let cool completely on a wire rack. Serve at room temperature or chilled.

The pie can be stored, covered, at room temperature for up to 1 day or refrigerated for up to 3 days.

Salted Honey Peanut Pie

PICTURED ON PAGE 196

The peanut is Georgia's official state crop, and the state produces close to half of the peanuts in America. The peanut is enjoyed in so many ways, from boiled to roasted. This pie, which is packed with plenty of peanuts in a gooey caramel filling, pays homage to the farmers who produce such a delicious product.

SERVES 8

¾ cup (150 g) packed dark brown sugar
4 large (200 g) eggs, at room temperature
6 tablespoons (85 g) unsalted butter, melted
⅔ cup (158 ml) honey
2 teaspoons pure vanilla extract
1 teaspoon fresh lemon juice
½ teaspoon fine sea salt
1½ cups (225 g) lightly salted dry-roasted peanuts
1 parbaked Extra-Flaky All-Butter Piecrust (page 237),
    cooled
About 1 teaspoon flaky sea salt, such as Maldon,
    for sprinkling

Position a rack in the middle of the oven and preheat the oven to 350°F (175°C).

In a medium bowl, stir together the brown sugar, eggs, butter, honey, vanilla, lemon juice, and salt until completely combined, 1 to 2 minutes. Fold in ½ cup (75 g) of the peanuts.

(Continued)

Pour the filling into the parbaked crust. Sprinkle the remaining 1 cup (150 g) peanuts on top.

Place the pie on a parchment-lined baking sheet and bake for 1 hour and 15 minutes, or until the filling is firm around the edges and just a bit loose in the center.

Remove the pie from the oven and sprinkle the flaky sea salt on top. Let cool for at least 1 hour on a wire rack before slicing.

The pie can be covered with plastic wrap and refrigerated for up to 3 days.

Sweet Potato Pie

This creamy custard pie made with golden baked sweet potatoes richly spiced with cinnamon, nutmeg, ginger, and orange zest is a staple in the South. It is always expected on the Thanksgiving dessert table, but most folks like to enjoy a slice or two all year long. Top the pie with the Meringue Topping, or serve with Chantilly Cream (page 373).

SERVES 8

1½ pounds (680 g) sweet potatoes (about 3 medium)
¾ cup (177 ml) heavy cream
2 large (100 g) eggs, lightly beaten
2 tablespoons cane syrup
2 tablespoons unsalted butter, melted
¾ cup (150 g) packed light brown sugar
1 teaspoon freshly grated nutmeg
½ teaspoon ground cinnamon
½ teaspoon ground ginger
½ teaspoon fine sea salt
1 teaspoon pure vanilla extract
1 parbaked Extra-Flaky All-Butter Piecrust (page 237), cooled
Meringue Topping (recipe follows; optional)

OPTIONAL SPECIAL EQUIPMENT
Kitchen blowtorch if making the Meringue Topping

Position a rack in the middle of the oven and preheat the oven to 375°F (190°C).

Wrap each sweet potato in aluminum foil. Place directly on an oven rack and bake for 40 to 50 minutes, or until soft enough to pierce with a fork. Remove from the oven and let cool slightly. Turn the oven down to 325°F (165°C).

Once the sweet potatoes are cool enough to handle, peel them and mash them. Measure out 2 cups (500 g) of the flesh for this recipe.

In the bowl of a stand mixer fitted with the paddle attachment (or in a large mixing bowl, using a handheld mixer), beat the sweet potato flesh on medium speed until smooth. Lift up the paddle (or beaters) and remove and discard any strings from the sweet potatoes, so they don't make it into your pie.

Add the heavy cream, eggs, cane syrup, and butter to the sweet potatoes and mix until fully incorporated. Add the sugar, nutmeg, cinnamon, ginger, salt, and vanilla, mixing until smooth.

Pour the filling into the prepared piecrust and place on a parchment-lined baking sheet. Bake for 40 to 45 minutes, until the filling is firm around the edges and the center wobbles slightly if jiggled.

Top the pie with the meringue, if desired. Pile the meringue sky-high on top of the filling, making sure it touches the crust all the way around. Toast lightly with a kitchen blowtorch.

The pie can be stored in an airtight container in the refrigerator for up to 3 days.

MERINGUE TOPPING

MAKES ENOUGH FOR ONE 9-INCH (23 CM) PIE

3 large (90 g) egg whites
¾ cup (150 g) granulated sugar
¼ teaspoon cream of tartar
½ teaspoon pure vanilla extract

Put the egg whites, sugar, and cream of tartar in the bowl of a stand mixer (or a medium heatproof bowl), set the bowl over a medium saucepan of simmering water (do not let the bottom of the bowl touch the water), and whisk constantly until the sugar is completely dissolved and the egg whites are warm to the touch, 3 to 4 minutes. The mixture should appear pale and opaque. Rub a little bit of it between your fingers to make sure all the sugar is dissolved; it should feel smooth, without any grittiness.

Attach the bowl to the mixer stand (if using) and fit it with the whisk attachment (or use a handheld mixer). Add the vanilla and, starting on low speed, whip the egg whites, gradually increasing the speed to high, until the meringue is glossy and forms stiff peaks, 5 to 7 minutes.

Pecan Pie

Georgia doesn't just lead the United States in peanut production; since the 1800s, it's been the number one producer of pecans as well. The area around Albany grows more than half of the total US crop, and Southerners can always find ways to use that bounty. This bourbon pecan pie features a toffee-like interior and beautiful bronzed top layer of pecan halves.

SERVES 8

½ cup (100 g) granulated sugar
¼ cup (50 g) packed light brown sugar
1½ cups (355 ml) cane, sorghum, or dark corn syrup
½ teaspoon fine sea salt
1½ teaspoons unbleached all-purpose flour
4 large (200 g) eggs, at room temperature
2 tablespoons bourbon
2 teaspoons pure vanilla extract
1½ tablespoons unsalted butter, melted
1¾ cups (175 g) pecan halves
1 parbaked Shortcut Piecrust (page 236) or Extra-Flaky
    All-Butter Piecrust (page 237), cooled

Position a rack in the lower third of the oven and preheat the oven to 350°F (175°C).

In a medium bowl, stir together both sugars, the syrup, salt, flour, and eggs, mixing until completely combined, 1 to 2 minutes. Stir in the bourbon, vanilla, and butter until well combined. Fold in the pecans.

Pour the filling into the parbaked crust and place on a parchment-lined baking sheet. Bake for 1 hour and 15 minutes, or until the filling is firm around the edges and just a bit loose in the center.

Let the pie cool for at least 1 hour on a wire rack before slicing.

This pie is best served the same day it's baked, but it can be covered with plastic wrap and refrigerated for up to 3 days.

Pecan Galette

A galette is an unpretentious free-form pie that can be made on a baking sheet. Serve this pecan version with good old-fashioned Custard Hard Sauce.

SERVES 8

1 disk dough for Extra-Flaky All-Butter Piecrust
    (page 237), in one piece, chilled

4 tablespoons (57 g) unsalted butter

½ cup (100 g) packed light brown sugar

½ cup (118 ml) light corn syrup

½ teaspoon grated orange zest

¼ teaspoon fine sea salt

2 large (100 g) eggs, at room temperature

2 cups (200 g) pecan halves

1 teaspoon pure vanilla extract

1 tablespoon heavy cream

1 tablespoon granulated or sanding sugar

1 recipe Custard Hard Sauce (page 380)

Remove the dough from the refrigerator. If it has been chilled overnight, let it sit at room temperature for 10 to 15 minutes before you roll it out.

Line a baking sheet with parchment.

On a lightly floured work surface, with a lightly floured rolling pin, roll the dough into a 14-inch (36 cm) circle. Place the dough on the prepared baking sheet. The dough will hang over the edges of the pan for now, but that's okay. Refrigerate the dough while you make the filling.

In a medium saucepan, melt the butter over low heat. Add the brown sugar and corn syrup and stir until the sugar is dissolved. Add the orange zest and salt. Whisk in the eggs until completely incorporated. Fold in the pecans. Remove from the heat, stir in the vanilla, and let cool slightly, about 10 minutes.

Pour the filling onto the center of the chilled dough, leaving a 3-inch (8 cm) border all around. Gently fold the edges of the dough up and over the filling, overlapping the dough to create loose pleats and leaving an opening in the center of the galette no larger than 6 inches (15 cm). Refrigerate the galette until the dough is firm, about 30 minutes.

Position a rack in the middle of the oven and preheat the oven to 400°F (205°C).

Brush the edges of the dough with the heavy cream and sprinkle with the granulated sugar. Bake for 35 to 40 minutes, until the crust is golden and the juices are bubbling.

Let the galette cool completely on a wire rack.

Serve the galette with the hard sauce.

The galette can be stored, covered, at room temperature for up to 1 day or refrigerated for up to 2 days.

Nectarine and Raspberry Galette

PICTURED ON PAGE 226

Topping this galette with grape jelly adds a glossy sheen to the pastry—a quintessential summer dessert.

SERVES 8

1 disk dough for Extra-Flaky All-Butter Piecrust
(page 237), in one piece, chilled
1½ pounds (680 g) firm but ripe nectarines, halved,
pitted, and sliced into ½-inch (1.5 cm) wedges
2 cups (240 g) fresh raspberries
3 tablespoons granulated sugar
1 tablespoon cornstarch
½ teaspoon fine sea salt
¼ teaspoon ground cardamom
1 large (50 g) egg, lightly beaten with a pinch of
fine sea salt, for egg wash
Turbinado sugar for sprinkling
¼ cup (85 g) grape jelly
1 tablespoon water

Remove the dough from the refrigerator. If it has been chilled overnight, let it sit at room temperature for 10 to 15 minutes before you roll it out.

Line a baking sheet with parchment.

Put the nectarines and raspberries in a medium bowl, add the granulated sugar, cornstarch, salt, and cardamom, and gently toss to coat the fruit. Set aside.

On a lightly floured work surface, with a lightly floured rolling pin, roll the dough into a 14-inch (36 cm) circle. Place the dough on the prepared baking sheet.

Arrange the fruit in the center of the prepared dough, leaving a 3-inch (8 cm) border all around. Gently fold the edges of the dough up and over the filling, overlapping the dough to create loose pleats and leaving an opening in the center of the galette no larger than 6 inches (15 cm). Refrigerate the galette until the dough is firm, about 30 minutes.

Position a rack in the middle of the oven and preheat the oven to 400°F (205°C).

Brush the edges of the dough with the egg wash and sprinkle with the turbinado sugar. Bake for 25 to 35 minutes, until the crust is golden and the juices are bubbling.

Meanwhile, a few minutes before the galette is done, in a small saucepan, heat the grape jelly with the water, stirring, until the jelly is melted and smooth. Remove from the heat.

Remove the galette from the oven and brush the fruit with the grape syrup. Let cool for at least 5 minutes. Serve warm or at room temperature.

The galette can be stored, covered, at room temperature for up to 1 day or refrigerated for up to 2 days.

Bourbon Peach Hand Pies

PICTURED ON PAGE 227

When peach season arrives, it's cause for celebration in the South. You'll find peaches at roadside stands from Georgia to Tennessee. These mini pies are a big part of Southern culture, and they're perfect for picnics. You can assemble them in advance, freeze them, and bake them whenever you're ready; see Tip.

MAKES 8 HAND PIES

1 recipe dough for Extra-Flaky All-Butter Piecrust
(page 237), chilled

FOR THE FILLING

2 cups (310 g) sliced (¼-inch/6 mm) fresh peaches
(about 5 peaches)

2 teaspoons grated lemon zest

1 tablespoon fresh lemon juice

2 tablespoons bourbon

½ cup (100 g) packed light brown sugar

½ teaspoon ground cardamom

½ teaspoon freshly grated nutmeg

2 tablespoons unbleached all-purpose flour

¼ teaspoon fine sea salt

1 large (50 g) egg, lightly beaten with a pinch of
fine sea salt, for egg wash

Turbinado sugar for sprinkling

Remove the dough from the refrigerator. If it has been chilled overnight, let it sit at room temperature for 10 to 15 minutes before you roll it out.

Line two baking sheets with parchment. On a floured surface, roll out each disk of dough into a 10-inch (25 cm) square, about ¼ inch (6 mm) thick. Cut each one into 4 equal squares. Transfer the squares to the prepared baking sheets, 4 to a pan. Cover with plastic wrap and refrigerate while you make the filling.

To make the filling: In a large bowl, combine the peaches, lemon zest and juice, bourbon, brown sugar, cardamom, nutmeg, flour, and salt and toss to combine.

Remove the dough from the refrigerator and lightly brush the edges of each square with the egg wash. Divide the filling among the squares, using a scant ¼ cup (59 ml) for each, leaving a ½-inch (1.5 cm) border around the edges. Gently fold each square of dough over to make a triangle and press the edges with your fingers to seal; make sure the filling does not ooze out of the sides. Crimp the edges of each hand pie with your fingers or a fork.

Lightly brush the tops of the pies with the egg wash and sprinkle with the turbinado sugar. Cut 3 small (about ⅓-inch-long/8 mm) slits for steam vents in the top of each pie. Chill the pies, uncovered, for 30 minutes, or up to 2 hours, to set the crust.

Position the racks in the middle and lower third of the oven and preheat the oven to 400°F (205°C).

Bake the hand pies for 20 to 25 minutes, rotating the pans halfway through and switching their positions, until deep golden brown.

Serve warm or at room temperature.

Tip

You can assemble the hand pies in advance and freeze them for up to 1 month. Freeze on the baking sheets until the pies have set, then place them in ziplock bags. Cut the steam vents in the tops before freezing, but don't brush the pies with the egg wash until after you pull them out of the freezer. Bake directly from the freezer, adding 5 to 8 minutes to the baking time.

Blueberry Cardamom Hand Pies

You find portable snacks like these, whether sweet or savory, baked or fried, all over the South, at picnics and church bake sales, in grandmothers' kitchens, and even on restaurant menus. These simple blueberry hand pies are a do-ahead dream. You can assemble them in advance, freeze them, and bake them whenever you're ready (see Tip, opposite).

MAKES 8 HAND PIES

1 recipe dough for Extra-Flaky All-Butter Piecrust
    (page 237), chilled

FOR THE FILLING

2 cups (290 g) fresh blueberries

½ cup (100 g) granulated sugar

¼ teaspoon fine sea salt

¼ teaspoon ground cardamom

2 tablespoons cornstarch

1 teaspoon grated lemon zest

4 teaspoons fresh lemon juice

1 large (50 g) egg, lightly beaten with a pinch of
    fine sea salt, for egg wash

FOR THE GLAZE

1½ cups (188 g) confectioners' sugar

½ teaspoon pure vanilla extract

¼ teaspoon fine sea salt

2 to 3 tablespoons warm water

Remove the dough from the refrigerator. If it has been chilled overnight, let it sit at room temperature for 10 to 15 minutes before you roll it out.

Line two baking sheets with parchment. Cut each disk of dough into 4 equal pieces. On a floured surface, roll out each piece of dough into a rough 7-inch (18 cm) round, a scant ¼ inch (6 mm) thick. Transfer the rounds to the prepared baking sheets, 4 to a pan. Cover with plastic wrap and refrigerate while you make the filling.

To make the filling: Put the blueberries in a medium bowl, add the sugar, salt, cardamom, cornstarch, and lemon zest and juice, and gently toss together until combined.

Remove the sheets of dough from the refrigerator and lightly brush the edges of each round with the egg wash. Divide the filling among the rounds, using a scant ¼ cup (59 ml) for each, leaving a ½-inch (1.5 cm) border around the edges. Gently fold each circle of dough over to make a half-moon shape and press the edges with your fingers to seal; make sure the filling does not ooze out of the sides. Crimp the edges of each hand pie with your fingers or a fork.

Lightly brush the tops of the pies with the egg wash. Cut 3 small (about ⅓-inch-long/8 mm) slits for steam vents in the top of each pie. Chill the pies, uncovered, for at least 30 minutes, and up to 2 hours, to set the crust.

Position the racks in the middle and lower third of the oven and preheat the oven to 400°F (205°C).

Bake the hand pies for 25 to 30 minutes, rotating the pans halfway through and switching their positions, until golden brown. Let cool on the pans on wire racks while you make the glaze.

To make the glaze: In a medium bowl, whisk the confectioners' sugar, vanilla, salt, and 2 tablespoons water together until thick and smooth, adding up to 1 tablespoon more water if needed. One at a time, dip the top sides of the slightly warm hand pies in the glaze, letting the excess drip back into the bowl. Transfer the pies to wire racks and let the glaze set before serving.

Any leftover hand pies can be stored in an airtight container in the refrigerator for up to 3 days. Reheat in a preheated 350°F (175°C) oven for 10 to 15 minutes.

OPPOSITE: NECTARINE AND RASPBERRY GALETTE (PAGE 223)
ABOVE: BOURBON PEACH HAND PIES (PAGE 224)

Country Captain Curry Hand Pies

PICTURED ON PAGE 230

Daisy Bonner was President Franklin Delano Roosevelt's beloved cook at the Little White House estate in Warm Springs, Georgia. If you take a tour today, you can see where she wrote on the kitchen wall to commemorate the fact that she cooked the first and last meals for the president at his special retreat.

Daisy was proud that a local specialty, a chicken curry called Country Captain, was his favorite dish. As the story goes, a ship from the West Indies carrying spices was forced to dock in Savannah, Georgia, because of a bad storm. A local cook used some of the spices to create a flavorful chicken curry. This recipe pays homage to the original dish, but in hand-pie form. The butter-rich flaky crust is filled with a curry-spiced sweet potato hash.

You can assemble the pies ahead and freeze them, then bake them when you are ready to serve; see the Tip on page 224.

MAKES 8 HAND PIES

1 recipe dough for Extra-Flaky All-Butter Piecrust
     (page 237), chilled

FOR THE FILLING

1 tablespoon Madras curry powder or garam masala
½ teaspoon ground cardamom
½ teaspoon fine sea salt
¼ teaspoon freshly ground black pepper
¼ teaspoon ground coriander
¼ cayenne pepper (optional)
⅛ teaspoon freshly grated nutmeg
½ teaspoon fresh thyme leaves
3 tablespoons mayonnaise, preferably Duke's
¼ cup (59 ml) water
3 tablespoons olive oil
1½ cups (165 g) diced sweet onions (¼-inch/6 mm pieces)
1 red pepper, cored, seeded, and cut into ¼-inch
     (6 mm) pieces
2 cups (270 g) diced peeled sweet potatoes
     (¼-inch/6 mm pieces)

¼ cup (36 g) raisins
½ cup (57 g) pecans, chopped

1 large (50 g) egg, beaten, for egg wash
3 tablespoons black sesame seeds

Remove the dough from the refrigerator. If it has been chilled overnight, let it sit at room temperature for 10 to 15 minutes before you roll it out.

Line two baking sheets with parchment. Cut each disk of dough into 4 pieces. On a floured surface, roll out each disk of dough into a rough 7-inch (18 cm) round, a scant ¼ inch (6 mm) thick. Transfer the rounds to the prepared baking sheets, 4 to a pan. Refrigerate while you make the filling.

To make the filling: In a small bowl, combine the curry powder (or garam masala), cardamom, salt, black pepper, coriander, cayenne, if using, nutmeg, and thyme. Add the mayonnaise and water and mix.

In a large skillet, heat the olive oil over medium heat. Add the onions and red pepper and cook, stirring occasionally, until tender, 5 to 10 minutes. Add the sweet potatoes and the spice mixture, stirring to distribute the ingredients evenly, and cook, stirring occasionally, until the sweet potatoes are fork-tender, 8 to 10 minutes. Stir in the raisins and pecans. Transfer to a medium bowl and set aside to cool completely.

Remove the sheets of dough from the refrigerator and lightly brush the edges of each round with the egg wash. Divide the filling among the rounds, leaving a ½-inch (1.5 cm) border around the edges. Gently fold each circle of dough over to make a half-moon shape and press the edges with your fingers to seal; make sure the filling does not ooze out of the sides. Crimp the edges of the hand pies with a fork or your fingers.

Lightly brush the tops of the pies with the egg wash. Cut 3 small (about ⅓-inch-long/8 mm) slits for steam vents in the top of each pie. Sprinkle the tops with the sesame seeds. Chill the pies, uncovered, for at least 30 minutes, and up to 2 hours, to set the crust.

Position the racks in the middle and lower third of the oven and preheat the oven to 400°F (205°C).

Bake the hand pies for 25 to 30 minutes, rotating the pans halfway through and switching their positions, until golden brown.

Let the hand pies cool for 10 minutes on wire racks, then serve warm.

Any leftover hand pies can be stored in an airtight container in the refrigerator for up to 3 days. Reheat in a preheated 350°F (175°C) oven for 10 to 15 minutes.

Summer Tomato Pie

This savory pie is a Southern tradition in the summer when tomatoes are at their peak. The recipe here mixes fresh heirloom tomatoes and roasted cherry tomatoes with thyme and basil, resulting in a filling that is bursting with all the flavors of the season. It is topped with a cheesy white sauce made with a combination of Parmesan, Fontina, and mayonnaise.

SERVES 8

3 cups (495 g) diced seeded heirloom tomatoes, plus 2 cups (330 g) cubed (1-inch/3 cm pieces) seeded heirloom tomatoes (about 2½ pounds/1.1 kg total)

2 teaspoons fine sea salt, or to taste

¼ teaspoon freshly ground black pepper, or to taste

1 teaspoon granulated sugar, or to taste

4 tablespoons (57 g) unsalted butter

4 medium sweet onions, thinly sliced

2 teaspoons balsamic vinegar

2 cups (290 g) halved heirloom cherry tomatoes

2 tablespoons olive oil

1 tablespoon fresh thyme leaves

¾ cup (177 ml) mayonnaise

⅓ cup (30 g) finely grated Parmesan cheese

⅓ cup (35 g) coarsely grated Fontina cheese

½ cup (40 g) chopped fresh basil

1 parbaked Extra-Flaky All-Butter Piecrust (page 237), cooled

Put the diced tomatoes in a bowl, add ½ teaspoon of the salt, the pepper, and the sugar, and toss well. Transfer the tomatoes to a sieve set over a bowl and let them drain for 1 hour. Give them a toss every 20 minutes or so to speed up the draining. (Set the cubed tomatoes aside for now.)

Meanwhile, in a large skillet, melt the butter over medium-high heat. Add the onions, season with 1 teaspoon salt, and cook, stirring occasionally, until tender and translucent, about 15 minutes. Reduce the heat to low and let the onions slowly caramelize, stirring occasionally, until they turn a medium brown color, 30 to 40 minutes. Remove from the heat, stir in the vinegar, and let cool to room temperature.

While the onions cook, position a rack in the middle of the oven and preheat the oven to 350°F (175°C). Line two baking sheets with parchment.

In a medium bowl, toss the cubed tomatoes and cherry tomatoes with the olive oil, the remaining ½ teaspoon salt, pepper to taste, and the thyme. Spread the tomatoes in a single layer on the prepared baking sheets and roast for 20 to 30 minutes, until caramelized but not burnt. Set aside.

In a medium bowl, combine the mayonnaise and the two cheeses, mixing well.

In a large bowl, combine the drained tomatoes, roasted tomatoes, caramelized onions, and basil.

(Continued)

CLOCKWISE FROM TOP LEFT: CHOCOLATE CHESS PIE (PAGE 217), BLACK BOTTOM CHOCOLATE CREAM PIE (PAGE 215), CHICKEN POTPIE (OPPOSITE), COUNTRY CAPTAIN CURRY HAND PIES (PAGE 228)

Tomatoes often need a good dose of seasoning to bring out the flavors: Taste and add more salt and/or sugar and pepper to your liking.

Place the parbaked piecrust on a parchment-lined baking sheet and spread the tomato mixture evenly in the crust. Top with the mayo-cheese mixture, spreading it to about 1 inch (3 cm) from the edges, leaving a border so you can see the tomatoes.

Bake the pie for 20 to 25 minutes, until the top is golden brown. Serve warm.

The pie can be refrigerated, tightly covered, for up to 3 days. Reheat in a preheated 350°F (175°C) oven before serving.

Chicken Potpie

PICTURED OPPOSITE

There is nothing more comforting than a potpie. This big pie is perfect for cold nights, and it's especially cozy when served right out of your favorite cast-iron skillet. The filling is loaded with chicken and vegetables, nestled in a creamy sauce, and enveloped in a flaky double crust.

SERVES 10

FOR THE FILLING

4 tablespoons (57 g) unsalted butter

1 medium sweet onion, diced

2 garlic cloves, minced

3 celery ribs, cut into 1-inch (3 cm) pieces

3 carrots, peeled and cut into 1-inch (3 cm) pieces

1 teaspoon ground coriander

1 teaspoon fine sea salt

1 teaspoon freshly ground black pepper

1 pound (454 g) Yukon Gold potatoes, peeled and cut into ½-inch (1.5 cm) cubes

1 cup (90 g) Brussels sprouts, cut in half

FOR THE CREAM SAUCE

8 tablespoons (1 stick/113 g) unsalted butter

½ cup (63 g) unbleached all-purpose flour

4 cups (946 ml) canned chicken broth

½ cup (118 ml) heavy cream

1 tablespoon fresh thyme leaves

One 16-ounce (454 g) bag frozen peas

2 teaspoons grated lemon zest

4 cups (500 g) shredded chicken from a store-bought rotisserie chicken

1 recipe dough for Extra-Flaky All-Butter Piecrust (page 237), chilled

1 large (50 g) egg, lightly beaten with a pinch of fine sea salt, for egg wash

To make the filling: In a large saucepan, melt the butter over medium-high heat. Add the onions, garlic, celery, carrots, coriander, salt, and pepper and sauté until the onions are translucent, about 10 minutes.

Add the potatoes and Brussels sprouts and stir to combine. Cook until the vegetables are tender and beginning to brown, 6 to 7 minutes. Transfer the vegetables to a large bowl and set aside.

To make the cream sauce: In a large saucepan, melt the butter over medium heat. Sprinkle the flour over the butter and cook, whisking, until a smooth paste forms. Turn the heat down to medium-low, add the chicken broth, heavy cream, and fresh thyme, and cook, stirring, until the sauce thickens slightly, about 10 minutes. Add the peas and lemon zest and remove from the heat.

Stir the chicken into the cream sauce until thoroughly combined, then pour the sauce over the vegetable mixture and stir to combine. Set aside to cool completely.

(Continued)

To assemble and bake the potpie: Remove the dough from the refrigerator. If it has been chilled overnight, let it sit at room temperature for 10 to 15 minutes before you roll it out.

Position a rack in the middle of the oven and preheat the oven to 400°F (205°C).

On a floured surface, roll out one disk of dough into a 14-inch (36 cm) round and fit it into a 10-inch (25 cm) cast-iron skillet or a 10-inch (25 cm) deep pie dish. Trim the edges of the dough, leaving a 1½-inch (4 cm) overhang. Roll out the second disk of dough into a 12-inch (30 cm) round.

Spoon the filling into the bottom crust. Place the second round of dough over the filling and trim to a 1-inch (3 cm) overhang. Roll the edge of the bottom crust forward tightly all around the pie, so that the bottom and top crusts are one rope. Make sure the crust is resting on the edge of the pie plate, and press the edges with your fingers to seal in loose pleats. Cut a few small steam vents in the top crust, then brush with the egg wash.

Bake until the crust is golden brown and the filling is bubbling, 50 to 60 minutes. Bring the skillet (or pie dish) to the table to serve.

Oyster Potpies

Filled with fresh oysters scalloped in a rich cream sauce flavored with thyme, coriander, and cayenne pepper, these little potpies are a comforting meal in themselves. You can assemble them in advance and freeze them to bake on a day when you need a special dose of comfort (see Tip).

MAKES 6 INDIVIDUAL POTPIES

FOR THE FILLING

4 slices thick-cut bacon, chopped
1 medium sweet onion, diced
3 celery ribs, cut into 1-inch (3 cm) pieces
2 garlic cloves, minced
Fine sea salt and freshly ground black pepper

FOR THE CREAM SAUCE

8 tablespoons (1 stick/113 g) unsalted butter
6 tablespoons (47 g) unbleached all-purpose flour
2 cups (473 ml) heavy cream
1 cup (237 ml) canned vegetable broth
¼ cup (59 ml) sherry
2 teaspoons fresh lemon juice
1 tablespoon fresh thyme leaves
½ teaspoon ground coriander
½ teaspoon fine sea salt

½ teaspoon cayenne pepper
1 quart (1 L) raw oysters, drained, oyster liquor reserved

1 disk dough for Extra-Flaky All-Butter Piecrust (page 237), chilled
1 large (50 g) egg, lightly beaten with a pinch of fine sea salt, for egg wash

SPECIAL EQUIPMENT
Six 6-inch (15 cm) ovenproof bowls

To make the filling: In a large saucepan, cook the bacon over medium heat until the fat has rendered and the bacon is crisp. Transfer to a plate lined with paper towels.

Add the onion, celery, garlic, and salt and pepper to taste to the saucepan and sauté until the onions are translucent and the celery is tender, 10 to 12 minutes. Remove from the heat.

To make the cream sauce: In a large saucepan, melt the butter over medium heat. Sprinkle the flour over the butter and cook, whisking, until a smooth paste forms. Add the heavy cream, broth, sherry, lemon juice, fresh thyme, coriander, salt, and cayenne, and cook, stirring frequently, until the sauce thickens slightly, 10 to 12 minutes. Stir in the bacon, sautéed vegetables, and oysters, along with their liquor. Remove from the heat and set aside.

To assemble and bake the potpies: Position a rack in the middle of the oven and preheat the oven to 375°F (190°C). Place six 6-inch (15 cm) ovenproof bowls on a parchment-lined baking sheet.

Lightly dust your work surface with flour. Roll the dough into a large rectangle about ¼ inch (6 mm) thick. Measure the diameter of the potpie bowls and cut out dough rounds large enough to cover the tops of the bowls with about a 1½-inch (4 cm) overhang. Gather the scraps together, reroll, and cut out more dough rounds as necessary.

Divide the filling evenly among the bowls, making them about three-quarters full. Lightly brush the rims of the bowls with the egg wash. Lay the dough rounds over the tops of the bowls, making sure the dough hangs evenly over the edges, and press to seal. Brush the dough with the egg wash. Cut a few slits for steam vents in the top of each pie.

Bake the pies for 35 to 40 minutes, until the crust is golden brown and the filling is bubbling. Serve hot.

Tip

You can assemble the potpies in advance and freeze them for up to 1 month. Freeze on the baking sheet until the pies have set, then wrap them in aluminum foil and then plastic wrap. Cut steam vents in the tops before freezing, but don't brush the potpies with egg wash until after you pull them out of the freezer. Remove the plastic wrap and leave the aluminum foil. Let them come to room temperature before baking.

Deep-Dish Spinach Quiche

This light, delicate quiche can be relied upon for a satisfying meal all year round. It's made for improvising, and you can use different vegetables or cheeses, depending on what you have on hand. Add a simple side salad, and it's an easy dinner any day of the week.

SERVES 8

1 disk dough for Extra-Flaky All-Butter Piecrust
(page 237), chilled

FOR THE FILLING
½ small shallot, thinly sliced
2 tablespoons extra-virgin olive oil
4 cups (120 g) spinach, roughly chopped
1½ cups (355 ml) heavy cream
4 large (200 g) eggs, at room temperature
2 large (38 g) egg yolks, at room temperature
½ teaspoon fine sea salt
¼ teaspoon freshly ground black pepper
¼ teaspoon freshly grated nutmeg
⅛ teaspoon cayenne pepper (optional)
One 5.2-ounce (150 g) package Boursin cheese (garlic
and fine herbs)
2 tablespoons chopped fresh thyme

SPECIAL EQUIPMENT
10-by-3-inch (25 by 8 cm) springform pan

(Continued on page 236)

Remove the dough from the refrigerator. If it has been chilled overnight, let it sit at room temperature for 10 to 15 minutes before you roll it out.

On a lightly floured surface, roll the dough into an approximately 14-inch-wide (36 cm) round that is a scant ¼ inch (6 mm) thick. Transfer it to a 10-by-3-inch (25 by 8 cm) springform pan, gently pressing over the bottom and up the sides of the pan. Place the pan in the freezer for at least 20 minutes to set the crust.

Position a rack in the lower third of the oven and preheat the oven to 375°F (190°C).

Remove the springform pan from the freezer, cover the dough with a piece of parchment, and weight the crust with dried beans, rice, or pie weights. Bake for 20 to 25 minutes, until you can see that the crust is golden brown when you peek under the parchment.

Remove the parchment and weights and set the crust aside to cool completely. Reduce the oven temperature to 350°F (175°C).

While the crust is cooling, make the filling: In a large skillet, cook the shallot in the oil over medium-high heat until tender, about 1 minute. Add the spinach and cook, stirring frequently, until wilted. Transfer to a large bowl and let cool.

Add the cream, whole eggs, egg yolks, salt, pepper, nutmeg, and cayenne, if using, to the spinach and whisk until well combined. Crumble in the Boursin cheese, add the thyme, and mix well.

Place the springform pan on a parchment-lined baking sheet and pour the filling into the crust. Bake until the filling is puffed up on the edges and the center no longer looks wet but still wobbles slightly when jiggled; it will continue to set as it cools.

Let the quiche cool on a wire rack for 30 to 40 minutes before serving.

Leftovers can be stored, tightly covered, in the refrigerator for up to 2 days. Reheat in a preheated 350°F (175°C) oven before serving.

Shortcut Piecrust

A press-in crust requires no rolling or chilling. It's buttery and flaky, and easy to prepare, allowing you to make a pie on a whim. You can use either granulated sugar or light brown sugar; both are equally delicious here.

MAKES ONE 9-INCH (23 CM) PIECRUST

1½ cups (188 g) unbleached all-purpose flour

¼ cup (50 g) granulated sugar or packed light brown sugar

½ teaspoon fine sea salt

11 tablespoons (1⅓ sticks/155 g) unsalted butter, melted

In a medium bowl, whisk together the flour, sugar, and salt. Slowly drizzle in the butter and stir with a fork until the mixture looks moist and crumbly.

Press the dough evenly over the bottom and up the sides of a 9-inch (23 cm) pie dish. You can crimp the edges decoratively or leave them rustic.

If the recipe calls for a prebaked piecrust, preheat the oven to 350°F (175°C). Dock the pie shell (prick it all over with a fork), then line with aluminum foil or parchment and fill with dried beans or rice or pie weights.

Bake for 15 to 20 minutes. Remove the foil and weights and bake for an additional 5 minutes, or until the crust is golden brown. Let cool completely before filling.

Extra-Flaky All-Butter Piecrust

This recipe produces a flavorful, super-tender flaky crust. Look for European-style butter, which has more butterfat and less water than other brands and yields a shatteringly flaky crust. The acidity in the vinegar weakens the gluten just enough to make rolling the crust a breeze, and it also prevents shrinkage when the crust is baked.

MAKES TWO 9-INCH (23 CM) PIECRUSTS OR 1 DOUBLE CRUST

2½ cups (313 g) unbleached all-purpose flour

1 tablespoon granulated sugar

1 teaspoon (4 g) baking powder, preferably
    aluminum-free

1 teaspoon fine sea salt

½ cup (118 ml) ice water

1 tablespoon apple cider vinegar

½ pound (2 sticks/227 g) cold unsalted butter,
    cut into 1-inch (3 cm) cubes

In a medium bowl, whisk together the flour, sugar, baking powder, and salt. Set aside.

In a large measuring cup or small bowl, combine the water and vinegar. Set aside.

Toss the pieces of butter in the flour mixture to coat. Then use a pastry blender to cut the butter into the flour. You should have various-sized pieces of butter ranging from coarse sandy patches to flat shaggy pieces to pea-sized chunks, with some larger bits as well. Drizzle in about half of the ice water mixture and stir lightly with a fork until the flour is evenly moistened and the dough starts to come together. If the dough seems dry, add a little more ice water, 1 to 2 tablespoons at a time. The dough will still look a bit shaggy at this point. If you grab a small piece of dough and press it lightly with your hand, it should mostly hold together.

Dump the dough out onto an unfloured work surface and gather it together into a tight mound. Using the heel of your hand, smear the dough a little at a time, pushing it away from you and working your way down the mass of dough to create flat layers of flour and butter. Then gather the dough back together with a bench scraper, layering the clumps of dough on top of one another. Repeat the process once or twice more; the dough should still have some big pieces of butter visible.

Cut the dough in half. Shape each piece into a disk and flatten it. Wrap the disks in plastic wrap and refrigerate for at least 1 hour, or overnight, to rest.

The dough can be stored, well wrapped, for up to 3 days in the refrigerator or up to 1 month in the freezer. If it's been frozen, defrost in the refrigerator overnight.

Whole Wheat Piecrust

A mixture of all-purpose and whole wheat dough adds a complex flavor to this buttery, flaky crust. Use it for the Mushroom Hand Pies (page 318), Sweet Potato Tarte Tatin (page 319), and galettes and skillet pies.

MAKES TWO 9-INCH (23 CM) PIECRUSTS OR 1 DOUBLE CRUST

1½ cups (188 g) unbleached all-purpose flour

1 cup (125 g) whole wheat flour

1 tablespoon light brown sugar

1 teaspoon (4 g) baking powder, preferably
    aluminum-free

1 teaspoon fine sea salt

½ cup (118 ml) ice water

1 tablespoon apple cider vinegar

½ pound (2 sticks/227 g) cold unsalted butter,
    cut into 1-inch (3 cm) cubes

In a medium bowl, whisk together both flours, the brown sugar, baking powder, and salt. Set aside.

In a large measuring cup or small bowl, combine the water and vinegar. Set aside.

Toss the butter in the flour mixture to gently coat it. Then use a pastry blender to cut the butter into the flour. You should have various-sized pieces of butter ranging from coarse sandy patches to flat shaggy pieces to pea-sized chunks, with some larger bits as well. Drizzle in about half of the ice water mixture and stir lightly with a fork until the flour is evenly moistened and the dough starts to come together. If the dough seems dry, add a little more ice water, 1 to 2 tablespoons at a time. The dough will still look a bit shaggy at this point. If you grab a small piece of dough and press it lightly with your hand, it should mostly hold together.

Dump the dough out onto an unfloured work surface and gather it together into a tight mound. Using the heel of your hand, smear the dough a little at a time, pushing it away from you and working your way down the mass of dough to create flat layers of flour and butter. Then gather the dough back together with a bench scraper, layering the clumps of dough on top of one another. Repeat the process once or twice more; the dough should still have some big pieces of butter visible.

Cut the dough in half. Shape each piece into a disk and flatten it. Wrap the disks in plastic wrap and refrigerate for at least 1 hour, and up to overnight, to rest.

The dough can be stored, tightly wrapped, for up to 3 days in the refrigerator or up to 1 month in the freezer. If it's been frozen, defrost in the refrigerator overnight.

Black Bottom Piecrust

This is an entry-level piecrust with advanced-level results. Cookie crusts can be made with just about any cookie crumb you like—even gluten-free cookies work great, making them a great alternative to regular crusts for folks with allergies. Use this crust for custard, cream, and icebox pies.

MAKES ONE 9-INCH (23 CM) PIECRUST

1½ cups (150 g) cream-filled chocolate cookie crumbs

2 tablespoons granulated sugar

¼ teaspoon fine sea salt

4 tablespoons (57 g) unsalted butter, melted

Position a rack in the middle of the oven and preheat the oven to 350°F (175°C).

In a medium bowl, blend together the cookie crumbs, sugar, and salt. Drizzle in the butter and mix with a fork until the crumbs are evenly moistened.

Press the mixture evenly over the bottom and about halfway up the sides of a 9-inch (23 cm) pie dish.

Bake the crust for 8 to 10 minutes. Remove from the oven and let cool completely before filling. The crust will firm up as it cools.

Graham Cracker Piecrust

Use this crust for cream pies.

MAKES ONE 9-INCH (23 CM) PIECRUST

2 cups (240 g) graham cracker crumbs (about 16 crackers)

2 tablespoons light brown sugar

½ teaspoon fine sea salt

8 tablespoons (1 stick/113 g) unsalted butter, melted

Position a rack in the lower third of the oven and preheat the oven to 350°F (175°C).

In a medium bowl, blend together the graham cracker crumbs, brown sugar, and salt. Drizzle in the butter and mix with a fork until the crumbs are evenly moistened.

Press the mixture evenly over the bottom and about halfway up the sides of a 9-inch (23 cm) pie dish.

Bake the crust for 6 to 8 minutes, until lightly golden. Let cool completely before filling.

Saltine Cracker Piecrust

This crust is not only for savory pies. It has just the right amount of saltiness to balance sweet custard fillings too, such as that of Bill Smith's Famous Atlantic Beach Pie (page 211). When you make the crumbs, be sure to leave a little texture, rather than making a fine dust.

MAKES ONE 9-INCH (23 CM) PIECRUST

2½ cups (190 g) saltine cracker crumbs (from about 1½ sleeves of crackers)

3 tablespoons granulated sugar

6 tablespoons (85 g) unsalted butter, at room temperature

Position a rack in the middle of the oven and preheat the oven to 350°F (175°C).

In a medium bowl, blend together the cracker crumbs and sugar. Drizzle in the butter and mix with a fork until the crumbs are moistened.

Press the mixture evenly over the bottom and about halfway up the sides of a 9-inch (23 cm) pie dish.

Bake the crust for 12 to 15 minutes, just until golden brown and firm. Remove from the oven and let cool completely before filling.

Slab Pie Crust

This crust is for a large-format pie made on a rimmed baking sheet.

MAKES ENOUGH FOR ONE DOUBLE-CRUST SLAB PIE

3¾ cups (469 g) unbleached all-purpose flour

1½ teaspoons granulated sugar

1 teaspoon fine sea salt

½ cup (118 ml) ice water

1 tablespoon apple cider vinegar

¾ pound (3 sticks/340 g) cold unsalted butter, cut into
    1-inch (3 cm) cubes

In a medium bowl, whisk together the flour, sugar, and salt. Set aside.

In a large measuring cup or small bowl, combine the water and vinegar.

Toss the butter in the flour mixture to lightly coat it. Then, using a pastry blender, cut the butter into the flour. You should have various-sized pieces of butter ranging from coarse sandy patches to flat shaggy pieces to pea-sized chunks, with some larger bits as well. Drizzle in about half of the ice water mixture and stir lightly with a fork until the flour is moistened. If the dough seems dry, add a little more ice water 1 to 2 tablespoons at a time. The dough will still look a bit shaggy at this point. If you grab a small piece and press it lightly with your hand, it should mostly hold together.

Dump the mixture onto an unfloured work surface and gather it together into a tight mound. Using the heel of your hand, smear the dough, pushing away from you and working your way down the mass to create flat layers of flour and butter. Then gather the dough back together with a bench scraper, laying the clumps of dough on top of one another. Repeat the process once or twice more; the dough should still have some big pieces of butter visible.

Divide the dough into 2 pieces, one slightly larger than the other. Shape each piece into a disk and flatten it. Wrap the disks in plastic wrap and refrigerate for at least 1 hour, and up to overnight, before using.

The dough can be stored, well wrapped, for up to 3 days in the refrigerator or up to 1 month in the freezer. If it's been frozen, defrost in the refrigerator overnight.

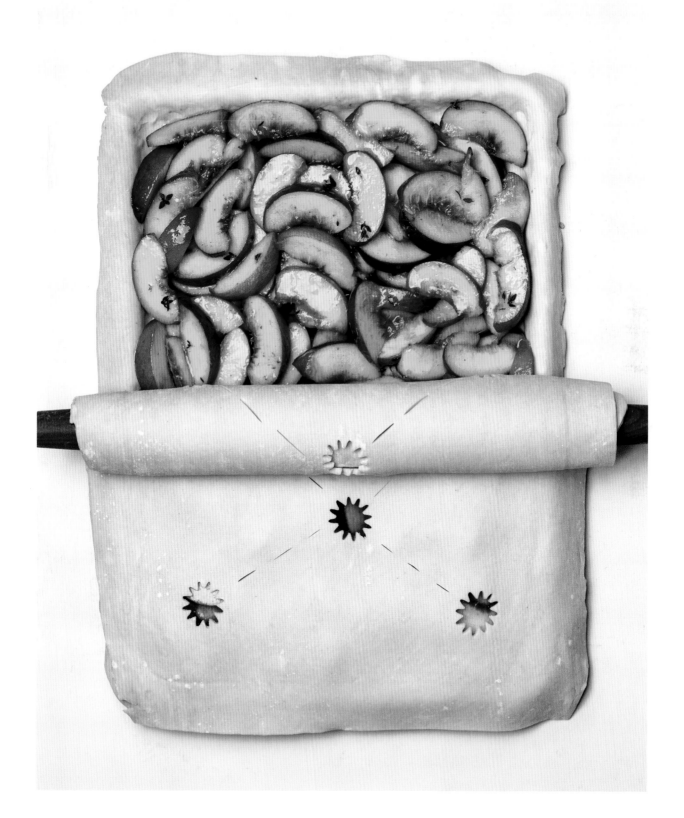

HINTS FOR MAKING PIES

EXPERIENCED PIE MAKERS KNOW THAT PIE DOUGH CAN SENSE FEAR.
So go into making your pie dough with a sense of calm, think happy thoughts before
you begin, and roll out the dough with confidence. With practice and patience, your
pie doughs will be tender and delicious, and you will have the shatteringly flaky crusts
you want. We all know it's the crust that makes the foundation for a great pie. Here
are some helpful tips to keep in mind.

Keep all the ingredients cold. Chilled ingredients are the key to flaky crusts. If the
butter starts to feel warm as you are mixing the dough, put the bowl in the refrigerator
for about 10 minutes, then start again once it has chilled. If any of the butter breaks
through the surface of the dough when you are rolling it, sprinkle a little flour over the
exposed butter, then brush away the excess.

Stay chill. All piecrusts bake best if they are chilled before baking. If you're refrigerating
a crust for more than an hour, wrap it in plastic wrap to prevent your dough from
drying out. Then remove the chilled dough from the refrigerator 10 to 15 minutes
before you want to roll it out to allow it to become pliable enough for rolling.

Go with the roll. Lightly dust your rolling pin with flour. Put the dough on a lightly
floured surface (or use a pastry cloth dusted with flour if you have one) and dust the
top of the dough with a little flour as well. Give the dough a good thwack with the
rolling pin before you start to roll. For a 9-inch (23 cm) pie, roll out the dough into
a 12-inch (30 cm) round. (You always want to roll dough into a round that is 2 to
3 inches/5 to 8 cm larger than the pie pan and about ⅛ inch/3 mm thick.) Roll from
the center out, using steady, even pressure, toward the edges, without going over
them, then rotate the dough 90 degrees, to prevent sticking and to keep it in a round
shape. Continue rolling, lightly dusting the dough and work surface with flour again
as necessary to prevent sticking, and rotating the dough as necessary.

Don't sweat it. If the dough becomes too warm, you may see melting butter peeking
through the crust. Chill it briefly, then dust it lightly with flour to seal and sweep off
the excess using a pastry brush.

Get the right fit. There are two ways to transfer your rolled-out dough to the pan: Roll the dough up around the pin and unfurl it into the pie dish. Or fold the round of dough in half and lay it over one side of the dish, making sure the folded edge is in the center. Gently unfold the dough and, with your fingertips, carefully ease the dough into the pan. Trim the dough overhang to about 1½ inches (4 cm).

Cover the crust with plastic wrap and chill for at least 30 minutes. Flaky piecrusts always bake best when they have been chilled before baking. You can also freeze it, wrapped airtight in plastic wrap, for up to 1 month.

Once the crust is fully chilled, dock it—prick the bottom of the crust all over with a fork.

Parbake or prebake the crust when appropriate. Some recipes call for parbaking or fully baking (blind-baking) a crust before filling it to prevent it from becoming soggy from the filling. To do so, position a rack in the lower third of your oven and preheat the oven to 375°F (190°C). **To parbake,** dock the bottom of the crust with the tines of a fork, then line the pie shell with parchment (or heavy-duty foil) and fill with dried beans, rice, or pie weights. This step prevents the crust from puffing up in the middle. Bake for 15 to 20 minutes, until the edges of the crust are lightly golden brown. Carefully remove the parchment and weights (the beans or rice can be used again for baking, but not for eating!). **For a prebaked crust,** bake for another 5 minutes, or until the crust is golden brown. Let cool completely before filling.

Create your signature style. A single piecrust needs a perfect finish. To create a deep fluted border, crimp the edges of the dough by using the index finger and thumb of one hand to make the letter C and pushing the thumb of your opposite hand against it, pressing gently into the pie dish as you go and working your way all around the edge of the crust. You can also dip the tines of a fork in flour and press them into the dough in any pattern that you like, creating a decorative edge. For a scalloped edge, crimp the pie first as described, then press the floured tines of a fork on the crimped edge resting on the pie dish. All of these methods work best when your dough is chilled, and cold dough will result in a more defined look when your pie is baked. If the dough gets too warm, return the crust to the refrigerator briefly before continuing.

Make your pie doubly delicious with a double crust. To make a pie with a top and a bottom crust, lightly flour your work surface and roll out one disk of dough into a 12-inch (30 cm) round that is ⅛ inch (3 mm) thick. Transfer the dough to a 9-inch (23 cm) pie dish, using your fingertips to ease the dough into the pie dish, leaving a 1½-inch (4 cm) overhang all around. Roll out the second disk of dough into a 10-inch (25 cm) round and transfer it to a parchment-lined baking sheet. Chill both crusts in the refrigerator until very cold, 15 to 20 minutes.

To finish the double crust, add the filling to the pie shell, place the top crust over the filling, and pinch the top and bottom crusts together all the way around. Trim any excess dough with kitchen scissors, leaving a ½-inch (1.5 cm) overhang. Roll the edge of the bottom crust forward tightly all around the pie, so that the bottom crust and the top crust are one rope. Make sure the crust is resting on the edge of the pie plate. Crimp your way around the entire crust, using both thumbs and your index finger to create the letter C for a ruffled effect. Be sure to cut small vents in the crust so that the steam can escape and the crust won't absorb too much of the juices, to keep your crust extra flaky.

You can also use small cookie cutters to make vent holes and save the cutouts to make decorations. Cut a few small decorative vent holes in the middle of the crust and set the cutouts aside. Brush the top of the crust with an egg wash or heavy cream, and position the cutouts however you like.

Make a lattice crust. Lattice crusts are great for juicy fruit pies. All those little windows provide extra vents to allow steam to evaporate and the juices inside to thicken. Roll out the second disk of dough into a circle approximately 12 inches (30 cm) in diameter and about ⅛ inch (3 mm) thick.

Using a pastry wheel, pizza cutter, or sharp knife, cut off a 1-inch-wide (3 cm) strip from two opposite sides of the circle. Cut the remaining dough into eight 1-inch-wide (3 cm) strips. Put the strips on a parchment-lined baking sheet and refrigerate until ready to use.

To make the lattice, starting with the longest strips, lay one strip across the center of the filled pie. Lay another strip across the middle of that strip (like a plus sign), then lay another strip perpendicular to that strip, about ½ inch (1.5 cm) away. Gently pull back one end of the bottom strip, lay another strip down perpendicular to it, and then put the strip back in place—it's like weaving. Repeat until you have used all the strips and covered your pie.

To finish the pie edges, trim the lattice strips even with the bottom crust, then roll the bottom crust and lattice top inward all around the pie, creating a rolled edge. Make sure the crust is resting on the edge of the pie dish. Then crimp the crust as directed above. Put the pie in the freezer to chill for 15 minutes to set the crust.

Give your pie a finishing touch. An egg wash or a brushing of milk or cream will give your pies a shiny finished appearance and will help any sugar you have sprinkled on top to adhere to the crust. The wash you choose will give a slightly different look to the top of the pie. A simple egg wash, made with 1 egg beaten with a pinch of fine sea salt, results in a nice shine. An egg-yolk-and-water wash creates a deep golden appearance. A brush of heavy cream or milk (including nondairy milks) will give the pie more of a matte finish.

Don't get burned. Remember that baking times are estimates. This is especially true when it comes to pies. You want to bake your pie until the crust is golden and flaky, but you certainly don't want to burn it. Turn on the oven light and set a timer so you can take a look at your pie at least 15 minutes before the shortest time given in the recipe. If you notice that the crust is browning too fast and the custard is not even close to being set, or the fruit filling is nowhere near bubbling, cut off a strip of aluminum foil and crimp the edges to make a foil ring to cover the edges of the pie while it finishes baking. Then continue to check it every 5 minutes or so, until it's done.

Cut clean slices of pie like a pro. The first slice of pie never comes out without a bit of a fuss. Ever. But here's a tip: Slice the first piece, but don't remove it from the pan. Slice the next piece, and once you've made that cut, it gives you enough flexibility to release that first slice of pie. Use a sturdy pie server to transfer that perfect slice of pie right onto the plate.

Cookies

Southern is a pitcher of lemonade, filled with
slices of lemon and a big piece of ice from
the icehouse, and served with buttermilk cookies.

—EDNA LEWIS

SOUTHERN BAKERS HAVE A SECRET that lets them shine at a moment's notice—cookies. Whether you are baking for a swap or to welcome last-minute guests, cookies are the answer. And there's something to match every craving: Cookies can be soft, crispy, chewy, delicate, or crunchy, and in every form you might want, from drop to rolled, from spritzed to slice and bake, and left plain or decorated. And you can make your favorite dough in advance and freeze it to bake whenever the craving for a freshly baked cookie hits you.

If you are a beginner baker, cookies are a great place to start learning about basic baking techniques. Let little hands join in the fun too; baking alongside your young ones is the best way to raise future Southern bakers. In this chapter, you'll find simple sugar cookies like Vanilla Wafers and Spritz Butter Cookies, classics like Oatmeal Cookie Creams and Chocolate Chip Cookies, and a host of others that feature key Southern ingredients: Benne Seed Wafers, Peanut Butter Cookies, and Sweet Potato Spice Cookies. Anytime you need a little pick-me-up, cookies are the answer.

Benne Seed Wafers

Benne seeds have been a staple in the cooking of Lowcountry South Carolina and Georgia since the 1700s, especially in the Gullah community, which is known for preserving African cultural heritage and foodways more so than any other African American community in the United States. The seeds are an agrarian treasure brought to the South by enslaved Africans who sowed the plants on cotton and rice plantations. The flavor becomes intensified when the seeds are toasted, and a sweet nutty aroma will fill your kitchen. Legend has it that eating these delicate cookies brings good luck.

MAKES 36 COOKIES

1 cup (150 g) benne seeds or white sesame seeds

1 cup (125 g) unbleached all-purpose flour

½ teaspoon (3 g) baking soda

¼ teaspoon fine sea salt

8 tablespoons (1 stick/113 g) unsalted butter, at room temperature

1 cup (200 g) packed light brown sugar

1 large (50 g) egg, at room temperature

1 teaspoon pure vanilla extract

Position the racks in the middle and lower third of the oven and preheat the oven to 350°F (175°C). Line two or three baking sheets with parchment.

Spread the seeds in a single layer on one of the prepared baking sheets and bake for about 5 minutes, until fragrant and lightly browned. Set aside to cool, then transfer to a small bowl.

In a medium mixing bowl, whisk together the flour, baking soda, and salt. Set aside.

In the bowl of a stand mixer fitted with the paddle attachment (or in a large mixing bowl, using a handheld mixer), cream the butter, brown sugar, egg, and vanilla together on medium speed until superlight and fluffy, 3 to 5 minutes. Turn the speed down to low and add the dry ingredients in thirds, beating until just combined, about 1 minute. Beat in the toasted seeds until just combined, about 1 minute.

Remove the bowl from the mixer stand (if using) and finish mixing by hand to make sure no bits of flour or butter are hiding on the bottom of the bowl and the dough is thoroughly mixed.

Use a small ice cream scoop or a tablespoon to form the cookies (about 1 rounded tablespoon each) and place on the prepared baking sheets, leaving 2 inches (5 cm) between them to allow for spreading.

Bake the cookies, rotating the pans halfway through and switching their positions, for 8 to 10 minutes, until lightly golden brown. Let cool completely on the pans on wire racks.

The cookies can be stored in an airtight container at room temperature for up to 1 week or in the freezer for up to 1 month.

Vanilla Wafers

These cookies are a nod to the store-bought ones you ate as a child, but nothing compares to the pure vanilla flavor of these made-from-scratch wafers. The dough freezes beautifully too; just bring it to room temperature before scooping the cookies.

MAKES ABOUT 48 COOKIES

½ pound (2 sticks/227 g) unsalted butter, at room temperature

1 cup (200 g) granulated sugar

(Continued)

¾ teaspoon fine sea salt

3 large (90 g) egg whites, at room temperature

1 large (50 g) egg, at room temperature

1½ teaspoons pure vanilla extract

½ vanilla bean, split lengthwise, seeds scraped out
    and reserved

2¾ cups plus 2 tablespoons (360 g) unbleached
    all-purpose flour

Position the racks in the middle and lower third of the oven and preheat the oven to 325°F (165°C). Line two baking sheets with parchment.

In the bowl of a stand mixer fitted with the paddle attachment (or in a large mixing bowl, using a handheld mixer), cream the butter, sugar, and salt together on medium speed until superlight and fluffy, 3 to 5 minutes.

In a medium bowl, whisk the egg whites, egg, and vanilla extract and seeds together until incorporated.

With the mixer on low, gradually add the egg mixture to the butter mixture in a steady stream, mixing until thoroughly incorporated. With the mixer still on low, add the flour in two batches, mixing until just combined.

Remove the bowl from the mixer stand (if using) and finish mixing by hand to make sure no bits of flour or butter are hiding on the bottom of the bowl and the dough is thoroughly mixed.

Use a small ice cream scoop or a tablespoon to form the cookies (about 1 rounded tablespoon each) and place on the prepared baking sheets, leaving 1 inch (3 cm) between them to allow for spreading.

Bake the cookies for 10 to 12 minutes, rotating the pans halfway through and switching their positions, until lightly golden on the edges. Let cool completely on the pans on wire racks.

The cookies can be stored in an airtight container at room temperature for up to 5 days.

Old-Fashioned Tea Cakes

These cookies are so popular that Zora Neale Hurston named a character Tea Cake in her book *Their Eyes Were Watching God*. The treats are known as tea cakes, but they are really soft, cakey cookies. Flavored with a hint of nutmeg and lemon, they are as good with coffee as with tea.

MAKES 24 COOKIES

3 cups (375 g) unbleached all-purpose flour

½ teaspoon (3 g) baking soda

¼ teaspoon freshly grated nutmeg

½ teaspoon fine sea salt

½ pound (2 sticks/227 g) unsalted butter,
    at room temperature

1½ cups (300 g) granulated sugar

2 large (100 g) eggs, at room temperature

1 tablespoon pure vanilla extract

1 tablespoon grated lemon zest

In a medium mixing bowl, whisk together the flour, baking soda, nutmeg, and salt. Set aside.

In the bowl of a stand mixer fitted with the paddle attachment (or in a large mixing bowl, using a handheld mixer), cream the butter and sugar together until superlight and fluffy, 3 to 5 minutes. Add the eggs one (50 g) at a time, mixing well after each addition and scraping down the sides and bottom of the bowl with a rubber spatula as necessary. Add the vanilla and lemon zest, mixing until just combined. Add the flour mixture in thirds, mixing until just incorporated.

Remove the bowl from the mixer stand (if using) and finish mixing by hand to make sure no bits of flour or butter are hiding on the bottom of the bowl and the dough is thoroughly mixed. Remove the dough from the bowl and wrap in plastic wrap. Chill until firm, about 20 minutes.

Position two racks in the middle and lower third of the oven and preheat the oven to 325°F (165°C). Line two baking sheets with parchment.

Use a small scoop to form the cookies (about 1 rounded tablespoon each) and place on the prepared baking sheets, leaving room between them to allow for spreading.

Bake the cookies for 8 to 10 minutes, rotating the pans halfway through and switching their positions, until lightly golden around the edges. Let cool completely on the pans on wire racks.

The cookies can be stored in an airtight container at room temperature for up to 5 days.

Oatmeal Cookie Creams

PICTURED ON PAGE 256

This filled oatmeal cookie is a throwback to lunch-box treats from childhood. Two soft and chewy oatmeal cookies spiced with cinnamon, allspice, and cloves and studded with plump golden raisins get sandwiched with a creamy vanilla filling. It's a classic treat folks of all ages will enjoy.

MAKES 12 SANDWICH COOKIES

FOR THE COOKIES

1½ cups (188 g) unbleached all-purpose flour

¼ teaspoon (1 g) baking soda

½ teaspoon fine sea salt

1 teaspoon ground cinnamon

½ teaspoon ground allspice

½ teaspoon ground cloves

12 tablespoons (1½ sticks/170 g) unsalted butter,
    at room temperature

½ cup (100 g) granulated sugar

¾ cup (150 g) packed light brown sugar

1 large (50 g) egg, at room temperature

2 teaspoons pure vanilla extract

1¾ cups (157 g) old-fashioned rolled oats

¾ cup (109 g) golden raisins

Turbinado sugar for sprinkling

FOR THE VANILLA CREAM FILLING

8 tablespoons (1 stick/113 g) unsalted butter,
    at room temperature

3 cups (375 g) confectioners' sugar

2 tablespoons heavy cream

1 teaspoon pure vanilla extract

¼ teaspoon fine sea salt

To make the cookies: Sift together the flour, baking soda, salt, cinnamon, allspice, and cloves into a medium mixing bowl. Set aside.

In the bowl of a stand mixer fitted with the paddle attachment (or in a large mixing bowl, using a handheld mixer), cream the butter and the granulated and brown sugars together on medium speed until superlight and fluffy, 3 to 5 minutes. Add the egg and vanilla and beat until completely incorporated, 1 to 2 minutes. Mix in the oats until just blended.

Add the dry ingredients in thirds, mixing until just combined. Sprinkle in the raisins and mix until just combined.

Remove the bowl from the mixer stand (if using) and finish mixing by hand to make sure no bits of flour or butter are hiding on the bottom of the bowl and the dough is thoroughly mixed. Cover the bowl with plastic wrap and chill until the dough is slightly firmer, about 30 minutes.

Position the racks in the middle and lower third of the oven and preheat the oven to 350°F (175°C). Line two baking sheets with parchment.

Use a large ice cream scoop or a ¼-cup (59 ml) measuring cup to form the cookies and place on the prepared baking sheets, leaving 2 inches (5 cm) between them to allow for spreading. Lightly press down on each cookie with the palm of your hand and sprinkle each one with just a pinch of turbinado sugar. (*If you want, you can freeze the cookies on the baking sheets until firm, then transfer to ziplock bags and freeze for up to 2 months. Sprinkle with the sugar before baking.*)

Bake the cookies for 12 to 15 minutes, rotating the pans halfway through and switching their positions, until lightly golden on the edges but still pale in the middle. Let cool completely on the pans on wire racks.

To make the filling: In the bowl of the stand mixer fitted with the paddle attachment (or in a large mixing bowl, using a handheld mixer), cream the butter, sugar, heavy cream, vanilla, and salt together on medium speed until superlight and creamy, 3 to 5 minutes.

To assemble the sandwich cookies: Put a dollop (about 1 rounded tablespoon) of vanilla filling on the bottom of one of the cookies, place another cookie right side up on top, and press together gently. Repeat with the remaining cookies and filling.

The unfilled cookies can be stored in an airtight container for up to 3 days at room temperature. The filled cookies can be stored for up to 2 days.

Peanut Butter Cookies

PICTURED ON THE FOLLOWING PAGE

Peanuts and peanut butter are ubiquitous in the South. It's not uncommon for folks to toss a bag of salty peanuts into an ice-cold cola—a tradition that started in the 1920s, when farmers with little time for breaks would eat and work at the same time. And today we still snack on handfuls of boiled peanuts bought from a vendor on the side of the road. These cookies are another way to get your peanut fix.

MAKES ABOUT 24 COOKIES

¾ cup (94 g) unbleached all-purpose flour

½ teaspoon (2 g) baking powder, preferably
    aluminum-free

½ teaspoon fine sea salt

¼ teaspoon (1 g) baking soda

8 tablespoons (1 stick/113 g) unsalted butter,
    at room temperature

½ cup (100 g) packed dark brown sugar

½ cup (100 g) granulated sugar

1 teaspoon cane syrup

1 cup (240 g) smooth peanut butter

1 large (50 g) egg

1 teaspoon pure vanilla extract

1 cup (150 g) honey-roasted peanuts

Flaky sea salt, such as Maldon, for sprinkling

Sift together the flour, baking powder, fine sea salt, and baking soda into a bowl. Set aside.

In the bowl of a stand mixer fitted with the paddle attachment (or in a large mixing bowl, using a handheld mixer), cream the butter, both sugars, and the cane syrup together on medium speed until superlight and fluffy, 3 to 5 minutes. Add the peanut butter, egg, and vanilla and mix until completely incorporated. Turn the speed down to low and gradually add half of the flour mixture, mixing until just combined. Gradually add the remaining flour, mixing until just combined, then add the peanuts, mixing until incorporated.

Remove the bowl from the mixer stand (if using) and finish mixing by hand to make sure no bits of flour or butter are hiding on the bottom of the bowl and the dough is thoroughly mixed. Cover the bowl with plastic wrap and chill the dough in the refrigerator until slightly firm, about 30 minutes.

Position the racks in the middle and lower third of the oven and preheat the oven to 325°F (165°C). Line two baking sheets with parchment.

Use a small ice cream scoop or a tablespoon to form the cookies (about 1 rounded tablespoon each) and place on the prepared baking sheets, leaving 2 inches (5 cm) between them to allow for spreading. Lightly touch each cookie with the tines of a fork to make a crisscross pattern (keeping it old-school). Top each cookie with a pinch of flaky sea salt. (*If you want, you can freeze the cookies on the baking sheets until firm, then transfer to ziplock bags and freeze for up to 2 months. Sprinkle the cookies with the salt just before baking.*)

Bake the cookies for 10 to 12 minutes, rotating the pans halfway through and switching their positions, until golden brown. Let cool completely on the pans on wire racks.

The cookies can be stored in an airtight container at room temperature for up to 3 days.

CLOCKWISE FROM TOP LEFT: OATMEAL COOKIE CREAMS (PAGE 254), PEANUT BUTTER COOKIES (PAGE 255), SPRITZ BUTTER COOKIES (OPPOSITE), JAM THUMBPRINT COOKIES (OPPOSITE)

Jam Thumbprint Cookies

PICTURED OPPOSITE

This simple, classic buttery cookie lets your favorite jam shine. It's the perfect vehicle for a jam you put up (see page 365), but don't fret if you don't have homemade; good-quality store-bought jam works fine here.

MAKES 24 COOKIES

2½ cups (313 g) unbleached all-purpose flour

½ teaspoon (2 g) baking powder, preferably aluminum-free

1 large (50 g) egg, at room temperature

½ teaspoon pure vanilla extract

12 tablespoons (1½ sticks/170 g) unsalted butter

1 cup (200 g) granulated sugar

½ teaspoon fine sea salt

About 1 cup (237 ml) good-quality jam, homemade (see page 347) or store-bought

Position the racks in the middle and lower third of the oven and preheat the oven to 350°F (175°C). Line two baking sheets with parchment.

Sift together the flour and baking powder into a medium bowl. Set aside.

In a large measuring cup or small bowl, whisk together the egg and vanilla. Set aside.

In the bowl of a stand mixer fitted with the paddle attachment (or in a medium mixing bowl, using a handheld mixer), cream the butter, sugar, and salt together on medium speed until superlight and fluffy, 3 to 5 minutes. Add the egg mixture and mix until fully incorporated and smooth, scraping down the sides and bottom of the bowl with a rubber spatula as necessary. With the mixer on low speed, add the flour mixture in thirds, mixing until just combined.

Remove the bowl from the mixer stand (if using) and finish mixing by hand to make sure no bits of flour or butter are hiding on the bottom of the bowl and the dough is thoroughly mixed.

Use a small ice cream scoop or a tablespoon to form the cookies (about 1 rounded tablespoon each) and place on the prepared baking sheets, leaving 1 inch (3 cm) between them to allow for spreading.

Using your thumb, make a well in the center of each cookie, then fill with a generous teaspoon of the jam.

Bake the cookies for 10 to 12 minutes, rotating the pans halfway through and switching their positions, until the cookies are lightly golden on the edges and the jam is bubbling. Let cool completely on the pans on wire racks.

The cookies can be stored in an airtight container at room temperature for up to 1 week.

Spritz Butter Cookies

PICTURED OPPOSITE

Do like a Southerner and present your summer guests with an assortment of butter cookies on a platter with a tall glass of lemonade for sipping alongside. This rich cookie is simply flavored with pure vanilla and a splash of buttermilk. You'll need a pastry bag and a star tip to pipe the dough; if you don't have a pastry bag, use a ziplock bag snipped at the corner.

MAKES 24 COOKIES

2 cups (250 g) unbleached all-purpose flour

½ teaspoon fine sea salt

½ pound (2 sticks/227 g) unsalted butter, at room temperature

1 cup (125 g) confectioners' sugar

1 vanilla bean, split lengthwise, seeds reserved

(Continued)

2 tablespoons buttermilk

1 teaspoon pure vanilla extract

SPECIAL EQUIPMENT

Pastry bag fitted with a large star tip
(such as Ateco 869) or a large ziplock bag

Position the racks in the middle and lower third of the oven and preheat the oven to 325°F (165°C). Line two baking sheets with parchment.

Sift together the flour and salt into a small bowl. Set aside.

In the bowl of a stand mixer fitted with the paddle attachment (or in a large mixing bowl, using a handheld mixer), cream the butter, confectioners' sugar, and vanilla seeds together on medium speed until superlight and fluffy, 3 to 5 minutes. Turn the mixer down to low and add half of the flour mixture, beating until just combined. Add the buttermilk and vanilla extract, mixing until combined, then mix in the remaining flour until just combined.

Remove the bowl from the mixer stand (if using) and finish mixing by hand to make sure no bits of flour or butter are hiding on the bottom of the bowl and the dough is thoroughly mixed.

Transfer the dough to a pastry bag fitted with a ½-inch (1.5 cm) star tip (or use a large ziplock bag with a bottom corner snipped off). Pipe the dough onto the prepared baking sheets in upside-down U shapes that are about 1½ by 3 inches (4 by 8 cm), spacing them 2 inches (5 cm) apart. Place the sheets of cookies in the freezer for 15 minutes to chill the dough so that it holds its shape when baked.

Bake the cookies for 20 to 25 minutes, rotating the pans halfway through and switching their positions, until lightly golden brown. Let cool completely on the pans on wire racks.

The cookies can be stored in an airtight container at room temperature for up to 5 days.

Brown Butter Lime Cookies

These golden cutout sugar cookies are infused with lime zest and brown butter, which gives them a rich, nutty, toasty flavor. The sugar and flaky sea salt mixture sprinkled on top is a lovely touch.

MAKES 24 COOKIES

10 ounces (2½ sticks/284 g) unsalted butter

2¼ cups (281 g) unbleached all-purpose flour

¾ teaspoon fine sea salt

½ cup (100 g) granulated sugar, plus 1½ tablespoons for
    sprinkling

6 tablespoons (47 g) confectioners' sugar

Grated zest of 1 lime

3 large (57 g) egg yolks

1 teaspoon pure vanilla extract

½ teaspoon flaky sea salt, such as Maldon

SPECIAL EQUIPMENT

One or more 3- to 4-inch (8 to 10 cm) cookie cutters

To make the brown butter: Fill a large bowl with ice cubes and cold water to make an ice bath. Place a large heatproof bowl in it.

In a large saucepan, melt the butter over medium heat; the butter will bubble and foam up. Then continue to cook, watching closely and swirling the pan often for even cooking, until the butter turns a deep golden color. (For more detail, see Brown Butter, page 387.) Pour the butter, along with the browned milk solids, into the bowl in the ice bath and set aside, stirring occasionally, until cold. Remove the bowl from the ice bath.

Transfer the butter to an airtight container and refrigerate until ready to use. (*The brown butter can be refrigerated for up to 2 weeks or stored in the freezer for up to 3 months.*)

In a medium bowl, whisk together the flour and fine sea salt. Set aside.

Remove the browned butter from the refrigerator and cut into 1-inch (3 cm) cubes.

In the bowl of a stand mixer fitted with the paddle attachment (or in a large mixing bowl, using a handheld mixer), cream the brown butter, both sugars, and the lime zest together until superlight and fluffy, 3 to 5 minutes. Add the egg yolks one (19 g) at a time, beating well after each addition and scraping down the sides and bottom of the bowl with a rubber spatula as necessary, then beat in the vanilla. Add the flour mixture in thirds, mixing until just incorporated.

Remove the bowl from the mixer stand (if using) and finish mixing by hand to make sure no bits of flour or butter are hiding on the bottom of the bowl and the dough is thoroughly mixed. Scrape the dough from the bowl, divide it in half, and shape each piece into a disk. Wrap each piece in plastic wrap and place the disks in the refrigerator for at least 30 minutes, or until firm enough to roll. (*The dough can be refrigerated for up to 3 days, or frozen, well wrapped, for up to 1 month. Thaw in the refrigerator overnight before using.*)

To cut out the cookies, remove one of the disks of dough from the refrigerator and let it sit at room temperature until it is soft enough to roll out but still quite firm (it will continue to soften as you work with it). Line two baking sheets with parchment.

Transfer the dough to a lightly floured surface. Place a piece of plastic wrap or parchment on top and, using a rolling pin, roll the dough out to a ¼-inch (6 mm) thickness. Using a 3- to 4-inch (8 to 10 cm) cookie cutter, cut out the cookies. Place on the prepared baking sheets, leaving about ½ inch (1.5 cm) between the cookies to allow for spreading. Put the sheets of cookies in the refrigerator to chill for at least 1 hour before baking. (You can save the scraps, chill them, and reroll them to make more cookies.) Repeat with the remaining dough.

When you are ready to bake, position the racks in the middle and lower third of the oven and preheat the oven to 350°F (175°C).

In a small bowl, combine the 1½ tablespoons sugar and the flaky sea salt. Lightly sprinkle the tops with the mixture. Bake the cookies for 12 to 14 minutes, rotating the pans halfway through and switching their positions, until golden at the edges. Let cool completely on the pans on wire racks.

The cookies can be stored in an airtight container at room temperature for up to 5 days.

Milk-Jam Shortbread Sammies

The South is an ever-evolving cultural melting pot. These simple shortbread cookies are inspired by Latin American dulce de leche sandwich cookies. They are made with a blend of all-purpose and rice flour (instead of the more typical cornstarch) to give them a delicate texture. The cookies are sandwiched with homemade Milk Jam, a thick caramel made by cooking milk and sugar together low and slow that is a culinary marvel all by itself. Gild the lily and finish the cookies with a light dusting of confectioners' sugar.

MAKES 24 SANDWICH COOKIES

4¾ cups (594 g) unbleached all-purpose flour

½ cup (80 g) rice flour

1 teaspoon fine sea salt

(Continued)

1 pound (454 g) unsalted butter, at room temperature

1¼ cups (250 g) granulated sugar

1 teaspoon pure vanilla extract

About 1 cup (237 ml) Milk Jam (page 386)

About ¼ cup (31 g) confectioners' sugar for dusting

SPECIAL EQUIPMENT

2-inch (5 cm) round cookie cutter

In a medium bowl, whisk together both flours and the salt. Set aside.

In the bowl of a stand mixer fitted with the paddle attachment (or in a large mixing bowl, using a handheld mixer), cream the butter and granulated sugar together on medium speed until superlight and fluffy, 3 to 5 minutes. Beat in the vanilla. Turn the speed down to low and add the dry ingredients in three additions, mixing until just combined.

Remove the bowl from the mixer stand (if using) and finish mixing by hand to make sure no bits of flour or butter are hiding on the bottom of the bowl and the dough is thoroughly mixed.

Divide the dough in half, shape each piece into a disk, and wrap each one in plastic wrap. Chill the disks in the refrigerator until totally firm, at least 2 hours, and up to overnight. (*The dough can be frozen, tightly wrapped, for up to a month; thaw overnight in the refrigerator.*)

When you are ready to make the cookies, one at a time, remove the disks of dough from the refrigerator and let sit at room temperature for 10 to 15 minutes, until softened enough to roll out but still quite firm (the dough will continue to soften as you work with it).

Position the racks in the middle and lower third of the oven and preheat the oven to 325°F (165°C). Line two baking sheets with parchment.

Transfer the dough to a lightly floured surface. Place a piece of plastic wrap or parchment on top and, using a rolling pin, roll the dough out to a ¼-inch (6 mm) thickness. Using a 2-inch (5 cm) round cookie cutter, cut out the cookies and place about 1 inch (3 cm) apart on the prepared baking sheets. Gather up the scraps of dough, shape into a disk, and chill for at least 30 minutes, then reroll and cut out more cookies.

Bake the cookies for 15 to 18 minutes, rotating the pans halfway through and switching their positions, until golden brown. Let cool completely on the pans on wire racks.

To assemble the cookies: Put 1 rounded tablespoon of milk jam on the bottom of one of the cookies, place another cookie right side up on top, and press together gently. Repeat with the remaining cookies and filling.

Sprinkle the cookies generously with confectioners' sugar before serving.

The cookies (unfilled or filled) can be stored in an airtight container at room temperature for up to 3 days.

Jam Dumpling Cookies

Many cultures enjoy dumplings, both sweet and savory in a variety of shapes and sizes. In the South, dumplings range from balls of cornbread bobbing in a pot of braised collard greens to pastry clouds steaming in chicken soup to puffy spoonfuls of dough scattered over simmering stewed apples, peaches, or berries. These dumpling cookies are filled with jam and shaped like tiny hand pies.

MAKES 14 TO 16 COOKIES

1½ cups (188 g) cake flour (not self-rising)

½ teaspoon (2 g) baking powder, preferably aluminum-free

2 tablespoons granulated sugar, plus more for sprinkling

12 tablespoons (1½ sticks/170 g) cold unsalted butter, cut into 1-inch (3 cm) cubes

1 tablespoon pure vanilla extract

1 large (30 g) egg white, beaten, for egg wash

½ cup (118 ml) good-quality jam, homemade
(see page 347) or store-bought

SPECIAL EQUIPMENT

4-inch (10 cm) biscuit cutter or round cookie cutter

In a medium bowl, whisk together the flour, baking powder, and sugar.

Add the butter to the flour mixture and toss to gently coat it. Then use a pastry blender to cut the butter into the flour. You should have various-sized pieces of butter ranging from coarse sandy patches to flat shaggy pieces to pea-sized chunks. Drizzle the vanilla over the mixture and gently knead until the dough comes together.

Cut the dough in half. Shape each piece into a disk and then flatten it. Wrap the disks in plastic wrap and put in the refrigerator for at least 1 hour, and up to overnight, to rest. (*The dough can be stored in the refrigerator for up to 3 days or, well wrapped, in the freezer for up to 1 month. If it has been frozen, defrost in the refrigerator overnight.*)

One at a time, remove the disks of dough from the refrigerator. If the dough has been chilled overnight or longer, it will need to sit at room temperature for 10 to 15 minutes before you roll it out.

Position the racks in the middle and lower third of the oven and preheat the oven to 350°F (175°C). Line two baking sheets with parchment.

Transfer the dough to a lightly floured work surface. Using a rolling pin, roll the dough out to an ⅛-inch (3 mm) thickness. Dip a 4-inch (10 cm) biscuit cutter or round cookie cutter into flour, then press it into the dough and cut out as many

circles as you can, reflouring the cutter each time. Use an offset spatula to transfer the cookies to the prepared baking sheets, leaving about 1 inch (3 cm) between them. Gather the scraps together, chill them, reroll them, and cut out more rounds.

One at a time, lightly brush the edges of each circle with the egg wash. Place a generous teaspoon of the jam in the center of the circle, then gently fold the dough over to make a half-moon and press the edges with your fingers to seal; make sure the filling does not ooze out of the sides. Crimp the edges of each cookie with your fingers or a fork. Brush the tops of the cookies with egg wash and sprinkle generously with sugar.

Bake the cookies for 35 to 40 minutes, rotating the pans halfway through and switching their positions, until golden brown. Let cool completely on the pans on wire racks.

The cookies can be stored in an airtight container at room temperature for up to 3 days.

VARIATION

"CHICKEN DUMPLING" COOKIES

After you have filled each cookie and sealed the edges, shape one of the corners into a chicken's head, pinching out the beak. Press a raisin or cacao nib into the dough to make the chicken's eye. Shape the other corners of the cookie into tail feathers by flattening it and then using kitchen scissors to cut feathers in the dough. Cut into the beak to open it, and cut some wing marks all along the chicken's body. Bake the cookies for 25 to 30 minutes, until lightly golden. Let cool completely, then dust the cookies with confectioners' sugar before serving.

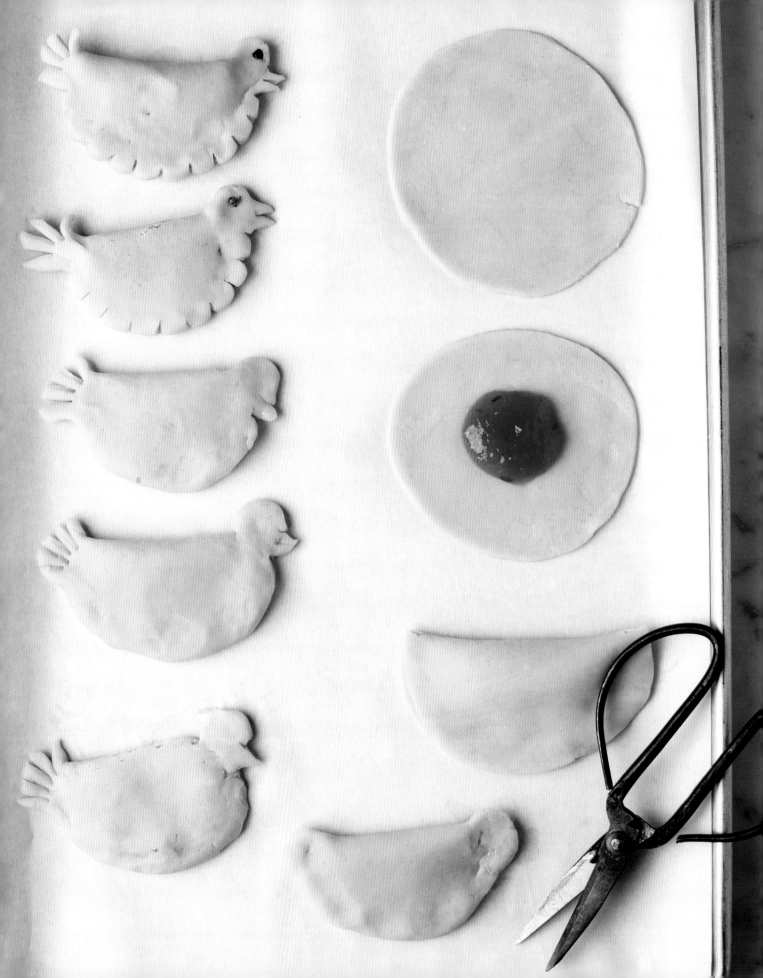

Moravian Ginger Cookies

These crisp, paper-thin ginger spice cookies are super addictive. Family recipes for this cookie have been passed down for generations, ever since the Moravians settled in Winston-Salem, North Carolina, in 1753. The dough is easy to put together, but the rolling takes time and patience, and you will have to return the dough to the refrigerator often during this period, so making the cookies is a true labor of love. Use a pastry cloth or clean tea towel to roll out the dough so you won't have to add too much flour.

This recipe makes dozens of cookies; they make great gifts.

MAKES ABOUT 100 COOKIES

3½ cups (438 g) unbleached all-purpose flour,
 plus more as needed
¾ teaspoon (4 g) baking soda
½ teaspoon fine sea salt
½ cup (100 g) packed light brown sugar
¾ teaspoon ground ginger
¾ teaspoon ground cinnamon
¾ teaspoon ground cloves
¼ teaspoon freshly grated nutmeg
¼ teaspoon ground allspice
⅛ teaspoon cayenne pepper
1 cup (237 ml) unsulfured molasses, such as Grandma's
½ cup (100 g) vegetable shortening (such as Crisco),
 at room temperature

SPECIAL EQUIPMENT
2-inch (5 cm) round cookie cutter

In a medium bowl, whisk together the flour, baking soda, and salt. Set aside.

In a small bowl, mix together the brown sugar, ginger, cinnamon, cloves, nutmeg, allspice, and cayenne. Set aside.

In a medium saucepan, heat the molasses to just below the boiling point. Turn off the heat, add the shortening, and stir until completely smooth. Set aside to cool slightly.

Transfer the molasses mixture to the bowl of a stand mixer fitted with the paddle attachment (or to a large mixing bowl, and use a handheld mixer) and, with the mixer on medium speed, add the sugar mixture and beat for 2 to 3 minutes, until the mixture has lightened in color and cooled. Add the flour mixture in thirds, then beat until the dough comes together in a ball.

Remove the bowl from the mixer stand (if using) and finish mixing by hand to make sure no bits of flour or shortening are hiding on the bottom of the bowl and the dough is thoroughly mixed. If the dough is still sticky, add a little bit more flour, a tablespoon or so at a time, and gently knead the dough until it no longer sticks to your hands.

Divide the dough into 4 pieces, shape each piece into a disk, and wrap each one in plastic wrap. Put the disks in the refrigerator to chill for at least 2 hours, and up to overnight. (*The dough can be frozen, tightly wrapped, for up to 1 month; thaw overnight in the refrigerator.*)

When you are ready to make the cookies, remove one of the disks of dough from the refrigerator and let it sit at room temperature for 10 to 15 minutes, until it is softened enough to roll out but still quite firm.

Transfer the dough to a lightly floured pastry cloth or clean tea towel. Place a piece of parchment on top and, using a rolling pin, roll out the dough paper-thin, about 1/16 inch (1.5 mm) thick. Transfer the dough, on the cloth, to one of the baking sheets and refrigerate for at least 15 minutes before cutting out the cookies.

Position the racks in the middle and lower third of the oven and preheat the oven to 375°F (190°C). Line two baking sheets with parchment.

Using a 2-inch (5 cm) round cookie cutter, cut out the cookies: Dip the cutter in flour first, then cut out the cookies. Use an offset spatula to transfer the cookies to the prepared baking sheets, leaving about ½ inch (1.5 cm) between them. Gather up the scraps of dough, shape into a disk, and chill for at least 15 minutes, then reroll and cut out more cookies (or save for another time).

Bake the cookies for 4 to 6 minutes, rotating the pans halfway through and switching their positions, until golden brown. Be careful: These cookies are superthin and bake quickly. Let cool completely on the pans on wire racks. Repeat with the remaining disks of dough.

The cookies can be stored in an airtight container at room temperature for up to 1 week or frozen for up to 1 month.

Sweet Potato Spice Cookies

These soft and chewy cookies are loaded with all of your favorite warm spices and honey.

MAKES 24 COOKIES

2 cups (250 g) unbleached all-purpose flour

1 teaspoon (6 g) baking soda

1 teaspoon ground cinnamon

½ teaspoon ground allspice

1 teaspoon ground ginger

½ teaspoon ground cardamom

½ teaspoon mace

½ teaspoon fine sea salt

10 ounces (2½ sticks/284 g) unsalted butter,
    at room temperature

1 cup (200 g) granulated sugar

2 cups (400 g) packed light brown sugar

1½ cups (375 g) mashed roasted sweet potatoes
    (from about 2 medium potatoes; see page 37
    for cooking instructions)

2 teaspoons honey

3 large (57 g) egg yolks, at room temperature

1 teaspoon pure vanilla extract

¾ cup (150 g) turbinado sugar for rolling

In a large bowl, whisk together the flour, baking soda, cinnamon, allspice, ginger, cardamom, mace, and salt. Set aside.

In the bowl of a stand mixer fitted with the paddle attachment (or in a medium mixing bowl, using a handheld mixer), cream the butter and the granulated and brown sugars together on medium speed until superlight and fluffy, 3 to 5 minutes. Add the sweet potato puree, honey, eggs, and vanilla, mixing until fully incorporated and smooth. With the mixer on low speed, add the flour mixture in thirds, mixing until just combined.

Remove the bowl from the mixer stand (if using) and finish mixing by hand to make sure no bits of flour or butter are hiding on the bottom of the bowl and the dough is thoroughly mixed. Cover the bowl with plastic wrap and chill until the dough is firm, at least 2 hours, and up to overnight.

When you are ready to bake, position the racks in the middle and lower third of the oven and preheat the oven to 350°F (175°C). Line two baking sheets with parchment. Pour the turbinado sugar into a shallow bowl.

Use a small ice cream scoop or a tablespoon to portion the cookies, then form each cookie into a ball with your hands. Roll the balls in the turbinado sugar and place them on the prepared baking sheets, leaving 2 inches (5 cm) between them to allow for spreading. Place the sheets of cookies in the refrigerator to chill for about 15 minutes before baking.

(Continued)

Bake for 16 to 18 minutes, rotating the pans halfway through and switching their positions. It's difficult to check darker cookies for doneness: Look for browner edges that are slightly firm to the touch; the middles should have started to puff and look dry. Let the cookies cool completely on the pans on wire racks.

The cookies can be stored in an airtight container at room temperature for up to 3 days.

Ginger Molasses Cookies

This old-fashioned molasses cookie is soft and chewy and loaded with comforting warm spices. The addition of coriander and cardamom is unexpected, and lemon zest adds a complementary citrus note.

MAKES 24 COOKIES

4¾ cups (594 g) unbleached all-purpose flour

2 tablespoons ground ginger

2 teaspoons ground cinnamon

¼ teaspoon ground coriander

¼ teaspoon ground cardamom

2 teaspoons (11 g) baking soda

1 teaspoon fine sea salt

Grated zest of 2 lemons

¾ pound (3 sticks/340 g) unsalted butter,
    at room temperature

2 cups (400 g) granulated sugar

½ cup (118 ml) dark molasses

2 large (100 g) eggs, at room temperature

¾ cup (150 g) turbinado sugar for rolling

In a large mixing bowl, whisk together the flour, ginger, cinnamon, coriander, cardamom, baking soda, salt, and zest. Set aside.

In the bowl of a stand mixer fitted with the paddle attachment (or in a large mixing bowl, using a handheld mixer), cream the butter and granulated sugar together on medium speed until superlight and fluffy, 3 to 5 minutes. Add the molasses and mix until blended. Add the eggs, beating well after each addition and scraping down the sides and bottom of the bowl with a rubber spatula as necessary. Add the flour mixture in thirds, mixing until just combined.

Remove the bowl from the mixer stand (if using) and finish mixing by hand to make sure no bits of flour or butter are hiding on the bottom of the bowl and the dough is thoroughly mixed. Cover the bowl with plastic wrap and chill until the dough is firm, at least 2 hours, and up to overnight.

When you are ready to bake, position the racks in the middle and lower third of the oven and preheat the oven to 350°F (175°C). Line two baking sheets with parchment. Pour the turbinado sugar into a shallow bowl.

Use a large ice cream scoop or spoon to portion the cookies (about 3 tablespoons each), then shape each one into a ball with your hands. Roll the balls in the turbinado sugar and place them on the prepared baking sheets, leaving 2 inches (5 cm) between them to allow for spreading. Place the sheets of cookies in the refrigerator to chill for about 15 minutes before baking.

Bake the cookies for 12 to 17 minutes, rotating the pans halfway through and switching their positions. It's difficult to check darker cookies for doneness: Look for browner edges that are slightly firm to the touch; the middles should have started to puff and look dry. Let the cookies cool completely on the pans on wire racks.

The cookies can be stored in an airtight container at room temperature for up to 3 days.

Mexican Wedding Cookies

These cookies are found in many cultures and have different names all over the world: Italian wedding cakes, polvorones, pecan sandies, Napoleon hats, Swedish tea cakes, snowballs, and more. Culinary historians say that recipes referring to cookies called Russian tea cakes started disappearing from cookbooks after the 1950s because of the strained relationship between the United States and the Soviet Union at that time. No matter what you call them, they all start with the same buttery base. The variations are slight; different nuts can be used, and the shape may vary from crescent moons to balls. They are all melt-in-your-mouth delicious.

MAKES 24 COOKIES

1 cup (125 g) unbleached all-purpose flour
1 cup (125 g) cake flour (not self-rising)
½ pound (2 sticks/227 g) unsalted butter,
    at room temperature
½ cup (63 g) confectioners' sugar, plus 1 cup (125 g)
    for rolling
½ teaspoon fine sea salt
½ teaspoon pure vanilla extract
½ cup (60 g) chopped pecans, toasted

Sift together both flours into a medium bowl. Set aside.

In the bowl of a stand mixer fitted with the paddle attachment (or in a large mixing bowl, using a handheld mixer), cream the butter, confectioners' sugar, and salt together on medium speed until superlight and fluffy, 3 to 5 minutes. Beat in the vanilla. With the mixer on low speed, add the flour mixture in thirds, mixing until just incorporated. Beat in the pecans, mixing until incorporated.

Remove the bowl from the mixer stand (if using) and finish mixing by hand to make sure no bits of flour, butter, or nuts are hiding on the bottom of the bowl and the dough is thoroughly mixed. Cover the bowl with plastic wrap and chill until the dough is firm, at least 2 hours, and up to overnight.

When you are ready to bake, position the racks in the middle and lower third of the oven and preheat the oven to 350°F (175°C). Line two baking sheets with parchment.

Use a small ice cream scoop or a tablespoon to form the cookies (about 1 rounded tablespoon each) and place on the prepared baking sheets, leaving 1 inch (3 cm) between them to allow for spreading.

Bake the cookies for 14 to 18 minutes, rotating the pans halfway through and switching their positions, until lightly golden. Let cool on the pans on wire racks just until warm, about 10 minutes.

Put the 1 cup confectioners' sugar in a medium bowl. Working with a few cookies at a time, gently toss in the confectioners' sugar, coating them completely, and place them on another baking sheet. When you've coated all the cookies, set the bowl of confectioners' sugar aside.

Just before serving, toss the cookies again in confectioners' sugar.

The cookies can be stored in an airtight container at room temperature for up to 3 days.

Iced Sugar Cookies

PICTURED ON PAGE 275

Sugar cookies are very versatile. You can swap in another extract for the almond or add the grated zest of any citrus you have on hand to the dough. You can cut the cookies into any shapes you like. They can be enjoyed unadorned, but decorating sugar cookies is a great project for young bakers. If you like, tint the frosting with assorted food colorings and top the cookies with sprinkles galore.

MAKES 24 COOKIES

3 cups (375 g) unbleached all-purpose flour
1 teaspoon (4 g) baking powder, preferably
    aluminum-free
1 large (50 g) egg, at room temperature
½ teaspoon almond extract
½ pound (2 sticks/227 g) unsalted butter,
    at room temperature
1 cup (200 g) granulated sugar
½ teaspoon fine sea salt
½ recipe American Buttercream Frosting (page 132),
    tinted various colors with natural food coloring
    (see sidebar) or liquid gel food coloring,
    if desired
Assorted sprinkles (optional)

SPECIAL EQUIPMENT
2-inch (5 cm) biscuit cutter or cookie cutter

Sift together the flour and baking powder into a medium bowl. Set aside.

In a small bowl, whisk together the egg and almond extract. Set aside.

In the bowl of a stand mixer fitted with the paddle attachment (or in a large mixing bowl, using a handheld mixer), cream the butter, sugar, and salt together on medium speed until superlight and fluffy, about 5 minutes. Add the egg mixture and mix until fully incorporated and smooth. Scrape down the sides and bottom of the bowl with a rubber spatula as necessary. With the mixer on low, add the flour mixture in thirds, mixing until just combined.

Remove the bowl from the mixer stand (if using) and finish mixing by hand to make sure no bits of flour or butter are hiding on the bottom of the bowl and the dough is thoroughly mixed.

Divide the dough in half, shape each piece into a disk, and wrap each one in plastic wrap. Put the disks in the refrigerator to chill until totally firm, at least 4 hours, and up to overnight. (*The dough can be frozen, tightly wrapped, for up to a month. Thaw overnight in the refrigerator.*)

When you are ready to make the cookies, remove the dough from the refrigerator and let it sit at room temperature for 10 to 15 minutes, until it is soft enough to roll out but still quite firm. Line two baking sheets with parchment.

Transfer the dough to a lightly floured surface. Place a piece of parchment on top and, using a rolling pin, roll each disk of dough out to a ¼-inch (6 mm) thickness. Use a 2-inch (5 cm) biscuit cutter or cookie cutter in any shape you like (I love to use heart-shaped cutters) to cut out the cookies: Dip the cutter in flour before each cut, then press it into the dough to cut out the cookies and use an offset spatula to transfer them to the prepared baking sheets, leaving about 2 inches (5 cm) between them to allow for spreading. Gather up the scraps of dough, shape into a disk, and chill for at least 30 minutes, then reroll and cut out more cookies. Put the sheets of cookies in the refrigerator to chill for at least 20 minutes before baking.

Position the racks in the middle and lower third of the oven and preheat the oven to 375°F (190°C).

Bake the cookies for 10 to 12 minutes, rotating the pans halfway through and switching their positions, until the edges are lightly golden. Let cool completely on the pans on wire racks.

Using an offset spatula or a butter knife, frost the tops of the cookies with the buttercream frosting. Decorate with sprinkles, if you like.

The iced cookies can be stored in an airtight container at room temperature for up to 3 days. Undecorated cookies can be frozen in an airtight container for up to 2 weeks.

HOW TO MAKE NATURAL FOOD COLORING

Natural food coloring is easy to make and a great alternative to store-bought food coloring. The natural colors will tint icings and frostings for decorated sugar and gingerbread cookies in beautiful hues. Add the natural colorings to the icing or frosting a little at a time until you achieve the desired color. The food colorings can be stored in an airtight container in the refrigerator for up to 1 week.

RED

Add 1 teaspoon cranberry or strawberry powder to 1 tablespoon water, stirring to create a smooth paste.

PINK

In a small saucepan, combine 2 cups (290 g) strawberries with ¼ cup (59 ml) water and bring to a gentle boil, then simmer for about 5 minutes; let cool. Strain the liquid through a fine-mesh sieve, then return the liquid to the saucepan and simmer until reduced to about ¼ cup (59 ml). Let cool completely.

PURPLE

In a small saucepan, combine 2 cups (290 g) fresh blueberries with ¼ cup (59 ml) water and bring to a gentle boil. Reduce the heat slightly and simmer until the berries burst and break down. Mash the berries and strain through a fine-mesh sieve into a bowl, pressing on the berries to release as much liquid as possible; discard the solids. Return the liquid to the pan and boil until reduced to about ¼ cup (59 ml). Let cool completely.

BLUE

In a small saucepan, combine 2 cups (190 g) shredded purple cabbage with 1½ cups (355 ml) water and bring to a gentle boil. Remove from the heat, cover with a lid, and let steep for about 15 minutes. Strain the liquid through a fine-mesh sieve into a bowl (discard the solids), then return the liquid to the saucepan. Add ¼ cup (50 g) sugar, bring to a simmer, stirring to dissolve the sugar, and continue to simmer until the liquid is a deep purple color and has reduced by half. Stir in ¼ teaspoon (1 g) baking soda, which will turn the liquid blue. Let cool completely.

YELLOW

In a small saucepan, combine ¼ cup (59 ml) water with ½ teaspoon ground turmeric, bring to a gentle boil over medium heat, and boil until reduced by half. Let cool completely. Beware: Turmeric stains everything it touches.

GREEN

Add 1 teaspoon matcha powder to 2 tablespoons water, stirring to create a smooth paste.

Coconut Macaroons

When separating eggs for custards, puddings, and curds, resourceful Southerners are always looking for ways to use the leftover egg whites. These macaroons, sweet treats that are somewhere between delicate cookie and rich confection, are the perfect solution.

MAKES 24 COOKIES

8 cups (680 g) sweetened flaked coconut
    (from two 14-ounce/397 g bags)
2 cups (400 g) granulated sugar
1 cup (240 g) egg whites (about 8 large whites)
2 teaspoons pure vanilla extract

Position the racks in the middle and lower third of the oven and preheat the oven to 350°F (175°C). Line two baking sheets with parchment.

In a large mixing bowl, combine the coconut and sugar, tossing to break up any clumps of coconut. Add the egg whites and vanilla and mix until the coconut is completely moistened.

Use a small ice cream scoop or a tablespoon to form the macaroons (about 1 rounded tablespoon each) and place on the prepared baking sheets, leaving 1 inch (3 cm) between them to allow for spreading. Slightly flatten each macaroon with the palm of your hand.

Bake the macaroons for 12 to 15 minutes, rotating the pans halfway through and switching their positions, until lightly golden. Let cool completely on the pans on wire racks.

The macaroons can be stored in an airtight container at room temperature for up to 5 days.

Meringue Cloud Cookies

Crisp on the outside with a cloudlike chewy interior, these meringue cookies are a delicious gluten-free offering. You can eat them on their own or arrange in bowls and top them with sliced fresh peaches or berries and fresh whipped cream. These confections are simple to make, but you do need an electric mixer, preferably a stand mixer. Whipping the egg whites can take up to 10 minutes. Meringues are also a great way to use up leftover egg whites.

MAKES 12 COOKIES

8 large (240 g) egg whites, at room temperature
½ teaspoon cream of tartar
2 cups (400 g) granulated sugar
4 teaspoons cornstarch
1 tablespoon pure vanilla extract
2 teaspoons white vinegar
3 tablespoons freeze-dried-strawberry powder
    (see Resources, page 389), plus more for dusting
    (optional)

Position the racks in the middle and lower third of the oven and preheat the oven to 250°F (120°C). Line two baking sheets with parchment. Using a 3-inch (8 cm) round cookie cutter (or an upturned small bowl) as a guide, trace 12 circles at least 1 inch (3 cm) apart on the parchment, then turn the parchment over on the baking sheets.

In the bowl of a stand mixer fitted with the whisk attachment (or in a large mixing bowl, using a handheld mixer), whip the egg whites and cream of tartar on high speed until the whites form soft

peaks. Gradually add the sugar and cornstarch, then whip until the meringue forms stiff, shiny peaks, 2 to 3 minutes.

Remove the bowl from the mixer stand (if using) and gently fold in the vanilla and vinegar. Fold in the freeze-dried-strawberry powder, if using.

Using a large ice cream scoop or spoon, gently scoop mounds of meringue, about 2 inches

(5 cm) high, into the traced circles on the prepared baking sheets. Use the back of the scoop or spoon to form peaks.

Slide the pans into the oven and turn the oven down to 200°F (95°C). Bake the meringues for 1 to 1½ hours, switching the positions of the pans halfway through, until set to the touch. You should be able to pull a meringue off the parchment easily, without resistance. Turn the oven off and let the meringues cool in the turned-off oven for 30 minutes.

Remove the meringues from the oven and let cool completely.

If desired, dust the tops of the meringues with strawberry powder before serving.

The meringues are best eaten the same day they're made, but they can be stored in an airtight container at room temperature for up to 1 week.

Chocolate Chip Cookies

PICTURED ON PAGE 248

Crisp on the edges, soft and chewy in the middle, and loaded with chocolate chunks, with just the right amount of salt to bring out the other flavors—this cookie has everything you crave in the iconic treat. And you can freeze the unbaked cookies for later, so you can bake off just a few at a time on a whim.

MAKES 24 COOKIES

2½ cups (313 g) unbleached all-purpose flour

1¼ (7 g) teaspoons baking soda

1¼ teaspoons fine sea salt

½ pound (2 sticks/227 g) unsalted butter, at room temperature

1 cup (200 g) granulated sugar

1 cup (200 g) packed light brown sugar

1 teaspoon pure vanilla extract

1 teaspoon cane syrup

2 large (100 g) eggs, at room temperature

2 cups (12 ounces/340 g) semisweet chocolate chunks or chocolate wafers, such as Guittard

Flaky sea salt, such as Maldon, for sprinkling

Sift together the flour, baking soda, and fine sea salt into a medium bowl. Set aside.

In the bowl of a stand mixer fitted with the paddle attachment (or in a large mixing bowl, using a handheld mixer), cream the butter and both sugars together on medium speed until superlight and fluffy, 3 to 5 minutes. Beat in the vanilla and cane syrup, then add the eggs one (50 g) at a time, mixing well after each addition and scraping down

the sides and bottom of the bowl with a rubber spatula as necessary. Turn the speed down to low and add the flour mixture in thirds, mixing until just combined. With the mixer running, add the chocolate chunks and mix until evenly incorporated.

Remove the bowl from the mixer stand (if using) and finish mixing by hand to make sure no bits of flour or butter are hiding on the bottom of the bowl and the dough is thoroughly mixed.

Cover the bowl with plastic wrap and chill the dough in the refrigerator until slightly firm, about 30 minutes. Position the racks in the middle and lower third of the oven and preheat the oven to 350°F (175°C). Line two baking sheets with parchment.

Use a large ice cream scoop or a ¼-cup (59 ml) measuring cup to form the cookies and place on the prepared baking sheets, leaving 2 inches (5 cm) between them to allow for spreading. Lightly tap each cookie with the palm of your hand to flatten it slightly and lightly sprinkle the cookies with flaky sea salt. (*If you like, you can freeze the cookies on the baking sheets until firm, then transfer them to ziplock bags and freeze for up to 1 month. Sprinkle the cookies with salt before baking and bake from frozen, adding about 2 minutes to the baking time.*)

Bake the cookies for 15 to 18 minutes, rotating the pans halfway through and switching their positions, until golden brown around the edges but still paler in the centers. Let cool completely on the pans on wire racks.

The cookies can be stored in an airtight container at room temperature for up to 3 days.

Lemon Lavender Crinkles

PICTURED ON PAGE 275

The subtle floral aroma and taste of lavender work beautifully in these bright, lemon-flavored cookies. Tender and chewy, they make a lovely addition to any cookie platter.

MAKES 24 COOKIES

2 cups (250 g) unbleached all-purpose flour

1 cup (200 g) granulated sugar

1½ teaspoons (7 g) baking powder, preferably
    aluminum-free

1 teaspoon dried culinary lavender
    (see Resources, page 389)

½ teaspoon fine sea salt

1 tablespoon grated lemon zest

2 large (100 g) eggs, at room temperature

¼ cup (59 ml) fresh lemon juice

½ teaspoon pure vanilla extract

8 tablespoons (1 stick/113 g) unsalted butter,
    at room temperature

½ cup (63 g) confectioners' sugar

In a medium bowl, whisk together the flour, granulated sugar, baking powder, lavender, salt, and zest. Set aside.

In a large measuring cup or small bowl, whisk together the eggs, lemon juice, and vanilla. Set aside.

In the bowl of a stand mixer fitted with the paddle attachment (or in a medium mixing bowl, using a handheld mixer), beat the butter on medium speed until creamy and pale, about 1 minute. With the mixer on low speed, slowly stream in the egg mixture, mixing until fully incorporated and smooth. On low speed, add the flour mixture in thirds, mixing until just combined.

Remove the bowl from the mixer stand (if using) and mix by hand to make sure no bits of flour or butter are hiding on the bottom of the bowl and the dough is thoroughly mixed.

Cover the bowl with plastic wrap and chill the dough in the refrigerator until firm, about 1 hour.

When you are ready to bake, position the racks in the middle and lower third of the oven and preheat the oven to 350°F (175°C). Line two baking sheets with parchment.

Put the confectioners' sugar in a small bowl.

Use a small ice cream scoop or a tablespoon to form the cookies (about 1 rounded tablespoon each). Roll each one in the confectioners' sugar, coating it completely, and place on the prepared baking sheets, leaving 2 inches (5 cm) between the cookies to allow for spreading.

Bake the cookies for 10 to 12 minutes, rotating the pans halfway through and switching their positions, until lightly golden and puffed up. Let cool completely on the pans on wire racks.

The cookies can be stored in an airtight container at room temperature for up to 3 days.

Double Chocolate Cookies

PICTURED OPPOSITE

This cookie is a chocolate lover's delight. The secret is to use good-quality dark chocolate bars, with at least 65 to 75% cacao, and chop it into chunks by hand. Chocolate chips are formulated to keep their shape and not melt completely. It's well worth the extra effort when you take that first bite and the chocolate is still ooey-gooey inside.

MAKES 30 COOKIES

2 cups (250 g) unbleached all-purpose flour

1¾ cups (140 g) Dutch-processed cocoa powder, sifted

2 teaspoons (11 g) baking soda

1 teaspoon fine sea salt

½ pound (2 sticks/227 g) unsalted butter,
    at room temperature

1 cup (200 g) granulated sugar

1 cup (200 g) packed light brown sugar

1 teaspoon pure vanilla extract

1 teaspoon cane syrup

2 large (100 g) eggs, at room temperature

1½ cups (9 ounces/255 g) chopped chocolate
    (at least 65 to 75% cacao; see headnote)

Flaky sea salt, such as Maldon, for sprinkling

In a large bowl, whisk together the flour, cocoa, baking soda, and fine sea salt. Set aside.

In the bowl of a stand mixer fitted with the paddle attachment (or in a large mixing bowl, using a handheld mixer), cream the butter and both sugars together on medium speed until superlight and fluffy, 3 to 5 minutes. Beat in the vanilla and cane syrup. Add the eggs, beating well after each addition and scraping down the sides and bottom of the bowl with a rubber spatula

as necessary. Turn the speed down to low and add the flour mixture in thirds, mixing until just combined, 1 to 2 minutes. With the mixer running, add the chopped chocolate, mixing until evenly incorporated.

Remove the bowl from the mixer stand (if using) and finish mixing by hand to make sure no bits of flour or butter are hiding on the bottom of the bowl and the dough is thoroughly mixed.

Cover the bowl with plastic wrap and chill the dough in the refrigerator until slightly firm, about 30 minutes.

Position the racks in the middle and lower third of the oven and preheat the oven to 350°F (175°C). Line two baking sheets with parchment.

Use a large ice cream scoop or a ½-cup (118 ml) measuring cup to form the cookies and place on the prepared baking sheets, leaving 2 inches (5 cm) between them to allow for spreading. Lightly tap each cookie with the palm of your hand to flatten it slightly and sprinkle with a few grains of flaky sea salt. (*If you like, you can freeze the cookies on the baking sheets until firm, then transfer them to ziplock bags and freeze for up to 1 month. Sprinkle the cookies with salt before baking and bake from frozen, adding about 2 minutes to the baking time.*)

Bake the cookies for 15 to 18 minutes, rotating the pans halfway through and switching their positions. It's difficult to check darker cookies for doneness: Look for browner edges that are slightly firm to the touch. Let the cookies cool completely on the pans on wire racks.

The cookies can be stored in an airtight container at room temperature for up to 3 days.

CLOCKWISE FROM TOP LEFT: LEMON LAVENDER CRINKLES (PAGE 273), ICED SUGAR COOKIES (PAGE 268), DOUBLE CHOCOLATE COOKIES (OPPOSITE), MERINGUE CLOUD COOKIES (PAGE 270)

Marshmallow Pies

The first moon pies (aka marshmallow pies) were made by the Chattanooga Bakery in Tennessee in 1917. Legend has it that the sweet Southern snack was named when a salesman asked a coal miner how big the treat should be and the miner framed his hands around the moon hanging in the sky and said, "About that big!" In the 1930s, the combination of a moon pie and an RC Cola became known as a "workingman's lunch," because both were cheap and easy to pack. The treat was also popular during World War II in care packages for servicemen and -women wanting a taste of home. You can buy packaged moon pies, but you'll like this homemade version so much better.

Note that you need a good amount of melted chocolate to coat the pies easily and thoroughly. Any leftover chocolate coating can be refrigerated for up to 5 days and reheated to drizzle over other cookies.

MAKES ABOUT 12 SANDWICH COOKIES

FOR THE COOKIES

3 cups (375 g) unbleached all-purpose flour

2½ cups (300 g) fine graham cracker crumbs
(about 20 crackers)

1½ teaspoons fine sea salt

1 teaspoon (4 g) baking powder, preferably
aluminum-free

1 teaspoon (6 g) baking soda

¾ teaspoon ground cinnamon

¾ pound (3 sticks/340 g) unsalted butter,
at room temperature

½ cup (100 g) packed light brown sugar

½ cup (118 ml) cane syrup

½ teaspoon pure vanilla extract

¼ cup (59 ml) whole milk

FOR THE MARSHMALLOW FILLING

¾ cup (150 g) granulated sugar

6 tablespoons (89 ml) water

¼ cup (59 ml) light corn syrup

1 tablespoon honey

⅛ teaspoon fine sea salt

1 envelope (0.25 ounce/7 g) unflavored powdered gelatin

1 teaspoon pure vanilla extract

FOR THE CHOCOLATE COATING

2 pounds (907 g) dark chocolate (60 to 75% cacao),
chopped, or chocolate baking wafers,
such as Guittard

½ cup (118 ml) vegetable oil

SPECIAL EQUIPMENT

3-inch (8 cm) round cookie cutter

Candy thermometer

Pastry bag fitted with a ½-inch (1.5 cm) plain tip or
a large ziplock bag

To make the cookies: In a large mixing bowl, whisk together the flour, graham cracker crumbs, salt, baking powder, baking soda, and cinnamon. Set aside.

In the bowl of a stand mixer fitted with the paddle attachment (or in a large mixing bowl, using a handheld mixer), cream the butter and brown sugar together on medium speed until superlight and fluffy, 3 to 5 minutes. Beat in the cane syrup and vanilla. Turn the speed down to low and gradually add the flour and graham cracker mixture, beating until combined; scrape down the sides and bottom of the bowl with a rubber spatula as necessary. Add the milk and mix until just incorporated.

Divide the dough in half. Place one piece on a sheet of parchment. Place a piece of plastic wrap (or parchment) on top of the dough and use a rolling pin to roll it out to about a ½-inch (1.5 cm) thickness. Remove the plastic wrap and slide the dough, on the parchment, onto a baking sheet. Repeat with the remaining dough. Cover with plastic wrap and chill for at least 30 minutes. (*The dough can be refrigerated for up to 2 days.*)

Remove one baking sheet of dough from the refrigerator and transfer the dough, on the parchment, to the counter; line the baking sheet with fresh parchment. Cut out cookies with a 3-inch (8 cm) round cookie cutter and place the cutout cookies on the lined baking sheet, leaving about 1 inch (3 cm) between them to allow for spreading. Chill the cookies in the refrigerator while you cut out the second sheet of cookies. You can gather all the scraps of dough together, shape into a disk, reroll, and cut out more cookies. Chill the cookies for at least 15 minutes before baking.

Position the racks in the middle and lower third of the oven and preheat the oven to 325°F (165°C).

Bake the cookies for 10 to 12 minutes, rotating the pans halfway through and switching their positions, until firm to the touch and lightly golden. Let cool completely on the pans on wire racks.

To make the filling: In a large saucepan, combine the sugar, 3 tablespoons of the water, the corn syrup, honey, and salt and cook, stirring, over medium heat until the sugar is dissolved. Clip a candy thermometer to the side of the pan and bring to a boil, without stirring, then cook until the syrup reaches 240°F (115°C), about 10 minutes.

Meanwhile, pour the remaining 3 tablespoons water into the bowl of a stand mixer fitted with the whisk attachment (or use a large mixing bowl and a handheld mixer), sprinkle the gelatin over it, and let the gelatin stand for about 5 minutes to soften, then mix on low speed until the gelatin dissolves.

With the mixer on low speed, gradually pour the hot sugar syrup into the gelatin mixture, then beat, gradually increasing the speed to high, until the mixture holds stiff peaks and has cooled to room temperature, 10 to 12 minutes. Turn the speed down to low, add the vanilla, and mix to incorporate.

To assemble the cookies: Fill a pastry bag fitted with a plain ½-inch (1.5 cm) tip with the filling (or use a large ziplock bag with a bottom corner snipped off) and pipe about 2 rounded tablespoons of the filling onto the bottom of one cookie. Place another cookie right side up on top and gently press down to seal. Repeat with the remaining cookies and filling.

To coat the cookies: Set a heatproof bowl over simmering water (make sure the bowl does not touch the water), add the chocolate and oil, and stir frequently until the chocolate has completely melted. Remove the bowl from the heat.

Set a wire rack on a parchment-lined baking sheet to catch the chocolate drips. Using two forks, dunk each cookie sandwich into the warm chocolate, turning to coat, then gently place on the wire rack. If the dipping chocolate begins to harden, return it to the simmering water and stir until smooth again. Let the cookies stand until set before serving.

The cookies can be stored in an airtight container at room temperature for up to 3 days.

Brownies and Bars

*You cannot be afraid if you want to accomplish
anything. You got to have the willing, the spirit,
and, above all, you got to have the get-up.*

—GEORGIA GILMORE

BROWNIES FIRST APPEARED in American cookbooks in the early twentieth century, and they have continued to gain in popularity ever since. It didn't take long for home bakers to figure out how creative and convenient it can be to make all kinds of dessert bars. These handheld treats fit nicely into the ethos of the Southern lifestyle. Bars travel well, which makes them easy companions for lunch-box snacks and picnic baskets, and they are a good choice for a community gathering table or at bake sales any time of the year.

Folks are very particular about the way they like their bars. Fudgy or cakey. Middles or corners. Dusted with confectioners' sugar or slathered in frosting. But bars are so easy to make: no rolling, slicing, or dropping, and all you need is one baking pan. You can customize them easily too. Honestly, the hardest part is waiting for them to cool before you dig in.

In this chapter, you will find classic bars with a Southern spin and some creative twists as well. Chocolate Fudge Brownies and Brown Sugar–Jam Blondies are favorite after-school treats. S'mores Bars and Hello Dolly Bars will satisfy any chocolate craving. Try the Salty Honey Bars or Tres Leches Cheesecake Bars for something a little unexpected.

Chocolate Fudge Brownies

PICTURED ON PAGE 278

This is the quintessential bake-sale brownie—soft, chewy, and fudgy—but it's a classic for any occasion. Finishing the brownies with a heavenly chocolate glaze pushes the decadence level of this already delicious treat into its own category.

MAKES 12 TO 16 BROWNIES

FOR THE BROWNIES

½ pound (2 sticks/227 g) unsalted butter, cut into 1-inch (3 cm) cubes

½ pound (227 g) unsweetened chocolate, chopped (about 3 cups)

2½ cups (500 g) granulated sugar

1½ teaspoons fine sea salt

1 tablespoon pure vanilla extract

4 large (200 g) eggs, at room temperature

1 cup (125 g) unbleached all-purpose flour

FOR THE CHOCOLATE GLAZE

¾ pound (340 g) dark chocolate (at least 60 to 70% cacao), chopped

4 tablespoons (57 g) unsalted butter, at room temperature

1 teaspoon pure vanilla extract

Flaky sea salt, such as Maldon, for sprinkling

To make the brownies: Position a rack in the middle of the oven and preheat the oven to 350°F (175°C). Butter a 9-by-13-inch (23 by 33 cm) baking pan or spray with nonstick spray. Line the pan with parchment, leaving an overhang on two opposite sides.

Set a medium heatproof bowl over a saucepan of simmering water (make sure the bowl does not touch the water), add the butter and chocolate, and stir frequently until both are melted and the mixture is smooth.

Remove the bowl from the heat, add the sugar, fine sea salt, and vanilla, and stir with a heatproof spoon until thoroughly combined. Add the eggs one (50 g) at a time, mixing until each one is fully incorporated before adding the next. Add the flour and fold it into the batter until just combined.

Pour the batter into the prepared baking pan. Bake for 40 to 45 minutes, until a slight crack forms around the edges of the brownies. Remove from the oven and let cool completely on a wire rack.

Using the parchment "handles," remove the brownies from the pan.

To make the glaze: In a small saucepan, combine the chocolate and butter and heat over low heat, stirring, until the chocolate is almost melted.

Remove the pan from the heat and add the vanilla. Stir the mixture until the chocolate is completely melted, smooth, and shiny (partially melting the chocolate over the heat and then finishing it off the heat will "quick-temper" it, keeping it shiny). Set aside to cool slightly.

Pour the glaze over the brownies, spreading it evenly with a spatula or a butter knife into a thick layer over the top. Let the brownies stand until the glaze is completely set, then sprinkle the top lightly with the flaky sea salt and cut into squares.

The brownies can be stored in an airtight container at room temperature for up to 3 days or refrigerated for up to 1 week.

Raspberry Chess Pie Bars

This is an old-fashioned Southern dessert in bar form. Because the recipe makes a lot, it would be a welcome addition to any potluck table. A delicious buttermilk custard hides beneath sweet ripe raspberries—you can make this with other berries too. Use fresh berries if you can, but frozen berries will work just fine (do not thaw them before using).

MAKES 16 TO 24 BARS

FOR THE FILLING

1 cup (125 g) unbleached all-purpose flour

¼ cup (45 g) fine-ground yellow cornmeal

1 teaspoon fine sea salt

10 ounces (2½ sticks/284 g) unsalted butter, at room temperature

2 cups (400 g) granulated sugar

2 teaspoons pure vanilla extract

8 large (400 g) eggs, at room temperature

2½ cups (592 ml) buttermilk

1 Brown Sugar Bar Crust (recipe follows), cooled

4 cups (480 g) raspberries

About 2 tablespoons granulated sugar for sprinkling

Position a rack in the lower third of the oven and preheat the oven to 325°F (165°C).

To make the filling: In a small bowl, whisk together the flour, cornmeal, and salt. Set aside.

In the bowl of a stand mixer fitted with the paddle attachment (or in a large mixing bowl, using a handheld mixer), cream the butter and sugar together on medium speed until superlight and fluffy, 3 to 5 minutes. Beat in the vanilla. Add the eggs one (50 g) at a time, beating well after each addition and scraping down the sides and bottom of the bowl with a rubber spatula as necessary. Reduce the speed to low and add the flour mixture in thirds, beating until just well blended. Slowly add

the buttermilk, beating until thoroughly combined, scraping down the sides and bottom of the bowl as necessary.

Pour the filling into the prepared crust. Arrange the berries on top of the filling, then sprinkle with the sugar.

Bake for 40 to 45 minutes, until the filling is golden and puffed up at the edges and the center no longer looks wet but still wobbles slightly when jiggled; it will continue to set as it cools. Let cool completely on a wire rack before cutting into bars.

The bars can be stored in an airtight container in the refrigerator for up to 1 week.

BROWN SUGAR BAR CRUST

This is also a great base for the Salty Honey Bars (page 297).

MAKES ONE 12-BY-17-INCH (30 BY 43 CM) CRUST

4½ cups (563 g) unbleached all-purpose flour

¾ cup (150 g) packed light brown sugar

¾ teaspoon fine sea salt

1 pound (454 g) unsalted butter, melted and slightly cooled

Position a rack in the middle of the oven and preheat the oven to 350°F (175°C). Lightly butter the bottom and sides of a 12-by-17-inch (30 by 43 cm) rimmed baking sheet, then line with parchment, leaving an overhang on two opposite sides of the pan.

In a large bowl, use your hands or a fork to combine the flour, brown sugar, and salt. Slowly drizzle in the butter and stir with a fork until the mixture looks moist and crumbly.

Using your hands, press the dough evenly over the bottom and up the sides of the baking sheet. You can decorate the edges by crimping them with a fork or leave them rustic. Refrigerate for 15 minutes to set the crust.

Line the crust with parchment and fill with dried beans, rice, or pie weights. Bake for 12 to 15 minutes, until the crust is just set and lightly browned. Remove the parchment and weights and set the crust on a wire rack to cool completely before filling.

Brown Sugar–Jam Blondies

PICTURED ON PAGE 292

Big dollops of jam are swirled throughout a classic butterscotch blondie batter, adding a sweet note and visual delight.

MAKES 12 TO 16 BLONDIES

2 cups (250 g) unbleached all-purpose flour

1 teaspoon (4 g) baking powder, preferably aluminum-free

¾ teaspoon fine sea salt

1½ cups (300 g) packed light brown sugar

2 large (100 g) eggs, at room temperature

½ pound (2 sticks/227 g) unsalted butter, melted and
    slightly cooled

2 teaspoons pure vanilla extract

¾ cup (177 ml) good-quality jam, homemade
    (see page 347) or store-bought

Position a rack in the middle of the oven and preheat the oven to 350°F (175°C). Lightly butter a 9-by-13-inch (23 by 33 cm) baking pan. Line with parchment, leaving an overhang on two opposite sides of the pan.

In a small bowl, whisk together the flour, baking powder, and salt. Set aside.

In the bowl of a stand mixer fitted with the paddle attachment (or in a large mixing bowl, using a handheld mixer), combine the brown sugar and eggs and mix until thoroughly blended and lightened in color. Mix in the butter and vanilla. Add the flour mixture in thirds, mixing until just combined.

Remove the bowl from the mixer stand (if using) and finish mixing by hand to make sure no bits of flour or butter are hiding on the bottom of the bowl and the dough is thoroughly mixed.

Transfer the batter to the prepared pan and spread it evenly, making sure to get into the corners. Drop small dollops of the jam (about 1 tablespoon) all over the top of the batter. Run a butter knife randomly back and forth, from side to side, all the way down the length of the pan and back, to create ribbons of jam into the batter.

Bake the blondies for 30 to 35 minutes, until golden brown on top. Let cool completely on a wire rack before cutting into bars.

The blondies can be stored in an airtight container in the refrigerator for up to 1 week or in the freezer for up to 2 months.

Butterscotch Pecan Blondies

These blondies are moist, cakey, and chewy, and brimming with pecans. The butterscotch frosting is an irresistible bonus.

MAKES 24 BLONDIES

FOR THE BLONDIES

3 cups (375 g) unbleached all-purpose flour

1 tablespoon (13 g) baking powder, preferably
    aluminum-free

1 teaspoon fine sea salt

½ pound (2 sticks/227 g) unsalted butter,
    at room temperature

3 cups (600 g) packed light brown sugar

4 large (200 g) eggs, at room temperature

1 tablespoon pure vanilla extract

2 cups (240 g) chopped pecans

FOR THE FROSTING

½ pound (2 sticks/227 g) unsalted butter, at room
    temperature

2 cups (400 g) packed light brown sugar

2 cups (250 g) confectioners' sugar

½ teaspoon fine sea salt

⅓ cup (79 ml) half-and-half

1 tablespoon pure vanilla extract

To make the blondies: Position a rack in the middle of the oven and preheat the oven to 350°F (175°C). Lightly butter the bottom and sides of a 12-by-17-inch (30 by 43 cm) rimmed baking sheet. Line with parchment, leaving an overhang on two opposite sides of the pan.

In a medium bowl, whisk together the flour, baking powder, and salt. Set aside.

In the bowl of a stand mixer fitted with the paddle attachment (or in a large mixing bowl, using a handheld mixer), cream the butter and brown sugar together on medium-high speed until superlight and fluffy, 2 to 3 minutes. Beat in the eggs and vanilla, scraping down the sides and bottom of the bowl with a rubber spatula as necessary. Turn the speed down to low and add the flour mixture in thirds, mixing until just incorporated. Add the pecans, mixing until incorporated.

Remove the bowl from the mixer stand (if using) and finish mixing by hand to make sure no bits of flour or butter are hiding on the bottom of the bowl and the dough is thoroughly mixed.

Spread the batter evenly in the prepared pan and smooth the top with a spatula. Bake for 25 to 30 minutes, until the blondies are slightly puffed up and golden. Let cool completely on a wire rack before frosting.

To make the frosting: In a large saucepan, cook the butter and brown sugar over medium-low heat, stirring, until the sugar is dissolved and the mixture is gently bubbling. Reduce the heat to low and continue to cook until the mixture turns a golden caramel color, about 2 minutes. Remove from the heat and set aside.

In the bowl of the stand mixer fitted with the paddle attachment (or in a large mixing bowl, using a handheld mixer), beat the confectioners' sugar, salt, half-and-half, and vanilla together on medium speed until smooth and creamy, about 1 minute. Add the brown sugar mixture and mix until combined.

Spread the frosting over the cooled blondies. Let the frosting set for at least 20 minutes before cutting into squares.

The blondies can be stored in an airtight container at room temperature for up to 3 days.

Pecan Bars

In the South, we don't take pecans for granted because we know how much work goes into processing the nutmeats out of their shells and hulls. If you are lucky, you can buy them from a local farmer at a food stand, and they will be as fresh as can be. The flavor of pecans really blooms when they are baked in a dessert. For these delicious bars, a filling made with pecans in all their glory, brown sugar, and coconut sits atop a golden shortbread crust.

MAKES 12 TO 16 BARS

FOR THE CRUST

2 cups (250 g) unbleached all-purpose flour

½ teaspoon fine sea salt

12 tablespoons (1½ sticks/170 g) unsalted butter, at room temperature

½ cup (100 g) packed light brown sugar

FOR THE FILLING

4 large (200 g) eggs, at room temperature

2 cups (400 g) packed light brown sugar

(Continued)

1 cup (237 ml) cane syrup or dark corn syrup

3 tablespoons unsalted butter, melted

1 tablespoon pure vanilla extract

½ cup (63 g) unbleached all-purpose flour

½ teaspoon fine sea salt

1½ cups (128 g) sweetened flaked coconut

2½ cups (250 g) pecan halves

Position a rack in the middle of the oven and preheat the oven to 350°F (175°C). Butter a 9-by-13-inch (23 by 33 cm) baking pan. Line with parchment, leaving an overhang on two opposite sides of the pan.

To make the crust: Sift together the flour and salt into a small bowl. Set aside.

In the bowl of a stand mixer fitted with the paddle attachment (or in a large mixing bowl, using a handheld mixer), cream the butter and brown sugar together on medium speed until superlight and fluffy, 3 to 5 minutes. Slowly add the flour mixture, beating on low speed until well blended; the mixture should still be crumbly.

Press the crust mixture evenly over the bottom of the prepared pan. Bake for 15 to 20 minutes, until golden brown. Set aside while you make the filling. (Leave the oven on.)

To make the filling: In a large bowl, whisk together the eggs and brown sugar. Add the cane syrup, butter, and vanilla, whisking to blend, then add the flour and salt, whisking until completely incorporated. Fold in the coconut and pecans.

Pour the filling over the cooled crust. Bake the bars for 25 to 30 minutes, until golden brown. Let cool completely on a wire rack, about 1 hour, before cutting into bars.

The bars can be stored in an airtight container in the refrigerator for up to 1 week or in the freezer for up to 3 weeks.

Peanut Brittle

PICTURED ON PAGE 292

In the South, brittle is served alongside a big scoop of ice cream. This recipe is a great base for other nuts, benne seeds, pumpkin seeds, or even cacao nibs. If substituting seeds, use just ¾ cup (100 g).

MAKES ABOUT 36 PIECES

1 cup (200 g) granulated sugar

⅓ cup (79 ml) light corn syrup

¼ cup (59 ml) water

¾ teaspoon fine sea salt

1⅔ cups (175 g) peanuts

1 tablespoon unsalted butter, cut into small pieces

1 teaspoon pure vanilla extract

1 teaspoon (6 g) baking soda

SPECIAL EQUIPMENT

Candy thermometer

Line a baking sheet with parchment and spray the parchment lightly with nonstick spray.

In a deep heavy-bottomed saucepan, combine the sugar, corn syrup, water, and salt and cook over low heat, stirring with a wooden spoon, until the sugar dissolves. Clip a candy thermometer to the side of the pan, increase the heat to high, and bring to a boil, without stirring, then cook until the mixture registers 264°F (130°C), 6 to 8 minutes. Add the peanuts and stir constantly until the mixture registers 310°F (155°C) on the thermometer.

Remove from the heat and add the butter and vanilla, stirring until combined. Sprinkle in the baking soda, stirring briskly until incorporated.

Pour the mixture into the prepared pan and use an oiled spatula to spread it evenly. Let cool completely before breaking the brittle into pieces.

The brittle can be stored in an airtight container in a cool dry place for up to 2 weeks.

S'mores Bars

Every year, thousands of green-sashed girls make a pilgrimage to Savannah, Georgia, to visit the birthplace of Juliette Gordon Low, founder of the Girl Scouts of America. These bars are a nod to the classic campfire treat. A salty, crunchy graham cracker crust is topped with a rich, melt-in-your mouth chocolate filling and a fluffy, light marshmallow meringue, which is toasted for the full experience.

MAKES 12 BARS

FOR THE CRUST

3 cups (360 g) graham cracker crumbs (about 24 crackers)

2 tablespoons light brown sugar

½ teaspoon fine sea salt

12 tablespoons (1½ sticks/170 g) unsalted butter, melted

FOR THE FILLING

8 tablespoons (1 stick/113 g) cold unsalted butter, cut into 1-inch (3 cm) cubes

¼ pound (113 g) unsweetened chocolate, chopped (about ½ cup)

1¼ cups (250 g) granulated sugar

¼ teaspoon fine sea salt

2 teaspoons pure vanilla extract

2 large (100 g) eggs, at room temperature

½ cup (63 g) unbleached all-purpose flour

FOR THE MARSHMALLOW MERINGUE

3 large (90 g) egg whites

¾ cup (150 g) granulated sugar

¼ teaspoon cream of tartar

½ teaspoon pure vanilla extract

SPECIAL EQUIPMENT (OPTIONAL)

Kitchen blowtorch

Position a rack in the middle of the oven and preheat the oven to 350°F (175°C). Butter a 9-by-9-inch (23 by 23 cm) baking pan. Line with foil, leaving an overhang on two opposite sides of the pan.

To make the crust: In a medium bowl, combine the graham cracker crumbs, brown sugar, and salt. Drizzle in the butter and blend with a fork until the crumbs are evenly moistened.

Press the crumb mixture firmly and evenly over the bottom of the prepared pan. Bake the crust for about 8 minutes, until lightly golden. Set aside to cool completely.

To make the filling: Set a medium heatproof bowl over a saucepan of simmering water (do not let the bottom of the bowl touch the water), add the cubed butter and chocolate, and heat, stirring frequently, until melted and smooth.

Remove the bowl from the heat, add the sugar, salt, and vanilla, and stir until completely combined, about 2 minutes. Add the eggs and stir until thoroughly incorporated and smooth. Add the flour and fold into the batter until combined.

Pour the batter into the prepared baking pan. Bake for 20 to 22 minutes, until a slight crack forms around the edges of the bars. Let cool completely on a wire rack.

To make the meringue: Put the egg whites, sugar, and cream of tartar in the bowl of a stand mixer (or a medium heatproof bowl), set the bowl over a medium saucepan of simmering water (do not let the bottom of the bowl touch the water), and whisk constantly until the sugar is completely dissolved and the egg whites are warm to the touch, 3 to 4 minutes. The mixture should appear pale and opaque. Rub a little bit of it between your fingers to make sure all the sugar is dissolved; it should feel smooth, without any grittiness.

Attach the bowl to the mixer stand (if using) and fit it with the whisk attachment (or use a handheld mixer). Add the vanilla and, starting on low speed, whip the egg whites, gradually

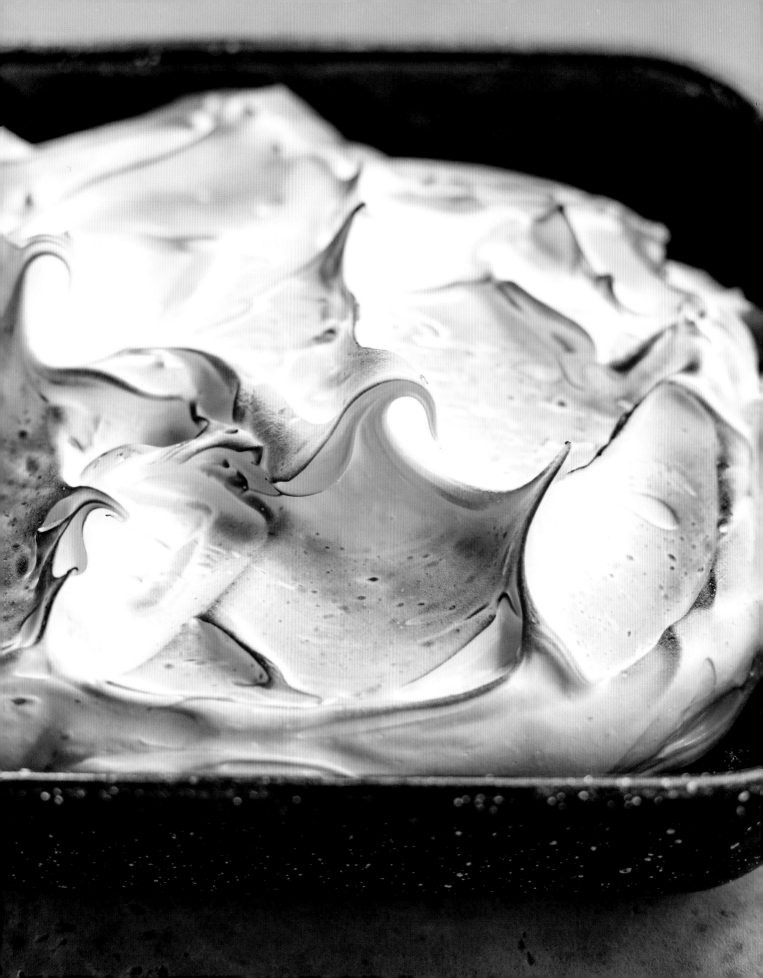

increasing the speed to high, until the meringue is glossy and forms stiff peaks, 5 to 7 minutes.

Loosely pile the meringue onto the bars and spread it evenly over them. Toast the meringue with a kitchen blowtorch until golden in spots, or broil 8 inches (20 cm) from the heat source, watching carefully until toasted and golden, 2 to 3 minutes. Let cool completely before cutting into bars.

The bars can be refrigerated in an airtight container for up to 2 days.

Tres Leches Cheesecake Bars

PICTURED ON PAGE 292

Tres leches cake, or "three milks cake," is a rich, sweet Latin American dessert that is beloved. The traditional recipe includes whole milk (or heavy cream), condensed milk, and evaporated milk. This bar version gets some Southern flair with the addition of sweet, tangy buttermilk to the cream cheese filling. If you like, gild the lily and top with sliced strawberries and Chantilly Cream.

MAKES 12 TO 16 BARS

FOR THE CRUST

2 cups (240 g) graham cracker crumbs (about 16 crackers)

1 tablespoon granulated sugar

½ teaspoon fine sea salt

8 tablespoons (1 stick/113 g) unsalted butter, melted

FOR THE FILLING

2 pounds (four 8-ounce/227 g packages) cream cheese, at room temperature

One 14-ounce (300 ml) can sweetened condensed milk

6 large (300 g) eggs, at room temperature

¼ cup (59 ml) buttermilk

1½ teaspoons pure vanilla extract

1 teaspoon ground cinnamon

Sliced fresh strawberries for serving

1 recipe Chantilly Cream (page 373) for serving

Position a rack in the middle of the oven and preheat the oven to 350°F (175°C). Butter a 9-by-13-inch (23 by 33 cm) baking pan. Line with aluminum foil, leaving an overhang on two opposite sides of the pan.

To make the crust: In a medium bowl, blend the graham cracker crumbs, sugar, and salt. Drizzle in the butter and mix with a fork until the crumbs are evenly moistened.

Press the mixture evenly over the bottom of the prepared pan. (You can use a piece of parchment to press on the crust to make sure it is completely level.) Bake for 6 to 8 minutes, until lightly golden. Transfer to a wire rack to cool completely before filling. Increase the oven temperature to 400°F (205°C).

To make the filling: In the bowl of a stand mixer fitted with the paddle attachment (or in a large mixing bowl, using a handheld mixer), beat the cream cheese on medium-high speed until smooth and creamy, 5 to 8 minutes. Reduce the speed to low and gradually add the sweetened condensed milk, then beat until light and fluffy, 3 to 5 minutes. Add the eggs 3 (150 g) at a time, beating well after each addition. Scrape down the sides and bottom of the bowl with a rubber spatula as necessary. Add the buttermilk, vanilla, and cinnamon and mix until the filling is the consistency of sour cream, 3 to 5 minutes.

Pour the filling into the cooled crust. Bake for 10 minutes, then turn the oven temperature down to 225°F (105°C) and bake for another 50 to

65 minutes, until the filling is firm at the edges and the center no longer looks wet but still wobbles slightly when jiggled. It will continue to bake as it cools.

Turn the oven off and leave the bars in the oven, with the door partially open, for 1 hour, allowing it to cool slowly and prevent cracking.

Remove the bars from the oven and allow to cool to room temperature on a wire rack, 2 hours. Once they have cooled, cover the pan with aluminum foil and refrigerate overnight to chill completely before serving.

Cut into bars and serve with the fresh strawberries and Chantilly cream.

Classic Lemon Bars

For these bars, a crisp, golden shortbread crust is topped with bright, tangy lemon curd.

MAKES 12 BARS

FOR THE CRUST
½ pound (2 sticks/227 g) unsalted butter, melted
½ cup (100 g) granulated sugar
1½ teaspoons pure vanilla extract
1½ teaspoons fine sea salt
2 cups (250 g) unbleached all-purpose flour

FOR THE FILLING
2¼ cups (450 g) granulated sugar
6 tablespoons (47 g) unbleached all-purpose flour
6 large (300 g) eggs, at room temperature
1 cup (237 ml) fresh lemon juice (from 5 to 6 lemons)

Confectioners' sugar for dusting

Position a rack in the middle of the oven and preheat the oven to 350°F (175°C). Butter a 9-by-13-by-2-inch (23 by 33 by 5 cm) baking pan or spray with nonstick spray. Line the pan with parchment, leaving an overhang on two opposite sides.

To make the crust: In a medium bowl, combine the butter, sugar, vanilla, and salt and stir until well blended. Gradually add the flour, stirring until it is just incorporated.

Press the mixture evenly over the bottom of the prepared pan. Bake for 15 to 18 minutes, until the crust is lightly golden.

While the crust is baking, make the filling: In a medium mixing bowl, whisk the sugar and flour together until thoroughly combined. Add the eggs and lemon juice and whisk until well mixed.

When the crust is baked, remove from the oven, set the pan on a heatproof surface, and pour the lemon filling over the hot crust. Turn the oven temperature down to 300°F (150°C), return the pan to the oven, and bake for 20 to 25 minutes, until the filling looks puffy on top and the center wobbles slightly if jiggled.

Let the bars cool completely on a wire rack, then refrigerate for at least 3 hours.

Cut into bars and dust the tops with confectioners' sugar. Serve chilled.

The bars can be stored in an airtight container in the refrigerator for up to 5 days.

CLOCKWISE FROM TOP LEFT: TRES LECHES CHEESECAKE BARS (PAGE 290), FRUIT PIE BARS (OPPOSITE), PEANUT BRITTLE (PAGE 286), BROWN SUGAR–JAM BLONDIES (PAGE 284)

Fruit Pie Bars

PICTURED OPPOSITE

These fruit bars are very versatile and easy to make. Start with a buttery press-in crust—reserve some for the topping—and fill it with creamy custard and the fruit of your choice. You can use a variety of berries or sliced peaches or plums, or whatever is in season. The bars are also good made with frozen berries.

MAKES 12 TO 16 BARS

FOR THE CRUST AND TOPPING

3 cups (375 g) unbleached all-purpose flour

1½ cups (300 g) granulated sugar

¼ teaspoon fine sea salt

¾ pound (3 sticks/340 g) unsalted butter, cut into
    1-inch (3 cm) cubes

FOR THE FRUIT FILLING

2 cups (400 g) granulated sugar

¾ cup (94 g) unbleached all-purpose flour

¼ teaspoon fine sea salt

4 large (200 g) eggs, at room temperature

1 cup (240 g) sour cream

2 cups (290 g) fresh berries or sliced fruit
    or two 16-ounce (454 g) packages
    frozen berries, thawed and drained

Position a rack in the middle of the oven and preheat the oven to 350°F (175°C). Butter a 9-by-13-inch (23 by 33 cm) baking pan. Line with parchment, leaving an overhang on two opposite sides of the pan.

To make the crust and topping: In the bowl of a stand mixer fitted with the paddle attachment (or in a large mixing bowl, using a handheld mixer), combine the flour, sugar, and salt and mix on low speed until thoroughly blended. With the mixer running, add the cubed butter a few pieces at a time, mixing until the mixture looks crumbly.

Transfer 1½ cups (250 g) of the mixture (for the crumb topping) to a container and refrigerate while you bake the crust.

Press the rest of the mixture evenly over the bottom of the prepared pan. Bake for 12 to 15 minutes, until lightly golden. Let cool for at least 10 minutes on a wire rack. (Leave the oven on.)

To make the filling: In a large mixing bowl, whisk together the sugar, flour, and salt. Add the eggs and sour cream and whisk until smooth. Gently fold in the fruit.

Pour the filling over the baked crust. Sprinkle the reserved crumb topping evenly on top.

Bake the bars for 45 to 55 minutes, until the top is golden brown and bubbly. Cool on a wire rack for at least an hour before cutting into squares. The bars can be stored in an airtight container in the refrigerator for up to 3 days.

Caramel Crispy Treats

When it's too hot to turn on the oven but you are craving something sweet, try these good old-fashioned rice cereal treats. Brown butter adds a warm nutty flavor, and salted caramel takes them over the top. Cut into squares, and try to resist eating more than one.

MAKES 12 BARS

2 tablespoons unsalted butter

One 12-ounce (340 g) bag marshmallows

½ cup (118 ml) Salted Caramel Sauce (page 380)

9 cups (252 g) puffed rice cereal, such as Rice Krispies

Butter a 9-by-13-by-2-inch (23 by 33 by 5 cm) baking pan.

In a large heavy-bottomed pot, melt the butter over medium heat, then cook until it starts to make a crackling sound and begins to color. A nutty aroma will start to fill your kitchen. Add the marshmallows and, using a heatproof spoon, stir to coat them with the browned butter and the bits on the bottom of the pot. Then heat, stirring frequently, until completely melted and smooth. Add the caramel sauce and stir until well blended. Fold in the rice cereal, stirring until completely coated.

Carefully pour the mixture into the prepared pan; the mixture will be very hot. Lightly butter your hands or spray a piece of parchment with nonstick spray and press the mixture evenly over the bottom of the pan.

Place the pan in the refrigerator to chill for at least 1 hour, before cutting into squares.

Carmelita Bars

This bar has a chewy oatmeal crumb crust and topping layered with homemade caramel sauce, chocolate, and pecans. It's rich and gooey in every bite.

MAKES 12 TO 16 BARS

FOR THE CRUST AND TOPPING

2 cups (250 g) unbleached all-purpose flour

2 cups (180 g) old-fashioned rolled oats

1 cup (200 g) packed light brown sugar

1 teaspoon (6 g) baking soda

¾ teaspoon fine sea salt

10 ounces (2½ sticks/284 g) unsalted butter, cut into 1-inch (3 cm) cubes

FOR THE FILLING

1 recipe Salted Caramel Sauce (page 380), at room temperature

1 cup (120 g) chopped pecans

1 cup (175 g) semisweet chocolate chips

Butter a 9-by-13-inch (23 by 33 cm) baking pan. Line with parchment, leaving an overhang on two opposite sides of the pan.

To make the crust and topping: In the bowl of a stand mixer fitted with the paddle attachment (or in a large mixing bowl, using a handheld mixer), combine the flour, oats, brown sugar, baking soda, and salt and mix on low speed until blended. Gradually add the butter cubes and mix until the mixture looks dry and crumbly.

(Continued)

Transfer half of the mixture to a bowl and reserve in the refrigerator for the topping.

Press the remaining mixture evenly over the bottom of the prepared pan. Bake the crust for 10 minutes. Remove from the oven (leave the oven on).

To assemble the bars: Pour the caramel sauce over the baked crust, then sprinkle the pecans evenly over the caramel, followed by the chocolate chips. Sprinkle the reserved oatmeal mixture evenly all over the top (do not press it in).

Bake the bars for 10 to 12 minutes, until lightly golden. Let cool completely on a wire rack before cutting into bars.

The bars can be stored in an airtight container at room temperature for up to 3 days or refrigerated for up to 1 week.

Hello Dolly Bars

These creamy, chewy, ooey-gooey, delicious bars are also known as Dream Bars. The recipe became popular in the mid-1960s when *Hello, Dolly!* was playing on Broadway. The layers—of graham cracker crumbs, chocolate chips, pecans, and coconut—make this confection far greater than the sum of its parts.

MAKES 12 TO 16 BARS

FOR THE CRUST

3 cups (297 g) finely crushed graham crackers (about 24 crackers)

2 tablespoons light brown sugar

¾ teaspoon fine sea salt

12 tablespoons (1½ sticks/170 g) unsalted butter, melted

2 cups (350 g) semisweet chocolate chips

2 cups (240 g) chopped pecans, toasted

3 cups (255 g) sweetened flaked coconut

One 14-ounce (300 ml) can sweetened condensed milk

Position a rack in the middle of the oven and preheat the oven to 350°(175°C). Butter a 9-by-13-by-2-inch (23 by 33 by 5 cm) baking pan. Line with parchment, leaving an overhang on two opposite sides of the pan.

To make the crust: In a medium bowl, blend together the graham cracker crumbs, brown sugar, and salt. Drizzle in the melted butter and mix with a fork until the crumbs are evenly moistened. When you squeeze a handful of the mixture, it should hold its shape.

Press the mixture firmly and evenly over the bottom of the prepared pan. (You can use a piece of parchment to press on the crust with the palms of your hands to make sure it is completely even). Bake the crust for 6 to 8 minutes, until lightly golden. Let cool completely on a wire rack. (Leave the oven on.)

Sprinkle the chocolate chips evenly over the cooled crust, followed by the pecans, and then the coconut. Drizzle the condensed milk evenly over the top.

Bake the bars for 25 to 30 minutes, until lightly golden on top. Let cool completely before cutting into squares.

The bars can be stored in an airtight container at room temperature for up to 3 days.

Salty Honey Bars

If you like a balance of salty and sweet in your dessert treats, this is the bar for you. The smooth, luscious filling, made with a browned butter–honey custard and cornmeal, develops a shiny, crunchy top as the bars bake, a delightful surprise.

MAKES 12 TO 16 BARS

FOR THE FILLING

½ pound (2 sticks/227 g) unsalted butter, cut into ½-inch (1.5 cm) cubes

1 cup (200 g) granulated sugar

⅔ cup (158 ml) honey

¼ cup (45 g) fine cornmeal

2 teaspoons fine sea salt

6 large (300 g) eggs plus 2 large (38 g) egg yolks, beaten

1 cup (237 ml) cane syrup

1 cup (237 ml) heavy cream

1 tablespoon pure vanilla extract

4 teaspoons apple cider vinegar

1 Brown Sugar Bar Crust (page 282), cooled

2 teaspoons flaky sea salt, such as Maldon, for sprinkling

To make the filling: In a large light-colored skillet or saucepan (the light color makes it easier to see the browning), melt the butter over medium-high heat, stirring with a heatproof spatula as the butter begins to foam up. Continue to cook, stirring to make sure the flavorful brown bits do not stick to the bottom of the pan and swirling the pan frequently to check the color, until the butter turns lightly golden, 1 to 3 minutes. Use all of your senses here, waiting for a nutty aroma to develop as the melted butter snaps and crackles, and watching carefully as the butter starts to brown.

Remove the butter from the heat and scrape it, along with any browned bits in the bottom of the pan, into a large heatproof bowl. Set aside to cool for about 15 minutes, stirring occasionally.

Whisk the sugar, honey, cornmeal, and fine sea salt into the browned butter. Add the beaten eggs and yolks, slowly whisking until the ingredients are blended and fully combined. Whisk in the cane syrup, cream, vanilla, and vinegar, in that order, until smooth.

Pour the filling into the baked crust. Bake for 40 to 45 minutes, until the edges of the filling have puffed up and the center wobbles slightly if jiggled.

Remove the bars from the oven and sprinkle the top with the flaky sea salt. Let cool on a wire rack for at least 3 hours before cutting into bars.

The bars can be stored in an airtight container at room temperature for up to 3 days.

Grits and Grains

THE SOUTH IS EXPERIENCING a regional grain renaissance, milling flours ranging from Appalachian White Whole Wheat to spelt, rice, and rye. These heirloom grains allow us to bring back the old flavors and textures to our biscuits, cookies, cakes, and pies with the signature tenderness, flakiness, and loft. Folks like Social Roots, Carolina Ground, and Anson Mills have all taken on the challenge of making Southern heritage grits, grains, and flours readily available. They are cultivating a movement to create historic awareness in the food industry and have helped farmers rebuild regional grain systems. So now our amber waves of grain can be accessible from sea to shining sea!

The first thing you'll notice about cooking with whole-grain flours is the texture; some need more liquid when you mix them. Once you learn the nuances of working with these flours, you'll have the confidence to incorporate them in other recipes too. Keep in mind that these specialty flours can spoil more readily than all-purpose flour, so store them in the freezer to keep them fresh.

In this chapter, you'll find whole heritage grains and flours from grits and cornmeal to graham, rice, oat, rye, and spelt. You can make the delicious Rice Pudding with Jam or Toasted Rice Panna Cotta using the heritage rice called Carolina Gold. Cornmeal gives Lemon-Cornmeal Shortbread Cookies and Cornmeal Madeleines a delicious sweet, nutty flavor. Savor the malty flavors of rye flour in the Rye Brownies with Cacao Nibs, and discover some new baking ingredients to add to your pantry with delicious results.

Honey Graham Cracker Squares

PICTURED ON PAGE 298

There is something so satisfying and nostalgic about a graham cracker made from scratch. Graham flour is more coarsely ground than whole wheat flour. You can order it online from Anson Mills or find it in your local grocery store from Bob's Red Mill. The squares are finished with cinnamon sugar. Save any leftover cinnamon sugar to sprinkle on toast another day.

MAKES 24 SQUARES

FOR THE GRAHAM CRACKERS

3 cups (360 g) graham flour

1 cup (220 g) packed dark brown sugar

1 teaspoon (6 g) baking soda

1 teaspoon fine sea salt

½ teaspoon ground cinnamon

¼ cup (59 ml) whole milk

¼ cup (59 ml) honey

2 teaspoons pure vanilla extract

8 tablespoons (1 stick/113 g) cold unsalted butter,
    cut into ½-inch (1.5 cm) cubes

FOR THE CINNAMON SUGAR

¼ cup (50 g) granulated sugar

1 tablespoon ground cinnamon

To make the graham crackers: In a large bowl, whisk the graham flour, brown sugar, baking soda, salt, and cinnamon together until completely blended.

In a large measuring cup or small bowl, combine the milk, honey, and vanilla and stir until blended.

Add the butter to the flour mixture and toss to gently coat it. Then, using your fingertips, pinch and smear the butter into the flour. You should have various-sized pieces of butter ranging from sandy patches to pea-sized chunks, with some larger bits as well. Gradually add the milk mixture, stirring until the dough comes together.

Turn the dough out and divide it in half. Shape each piece into a disk, wrap the disks in plastic wrap, and refrigerate for at least 1 hour, and up to overnight, to rest. (*The dough can be refrigerated for up to 5 days or frozen, well wrapped, for up to 1 month. If frozen, defrost in the refrigerator overnight.*)

Position the racks in the middle and lower third of the oven and preheat the oven to 375°F (190°C). Line two baking sheets with parchment.

To make the cinnamon sugar: Combine the sugar and cinnamon in a small cup.

Remove the dough from the refrigerator. If it has been refrigerated overnight, let stand for 10 to 15 minutes before you roll it out.

On a floured surface, one at a time, roll out each piece of dough to a ⅛-inch (3 mm) thickness. Cut into 24 squares. Prick the squares with a fork and place them on the prepared baking sheets, spacing them 1 inch (3 cm) apart to allow for spreading. Sprinkle with the cinnamon sugar.

Bake for 14 to 16 minutes, rotating the pans halfway through and switching their positions, until the squares are dark golden. Let cool completely on the pans on wire racks.

The squares can be stored in an airtight container at room temperature for up to 5 days.

Lemon-Cornmeal Shortbread Cookies

PICTURED ON PAGE 308

This delicate butter shortbread cookie has an appealing balance of flavors and textures. Use your favorite cookie cutters.

MAKES 24 COOKIES

3 cups (375 g) unbleached all-purpose flour

1 cup (120 g) yellow cornmeal

2 teaspoons (9 g) baking powder, preferably
    aluminum-free

¼ teaspoon freshly grated nutmeg

1½ teaspoons fine sea salt

1 pound (454 g) unsalted butter, at room temperature

1½ cups (188 g) confectioners' sugar, plus more
    for dusting

1 tablespoon pure vanilla extract

Grated zest of 2 lemons

SPECIAL EQUIPMENT
One or more 3- to 4-inch (8 to 10 cm) cookie cutters

In a medium bowl, whisk together the flour, cornmeal, baking powder, nutmeg, and salt. Set aside.

In the bowl of a stand mixer fitted with the paddle attachment (or in a large mixing bowl, using a handheld mixer), cream the butter, confectioners' sugar, vanilla, and lemon zest together until light and fluffy, about 3 minutes. Add the flour mixture in thirds, mixing until just incorporated.

Scrape the dough out, divide it in half, and shape each piece into a disk. Wrap each one in plastic wrap and place in the refrigerator for at least 30 minutes. (*The dough can be refrigerated for up to 3 days. It can also be frozen, well wrapped, for up to 1 month; thaw overnight in the refrigerator before using.*)

To shape the cookies, remove one of the disks of dough from the refrigerator and let it sit at room temperature until it is soft enough to roll out but still quite firm (it will continue to soften as you work with it). Line two baking sheets with parchment.

Transfer the dough to a lightly floured surface. Place a piece of plastic wrap or parchment on top of it and, using a rolling pin, roll the dough out to a ¼-inch (6 mm) thickness. Using a 3- to 4-inch (8 to 10 cm) cookie cutter, cut out the cookies and arrange on the prepared baking sheets, leaving 1 inch (3 cm) between them to allow for spreading. Put the cookies in the refrigerator to chill for at least 30 minutes. Repeat with the remaining dough. Gather the scraps together and shape into a disk, chill, and then roll out and cut out more cookies.

Position the racks in the middle and lower third of the oven and preheat the oven to 325°F (165°C).

Bake the cookies for 12 to 14 minutes, rotating the pans halfway through and switching their positions, until lightly golden at the edges. Let the cookies cool completely on the pans on wire racks.

The cookies can be stored in an airtight container at room temperature for up to 5 days.

Cornmeal Madeleines

These delicate little butter cakes are delightful. Eat them topped with scoops of Vanilla Bean Ice Cream (page 344) or simply dusted with confectioners' sugar to accompany a cup of your favorite tea.

Starting the madeleines in cold pans helps with oven spring, giving them greater lift. You can bake these in corn stick or madeleine pans. If you use corn stick pans, which have only six molds each, you will have to cook the madeleines in batches; let the corn stick pans cool after baking the first batch, then wash them thoroughly and butter and flour them for the second batch. Or just bake one batch of madeleines and refrigerate the remaining batter to make another batch later; it will keep, tightly covered, for up to three days.

MAKES 24 MADELEINES

¾ cup (100 g) medium-grind white cornmeal

¾ cup (94 g) unbleached all-purpose flour

½ teaspoon (2 g) baking powder, preferably
    aluminum-free

¼ teaspoon fine sea salt

A few gratings of nutmeg

¼ cup (59 ml) whole milk

1 teaspoon rose water (see Resources, page 389)

8 tablespoons (1 stick/113 g) unsalted butter,
    at room temperature

½ cup (100 g) packed light brown sugar

¼ cup (50 g) granulated sugar

2 teaspoons grated orange zest

4 large (200 g) eggs, at room temperature

Confectioners' sugar for dusting

SPECIAL EQUIPMENT

Two madeleine pans or corn stick pans

Position a rack in the middle of the oven and preheat the oven to 350°F (175°C). Butter and flour two madeleine pans or corn stick pans and place them in the freezer.

Sift together the cornmeal, flour, baking powder, salt, and nutmeg into a small bowl. Set aside.

In a large measuring cup or small bowl, combine the milk and rose water. Set aside.

In the bowl of a stand mixer fitted with the paddle attachment (or in a large mixing bowl, using a handheld mixer), cream the butter, both sugars, and the orange zest together on medium-high speed until superlight and fluffy, 3 to 5 minutes. Add the eggs one (50 g) at a time, beating well after each addition. Using a rubber spatula, scrape down the sides and bottom of the bowl and mix for another minute.

With the mixer on low speed, add the flour mixture in thirds, alternating with the milk mixture and beginning and ending with the flour, mixing until just combined. Scrape down the sides and bottom of the bowl as necessary.

Spoon the batter into the prepared molds, filling each one about three-quarters full. Bake for 18 to 20 minutes, until the madeleines are golden and spring back to the touch. Gently unmold the madeleines onto a parchment-lined wire rack and let cool slightly.

Sprinkle the madeleines with confectioners' sugar and serve warm.

The madeleines can be stored in an airtight container at room temperature for up to 3 days.

Georgia Peach Cornmeal Cake

PICTURED ON PAGE 308

In early spring, the seas of pink peach blossoms lining Georgia highways are quite a sight, and they mean that in five to six months, it will be peach season once again—the time to make this treat. Cornmeal adds a great texture to the cake and balances the sweetness of the juicy ripe peaches.

SERVES 10

1 cup (200 g) granulated sugar

¾ cup (94 g) whole wheat flour

¾ cup (100 g) medium-grind yellow cornmeal

1½ teaspoons (7 g) baking powder, preferably
    aluminum-free

¼ teaspoon fine sea salt

¼ teaspoon ground mace

1 large (50 g) egg, lightly beaten

½ cup (118 ml) whole milk

6 tablespoons (85 g) unsalted butter, melted

1 teaspoon pure vanilla extract

5 large ripe peaches, halved, pitted, and sliced

Preheat the oven to 325°F (165°C). Generously grease a 9-inch (23 cm) square baking dish with butter.

In a large bowl, whisk together the sugar, flour, cornmeal, baking powder, salt, and mace.

In a medium bowl, stir together the egg, milk, butter, and vanilla.

Add the wet ingredients to the dry ingredients, gently folding them in until just combined. Pour the batter into the prepared baking dish. Top the batter with the sliced peaches.

Bake the cake for 55 to 65 minutes, until puffed up and golden brown. Let the cake cool in the pan on a wire rack for 20 minutes, then invert it onto another rack and turn right side up to cool.

Serve warm or at room temperature, with your favorite ice cream.

The cake can be stored in an airtight container at room temperature for up to 3 days.

Dried-Apple Oat Bars

Apples are high on the list of ingredients Southerners "put up" for the winter months. Traditionally the apples were either wrapped in newspaper and stored in boxes in a cold room or peeled and sliced, then dried in the sun or on racks over the kitchen stove. Thankfully, you can buy dried apples at the grocery store, or online, now. The combination of whole wheat flour and oats makes this a hearty apple-season treat.

MAKES 12 BARS

FOR THE APPLE FILLING

4 cups (946 ml) unsweetened apple cider

3 cups (255 g) dried apple slices

3 tablespoons light brown sugar

1 teaspoon ground cinnamon

¼ teaspoon ground mace

2 teaspoons fresh lemon juice

2 dashes Angostura bitters

FOR THE CRUST AND TOPPING

1¼ cups (156 g) whole wheat flour

1 teaspoon ground cinnamon

½ teaspoon fine sea salt

½ teaspoon (3 g) baking soda

¼ teaspoon ground mace

2¼ cups (202 g) old-fashioned rolled oats

10⅔ tablespoons (1⅓ sticks/151 g) unsalted butter

⅔ cup (133 g) packed light brown sugar

2 generous tablespoons cane syrup

To make the filling: In a large saucepan, combine the apple cider and apple slices. Cover and set aside for 1 hour.

Uncover the saucepan and bring the apple mixture to a boil over medium heat. Boil, stirring frequently, for about 10 minutes. Then reduce the heat and simmer, stirring occasionally, until the apples are soft and have absorbed most of the liquid, about 40 minutes. Remove from the heat.

Stir in the brown sugar, cinnamon, mace, lemon juice, and bitters. Cover with plastic wrap and set aside.

Position a rack in the middle of the oven and preheat the oven to 350°F (175°C). Lightly butter a 9-by-13-inch (23 by 33 cm) baking pan. Line with parchment, leaving an overhang on two opposite sides of the pan.

To make the crust and topping: In a large mixing bowl, combine the flour, cinnamon, salt, baking soda, mace, and oats. Set aside.

In a small saucepan, combine the butter, brown sugar, and cane syrup and stir over low heat until the butter is melted and the mixture is completely combined.

Pour the butter mixture over the oat mixture, stirring until well mixed but still crumbly.

Press half of the mixture evenly over the bottom of the prepared pan. Spread the apple filling evenly over the top. Scatter the remaining oat mixture on top of the fruit, pressing down as necessary, until the apples are completely covered.

Bake the bars for 30 to 40 minutes, until the topping is golden brown. Let cool completely in the pan on a wire rack.

Use the parchment "handles" to remove the bars from the pan, and cut into 12 squares.

The bars can be stored in an airtight container at room temperature for up to 1 day or refrigerated for up to 5 days.

Blueberry Spelt Crisp

PICTURED ON THE FOLLOWING PAGE

Spelt is an ancient grain similar to wheat without the bitterness. It will add a mild, slightly sweet, nutty flavor to your baked goods. Spelt flour also provides a bit more texture than wheat flour does, making it a good choice for the topping for this crisp. The filling is made with plump juicy blueberries, bright lemon zest, and fresh mint.

SERVES 8

FOR THE FILLING

5 cups (725 g) fresh blueberries

Grated zest of 1 lemon

1 tablespoon fresh lemon juice

⅓ cup (67 g) turbinado sugar

¼ teaspoon fine sea salt

1 tablespoon roughly chopped fresh mint

3 tablespoons unbleached all-purpose flour

FOR THE TOPPING

1 cup (90 g) old-fashioned rolled oats

¾ cup (100 g) spelt flour

¼ cup (50 g) turbinado sugar

½ teaspoon fine sea salt

½ teaspoon ground cinnamon

6 tablespoons (85 g) unsalted butter, melted and slightly cooled

Position a rack in the middle of the oven and preheat the oven to 400°F (205°C). Grease a

CLOCKWISE FROM TOP LEFT: GEORGIA PEACH CORNMEAL CAKE (PAGE 306), LEMON-CORNMEAL SHORTBREAD COOKIES (PAGE 302), RYE BROWNIES WITH CACAO NIBS (OPPOSITE), BLUEBERRY SPELT CRISP (PAGE 307)

2-quart (1.9 L) baking dish generously with butter. Line a baking sheet with parchment.

To make the filling: In a medium bowl, combine the blueberries, lemon zest and juice, sugar, salt, and mint and toss well. Cover with plastic wrap and set aside for 10 to 15 minutes to allow the berries to release some juices.

Meanwhile, make the topping: In a medium bowl, combine the oats, spelt flour, sugar, salt, and cinnamon and toss until well mixed. Slowly drizzle the butter over the mixture and toss with your hands until the dry ingredients are completely coated and the texture is crumbly. Spread on the prepared baking sheet in an even layer and set aside, uncovered, for 10 to 15 minutes to set up and dry out a bit.

Once the berries have macerated, sprinkle in the flour and toss until the flour is no longer visible. Pour the filling into the prepared baking dish.

Sprinkle the topping evenly over the filling, squeezing some of the topping together with your hands but leaving some loose bits too, so the baked topping will be both chewy and crisp.

Line the baking sheet with another sheet of parchment and put the baking dish on it. Bake the crisp for 35 to 45 minutes, until the topping is golden and the juices are bubbling.

Serve the crisp warm or at room temperature, maybe with a big scoop of ice cream.

The crisp is best the day it is made, but leftovers can be stored in the refrigerator, covered, for up to 2 days.

Rye Brownies with Cacao Nibs

The flavor of rye flour complements chocolate, adding subtle nuttiness and malt and caramel notes to make these fudgy brownies even better. Be sure to use good-quality chocolate here. The bars are topped off with cacao nibs and flaky sea salt for the ultimate chewy-crunchy-sweet-salty experience.

MAKES 12 BROWNIES

12 tablespoons (1½ sticks/170 g) unsalted butter, cut into
    1-inch (3 cm) cubes

10½ ounces (298 g) dark chocolate (60 to 70% cacao),
    chopped (about 1¾ cups)

1⅓ cups (136 g) whole-grain rye flour

½ cup (40 g) Dutch-processed cocoa powder

1 teaspoon fine sea salt

½ teaspoon (2 g) baking powder, preferably
    aluminum-free

2 cups (400 g) packed light brown sugar

5 large (250 g) eggs, at room temperature

1 tablespoon pure vanilla extract

2 tablespoons cacao nibs

1 teaspoon flaky sea salt, such as Maldon

Position a rack in the middle of the oven and preheat the oven to 350°F (175°C). Lightly butter a 9-by-13-inch (23 by 33 cm) baking pan. Line with parchment, leaving an overhang on two opposite sides of the pan.

Set a medium heatproof bowl over a saucepan of simmering water (make sure the bowl does not touch the water), add the butter and chocolate, and stir frequently until melted and smooth. Remove from the heat.

Sift together the rye flour, cocoa, fine sea salt, and baking powder into a medium bowl. Set aside.

In the bowl of a stand mixer fitted with the whisk attachment (or in a large mixing bowl, using a handheld mixer), whisk the brown sugar, eggs, and vanilla together until light and fluffy. Slowly add the chocolate mixture, whisking to combine. Gradually add the flour mixture in thirds,

Grits and Grains 309

mixing until no dry bits of flour remain. Rye has a reputation for being difficult to work with, so don't freak out if the batter looks grainy at this point.

Pour the batter into the prepared baking pan and smooth the top with a spatula. Tap the pan firmly on the countertop to remove any air pockets in the batter. Sprinkle the top evenly with the cacao nibs, followed by the flaky sea salt.

Bake for 25 to 30 minutes, until the brownies are set around the edges but still wiggle slightly in the center when jiggled. It's best to underbake these brownies, so they remain chewy and fudgy once cooled. Let cool completely in the pan on a wire rack.

Use the parchment "handles" to remove the brownies from the pan, and cut into 12 squares.

The brownies can be stored in an airtight container at room temperature for up to 1 day or refrigerated for up to 5 days.

Toasted Rice Panna Cotta

Panna cotta, or, literally, "cooked cream," is a pure and simple Italian dessert, traditionally made with little more than sweetened cream and gelatin. This version includes toasted rice, which is infused with sweet cream and vanilla. The flavor of the rice will surprise you; it takes on a floral quality that is present in every bite. This is a quick, light summer dessert that you can make in advance, and you don't even need to turn on the oven. Serve with fruit and a crisp brittle (see page 286).

SERVES 6

¼ cup (50 g) Carolina Gold or jasmine rice

½ cup (118 ml) whole milk

3 cups (710 ml) heavy cream

6 tablespoons (75 g) granulated sugar

1 plump vanilla bean, split lengthwise,
    seeds scraped out and reserved

¼ teaspoon fine sea salt

2 teaspoons (6 g) unflavored powdered gelatin

1 tablespoon cold water

SPECIAL EQUIPMENT

Six 4-ounce (118 ml) ramekins or a 2-quart (1.9 L)
    baking dish

In a large skillet or saucepan, toast the rice over medium-low heat, swirling the pan to prevent it from burning, just until the grains are aromatic and starting to color a little, about 5 minutes. Stir in the milk and cream and give it a good stir.

Transfer the milk-cream mixture to a bowl, cover with plastic wrap, and set aside to steep and cool slightly. Then place the bowl in the refrigerator to chill and steep for at least 1 hour, or, preferably, overnight.

Drain the rice in a fine-mesh strainer set over a bowl and discard the rice. You will be left with fragrant rice cream.

In a large heavy-bottomed saucepan, combine the cream mixture, sugar, vanilla seeds, and salt and bring to a simmer over medium-low heat, stirring frequently to prevent scorching.

Meanwhile, in a cup, sprinkle the gelatin evenly over the 1 tablespoon cold water and let stand until softened, about 5 minutes. Fill a large bowl with ice and water; set aside.

When the cream mixture has come to a simmer, remove from the heat and whisk in the gelatin until dissolved. Pour the mixture into a heatproof bowl, set it in the bowl of ice water, and chill, stirring often with a spatula, until very cold, 5 to 8 minutes.

Ladle the cream mixture into six 4-ounce (118 ml) ramekins or a 2-quart (1.9 L) baking dish. Cover with plastic wrap and refrigerate for at least 6 hours before serving.

If you used ramekins, to unmold the panna cotta, run a paring knife around the inside of each ramekin and release the panna cotta onto serving plates; or serve in the ramekins. Or spoon the panna cotta out of the baking dish to serve.

The panna cotta can be stored, tightly covered, in the refrigerator for up to 3 days.

Rice Pudding with Jam

Carolina Gold rice, a favorite in the South, makes an excellent rice pudding, but you can use jasmine rice instead if you prefer. In this recipe, the sweetened milky custard is flavored with a hint of orange liqueur, orange zest, and nutmeg. Serve the pudding topped with a spoonful of your favorite jam—any flavor you like—and a few slices of sweet peaches or pears, or layer the pudding with jam to make a parfait.

SERVES 12

¾ cup (145 g) Carolina Gold or jasmine rice

1½ cups (355 ml) water

½ teaspoon fine sea salt

4½ cups (1 L) half-and-half

½ cup (100 g) granulated sugar

1 large (50 g) egg

1 tablespoon triple sec or Grand Marnier

2 teaspoons pure vanilla extract

2 teaspoons grated orange zest

¼ teaspoon freshly grated nutmeg

1 cup (237 ml) good-quality jam, homemade
(see page 347) or store-bought, for serving
(optional)

Sliced peaches or pears for serving (optional)

In a large heavy saucepan, combine the rice, water, and salt and bring to a boil over medium heat. Give the rice a good stir, then turn the heat down to low and simmer, covered, for 6 to 8 minutes, until the rice has absorbed some of the liquid.

Stir in 4 cups (946 ml) of the half-and-half and the sugar and bring to a gentle boil over medium heat, then turn the heat down to low and simmer, uncovered, for 25 to 30 minutes, stirring occasionally to make sure the pudding is not sticking to the pan.

In a small bowl, combine the egg, triple sec, vanilla, orange zest, and nutmeg, then add the remaining ½ cup (118 ml) half-and-half, whisking until completely incorporated. Stir this mixture into the rice and cook until thickened, another 8 to 10 minutes. The rice should be soft but not mushy.

Transfer the pudding to a bowl and place a piece of plastic wrap directly on top of it to prevent a skin from forming as it cools.

Serve warm or chilled, with spoonfuls of jam and a few slices of fresh fruit, if desired.

The pudding can be stored, tightly covered, in the refrigerator for up to 3 days.

Cheesy Baked Grits

Grits are a staple that warms the soul in the morning or complements a good ol' Sunday meal. Grits are creamy and delicious, and baking them in a cheesy, eggy custard makes them even more so.

SERVES 12

1½ cups (255 g) coarse stone-ground grits

3½ cups (828 ml) whole milk

1 cup (237 ml) cold water

1½ teaspoons fine sea salt, plus more if needed

2 tablespoons unsalted butter

½ cup (118 ml) buttermilk or heavy cream

6 ounces (170 g) extra-sharp cheddar cheese, grated

6 ounces (170 g) Gruyère cheese, grated

¼ teaspoon freshly ground black pepper

5 large (250 g) eggs

Position a rack in the middle of the oven and preheat the oven to 325°F (165°C). Butter a 2½-quart (2.4 L) baking dish.

Place the grits in a sieve and rinse under cold water for a few minutes. Drain well.

In a large saucepan, combine 1½ cups (355 ml) of the milk, the water, and salt and set over medium heat. Slowly pour in the grits, whisking frequently to prevent lumps, then cook, stirring occasionally, until the mixture is thickened and the grits are tender but still have some bite, 15 to 20 minutes.

Whisk in the butter, followed by the buttermilk. Reduce the heat to low and simmer until the grits are tender and have thickened, 15 to 20 minutes. Remove from the heat and stir in the cheeses, a little at a time. Taste and add a pinch or two of salt if needed.

GRISTMILLS AND COMMUNITY

The gristmill, the place where farmers would bring grains they had grown to have them ground into meal and flour, was at one time the natural town center for news gathering, information, and fellowship. The community mill often shared space with a general store or the post office, and farmers could take care of business, socialize, and trade while their corn or wheat was milled. Many mills were built alongside a creek or river, so the mill could be water-powered. Some folks might also fish or swim near the mill, and local churches often used millponds for baptisms.

By the early 1900s, flour production had become industrialized, the grains going to larger companies using more efficient steel-roller mills. So most gristmills became a thing of the past. And thus, regional grains and their unique flavors were lost.

We are experiencing a regional grain renaissance in the South, and others across the country are following suit. You can now buy flours from community mills from folks like Carolina Ground in Asheville, North Carolina, and Old Mill of Guilford in Oak Ridge, North Carolina, among others all over the country. Seek them out.

In a large bowl, whisk together the remaining 2 cups (473 ml) milk, the pepper, and eggs. Slowly add the hot grits, whisking vigorously to combine. Pour the grits into the prepared dish. (*You can assemble this a day in advance and refrigerate it overnight, covered. Bake it directly from the refrigerator, adding about 15 minutes to the baking time.*)

Bake the grits for 45 minutes, or until lightly golden and puffed up on the edges. Serve warm.

Leftovers can be covered with plastic wrap and refrigerated for up to 3 days.

Sweet Grits Pie Bars

This bar cookie recipe takes grits into the sweet realm: A rich creamy custard is thickened with grits instead of flour, flavored with lemon zest and vanilla seeds, and poured atop a shortbread crust. Serve the bars with fresh summer berries and whipped cream.

MAKES 12 BARS

FOR THE CRUST

3 cups (375 g) unbleached all-purpose flour

½ cup (100 g) granulated sugar

½ teaspoon fine sea salt

½ pound (2 sticks/227 g) unsalted butter, melted and slightly cooled

FOR THE FILLING

8 large (400 g) eggs, at room temperature

3 cups (600 g) granulated sugar

¼ cup (45 g) medium-ground white grits

½ teaspoon fine sea salt

½ pound (2 sticks/227 g) unsalted butter, melted and cooled

1 plump vanilla bean, split lengthwise, seeds scraped out and reserved

Grated zest of 1 lemon

1 cup (237 ml) buttermilk

Position a rack in the middle of the oven and preheat the oven to 350°F (175°C). Lightly butter the bottom and sides of a 9-by-13-inch (23 by 33 cm) baking pan, then line with parchment, leaving an overhang on two opposite sides of the pan.

To make the crust: Sift together the flour, sugar, and salt into a large bowl. Slowly drizzle in the butter, stirring with a fork until the mixture looks moist and crumbly.

Using your hands, press the dough evenly over the bottom and up the sides of the baking pan. You can decorate the edges by crimping them with a fork or leave them rustic. Chill for about 15 minutes to set the crust.

Line the crust with parchment and fill with dried beans or rice or pie weights. Bake for 15 to 18 minutes, until the crust is just set and lightly browned. Remove the parchment and weights and set the crust on a wire rack to cool to room temperature. (Leave the oven on.)

To make the filling: In a large bowl, whisk together the eggs, sugar, grits, and salt. Add the butter, vanilla seeds, lemon zest, and buttermilk and whisk briskly until combined.

Pour the filling into the crust and bake for 35 to 40 minutes, until the filling is golden and puffed up at the edges and the center no longer looks wet but still wobbles slightly if jiggled; it will continue to set as it cools. Remove the bars from the oven and let cool completely in the pan on a wire rack.

Cut the bars and serve at room temperature or chilled.

The bars can be stored in an airtight container at room temperature for up to 1 day or refrigerated for up to 3 days.

Whole Wheat Chocolate Chip Cookies

Whole wheat flour and Southern cane syrup give these cookies a more complex flavor than their original nostalgic counterpart. Loaded with chocolate chunks and topped with flaky sea salt, they create a gooey-chewy close-your-eyes moment when you take a bite, especially if you enjoy them warm out of the oven.

MAKES 24 COOKIES

2½ cups (313 g) whole wheat flour

1⅓ cups (167 g) unbleached all-purpose flour, plus 1 tablespoon

1½ teaspoons fine sea salt

¾ teaspoon (4 g) baking soda

¾ pound (3 sticks/340 g) unsalted butter, at room temperature

1⅓ cups (267 g) packed light brown sugar

1 cup (200 g) granulated sugar

1 tablespoon cane syrup

1 teaspoon pure vanilla extract

2 large (100 g) eggs plus 1 large (19 g) egg yolk, at room temperature

3 cups (18 ounces/510 g) dark chocolate chunks or baking wafers, such as Guittard

Sift together both flours, the salt, and baking soda into a bowl. Set aside.

In the bowl of a stand mixer fitted with the paddle attachment (or in a large mixing bowl, using a handheld mixer), cream the butter and both sugars together on medium speed until superlight and fluffy, 3 to 5 minutes. Beat in the cane syrup and vanilla. Add the eggs one (50 g) at a time, mixing well after each addition and scraping down the sides and bottom of the bowl with a rubber spatula as necessary. Turn the speed down to low and add the flour mixture in thirds, mixing until just combined. With the mixer running, add the chocolate chunks and mix until they are evenly distributed throughout the dough.

Remove the bowl from the mixer stand (if using) and finish mixing by hand to make sure no bits of flour or butter are hiding on the bottom of the bowl and the dough is thoroughly mixed.

Cover the bowl with plastic wrap and chill the dough in the refrigerator until slightly firm, about 30 minutes. Position the racks in the middle and lower third of the oven and preheat the oven to 350°F (175°C). Line two baking sheets with parchment.

Use a large ice cream scoop or a ¼-cup (59 ml) measuring cup to form the cookies and place on the prepared baking sheets, leaving 2 inches (5 cm) between them to allow for spreading. (*If you like, you can freeze the cookies on the baking sheets until firm, then transfer to ziplock bags and freeze for up to 6 months. Bake directly from the freezer, adding 4 minutes to the baking time.*)

Bake the cookies for 15 to 18 minutes, rotating the pans halfway through and switching their positions, until golden brown around the edges but still pale in the centers. Let the cookies cool completely on the pans on wire racks.

The cookies can be stored in an airtight container at room temperature for up to 3 days.

Mushroom Hand Pies

For these savory hand pies, a flaky whole wheat pastry crust holds a filling of wild mushrooms and herbs. They are the perfect pass-around for a dinner party, or take them on a weekend picnic.

MAKES 24 HAND PIES

1 recipe dough for Whole Wheat Piecrust (page 238), chilled

FOR THE FILLING

2 tablespoons olive oil

½ pound (227 g) mixed mushrooms, washed, trimmed, and finely chopped

1 small yellow onion, diced (¼-inch/6 mm pieces)

½ teaspoon fine sea salt

1 tablespoon unbleached all-purpose flour

1½ tablespoons sherry

1 tablespoon finely chopped fresh rosemary

¼ teaspoon freshly ground black pepper

A few gratings of nutmeg

¼ cup (25 g) coarsely grated Parmesan cheese

¼ cup (60 g) sour cream

1 large (50 g) egg, lightly beaten with a pinch of fine sea salt, for egg wash

SPECIAL EQUIPMENT

4-inch (10 cm) biscuit cutter or round cookie cutter

Line two baking sheets with parchment. If the dough has been chilled for longer than an hour, it may need to sit at room temperature for 10 to 15 minutes before you roll it out.

On a lightly floured surface, roll out one disk of dough at a time to a ⅛-inch (3 mm) thickness. Using a 4-inch (10 cm) biscuit cutter or round cookie cutter, cut out 16 rounds (reroll the scraps, to get 24 rounds total). Place the rounds on the baking sheets, cover, and refrigerate while you make the filling.

To make the filling: In a large skillet, heat the oil over medium-high heat until hot. Add the mushrooms, onion, and salt and cook until the liquid the mushrooms release has evaporated and the mushrooms and onions are caramelized, about 5 minutes.

Sprinkle in the flour, stirring well. Add the sherry, rosemary, pepper, nutmeg, and Parmesan, stirring well. Stir in the sour cream. Remove from the heat.

Remove the dough rounds from the refrigerator. Divide the filling among them, placing 1 rounded teaspoon on each one. Lightly brush the edges of each circle with egg wash (reserve the remaining egg wash). Fold the dough over the filling to make a half-moon shape and press the edges of the dough to seal. Use a fork or your fingers to crimp the edges of the hand pies. With a sharp knife, make several small slits for steam vents in the top of each hand pie.

Refrigerate the hand pies for about 30 minutes. (*They can also be frozen for up to 1 month. Bake straight from the freezer, adding 5 to 8 minutes to the baking time.*)

Position the racks in the middle and lower third of the oven and preheat the oven to 375°F (190°C).

Remove the hand pies from the refrigerator and brush the tops with the egg wash. Bake for 18 to 20 minutes, rotating the pans halfway through and switching their positions, until the hand pies are golden brown. Let cool for 10 minutes, then serve warm.

Once cooled, the hand pies can be stored in an airtight container in the refrigerator for up to 3 days. Reheat in a preheated 350°F (175°C) oven for 10 to 15 minutes before serving.

Sweet Potato Tarte Tatin

The crust of this savory tarte Tatin is made with whole wheat dough. Pairing fresh herbs and goat cheese with savory vegetables that caramelize in the pan results in a delicious dish that is irresistible.

SERVES 12

FOR THE FILLING

2 medium sweet potatoes, peeled and sliced into
     ½-inch (1.5 cm) rounds

2 medium carrots, peeled and sliced into ½-inch
     (1.5 cm) rounds

1 medium parsnip, peeled and sliced into ½-inch
     (1.5 cm) rounds

1 small sweet onion, sliced into ½-inch (1.5 cm) rounds

¼ cup (59 ml) olive oil

½ teaspoon fine sea salt, plus a pinch

½ teaspoon freshly ground black pepper

½ teaspoon smoked paprika

⅓ cup (67 g) packed light brown sugar

2 tablespoons water

1 tablespoon rice wine vinegar

1 tablespoon unsalted butter

1 tablespoon chopped fresh rosemary

1 tablespoon chopped fresh sage

¼ pound (113 g) soft goat cheese

1 disk dough for Whole Wheat Piecrust (page 238), chilled

Position a rack in the middle of the oven and preheat the oven to 400°F (205°C). Line two baking sheets with parchment. Have a 10-inch (25 cm) cast-iron or ovenproof skillet at hand.

To make the filling: In a large bowl, toss the sweet potatoes, carrots, parsnip, and onion with the oil. Season with the salt, pepper, and paprika and give it all another good toss with a large spoon.

Transfer the vegetables to one of the prepared baking sheets, spreading them out in a single layer.

Roast for 30 to 35 minutes, until lightly golden and tender. Let cool. (*The vegetables can be roasted up to 4 hours in advance and set aside, covered, at room temperature until ready to use.*)

Meanwhile, roll out the dough. If it has been chilled, it will need to sit at room temperature for 15 to 20 minutes before you roll it out.

On a lightly floured work surface, with a lightly floured rolling pin, roll the dough into a 13-inch (33 cm) circle that is ⅛ inch (3 mm) thick. Place the dough on the second prepared baking sheet and set aside.

In a medium saucepan, combine the sugar and water and cook over medium-high heat, stirring, until the sugar dissolves. Then continue to cook, without stirring but swirling the pan occasionally to check the color, until the caramel is amber colored, 5 to 7 minutes. Watch carefully so it does not burn.

Remove the pan from the heat and add the vinegar and a pinch of salt. Add the butter and stir until melted and completely combined.

Pour the caramel into the skillet, swirling the pan to completely coat the bottom. Sprinkle the rosemary and sage evenly over the caramel. Arrange the sweet potatoes, carrots, and parsnip over the caramel. Layer on the sweet onions. Crumble the goat cheese on top.

Drape the crust over the vegetables and tuck the edges into the skillet. Dock the dough all over with the tines of a fork.

Bake the tarte Tatin for 20 minutes, then reduce the oven temperature to 350°F (175°C) and bake for 18 to 20 minutes longer, until the crust is golden brown.

Remove from the oven and let cool for about 5 minutes, then very, very carefully invert the tart onto a large serving plate. Cut into wedges and serve.

Custards, Puddings, and Cobblers

OLD RECIPE CARDS should be treated like family heirlooms. The best ones have dog-eared edges, notes, and splatters, like works of art. Whether they are shared among friends, found hidden in old cookbooks, or passed down for generations, they are a treasure to behold. Old recipes tell a story of days gone by and are a glimpse into the lives of our ancestors. But instructions on old recipe cards tend to be vague at best, and sometimes they show only a list of ingredients (yikes!). When that is the case, the cards are best used for inspiration to spark an idea. Skilled bakers often know the secret code and can use such old recipes as a starting point to imagine their own re-creation of the dish.

Fortunately, though, most custards, puddings, and cobblers follow tried-and-true methods. These passed-down recipes can be helpful enough to imagine the tastes and textures of old Southern recipes—even when the ingredients and recipe steps aren't explicitly spelled out. The ingredients are few, but the flavors are so easy to customize to make a standout dish. The recipes in this chapter range from Cleora's Baked Fudge and Banana Pudding to Strawberry Custard and Creole Bread Pudding. Apple Brown Betty, Blackberry Sonker, Peach Cobbler, Profiteroles, and Mini Baked Alaskas are other highlights in this diverse assortment of recipes and history to add to your baking repertoire.

Butterscotch Pudding

PICTURED ON PAGE 320

How can a few simple ingredients create something so sublime? This recipe requires a bit of finesse and patience to wait for the caramelized sugar to be just right. But the result is a creamy, sweet, and salty pudding with a rich caramel flavor.

SERVES 8

3½ cups (828 ml) heavy cream

½ vanilla bean, split lengthwise, seeds scraped
   out and reserved (see Tip)

9 large (171 g) egg yolks, at room temperature

1¼ cups (250 g) packed light brown sugar

1 tablespoon water

4 tablespoons (57 g) unsalted butter

1 teaspoon fine sea salt

SPECIAL EQUIPMENT
Eight 4-inch (10 cm) ramekins

Position a rack in the lower third of the oven and preheat the oven to 300°F (150°C). Arrange eight 4-inch (10 cm) ramekins in a large deep roasting pan that will hold them comfortably; set aside.

In a large measuring cup or medium bowl, combine the cream and vanilla bean seeds. Set aside to infuse and to allow the cream to come up to room temperature.

In a large heatproof bowl, whisk the egg yolks just to blend. Set aside.

In a medium saucepan, combine the brown sugar, water, and butter and cook over medium heat, stirring, just until the sugar has dissolved and the butter has melted. Then continue cooking, without stirring, swirling the pan occasionally to check the color, until it becomes a golden caramel color, about 5 minutes; watch carefully, because the color can change quickly. Gradually whisk in the cream, being careful, as it will bubble and splatter briskly, then whisk constantly until combined. Remove the pan from the heat and stir in the salt.

Add the caramel mixture to the egg yolks in a slow, steady stream, whisking constantly.

Strain the custard through a fine-mesh sieve into a large liquid measuring cup.

Divide the mixture among the ramekins, then add enough hot water to the roasting pan to come halfway up the sides of the ramekins. Cover the pan tightly with heavy-duty aluminum foil and bake for 45 minutes to 1 hour, until the puddings are set around the edges but still wiggle slightly in the center when jiggled.

Remove the roasting pan from the oven and, as soon as the ramekins are cool enough to handle, remove the puddings from the water bath and set on a wire rack to cool completely. Then chill for at least 3 hours, and up to overnight, covered, before serving.

The puddings can be stored, tightly covered, in the refrigerator, for up to 1 week.

Tip: Vanilla Sugar

When a recipe calls for just the seeds from a vanilla bean, don't discard that bean!
Use it for Vanilla Bean Sugar—see page 376.

Cleora's Baked Fudge

This baked fudge was one of the specialties at Cleora's Pastry Shop and Catering company, which opened in 1962, in Tulsa, Oklahoma. Cleora Butler was a Black cook and caterer known for her elaborate high-society parties and special brunches. Her home was also a favorite destination of Black musicians like Cab Calloway, who had to eat in private homes when they were traveling through the segregated South. The famous fudge is actually a rich chocolate custard with pecans that is baked in a water bath so that a delicious crusty top develops. Serve it with Chantilly Cream.

SERVES 6

4 large (200 g) eggs, at room temperature

2 cups (400 g) granulated sugar

¼ teaspoon fine sea salt

¼ cup (20 g) Dutch-processed cocoa powder

4 teaspoons unbleached all-purpose flour

2 teaspoons pure vanilla extract

½ pound (2 sticks/227 g) unsalted butter, melted

1 cup (120 g) chopped pecans

1 recipe Chantilly Cream (page 373) for serving

SPECIAL EQUIPMENT

Six 4-inch (10 cm) ramekins

Position a rack in the middle of the oven and preheat the oven to 325°F (165°C). Arrange six 4-inch (10 cm) ramekins in a deep roasting pan large enough to hold them comfortably; set aside.

In the bowl of a stand mixer fitted with the whisk attachment (or in a large mixing bowl, using a handheld mixer), beat the eggs on medium-high speed until super pale in color, about 3 minutes. Turn the mixer down to low and add the sugar and salt, mixing until well blended. Add the cocoa and flour and mix until just combined. Add the vanilla. With the mixer still running on low, gradually pour in the melted butter, mixing until just combined. Add the pecans and mix until just incorporated.

Using an ice cream scoop or a large spoon, divide the batter among the ramekins. Add enough hot water to the roasting pan to come about halfway up the sides of the ramekins.

Bake for 40 to 50 minutes, until the tops form a crust but the custard still wiggles slightly when jiggled. Do not overbake. The custard will continue to set as it cools. Remove the roasting pan from the oven and, as soon as they are cool enough to handle, carefully remove the ramekins from the water bath.

Serve with big dollops of the Chantilly cream. The fudge is best eaten the same day it's made, but leftovers can be covered and stored in the refrigerator for up to 3 days.

Strawberry Custard

PICTURED ON PAGE 332

This custard is lighter than most, because the eggs are separated and then the whites folded into it, suspending the slices of fruit in a rich cloud of heaven. The custard comes together quickly, making it a great dessert to whip up and bake just before dinner.

SERVES 6 TO 8

1 cup (165 g) sliced fresh strawberries

4 large (200 g) eggs, separated

1 cup (200 g) granulated sugar

2 tablespoons unsalted butter, melted

1 tablespoon unbleached all-purpose flour

½ teaspoon fine sea salt

1 teaspoon pure vanilla extract

1 cup (237 ml) whole milk, at room temperature

1 recipe Chantilly Cream (page 373), flavored with
   rose water, for serving

Position a rack in the middle of the oven and preheat the oven to 350°F (175°C).

Spread the strawberries evenly over the bottom of a 9-inch (23 cm) square baking dish.

In a medium bowl, whisk the egg yolks and sugar together until blended. Add the melted butter, flour, salt, vanilla, and milk, in that order, whisking until thoroughly combined.

In the bowl of a stand mixer fitted with the whisk attachment (or in a large mixing bowl, using a handheld mixer), whip the egg whites until soft peaks have formed. Whisk in the egg yolk mixture and continue whisking until the mixture has the appearance of a light custard, about 2 minutes.

Pour the custard over the strawberries. Bake for 25 to 35 minutes, until the custard is set around the edges and the center wobbles just slightly if jiggled. Remove the custard from the oven and let it cool slightly.

Serve warm with big dollops of the Chantilly cream.

Banana Pudding with Billowy Meringue

Banana pudding is ubiquitous at gatherings across all regions of the South. This classic dessert is a rich vanilla custard layered with bananas and vanilla wafer cookies (homemade are best, but store-bought wafers will work in a pinch). The Billowy Meringue is baked right atop the pudding. Serve hot or cold; it's delicious either way.

SERVES 12

FOR THE PUDDING

8 large (152 g) egg yolks

1 cup (200 g) granulated sugar

6 tablespoons (50 g) cornstarch

½ teaspoon fine sea salt

4 cups (946 ml) half-and-half

½ teaspoon ground cardamom

1 vanilla bean, split lengthwise,
   seeds scraped out and reserved

6 tablespoons (85 g) unsalted butter, cut into
   tablespoon-sized pieces, at room temperature

24 vanilla wafers, homemade (page 251) or store-bought

8 large bananas, peeled and sliced

Billowy Meringue (page 214), just prepared

To make the pudding: In a large heatproof bowl, whisk the egg yolks, sugar, cornstarch, and salt together until well blended. Set aside.

In a large heavy-bottomed saucepan, combine the half-and-half, cardamom, split vanilla bean, and vanilla seeds and bring to just under a boil. Whisk about 1 cup (237 ml) of the half-and-half mixture into the egg yolk mixture to temper the eggs, so they don't curdle. Then whisk the egg yolk mixture into the pan with the remainder of the half-and-half mixture. Discard the vanilla bean.

Cook over medium heat, whisking frequently and being careful to whisk all over the bottom of the pan to prevent burning, until the mixture has thickened, 5 to 8 minutes. The surface will start to steam and burp a little. Remove from the heat and whisk in the butter 2 tablespoons at a time until it is melted and the pudding is smooth and silky.

(Continued)

Place a piece of plastic wrap directly on top of the pudding so that a skin does not form. Set aside to cool for about 30 minutes, or until it reaches room temperature.

Position a rack in the middle of the oven and preheat the oven to 350°F (175°C).

To assemble the pudding: Spoon a thin layer of the pudding over the bottom of a 9-by-13-inch (23 by 33 cm) baking dish. Top with a layer of vanilla wafers. Arrange a layer of sliced bananas over the cookies. Spoon on more pudding and continue layering, ending with custard.

Spoon the meringue over the entire surface of the pudding and use a spatula to spread it in big, luscious swirls. Bake for 8 to 10 minutes, until the meringue is golden brown.

The pudding can be stored, loosely covered, in the refrigerator for up to 2 days.

Chocolate Custard Pots

These dense, dark, creamy baked custards, like French pots de crème, are a chocolate lover's dream. You can make them up to five days in advance, for easy-peasy entertaining. Serve with Chantilly Cream.

SERVES 8

1½ cups (355 ml) heavy cream

1 cup (237 ml) whole milk

½ cup (100 g) granulated sugar

1½ teaspoons fine sea salt

1 cup (6 ounces/170 g) coarsely chopped good-quality
    dark chocolate (at least 60 to 70% cacao)

1 teaspoon pure vanilla extract

6 large (114 g) egg yolks, at room temperature

1 recipe Chantilly Cream (page 373) for serving

SPECIAL EQUIPMENT

Eight 4-inch (10 cm) ramekins

Position a rack in the lower third of the oven and preheat the oven to 250°F (120°C). Arrange eight 4-inch (10 cm) ramekins in a large deep roasting pan that holds them comfortably; set aside.

In a medium saucepan, combine the cream, milk, sugar, and salt and bring to a boil over medium heat, whisking to dissolve the sugar and salt. Add the chopped chocolate and whisk gently until it has melted. Remove from the heat and stir in the vanilla.

In a medium bowl, lightly beat the egg yolks. Pour the egg yolks in a slow, steady stream into the chocolate-cream mixture, whisking until smooth.

Divide the mixture among the ramekins. Pour enough hot water into the roasting pan to come halfway up the sides of the ramekins. Cover the pan tightly with heavy-duty aluminum foil and bake for 1 hour and 15 minutes, or until the custards just wobble slightly in the center when jiggled.

Remove the roasting pan from the oven and, as soon as the ramekins are cool enough to handle, remove the custards from the water bath and set on a wire rack to cool completely. Then chill for at least 3 hours, and up to overnight, covered, before serving with the Chantilly cream.

The custards can be stored, tightly covered, in the refrigerator, for up to 5 days.

Boiled Custard

It's a sweet Southern tradition to give jars of custard as gifts during the holiday season. Some folks add a little bourbon (a tablespoon or so) in addition to the vanilla in this boiled custard. It is such a simple recipe to make, and yet, like all good things, it takes care to get it just right.

SERVES 6 TO 8

6 large (114 g) egg yolks, at room temperature

1½ cups (300 g) granulated sugar

1 teaspoon fine sea salt

6 cups (1.4 L) whole milk

2 cups (473 ml) heavy cream

1 vanilla bean, split lengthwise,
    seeds scraped out and reserved

In a large heatproof bowl, whisk together the egg yolks, sugar, and salt. Set aside.

In a medium saucepan, combine the milk, cream, split vanilla bean, and vanilla seeds and bring to just under a boil. Whisk about 1 cup (237 ml) of the hot milk mixture into the egg yolk mixture to temper the yolks, so they don't curdle. Whisk the egg yolk mixture back into the pan with the remainder of the milk mixture; remove the vanilla bean.

Cook over very low heat, whisking frequently and making sure to whisk all over the bottom of the pan to prevent burning, until the mixture has thickened, 5 to 7 minutes. The surface will start to steam and burp a little.

Remove from the heat and place a piece of plastic wrap directly on top of the custard so that a skin does not form. Set aside to cool to room temperature, then refrigerate for at least 2 hours, or up to overnight, covered, before serving.

The custard can be stored, tightly covered, in the refrigerator for up to 3 days.

Sweet Tea Custard

This recipe is a nod to that enduring symbol of Southern hospitality: a tall cold glass of sweet tea. The rich, creamy egg custard is infused with your favorite loose tea and sweetened with honey.

SERVES 6 TO 8

1⅓ cups (315 ml) heavy cream

3½ tablespoons honey

⅓ cup (67 g) granulated sugar

½ teaspoon fine sea salt

1 vanilla bean, split lengthwise, seeds scraped out and reserved

2 tablespoons of your favorite loose tea, such as Darjeeling, chamomile, or Earl Grey

5 large (95 g) egg yolks, at room temperature

SPECIAL EQUIPMENT

Six to eight 4-inch (10 cm) ramekins

Preheat the oven to 300°F (150°C). Arrange six to eight 4-inch (10 cm) ramekins in a large deep roasting pan that holds them comfortably; set aside.

In a large saucepan, combine the cream, honey, sugar, salt, and vanilla bean and seeds and bring to just under a boil over medium-high heat; steam will start to rise from the surface. Remove from the heat, add the tea, cover with plastic wrap, and let steep for 10 minutes.

In a medium bowl, whisk the egg yolks to blend. Whisking constantly, add a little of the hot cream mixture to temper the eggs, so they don't curdle. Gradually whisk in the remaining cream mixture. Strain the mixture through a fine-mesh sieve set over a large measuring cup.

Divide the mixture among the ramekins. Add enough hot water to the roasting pan to come halfway up the sides of the ramekins. Cover the pan with heavy-duty aluminum foil and bake for 45 to 55 minutes, until the custards are set around the edges and just wobble slightly in the center when jiggled.

Remove the roasting pan from the oven and, as soon as the ramekins are cool enough to handle, remove the custards from the water bath and set on a wire rack to cool completely. Then chill for at least 3 hours, and up to overnight, covered, before serving.

The custards can be stored, tightly covered, in the refrigerator for up to 5 days.

Tipsy Squire Trifle

PICTURED ON PAGE 332

This is a Southern interpretation of a classic English dessert. Pound cake squares sandwiched with jam are layered with macerated fresh berries—given a shot of sherry, if desired—and a velvety vanilla custard. To save time, you can prepare the trifle ahead and refrigerate it overnight. You can make the trifle in one large bowl or treat your guests to their own trifle in tall parfait glasses. Top with dollops of Chantilly Cream.

SERVES 8

FOR THE CUSTARD

5 large (95 g) egg yolks, at room temperature

6 tablespoons (75 g) granulated sugar

3 tablespoons cornstarch, sifted

¼ teaspoon fine sea salt

2 cups (473 ml) whole milk

1 tablespoon pure vanilla extract

2½ tablespoons unsalted butter, cut into
    ½-inch (1.5 cm) cubes, at room temperature

FOR THE FRUIT

5 cups (600 g) mixed fresh berries, such as raspberries,
    blueberries, blackberries, and sliced strawberries

½ cup (100 g) granulated sugar or 3 tablespoons flavored
    syrup (see Resources, page 389)

¼ cup (59 ml) sweet sherry or your favorite liquor (optional)

1 recipe Cold-Oven Pound Cake (page 80)

½ cup (118 ml) jam (any flavor)

1 recipe Chantilly Cream (page 373)

SPECIAL EQUIPMENT

3-quart (2.8 L) trifle bowl or large glass bowl

To make the custard: In a large heatproof bowl, whisk the egg yolks, sugar, cornstarch, and salt together until thick and pale in color. Set aside.

In a medium saucepan, heat the milk over medium heat to just under a boil. While whisking, pour about 1 cup (237 ml) of the hot milk into the egg yolk mixture to temper the eggs, so they won't curdle. Continuing to whisk, add the remainder of the milk in a steady stream. Transfer the mixture to the saucepan and cook over medium heat, whisking constantly, until the custard has thickened, 4 to 6 minutes.

Remove from the heat and whisk in the vanilla. Let the custard sit for about 2 minutes to cool slightly, then whisk in the butter until it is melted and the custard is smooth and silky. Pour the custard into a clean bowl.

Place a piece of plastic wrap directly on top of the custard so that a skin does not form and let cool to room temperature, about 30 minutes, then cover the bowl with plastic wrap and refrigerate for at least 2 hours, and up to overnight. (If you are in a hurry, you can set the bowl of custard in a larger bowl filled with ice and whisk occasionally for about 15 minutes, until chilled.)

Meanwhile, macerate the fruit: In a large bowl, toss the fruit with the sugar and the sherry or liquor, if using, until well combined. Refrigerate for at least 30 minutes, and up to 2 hours.

To assemble the trifle: Cut the pound cake into eight 1-inch-thick (3 cm) slices, and then slice each piece into quarters. Top each of 8 squares of cake with about 1 rounded teaspoon of the jam and place 8 plain cake squares on top to make sandwiches. Repeat with the remaining cake and jam.

Arrange a layer of cake sandwiches over the bottom of the trifle bowl. (The proportions of the layers will vary depending on the size of your bowl.) Add a layer of berries, with some of their juices, then spoon on a layer of custard. Repeat with the remaining cake, berries, and custard. Cover with plastic wrap and chill until ready to serve.

Just before serving, top the trifle with big, heaping dollops of the Chantilly cream.

The trifle can be stored, tightly covered, in the refrigerator for up to 3 days.

Corn Pudding

Also known as corn soufflé or spoon corn, this dish is a staple on the Southern sideboard, especially during the holidays. If you don't have "put up" fresh corn, frozen corn will work just fine, but the can of creamed corn is essential to get the creamy custardy texture. Serve as a side dish or, as in the South, a dessert.

SERVES 8

¼ cup (50 g) granulated sugar

3 tablespoons unbleached all-purpose flour

2 teaspoons (9 g) baking powder, preferably
   aluminum-free

1½ teaspoons fine sea salt

½ teaspoon freshly grated nutmeg

6 large (300 g) eggs, at room temperature

2 cups (473 ml) heavy cream

8 tablespoons (1 stick/113 g) unsalted butter, melted

5 cups (725 g) fresh (from 6 to 7 large ears)
   or frozen corn kernels

One 15-ounce (425 g) can creamed corn, not drained

Butter a 2-quart (1.9 L) baking dish.

In a large bowl, whisk together the sugar, flour, baking powder, salt, and nutmeg. Set aside.

In a medium bowl, whisk together the eggs, cream, and butter.

Make a well in the center of the dry ingredients and gently fold in the cream mixture until just combined. Stir in the corn kernels and creamed corn until thoroughly blended. Pour the mixture into the prepared baking dish.

Bake until puffed up and lightly golden, about 30 minutes. Serve hot.

Creole Bread Pudding

PICTURED ON PAGE 332

This recipe was inspired by Louisiana Creole cuisine, and using day-old crusty French bread is the key to its success. As the pudding bakes under a tent of foil, the bread softens in the rich, creamy custard. Once the foil is removed, the bread gets toasted just enough to give it some crispy edges and to add a bit of textural diversity. The boozy, buttery sauce takes it to the next level and makes it a grown-folks' dessert that is sure to please a crowd—Southern comfort at its best!

SERVES 12

FOR THE BREAD PUDDING

9 cups (270 g) 2-inch (5 cm) cubes crusty French
   baguette (1½ pounds/680 g bread)

4 cups (946 ml) half-and-half

12 tablespoons (1½ sticks/170 g) unsalted butter

1 cup (200 g) packed light brown sugar

½ cup (100 g) granulated sugar

3 tablespoons pure vanilla extract

5 large (250 g) eggs, lightly beaten

1 cup (145 g) golden raisins

FOR THE BOURBON BUTTER SAUCE

4 tablespoons (57 g) unsalted butter

2 tablespoons bourbon

1 cup (125 g) confectioners' sugar

½ cup (118 ml) heavy cream

To make the bread pudding: Position a rack in the middle of the oven and preheat the oven to 350°F (175°C). Lightly butter a 9-by-13-inch (23 by 33 cm) baking dish.

Put the bread in a large bowl and pour the half-and-half over it, tossing gently to moisten the bread. Set aside while you prepare the custard.

In a medium saucepan, melt the butter over medium heat. Remove from the heat, add both sugars and the vanilla, and stir until well combined and smooth. Add the beaten eggs, stirring until combined and smooth.

Pour the custard mixture over the bread, tossing gently until well combined.

Pour the bread mixture into the prepared baking dish and spread it evenly. Sprinkle the raisins over the top and gently work them into the pudding; press down on the mixture if necessary to make sure the bread is entirely covered by liquid.

Cover the baking dish with aluminum foil and bake for 55 minutes. Remove the foil and bake for an additional 10 to 15 minutes, until the bread pudding is golden brown on top. Remove from the oven and set aside while you prepare the sauce.

To make the bourbon butter sauce: In a medium saucepan, melt the butter over medium heat. Remove from the heat and add the bourbon and confectioners' sugar, stirring until smooth. Slowly whisk in the cream until smooth.

Pour the sauce over the top of the bread pudding and serve.

The pudding is best served warm, but leftovers can be covered and refrigerated for up to 3 days.

Sweet Potato Soufflé

Sweet potatoes always have a place on the Southern table. Here mashed sweet potatoes are baked into a soufflé laced with butter and warm spices, enriched with eggs and half-and-half, and covered in a toasted marshmallow–like meringue. Serve it as a side dish or as a dessert.

SERVES 12

FOR THE SOUFFLÉ
6 sweet potatoes (4 pounds/1.8 kg)
2 tablespoons vegetable oil
½ pound (2 sticks/227 g) unsalted butter
¼ cup (50 g) packed light brown sugar
¼ cup (59 ml) cane syrup
1 teaspoon grated orange zest or Citrus Paste
 (page 383), made with oranges
1 teaspoon fine sea salt
½ teaspoon ground cinnamon
¼ teaspoon ground ginger
¼ teaspoon freshly grated nutmeg
1½ cups (355 ml) half-and-half

2 large (100 g) eggs, lightly beaten
1 teaspoon pure vanilla extract

FOR THE MERINGUE TOPPING
3 large (90 g) egg whites
¼ teaspoon cream of tartar
½ cup (100 g) granulated sugar
¼ cup (50 g) packed light brown sugar
½ teaspoon pure vanilla extract

OPTIONAL SPECIAL EQUIPMENT
Kitchen blowtorch

To make the soufflé: Preheat the oven to 375°F (190°C). Line a baking sheet with aluminum foil or parchment. Butter a 2-quart (1.9 L) baking dish.

Peel the sweet potatoes and cut them into 1-inch (3 cm) cubes. Place the potatoes on the prepared baking sheet and toss them with the vegetable oil. Cover with foil and bake for 50 to 60 minutes, until tender. Set aside to cool. (Leave the oven on.)

(Continued)

CLOCKWISE FROM TOP LEFT: STRAWBERRY CUSTARD (PAGE 324), CREOLE BREAD PUDDING (PAGE 330),
TIPSY SQUIRE TRIFLE (PAGE 329), APPLE BROWN BETTY (OPPOSITE)

In the bowl of a stand mixer fitted with the paddle attachment (or in a large mixing bowl, using a handheld mixer), beat the sweet potatoes on medium speed until smooth. Pull off any stringy bits left on the paddle and discard. (You can also use a food processor to puree the sweet potatoes. Alternatively, you can mash them with a potato masher.)

Transfer the sweet potatoes to a large heavy-bottomed pot, add the butter, brown sugar, cane syrup, orange zest, salt, cinnamon, ginger, nutmeg, half-and-half, eggs, and vanilla, and cook over medium heat, stirring frequently, until the butter is melted and the mixture is smooth.

Transfer the sweet potato mixture to the prepared baking dish and smooth the top. Bake for 20 minutes.

Meanwhile, make the meringue topping: Put the egg whites, cream of tartar, and both sugars in the bowl of the stand mixer or a medium heatproof bowl, set the bowl over a medium saucepan of simmering water (do not let the bottom of the bowl touch the water), and whisk constantly until the sugar is completely dissolved and the egg whites are warm to the touch, 3 to 4 minutes. The mixture will appear pale and opaque. Rub a little bit of it between your fingers to make sure all the sugar is dissolved.

Attach the mixer bowl to the mixer stand and fit it with the whisk attachment (or use a handheld mixer to make the meringue). Add the vanilla and, starting on low speed and gradually increasing the speed to high, whip the egg whites until they are glossy and form stiff peaks, 5 to 7 minutes.

Top the sweet potatoes with big dollops of the meringue. Using a kitchen blowtorch, toast the meringue until golden brown. Alternatively, preheat the oven broiler to high. Place the baking dish about 4 inches (10 cm) from the heat source and broil for 3 to 6 minutes, watching carefully, until the meringue is toasted and golden brown.

Serve warm.

The soufflé is best eaten the same day it's made, but you can refrigerate leftovers, covered, for up to 3 days.

Apple Brown Betty

Apple Brown Betty was once called *pouding à la mulâtresse*, or mulatto pudding. It was a recipe found in the oldest Southern cookbooks. Many food historians believe the recipe was created by a biracial enslaved woman named Betty, the "brown" a reference to her skin color. Southern recipes were often the creative domain of Black folks, who were responsible for all aspects of a home or plantation's food system, from crop management and harvest to food preparation and service. In this recipe, layers of sugared spiced fruit and bread croutons are served with a luscious Custard Hard Sauce. Despite the simplicity of the ingredients, the dessert has an enjoyable complex flavor as intriguing as its history.

SERVES 8 TO 10

3 cups (90 g) 1-inch (3 cm) cubes crusty white bread

8 tablespoons (1 stick/113 g) unsalted butter, melted

½ cup (100 g) granulated sugar

3 pounds (1.4 kg) apples, such as Granny Smith, Pink Lady, or Honeycrisp, peeled, cored, and sliced about ½ inch (1.5 cm) thick

1 cup (200) packed light brown sugar

2 tablespoons unbleached all-purpose flour

Grated zest and juice of 1 lemon

1 tablespoon apple cider vinegar

1 teaspoon ground cinnamon

¼ teaspoon ground cardamom

¼ teaspoon ground mace

½ teaspoon fine sea salt

1 recipe Custard Hard Sauce (page 380)

Custards, Puddings, and Cobblers   333

Position a rack in the middle of the oven and preheat the oven to 350°F (175°C). Line a baking sheet with parchment. Butter a 2-quart (1.9 L) baking dish.

Spread the bread cubes in a single layer on the baking sheet. Bake for 5 to 7 minutes, until lightly toasted.

Transfer the toasted bread to a large mixing bowl. Pour the melted butter over it, followed by the granulated sugar, and toss to coat. Set aside.

In a large bowl, combine the apples, brown sugar, flour, lemon zest and juice, vinegar, cinnamon, cardamom, mace, and salt, tossing until thoroughly mixed.

Spread one-third of the bread in the bottom of the prepared baking dish, followed by one-third of the fruit mixture. Continue alternating layers of bread and fruit, ending with fruit.

Cover the dish with aluminum foil and bake for 30 minutes. Remove the foil and bake for an additional 25 to 35 minutes, until the fruit is bubbling and golden. Place on a wire rack to cool for about 20 minutes.

Serve the Betty warm with the hard sauce.

The Betty is best served the same day it's made, but it can be covered and refrigerated for up to 3 days.

Blackberry Sonker with Milk Dip

This dessert is so popular in Surry County, North Carolina, that it has an annual festival dedicated to it. As ever, there are several legends that attempt to explain the name. One theory links it to the Scottish word "sonker," or grassy knoll, referring to the shape of the dough on top. Or perhaps the name is a twisted pronunciation of the word "sunk," explaining what happens to the crust when it bakes over a deep dish of filling. Different kinds of fruit can be used, or even some vegetables such as sweet potato, but it's up for debate whether it should have a single or double crust and if the top should be a lattice crust or just a floating piece of pastry. All agree that there is always a sugary dip to accompany the sonker, but, of course, every family has a different recipe for that too.

SERVES 10 TO 12

1 recipe dough for Sonker Piecrust (recipe follows), chilled

2 tablespoons butter for the pan

FOR THE FILLING

12 cups (1.7 kg) fresh blackberries

2 cups (400 g) granulated sugar

⅓ cup (42 g) unbleached all-purpose flour

½ teaspoon fine sea salt

½ teaspoon ground cardamom

½ cup (118 ml) cold water

FOR THE MILK DIP

½ cup (100 g) granulated sugar

3 tablespoons cornstarch

¼ teaspoon fine sea salt

3 cups (710 ml) whole milk

½ teaspoon freshly grated nutmeg

½ teaspoon pure vanilla extract

On a lightly floured work surface, with a lightly floured rolling pin, roll the dough into a 16-by-12-inch (40 by 30 cm) rectangle. Using a ¾-inch (2 cm) cookie cutter, cut holes all over the dough, leaving a 2-inch (5 cm) border around the edges. Set aside.

Butter a 9-by-13-inch (23 by 33 cm) baking pan.

To make the filling: In a large saucepan, combine the blackberries and sugar and cook over medium heat, stirring occasionally, until the sugar is dissolved and the berries just begin to simmer and release some of their juices, about 10 minutes.

Meanwhile, in a large measuring cup or small bowl, whisk the flour, salt, cardamom, and cold water together to make a smooth slurry. Add the slurry to the blackberries and cook, stirring, until the mixture starts to thicken, 3 to 5 minutes. Remove from the heat and set aside to cool slightly.

Pour the filling into the prepared pan. Center the rectangle of dough on top of the berry filling. Roll the edges of the crust under, then crimp the edges. Put the sonker on a parchment-lined baking sheet and put in the refrigerator for 30 minutes to set the crust.

Position a rack in the middle of the oven and preheat the oven to 400°F (205°C).

Bake the sonker, on the baking sheet, for 15 minutes, then reduce the temperature to 350°F (175°C) and bake until the crust is golden brown and the juices are bubbling, 45 to 50 minutes.

Meanwhile, make the milk dip: In a medium saucepan, whisk the sugar, cornstarch, and salt together until completely combined. Gradually whisk in the milk, then bring to a boil over medium-high heat. Reduce the heat and simmer, stirring occasionally, until the dip starts to thicken, 3 to 5 minutes. Add the nutmeg and vanilla and remove from the heat. Reserve about ½ cup (118 ml) of the dip to pour over the sonker while it is baking, saving the rest for folks who will want a little more dip on the side. Set aside to cool.

Carefully remove the sonker from the oven and pour the reserved dip all over the top. Return to the oven for 5 to 10 minutes to allow the filling to absorb the dip. Remove from the heat and let cool slightly, or cool to room temperature.

Serve big scoops of the sonker in dessert bowls, and pass the reserved dip.

Leftovers can be stored, covered, in the refrigerator for up to 3 days.

SONKER PIECRUST

MAKES ENOUGH FOR ONE 9-BY-13-INCH (23 BY 33 CM) SONKER

¼ cup (59 ml) ice water
2 large (38 g) egg yolks
2 cups (250 g) unbleached all-purpose flour
¼ cup (32 g) confectioners' sugar
¼ teaspoon fine sea salt
½ pound (2 sticks/227 g) cold unsalted butter, cut into ½-inch (1.5 cm) cubes

In a large measuring cup or small bowl, combine the ice water and egg yolks.

In a large bowl, whisk together the flour, sugar, and salt. Add the butter, tossing with your hands to lightly coat it. Then, using a pastry blender, cut the butter into the flour. You should have various-sized pieces of butter ranging from coarse sandy patches to flat shaggy pieces to pea-sized chunks, with some larger bits as well. Drizzle in about half of the ice water mixture and stir lightly with a fork until the flour is moistened. If the dough seems dry, add more of the ice water mixture 1 to 2 tablespoons at a time. The dough should still look a bit shaggy at this point, but if you grab a small piece of dough and press it slightly with your hand, it should mostly hold together.

Dump the dough out onto an unfloured work surface and gather it together into a tight mound. Using the heel of your hand, smear the dough a little at a time, pushing it away from you and working your way down the mass to create flat layers of flour and butter. Then gather the dough back together with a bench scraper, layering the clumps of dough on top of one another. Repeat the process once or twice more; the dough should still have some big pieces of butter visible.

Shape the dough into a disk and flatten it. Wrap the disk in plastic wrap and place in the refrigerator for at least 1 hour, and up to overnight, to rest before rolling out.

The dough can be stored for up to 3 days in the refrigerator or up to 1 month in the freezer. If frozen, defrost in the refrigerator overnight.

Peach Cobbler

"Cobbler" is the name given to a variety of baked fruit desserts. Some folks say a cobbler is made in a deep-dish pie plate, with a filling of seasonal fruit baked between a bottom and a top layer of pastry. Others argue that a cobbler has only a top crust. From family to family, region to region, the dessert can vary, but everyone will agree that it's delicious in any form.

SERVES 10 TO 12

FOR THE CRUST

2 cups (250 g) unbleached all-purpose flour

3 tablespoons granulated sugar

1 tablespoon (13 g) baking powder, preferably
    aluminum-free

½ teaspoon fine sea salt

¼ teaspoon ground cardamom

6 tablespoons (85 g) cold unsalted butter,
    cut into ½-inch (1.5 cm) cubes

¾ cup (177 ml) heavy cream

FOR THE FILLING

2 pounds (907 g) peaches, peeled, halved, pitted,
    and cut into ¾-inch (2 cm) slices

½ cup (100 g) packed light brown sugar

1 tablespoon cornstarch

1 teaspoon ground cinnamon

¼ teaspoon ground ginger

¼ teaspoon freshly grated nutmeg

Grated zest and juice of 1 lemon

Heavy cream for brushing

1 tablespoon Cinnamon Sugar (page 376) or
    granulated sugar

Position a rack in the middle of the oven and preheat the oven to 350° F (175°C). Butter a 9-inch (23 cm) deep-dish pie plate.

To make the crust: In a large bowl, whisk together the flour, sugar, baking powder, salt, and cardamom. Drop in the butter and, working quickly, cut it in with a pastry blender. You should have various-sized pieces of butter ranging from sandy patches to flat shaggy pieces to pea-sized butter chunks, with some larger bits as well.

Pour the cream over the flour mixture and toss together with a rubber spatula or your hands until you have a very soft dough. If there are still a few bits of flour in the bottom of the bowl, gently knead the dough until they are fully incorporated. But be sure not to overwork the dough; it is better to have a few dry patches rather than a tough crust.

Turn the dough out onto a sheet of plastic wrap or parchment and cover with another sheet. Using a rolling pin, gently roll the dough into a 9-inch (23 cm) round. Slide the dough, still between the plastic wrap or parchment, onto a baking sheet and refrigerate while you make the filling. (*The dough can also be made in advance and refrigerated for up to 6 hours.*)

To make the filling: In a large mixing bowl, combine the peaches, brown sugar, cornstarch, cinnamon, ginger, nutmeg, and lemon zest and juice and toss together to mix. Pour the filling into the baking dish.

Remove the chilled dough from the refrigerator and cut a few slits in the top to create steam vents.

Gently place the dough on top of the filling. Brush the dough lightly with the cream and sprinkle with the cinnamon sugar.

Put the cobbler on a parchment-lined baking sheet. Bake for 60 to 75 minutes, until the top is golden and puffed and the juices are bubbling.

Transfer to a wire rack and let cool for at least 30 minutes before serving.

Serve the cobbler warm or at room temperature.

The cobbler is best served the same day it's made, but it can be covered and refrigerated for up to 3 days.

Apple Cobbler

When you need something quick to fix for dessert, this cobbler will do the trick. Warm spiced apples are tucked under a cookie-like crust. Choose a mix of at least two kinds of apples, sweet, tart, and/or crisp, such as Granny Smith, Arkansas Black, Golden Delicious, or Pink Lady.

SERVES 10 TO 12

FOR THE FILLING

4 tablespoons (57 g) unsalted butter

6 large apples (see headnote), peeled, cored, and cut into
     ½-inch (1.5 cm) pieces

Grated zest and juice of 1 lemon

½ cup (118 ml) apple cider

¼ cup (50 g) packed light brown sugar

1 teaspoon ground cinnamon

¼ teaspoon freshly grated nutmeg

¼ teaspoon ground allspice

FOR THE TOPPING

1 cup (125 g) unbleached all-purpose flour

1 teaspoon (4 g) baking powder, preferably
     aluminum-free

½ teaspoon fine sea salt

¾ cup (150 g) granulated sugar

8 tablespoons (1 stick/113 g) unsalted butter, melted

1 teaspoon pure vanilla extract

1 tablespoon Cinnamon Sugar (page 376)

Position a rack in the middle of the oven and preheat the oven to 350°F (175°C). Butter a 9-by-13-inch (23 by 33 cm) baking dish.

To make the filling: In a large saucepan, melt the butter over medium heat. Add the apples, lemon zest and juice, apple cider, brown sugar, cinnamon, nutmeg, and allspice and cook until the apples are coated in spices and slightly softened, 5 to 8 minutes. Pour the filling into the prepared baking dish and set aside.

To make the topping: In a medium bowl, whisk together the flour, baking powder, and salt.

In a large bowl, combine the sugar, butter, and vanilla and stir to mix. Add the flour mixture, stirring with a rubber spatula until the mixture resembles a soft cookie dough.

Place big dollops of dough all over the top of the apples. Sprinkle the dough with the cinnamon sugar.

Put the cobbler on a parchment-lined baking sheet. Bake until the topping is golden and the juices are bubbling, 35 to 40 minutes.

Serve the cobbler hot, warm, or at room temperature.

The cobbler is best eaten the same day it's made, but leftovers can be covered and stored in the refrigerator for up to 3 days.

Savory Chicken Cobbler

Drop biscuits steam on top of a fragrant chicken filling infused with coriander, thyme, sage, and nutmeg. This is a hearty and comforting dish to bring to a potluck dinner. You can also make it with leftover turkey.

SERVES 10 TO 12

FOR THE FILLING

12 tablespoons (1½ sticks/170 g) unsalted butter, at room
     temperature

1 cup (125 g) finely diced yellow onion

2 garlic cloves, finely chopped

5 cups (1.2 L) canned reduced-sodium chicken broth

3 carrots, peeled and cut into 1-inch (3 cm) pieces

3 celery ribs, cut into 1-inch (3 cm) pieces

1 teaspoon fine sea salt

1 teaspoon freshly ground black pepper

1½ cups (355 ml) heavy cream

½ cup (63 g) unbleached all-purpose flour

5 cups (625 g) shredded store-bought rotisserie chicken

1 cup (135 g) frozen peas, thawed

1 cup (135 g) frozen corn kernels, thawed

One 8-ounce (227 g) package frozen pearl onions, thawed

1 teaspoon ground coriander

1 teaspoon chopped fresh thyme

½ teaspoon ground sage

¼ teaspoon freshly grated nutmeg

¼ teaspoon cayenne pepper

FOR THE BISCUIT TOPPING

1½ cups (188 g) unbleached all-purpose flour

1½ cups (188 g) cake flour (not self-rising)

2 tablespoons granulated sugar

2 tablespoons (26 g) baking powder, preferably
    aluminum-free

1 teaspoon fine sea salt

¼ teaspoon freshly ground black pepper

8 tablespoons (1 stick/113 g) cold unsalted butter,
    cut into 1-inch (3 cm) cubes

¼ cup (59 ml) buttermilk, plus more for brushing

1 tablespoon fresh thyme leaves

SPECIAL EQUIPMENT

2-inch (5 cm) biscuit cutter

Butter a 9-by-13-by-2-inch (23 by 33 by 5 cm) baking dish or a 10-inch (25 cm) cast-iron skillet.

To make the filling: In a large pot, melt 4 tablespoons (57 g) of the butter over medium heat. Add the onion and garlic and sauté until tender, about 8 minutes. Add the chicken broth, carrots, celery, salt, and pepper, lower the heat to medium-low, partially cover the pot, and simmer, stirring occasionally, for 15 minutes.

Stir the cream into the pot, raise the heat to medium, and cook, covered, until all the vegetables are tender, 12 to 15 minutes.

Meanwhile, in a small bowl, blend the remaining 8 tablespoons (1 stick/113 g) butter and the flour to make a smooth paste.

When the vegetables are tender, lower the heat and whisk the flour paste bit by bit into the broth until thoroughly combined. Add the chicken, peas, corn, pearl onions, coriander, thyme, sage, nutmeg, and cayenne, cover the pot, and let the filling simmer, stirring occasionally, until thickened, about 10 minutes.

Transfer the filling to the prepared baking dish, spreading the vegetables and chicken out evenly. Set aside.

Position a rack in the middle of the oven and preheat the oven to 450°F (230°C).

To make the biscuit topping: In a large bowl, whisk together the flours, sugar, baking powder, salt, and pepper. Add the butter, tossing to coat, and then, working quickly, cut it in with a pastry blender (or pinch it with your fingertips and smear the butter into the flour). You should have various-sized pieces of butter ranging from sandy patches to flat shaggy pieces, to pea-sized butter chunks, with some larger bits as well. Make a well in the center of the flour mixture and pour in the buttermilk. Stir gently to incorporate the dry ingredients into the buttermilk until a shaggy dough forms.

Turn the dough out onto a lightly floured surface and pat it out until it's an even ½ inch (1.5 cm) thick. Using a 2-inch (5 cm) biscuit cutter, stamp out biscuits and arrange them over the filling, leaving about ¼ inch (6 mm) between them. Brush the biscuits with buttermilk and sprinkle with the thyme leaves.

Bake for 35 to 40 minutes, or until golden brown and the juices are bubbling. Remove from the oven and let stand for 5 minutes before serving.

Leftovers can be stored, covered, in the refrigerator for up to 3 days.

Profiteroles

Many traditional Southern desserts were influenced by French cuisine. This recipe was inspired by one of chef Edna Lewis's famous spring dinner dessert menus in *The Edna Lewis Cookbook*, written in her signature style that leaves you longing to pull up a chair to her table. Light choux pastry puffs, filled with pastry cream, as here, or with ice cream, make an impressive finish to any meal, and they are quite easy to make—especially with a bit of advance planning. You can pipe out the rounds of dough and freeze them for up to a month to bake off straight from the freezer. Fill them with the pastry cream and serve with Hot Fudge Sauce and Chantilly Cream.

MAKES ABOUT 12 PROFITEROLES; SERVES 6

FOR THE PUFFS

½ cup (118 ml) whole milk

8 tablespoons (1 stick/113 g) unsalted butter, cut into
    8 pieces

2 teaspoons granulated sugar

½ teaspoon fine sea salt

½ cup (118 ml) water

1 cup (125 g) unbleached all-purpose flour

4 large (200 g) eggs, at room temperature

1 egg, beaten with a pinch of fine sea salt, for egg wash

1 recipe Pastry Cream (page 386)

About ¾ cup (177 ml) Hot Fudge Sauce (page 379)

2 cups (473 ml) Chantilly Cream (page 373)

SPECIAL EQUIPMENT

1-ounce (30 ml) ice cream scoop

To make the puffs: Position the racks in the middle and lower third of the oven and preheat the oven to 450°F (230°C). Line two baking sheets with parchment.

In a medium saucepan, combine the milk, butter, sugar, salt, and water and bring to a boil over medium-high heat, stirring occasionally to encourage the butter to melt. Add the flour all at once, reduce the heat to medium-low, and stir briskly (you'll need a strong wooden spoon for this job) until a dough forms and pulls away from the sides of the pan, 1 to 2 minutes. Then continue to stir vigorously until you see a thin skin on the sides and bottom of the pan.

Transfer the mixture to the bowl of a stand mixer fitted with the paddle attachment (or use a large mixing bowl and a handheld mixer) and mix for about 30 seconds to cool the mixture down a bit. Add the eggs one (50 g) at a time, making sure each one is incorporated before adding the next, and beating until the mixture is smooth and shiny. When you pull the paddle (or beaters) out of the bowl, the dough should drop down in a V shape.

Using a 1-ounce (30 ml) ice cream scoop, scoop the dough onto the prepared baking sheets, leaving about 3 inches (8 cm) between the mounds of dough. Flatten any points with a damp finger to smooth them out (to ensure that the points do not burn in the oven). Gently brush the top of each mound with egg wash.

Bake the puffs for 20 to 25 minutes, rotating the pans halfway through and switching their positions, until puffed and golden brown. Transfer the puffs to wire racks to cool completely.

Just before serving, carefully cut the top third off each puff with a serrated knife; set the "lids" aside. Fill each puff with the pastry cream and place the lids back on top.

Arrange 2 profiteroles on each serving plate and pour 1 rounded tablespoon of the hot fudge sauce over each one. Finish each serving with a spoonful of the Chantilly cream.

The unfilled puffs can be stored in an airtight container in the refrigerator for up to 2 days or in the freezer for up to 1 month. Refresh in a preheated 350°F (175°C) oven for 5 to 8 minutes, then cool completely before filling.

Mini Baked Alaskas

This cake and ice cream dessert, topped off with a toasted meringue, is magical. The most common origin story claims that the pastry chef at Antoine's, the famous restaurant in New Orleans, created this celebratory dessert in 1867 to honor the Alaska Purchase. It makes a spectacular presentation. Make sure you cover the ice cream cakes completely with the meringue to insulate the ice cream from the final blast of heat.

SERVES 6

FOR THE CAKE

1¾ cups (219 g) unbleached all-purpose flour

1¾ cups (350 g) granulated sugar

¾ cup (60 g) Dutch-processed cocoa powder

2 teaspoons baking soda

1 teaspoon baking powder, preferably aluminum-free

1 teaspoon fine sea salt

½ cup (118 ml) vegetable oil

2 large (100 g) eggs plus 1 (19 g) yolk, at room temperature

1 cup (237 ml) buttermilk

1 teaspoon pure vanilla extract

1 cup (237 ml) brewed hot coffee, slightly cooled

¼ cup (2 ounces/57 g) semisweet chocolate, melted and slightly cooled

About ½ cup (118 ml) good-quality strawberry or raspberry jam, homemade (see pages 350 and 354) or store-bought

1 quart (1 L) of your favorite ice cream (or use two flavors), slightly softened

FOR THE MERINGUE

4 large (120 g) egg whites

1 cup (200 g) granulated sugar

1 teaspoon cream of tartar

1 teaspoon pure vanilla extract

SPECIAL EQUIPMENT

3-inch (8 cm) biscuit cutter or round cookie cutter

Kitchen blowtorch

To make the cake: Position a rack in the middle of the oven and preheat the oven to 350°F (175°C). Butter a baking sheet, then line it with parchment, leaving an overhang on the two short ends of the pan. Butter the parchment as well and dust with flour, tapping the pan on the counter to shake out the excess.

In the bowl of a stand mixer fitted with the paddle attachment (or in a large mixing bowl, using a handheld mixer), combine the flour, sugar, cocoa, baking soda, baking powder, and salt. Let the mixer run on low speed to incorporate and aerate the flour.

In a medium bowl, lightly whisk together the oil, eggs and yolk, buttermilk, vanilla, and coffee.

Gradually add the buttermilk-egg mixture to the dry ingredients in thirds, mixing on medium speed for 1 to 2 minutes. Beat in the melted chocolate until just combined.

Remove the bowl from the mixer stand (if using) and, using a rubber spatula, incorporate any ingredients hiding at the bottom of the bowl, making sure the batter is completely mixed.

Pour the batter into the prepared pan and gently smooth the top with a spatula. Tap the pan firmly on the counter to remove any air bubbles from the batter.

Bake for 20 to 25 minutes, until the cake is lightly golden and a cake tester inserted in the center comes out clean. Let the cake cool for 15 minutes, then carefully remove it from the pan, using the parchment "handles," and invert it onto a wire rack. Let cool completely.

To assemble the mini cakes: Line a baking sheet with aluminum foil. Peel the parchment off the cake. Cut out 12 disks of cake with a 3-inch (8 cm) biscuit cutter or round cookie cutter.

(Continued on page 344)

Top 6 rounds of cake with about 1 tablespoon of the jam each, then place the plain rounds on top to make sandwiches. Place the cake sandwiches on the prepared baking sheet. Place a large scoop of the softened ice cream on top of each mini cake round; you can fill the ice cream scoop with two different flavors, if you like. Wrap each mini cake in plastic wrap and freeze until the ice cream is very hard, at least 1 hour.

To make the meringue: Put the egg whites, sugar, and cream of tartar in the bowl of the stand mixer or a medium heatproof bowl, set the bowl over a medium saucepan of simmering water (do not let the bottom of the bowl touch the water), and whisk constantly until the sugar is completely dissolved and the egg whites are warm to the touch, 3 to 4 minutes. The mixture will appear pale and opaque. Rub a little bit of the mixture between your fingers to make sure all the sugar is dissolved.

Attach the mixer bowl to the stand and fit with the whisk attachment (or use a handheld mixer with the mixing bowl). Add the vanilla and, starting on low speed and gradually increasing the speed to high, whip the egg whites until they are glossy and form stiff peaks, 5 to 7 minutes.

Remove the cakes from the freezer, unwrap them, and place them on individual heatproof glass or ceramic plates. Working quickly, frost the ice cream cakes, going all the way down to the bottom edges, with the meringue, making peaks and swirls on top; the cakes should look like little domes covered in snow.

Toast the meringue with a kitchen blowtorch until golden. Serve immediately.

Vanilla Bean Ice Cream

Southerners love custards of all sorts, and this ice cream is as rich as they come. The ice cream base is allowed to infuse overnight for the ultimate pure vanilla bean flavor. Serve with Hot Fudge Sauce (page 379) or Berry Sauce (page 379) to dress up each scoop.

MAKES ABOUT 2 QUARTS (2 L)

4 cups (946 ml) heavy cream

2 cups (473 ml) whole milk

1¼ cups (250 g) granulated sugar

½ teaspoon fine sea salt

1 vanilla bean, split lengthwise, seeds scraped out and reserved

2 large (100 g) eggs, at room temperature

10 large (190 g) egg yolks, at room temperature

SPECIAL EQUIPMENT

Instant-read thermometer

Ice cream maker

In a large saucepan, combine the heavy cream, milk, sugar, salt, and vanilla bean and seeds and heat to just below the boiling point, stirring frequently to dissolve the sugar.

Remove from the heat and set aside to cool to room temperature, then transfer the mixture to an airtight container and refrigerate overnight so the vanilla can add maximum flavor.

The next day, set a fine-mesh sieve over a large bowl. Fill another large bowl with ice cubes and water and set a heatproof bowl inside it.

Pour the milk mixture into a large saucepan. Bring to just below the boiling point over medium heat, whisking constantly. Remove from the heat.

In a large bowl, whisk the eggs and egg yolks until thoroughly combined. Whisk in ½ cup (118 ml) of the hot cream mixture to temper the eggs, so they won't curdle, then whisk the eggs into the remaining cream mixture.

Return the saucepan to the stove and cook, whisking frequently and making sure to scrape the bottom of the pan, until the mixture becomes a silky custard and thickens enough to coat the back of a spoon, about 5 minutes.

Remove from the heat and strain through the fine-mesh sieve to remove the vanilla bean and any pesky bits of egg, then pour into the bowl in the prepared ice bath. Cool the mixture to 40°F (5°C), stirring occasionally.

Transfer the mixture to the bowl of a 2-quart-capacity (1.9 L) ice cream maker and churn according to the manufacturer's instructions.

Transfer the ice cream to a freezer container and store in the freezer for at least 5 hours before serving.

Jams and Preserves

The kitchen should always be neat and clean.
The table, pastry boards, pans, and everything
pertaining to cookery should be well cleansed.

—MALINDA RUSSELL,
A DOMESTIC COOKBOOK, 1866

WHEN RIPE SEASONAL FRUITS ARE ABUNDANT—whether in your own garden or at the farmers' market or grocery—it's time to make jam. The jam can be safely stored in your refrigerator for up to two weeks to enjoy with your morning toast or biscuits, but you can also use one of two canning methods presented in this chapter to keep the jam for much longer.

The craft of "putting up" plays an important role in the Southern pantry. Being resourceful has always been a part of daily life in the South, and it runs deep in the culture. The "waste not, want not" approach resonates just as much today as it did a century ago. This practice of preserving not only enriches what you put on the dinner table all year round (and gets you through a long winter) but also rewards you with beautiful bright jars of produce to enjoy when your favorite fruits and vegetables are not in season.

There are lessons we can all learn from Southerners' preserving prowess, whether it's using old jammers' techniques like finishing a pot of jam with a dab of butter to add shine and clarity, or cutting up scraps of fabric to decorate the top of a jar to sit pretty in a picnic basket. Celebrate nature's blessings at any time of year, whether it's with Apple Butter, Strawberry Chamomile Jam, or Blueberry Rhubarb Rose Jam. There are some very special preserves as well, from sweet Peach Lavender Jam to savory Hot-Pink Pepper Jelly or Green Tomato Preserves. Note that all of these recipes are made without commercial pectin.

Grape Jam

This recipe uses the seedless black grapes that you can find in grocery stores all year round. The lemon rind is a great source of natural pectin and when combined with vanilla also adds a great flavor.

MAKES ABOUT 1½ QUARTS (1.4 L);
OR SIX ½-PINT (237 ML) JARS

3¾ pounds (1.7 kg) seedless black grapes

3 cups (600 g) granulated sugar

3 tablespoons fresh lemon juice (reserve the squeezed lemon)

2 teaspoons pure vanilla extract

SPECIAL EQUIPMENT

Cheesecloth bag or a square of cheesecloth

Kitchen twine

Candy or digital thermometer

Immersion blender or food processor

Put two clean saucers and three metal spoons in the freezer.

Put the grapes in a large bowl and toss in the sugar, lemon juice, and vanilla. Using your hands, get in there and crush the grapes, leaving some whole to give your jam some variation in texture. Set aside for at least 1 hour, or refrigerate overnight.

Transfer the grape mixture to a preserving pot or other large heavy nonreactive pot. Put the squeezed lemon rind in a cheesecloth bag, or wrap in a square of cheesecloth, and tie the bag to one of the pot's handles so that it will be covered by the jam as it cooks. Cook over medium-low heat, stirring frequently, until all the sugar has dissolved and the grapes are releasing a lot of juice, about 20 minutes. If using an immersion blender, turn off the heat and blend the jam until it reaches the desired consistency.

Clip a candy thermometer, if using, to the side of the pot. Continue to cook, gradually raising the heat to high, stirring frequently and scraping the bottom of the pot to prevent sticking (if the mixture does begin to stick, turn down the heat just a bit), and skimming off any foam with a large spoon, until the jam registers 220°F (105°C) on the candy thermometer, about 20 minutes after it reaches a rolling boil; or check the temperature with a digital thermometer. The jam should look glossy and dark. Remove from the heat.

Pull a chilled saucer and spoon from the freezer. Drop a rounded tablespoon of jam onto the cold plate. Return it to the freezer for 1 minute. Now pull your finger through the jam. If it leaves a clean trail, the jam is set! If the jam is still too runny, cook for 2 to 3 minutes longer and test again; repeat if necessary until you are satisfied.

Carefully remove the bag with the lemon rind and squeeze any juices into the jam. If you did not use an immersion blender earlier, you can process the jam in a food processor now until it reaches the desired consistency. Or leave the jam as it is. Let cool completely.

You can store the jam in Mason jars or airtight containers in the refrigerator for up to 2 weeks. For longer storage, see Puttin' Up Days (page 365).

Blackberry Lemon Verbena Jam

PICTURED ON PAGE 359

Lemon verbena adds a lovely herbaceous quality to this sweet-tart blackberry jam.

MAKES ABOUT 1½ QUARTS (1.4 ML);
OR SIX ½-PINT (237 ML) JARS

3 pounds (1.4 kg) fresh blackberries

Juice of 1 lemon (reserve the squeezed lemon)

4¼ cups (850 g) granulated sugar

A bunch (about 60 g) of fresh lemon verbena

3 tablespoons (64 g) honey

SPECIAL EQUIPMENT

Cheesecloth bag or cheesecloth

Kitchen twine

Candy or digital thermometer

Put the berries and lemon juice in a large bowl and toss with the sugar. Put the squeezed lemon rind and lemon verbena in a cheesecloth bag, or wrap it in a square of cheesecloth, and place on top of the berries.

Cover the bowl with plastic wrap, or transfer the berry mixture to a large airtight container, and refrigerate for at least 12 hours, and up to 2 days.

When you are ready to make the jam, put two clean saucers and three metal spoons in the freezer.

Transfer the berries to a preserving pot or other large nonreactive heavy pot. Tie the cheesecloth bag to one of the pot's handles and tuck it under the berries. Cook over medium-low heat, stirring, until all the sugar is dissolved and the berries have released a lot of juice, about 10 minutes. Stir in the honey.

Clip a candy thermometer, if using, to the side of the pot. Continue to cook, gradually raising the heat to high, stirring frequently and gently scraping the bottom of the pan to prevent sticking (if the mixture does begin to stick, turn down the heat just a bit), until the jam registers 220°F (105°C) on the candy thermometer, 10 to 15 minutes after it reaches a rolling boil; or use a digital thermometer to check the temperature. The jam should look glossy and dark. Remove from the heat.

Pull a chilled plate and spoon from the freezer. Drop a rounded tablespoon of jam onto the cold plate. Return it to the freezer for 1 minute. Now pull your finger through the jam. It should leave a clean trail through the jam. If the jam is still too runny, cook for 2 to 3 minutes longer and test again; repeat if necessary until you are satisfied.

Remove the cheesecloth bag and carefully press any juices into the jam. Let cool completely.

You can store the jam in Mason jars or airtight containers in the refrigerator for up to 2 weeks. For longer storage, see Puttin' Up Days (page 365).

Strawberry Chamomile Jam

PICTURED ON PAGE 359

The scent of sweet strawberries and aromatic chamomile will fill your kitchen as this jam bubbles away on your stove. And it tastes just as good as it smells.

MAKES ABOUT 1½ QUARTS (1.4 L); OR
SIX ½-PINT (237 ML) JARS

3 pounds strawberries (1.4 kg), hulled and quartered

4½ cups plus 1 tablespoon (912 g) granulated sugar

Grated zest of 1 lemon

2 tablespoons fresh lemon juice (reserve the squeezed lemon)

1 tablespoon edible dried chamomile flowers (see Resources, page 389)

Cheesecloth bag or a square of cheesecloth

Kitchen twine

Candy or digital thermometer

Immersion blender or food processor

Put two clean saucers and three metal spoons in the freezer.

In a large bowl, combine the strawberries and sugar. Add the lemon zest and juice and the chamomile, stirring with a big spoon until combined. Cover tightly with plastic wrap, or transfer to a large airtight container, place in the refrigerator, and let macerate for at least 12 hours, and up to 3 days.

When you are ready to make the jam, transfer the strawberries to a preserving pot or other large heavy nonreactive pot. Put the squeezed lemon rind in a cheesecloth bag, or wrap it in a square of cheesecloth, tie the bag to one of the pot's handles, and tuck it under the berries.

Cook over medium-low heat, stirring, until all the sugar has dissolved and the strawberries have released a lot of juice, about 10 minutes. If using an immersion blender, turn off the heat and blend the jam until it reaches the desired consistency.

Clip a candy thermometer, if using, to the side of the pot and cook, gradually raising the heat to high, stirring frequently and scraping the bottom of the pot to prevent sticking (if the mixture does begin to stick, turn down the heat just a bit), and skimming off any foam with a fine-mesh skimmer or heatproof spoon, until the jam registers 220°F (105°C) on the candy thermometer, 10 to 15 minutes after it reaches a rolling boil; or use a digital thermometer to check the temperature. The jam should look glossy and dark. Remove from the heat.

Pull a chilled plate and spoon from the freezer. Scoop a small spoonful of jam onto the cold plate. Return it to the freezer for 1 minute. Now pull your finger through the jam. It should leave a clean trail through the jam. If the jam is still runny, cook for 2 to 3 minutes longer and test again; repeat if necessary until you are satisfied.

Remove the cheesecloth bag and carefully squeeze any juices into the jam. If you did not use an immersion blender earlier, you can process the jam now in a food processor until it reaches the desired consistency. Or leave the jam as it is. Let cool completely.

You can store the jam in Mason jars or in airtight containers in the refrigerator for up to 2 weeks. For longer storage, see Puttin' Up Days (page 365).

Peach Lavender Jam

When fruit stands start to pop up on the side of the road, it's a sign that summer has arrived. There is nothing quite like that first bite of a ripe, juicy peach on a hot summer day. Roasting fruit is a way to caramelize and amplify its flavor, creating a complex richness. This peach jam with a hint of lavender has a wonderful flavor.

MAKES ABOUT 1½ QUARTS (1.4 L); OR SIX ½-PINT (237 ML) JARS

3 pounds (1.4 kg) peaches

4½ cups (900 g) granulated sugar

1 tablespoon dried edible lavender flowers (see Resources, page 389)

2 tablespoons fresh lemon juice (reserve the squeezed lemon)

SPECIAL EQUIPMENT

Cheesecloth bag or a square of cheesecloth

Kitchen twine

Candy or digital thermometer

(Continued on page 354)

Preheat the oven to 350°F (175°C).

Cut the peaches in half. Remove the pits and place the pits in a cheesecloth bag or wrap them in a square of cheesecloth. Set aside.

Arrange the peaches cut side up in a large deep roasting pan. Roast for 45 to 50 minutes, until the peaches are softened and golden brown. Set aside to cool.

Peel off the peach skins and discard. Transfer the peaches to a large bowl. Add the sugar, lavender, and lemon juice to the peaches and give it all a good stir to combine. Add the squeezed lemon rind to the bag with the peach pits and place the bag on top of the peaches.

Cover the bowl with plastic wrap, or transfer the peaches to a large airtight container, and refrigerate for least 12 hours, and up to 2 days.

When you are ready to make the jam, put two clean saucers and three metal spoons in the freezer.

Transfer the peaches to a preserving pot or other large nonreactive heavy pot. Tie the bag of peach pits to one of the pan's handles and tuck it under the peaches. Cook over medium-low heat, stirring, until all the sugar is dissolved and the peaches have released a lot of juice, about 10 minutes.

Clip a candy thermometer, if using, to the side of the pot. Continue to cook, gradually raising the heat to high, stirring frequently, gently scraping the bottom of the pot to prevent sticking (if the mixture does begin to stick, turn down the heat just a bit), and skimming off any foam, until the jam registers 220°F (105°C) on the candy thermometer, 10 to 15 minutes after it reaches a rolling boil; or use a digital thermometer to check the temperature. Remove from the heat.

Pull a chilled plate and spoon from the freezer. Drop a rounded teaspoon of jam onto the cold plate. Return it to the freezer for 1 minute. Now pull your finger through the jam. It should leave a clean trail. If the jam is still runny, cook for 2 to 3 minutes longer and test again; repeat if necessary until you are satisfied.

Remove the bag of pits and lemon rind and carefully press out any juices into the jam. Let cool completely.

You can store the jam in Mason jars or airtight containers in the refrigerator for up to 2 weeks. For longer storage, see Puttin' Up Days (page 365).

Raspberry–Vanilla Bean Jam

Try this raspberry-vanilla jam on a slice of toasted sourdough on its own or with a smear of ricotta.

MAKES ABOUT 1½ QUARTS (1.4 L); OR SIX ½-PINT (237 ML) JARS

3½ pounds (1.6 kg) fresh raspberries

5 cups (1 kg) granulated sugar

1 vanilla bean, split lengthwise, seeds scraped out and reserved

2 tablespoons fresh lemon juice (reserve the squeezed lemon)

SPECIAL EQUIPMENT
Cheesecloth bag or cheesecloth
Kitchen twine
Candy or digital thermometer

Put the berries in a large bowl and add the sugar, vanilla bean and seeds, and lemon juice. Using your hands, get in there and crush the berries, leaving some berries whole to give your jam some variety in texture. Put the squeezed lemon rind in a cheesecloth bag, or wrap it in a square of cheesecloth, and place on top of the berries. Cover the bowl with plastic wrap, or transfer the berry mixture to a large airtight container, and refrigerate for at least 12 hours, and up to 2 days.

When you are ready to make the jam, put two clean saucers and three metal spoons in the freezer.

Transfer the berries to a preserving pot or other large heavy nonreactive pot. Tie the cheesecloth bag to one of the pot's handles and tuck it under the berries. Cook over medium-low heat, stirring, until all the sugar is dissolved and the berries have released a lot of juice, about 10 minutes.

Clip a candy thermometer, if using, to the side of the pot. Continue to cook, gradually raising the heat to high, stirring frequently and gently scraping the bottom of the pan to prevent sticking (if the mixture does begin to stick, turn down the heat just a bit), and skimming off any white foam with a fine-mesh skimmer or heatproof spoon, until the jam registers 220°F (105°C) on the candy thermometer, 10 to 15 minutes after it reaches a rolling boil; or use a digital thermometer to check the temperature. The jam should look glossy and dark. Remove from the heat.

Pull a chilled plate and spoon from the freezer. Drop a rounded tablespoon of jam onto the cold plate. Return it to the freezer for 1 minute. Now pull your finger through the jam. If it leaves a clean trail through the jam, it's set! If the jam is still runny, cook for 2 to 3 minutes longer and test again; repeat if necessary until you are satisfied.

Remove the cheesecloth bag and carefully squeeze any juices into the jam. Let cool completely.

You can store the jam in Mason jars or airtight containers in the refrigerator for up to 2 weeks. For longer storage, see Puttin' Up Days (page 365).

Fig Elderflower Jam

A ripe fig is perfection all on its own. The addition of elderflower liquor enhances the flavor of this jam. Figs are a low-acid fruit, so do not substitute fresh squeezed lemon juice for the bottled lemon juice in this recipe. Bottled juice has a standard pH, while the acidity of lemons varies; using bottled lemon juice ensures a safe level for this jam. Use it on yogurt, biscuits, and toast.

MAKES ABOUT 1½ QUARTS (1.4 L); OR
SIX ½-PINT (237 ML) JARS

3 pounds (1.4 kg) fresh figs, stemmed and cut into ¼-inch (6 mm) slices
4 cups (800 g) granulated sugar
2 tablespoons elderflower extract or liqueur, such as St-Germain
½ cup (118 g) bottled lemon juice

SPECIAL EQUIPMENT
Candy or digital thermometer

Put two clean saucers and three metal spoons in the freezer.

In a preserving pot or other large heavy nonreactive pot, combine the figs, sugar, elderflower extract, and lemon juice and cook over low heat until the figs start to release their juices, about 5 minutes. Turn the heat up to medium-low and cook, stirring, until all the sugar is dissolved and the figs have released a lot of juice, about 10 minutes.

Clip a candy thermometer, if using, to the side of the pot. Continue to cook, gradually raising the heat to high, stirring frequently and gently scraping the bottom of the pot to prevent sticking (if the mixture does begin to stick, turn down the

heat just a bit), and skimming off any foam, until the jam registers 220°F (105°C) on the candy thermometer, 10 to 15 minutes after it reaches a rolling boil; or use a digital thermometer to check the temperature. The jam should look glossy and dark. Remove from the heat.

Pull a chilled plate and spoon from the freezer. Scoop a small spoonful of jam onto the cold plate.

Return it to the freezer for 1 minute. Now pull your finger through the jam. It should leave a clean trail through the jam. If the jam is still runny, cook for 2 to 3 minutes longer and test again; repeat if necessary until you are satisfied.

You can store the jam in Mason jars or airtight containers in the refrigerator for up to 2 weeks. For longer storage, see Puttin' Up Days (page 365).

Blueberry Rhubarb Rose Jam

Juicy sweet blueberries and tart rhubarb make a winning combination. Rose water elevates the flavors of this beautiful jewel-colored jam.

MAKES ABOUT 1½ QUARTS (1.4 L); OR SIX ½-PINT (237 ML) JARS

1 pound, 6 ounces (624 g) rhubarb, cut into 1½-inch (4 cm) pieces

⅔ cup (158 ml) cold water

1 pound, 6 ounces (624 g) fresh blueberries

2 tablespoons fresh lemon juice (reserve the squeezed lemon)

2 cups (400 g) granulated sugar

1 teaspoon rose water (see Resources, page 389)

¼ teaspoon fine sea salt

SPECIAL EQUIPMENT

Cheesecloth bag or a square of cheesecloth

Kitchen twine

Candy or digital thermometer

Put two clean saucers and three metal spoons in the freezer.

In a preserving pot or other large heavy nonreactive pot, combine the rhubarb and water and cook over medium heat until the rhubarb begins to soften, about 10 minutes. Add the blueberries, lemon juice, and sugar and slowly bring to a boil, stirring until the sugar is completely dissolved. Add the rose water and salt and give it all a good stir.

Put the squeezed lemon rind in a cheesecloth bag, or wrap it in a square of cheesecloth, tie the bag to one of the pot's handles, and tuck it under the fruit. Clip a candy thermometer, if using, to the side of the pot and continue to cook, gradually raising the heat to high, stirring frequently and scraping the bottom of the pot to prevent sticking (if the mixture does begin to stick, turn down the heat just a bit), and skimming off any foam, until the jam registers 220°F (105°C) on the candy thermometer, 10 to 15 minutes after it reaches a rolling boil; or use a digital thermometer to check. The jam should look glossy and dark. Remove from the heat.

Pull a chilled plate and spoon from the freezer. Scoop a small spoonful of jam onto the cold plate. Return it to the freezer for 1 minute. Now pull your finger through the jam. It should leave a clean trail. If the jam is still too runny, cook for 2 to 3 minutes longer and test again; repeat if necessary until you are satisfied.

Remove the cheesecloth bag and carefully press any juices into the jam. Let the jam cool completely.

You can store the jam in airtight containers in the refrigerator for up to 2 weeks. For longer storage, see Puttin' Up Days (page 365).

Satsuma-Vanilla Marmalade

PICTURED ON PAGE 359

Satsumas are a type of mandarin orange that have thin skins, making them an excellent choice for marmalade. You can substitute clementines or another mandarin orange for Satsumas if necessary. The marmalade is just right for slathering on anything from biscuits to toast.

MAKES ABOUT 2¼ QUARTS (2.1 L); OR FIVE ½-PINT (237 ML) JARS

2 pounds (about 1 kg) Satsuma oranges (see headnote)

6 cups (1.4 L) cold water

Grated zest and juice of 2 lemons

(Continued)

4 cups (800 g) granulated sugar

1 vanilla bean, split lengthwise,
    seeds scraped out and reserved

½ teaspoon unsalted butter (optional)

SPECIAL EQUIPMENT

Candy or digital thermometer

Put two clean saucers and three metal spoons in the freezer.

Wash the oranges thoroughly. Quarter them and remove the seeds, then cut them into thin slices.

In a preserving pot or other large heavy nonreactive pot, combine the oranges, water, and lemon zest and juice and bring to a boil, then reduce the heat and simmer until the peels are tender, 40 to 45 minutes.

Add the sugar and vanilla bean and seeds and cook, stirring, until the sugar dissolves. Clip a candy thermometer, if using, to the side of the pot and continue cooking, gradually raising the heat to medium-high, stirring frequently and gently scraping the bottom of the pot to prevent sticking

(if the mixture does begin to stick, turn down the heat just a bit), and skimming off any white foam with a fine-mesh skimmer or heatproof spoon, until the jam registers 220°F (105°C) on the candy thermometer, 30 to 45 minutes after it reaches a rolling boil; or use a digital thermometer to check the temperature. Remove from the heat and remove and discard the vanilla bean.

Pull a chilled plate and spoon from the freezer. Scoop a small spoonful of marmalade onto the cold plate. Return it to the freezer for 1 minute. Now pull your finger through the liquid. It should leave a clean trail through the jam. If the marmalade is still runny, cook for 2 to 3 minutes longer and test again; repeat if necessary until you are satisfied.

If using, stir the butter into the jam to absorb and disperse any remaining foam and add a slight sheen and clarity to the marmalade. Let cool completely.

You can store the jam in Mason jars or in airtight containers in the refrigerator for up to 2 weeks. For longer storage, see Puttin' Up Days (page 365).

Hot-Pink Pepper Jelly

PICTURED OPPOSITE

Granny Smith apples, sweet red bell pepper, and spicy serrano or jalapeño peppers play well together, giving this jelly just the right amount of sweetness and heat. The hot-pink color from the cranberries makes it a striking highlight on a cheese board; serve it atop a mound of cream cheese with crackers alongside.

**MAKES ABOUT 1½ QUARTS (1.4 L); OR
SIX ½-PINT (237 ML) JARS**

4 pounds (1.8 kg) Granny Smith apples,
    stems removed and quartered

1 cup (95 g) cranberries

1 large red bell pepper, cored, seeded,
    and roughly chopped

¼ pound (113 g) hot red chiles (about 10 serranos or
    8 jalapeños), roughly chopped

1 lemon, cut into ¼ inch (6 mm) slices

3 cups (710 ml) cold water

3 cups (710 ml) white vinegar

3 cups (600 g) granulated sugar

SPECIAL EQUIPMENT

Candy or digital thermometer

Put two clean saucers and three metal spoons in the freezer.

In a preserving pot or other large heavy nonreactive pot, combine the apples, cranberries,

CLOCKWISE FROM TOP LEFT: STRAWBERRY CHAMOMILE JAM (PAGE 350), SATSUMA-VANILLA MARMALADE (PAGE 357), BLACKBERRY LEMON VERBENA JAM (PAGE 350), HOT-PINK PEPPER JELLY (OPPOSITE)

bell pepper, chiles, and lemon, add the water and vinegar, and bring to a boil over medium-high heat. Boil, stirring occasionally, until the cranberries have completely broken down, releasing all of their natural pectin, 10 to 15 minutes.

Set a fine-mesh sieve over a large heatproof bowl or pot and pour in the apple-cranberry mixture. Allow it to drain naturally, stirring occasionally, but not pushing down on it, until it has released all the liquid, at least 30 minutes.

Measure the liquid. You should have about 4 cups (946 ml) pink juice. If you have less than that, add a little water to the fruit mixture and continue to drain until you have enough liquid to make 4 cups (946 ml). (Discard the solids that remain in the sieve.)

Wash out the pot and pour in the juice. Pour in the sugar. Clip a candy thermometer, if using,

to the side of the pot, bring the juice to a boil over medium-high heat, and cook until the jelly reaches 220°F (105°C) on the candy thermometer, 10 to 15 minutes after it reaches a rolling boil; or use a digital thermometer to check the temperature. Remove from the heat.

Pull a chilled plate and spoon from the freezer. Drop a rounded tablespoon of jelly onto the cold plate. Return it to the freezer for 1 to 2 minutes. Now pull your finger through the jelly. If it leaves a clean trail, it's set. If it's still too runny, cook for 2 to 3 minutes and then test again; repeat if necessary until you are satisfied.

Let the jelly cool completely.

You can store the jelly in Mason jars or airtight containers in the refrigerator for up to 2 weeks. For longer storage, see Puttin' Up Days (page 365).

Green Tomato Preserves

In the South, green tomatoes are generally fried or mixed into a pickled chowchow relish. This sweet-and-savory preserve offers another way to enjoy them. The tomatoes caramelize as they cook, and the resulting preserves are delicious. Serve them to complement a snack tray of crackers and cheese or as a condiment alongside thick-cut pork chops.

MAKES ABOUT 2 QUARTS (2 L)

4 pounds (1.8 kg) green tomatoes, cored and finely chopped

5 cups (1 kg) granulated sugar

½ teaspoon fine sea salt

¼ cup (25 g) finely minced peeled fresh ginger

1 teaspoon red pepper flakes

1 tablespoon sherry vinegar

In a large bowl, combine the green tomatoes, sugar, salt, ginger, and red pepper flakes and give it all a good stir to mix. Cover with plastic wrap, or transfer to an airtight container, and refrigerate for at least 12 hours, and up to 24 hours.

Transfer the tomato mixture to a preserving pot or other large heavy nonreactive pot and bring to a boil over medium-high heat. Add the vinegar, reduce the heat to low, and simmer, stirring frequently, until the mixture begins to thicken and the tomatoes are caramelized, about 1 hour. Remove from the heat and let cool completely.

You can store the preserves in Mason jars or in airtight containers in the refrigerator for up to 2 weeks. For longer storage, see Puttin' Up Days (page 365).

Apple Butter

Making apple butter is a labor of love, but it's so worth it. You can make it in a big pot on the stovetop, but using a slow cooker, as in this recipe, makes the process much easier. Apple butter has a soft, spreadable texture that is achieved only by cooking low and slow for hours until it is a rich, dark mahogany brown. The result is complex, comforting, and buttery, just as the name says. Spread it on toast or biscuits.

MAKES ABOUT 2¼ QUARTS (2.1 L)

3 pounds (1.4 kg) apples, such as Granny Smith, Arkansas Black, or Pink Lady, peeled, cored, and cut into 1-inch (3 cm) chunks

4 cups (946 ml) cold water

1 cup (237 ml) apple cider

¾ cup (150 g) granulated sugar

1 teaspoon ground cinnamon

½ teaspoon freshly grated nutmeg

¼ teaspoon ground cloves

¼ teaspoon ground cardamom

¼ teaspoon freshly ground black pepper

SPECIAL EQUIPMENT

4- to 6-quart (3.8 to 5.7 L) slow cooker

Put the apples into a large heavy pot, add the water, cider, and sugar, and bring to a boil over medium-high heat. Continue to boil, stirring occasionally, until the apples are completely broken down, 40 to 50 minutes. Remove from the heat.

Puree the apples directly in the pot with an immersion blender, or puree in batches in a food processor or blender and return to the pot. Add the cinnamon, nutmeg, cloves, cardamom, and black pepper and stir to combine.

Put two clean saucers and three metal spoons in the freezer.

Pour the puree into a 4- to 6-quart (3.8 to 5.7 L) slow cooker and cook on the low setting, with the lid propped slightly open, for 9 to 12 hours, until thick and dark. Use an immersion blender to blitz the puree a few times during the process so the consistency is as smooth as butter. Or puree the finished apple butter in a food processor, in batches if necessary.

To check for doneness, pull a chilled saucer and a spoon from the freezer. Scoop a small spoonful of apple butter onto the cold plate. Return to the freezer for 1 minute. Now pull your finger through the butter; it should be thick and smooth, without any runny liquid at the edges. If the butter is not set enough, continue to cook and test again; repeat if necessary until you are satisfied.

Let the apple butter cool completely.

You can store the apple butter in Mason jars or airtight containers in the refrigerator for up to 2 weeks. For longer storage, see Puttin' Up Days (page 365).

Cardamom-Spiced Peach Cheese

Some foods that have fallen out of fashion over time are ripe for rediscovering. This one fits the bill. Fruit cheese is a spread that would nicely complement any charcuterie platter. Think of it as a pâté of fruit. Fruit cheese can be made with any seasonal stone fruits. Pour it into vintage jelly molds or small scalloped tart pans for a stunning display on your table, or use small ramekins or tiny bowls. You can also can the fruit cheese if you like (see Puttin' Up Days, page 365).

MAKES 4 SMALL RAMEKINS, SMALL JELLY MOLDS, OR TINY BOWLS OF CHEESE

3 pounds (1.4 kg) peaches, quartered and pitted

6 whole cardamom pods, crushed

1 tablespoon pickling spice

Water to cover

Granulated sugar as needed (see step 3)

3 tablespoons fresh lemon juice

¼ teaspoon fine sea salt

Vegetable oil or melted butter for the molds

Place the peaches in a large heavy-bottomed saucepan and add the cardamom and pickling spice, then add enough water to cover the fruit and bring to a boil over medium-high heat. Turn the heat down to low, cover, and simmer, stirring occasionally to prevent sticking, until the peaches are soft, about 45 minutes. Remove from the heat and let cool for 20 minutes.

Set a fine-mesh sieve over a large heatproof bowl. Pour the peach mixture into the sieve and press on it with the back of a spoon to release as much liquid as possible. Discard the solids left in the sieve.

Measure the liquid in a large measuring cup; the amount of liquid determines the amount of sugar you will need. For every 2 cups (473 ml) of liquid, you will add 2¼ cups (450 g) sugar.

Wash and dry the saucepan and add the strained liquid and the sugar. Cook over medium heat, stirring, until the sugar is completely dissolved. Add the lemon juice and bring the mixture to a boil, then turn the heat down to low and cook until the mixture has thickened, 35 to 40 minutes; the fruit cheese should be thick enough that you can draw a clear path with a spoon over the bottom of the saucepan. Remove from the heat and stir in the salt.

Brush the inside of the molds you are using with vegetable oil for easy unmolding. Ladle the fruit cheese into the molds.

Cover the molds tightly with plastic wrap or transfer them to a large airtight container and refrigerate for at least 4 hours, or overnight, before serving. (*The fruit cheese can be refrigerated for up to 2 weeks.*)

Serve the fruit cheese in the molds. Or, to unmold, dip each mold into a bowl of hot water, wipe the mold dry, and invert the fruit cheese onto a serving plate.

PUTTIN' UP DAYS

IF YOU WANT TO STOCK YOUR PANTRY WITH JAMS AND PRESERVES TO ENJOY for many months, you need to use a canning method to ensure that no bacteria forms in the jars and the food you preserve is safe to eat. Before you get started, clean your work space and your mind. Gather all of your tools (see below). Plan to make a day of preserving, maybe even with a companion you can send home with a bountiful selection of your day together.

There are two methods for canning. The most common one is the stovetop method known as **water-bath canning.** For this method, you will need Ball, Kerr, or other Mason-style canning jars with two-piece lids, a flat metal lid with a sealing compound and a metal screw band, or ring. These jars are cheap, sturdy, extremely reliable, and easy to find in stores or online. You can sterilize and reuse the jars multiple times, but use the lids only once. Before using any jars, wash them with warm soapy water and rinse well. Water-bath canning is the canning method approved by the USDA, and you can refer to their Complete Guide to Home Canning for more information (see nchfp .uga.edu/publications/publications_usda.html). The second method is the **oven-canning method.** This is the technique commonly used in professional kitchens, but it can be done in a home oven too. For this method, you will need jars with a one-part lid called a lug lid that has a sealing compound inside the lid. You will most likely need to order these online. If you want to read more about the oven-canning method, check out Preserved (preservedgoods.com), which is also a great resource for canning supplies.

Here are the tools you'll need. You can buy a preserving kit for a reasonable price that will include most of the tools you will need to get started canning at home. Or you can buy these items separately.

Preserving pot or other large heavy pot
Canning pot or other large pot
Candy or digital thermometer
Canning rack
Jars
Jar lifter

Tongs
Ladle
Canning funnel
Magnetic lid lifter
Heatproof gloves
Heatproof pitcher with a spout
Long heatproof spatula

(Continued)

2-quart (1.9 L) saucepan (for the jar lids)

Kitchen scale (optional but recommended)

Two clean tea towels (one for the hot empty jars, one for the filled jars)

To use the stovetop method: Put the canning rack in your canning pot and add enough water to cover the submerged jars by 1 to 2 inches (3 to 5 cm). Bring the water to a boil; this will take at least 30 minutes. Then reduce the heat to a simmer (180°F/80°C), cover, and keep warm until you're ready to process the jars.

To process the jars for sterilization, using tongs, lay the empty jars on their sides in the pot so that they fill with water, then turn them right side up and leave them in the boiling water for 10 minutes. Use the tongs to lift the hot jars out of the boiling water and place on the clean towel you have set aside. Cover the pot and keep the water hot for the final step of canning.

Fill a saucepan with water and add the flat lids and rings together in sets, making sure they aren't too crowded or stacked on top of one another. Bring the water to a simmer (180°F/80°C)—you just want to warm the lids enough soften the rubber gasket on the lids—then turn off the heat. Overheating will weaken the rubber and the lids' ability to seal properly. Prepare your jam (or preserves). As soon as it is ready, fill the jars: Ladle the hot jam into a heatproof pitcher with a spout. Using a canning funnel, pour the jam into the jars, leaving ¼ inch (6 mm) headspace in each one. If you have any jam left over that will not fill a jar, label and store it in an airtight container in the refrigerator; use within 2 weeks.

Wearing gloves, clean the rims of the jars with a damp paper towel. (Be careful—the jars will be hot!) Using the magnetic lid lifter, lift the lids out of the hot water and place them on the jars. Add the rings and screw them on just to the point of resistance known as "finger-tight," not too tight. The air in the jar needs to escape as the contents of the jars are heated in the canning pot. If the rings are too tight, the seal will fail or, worse, the jars will crack.

Using the jar lifter, lower the jars into the hot water, making sure they're standing upright on the rack and not touching one another or the sides of the pot. Add more water if needed so they are covered by 1 to 2 inches (3 to 5 cm).

Turn up the heat and bring the water back to a rolling boil, with big bubbles. Cover the pot and process for 10 minutes. Turn off the heat and let the jars rest in the pot for 10 minutes. Using the jar lifter, remove the jars and place them on the second clean towel to cool.

As the jars come to room temperature, the button in the canning lid will become concave. This is a sign of a safely preserved jar. Listen for the popping sound; if you still see the button on the top of the lid, that means the jar has not properly sealed. Remove the rings and check the seal on each one by lifting the jar by the lid. If it remains in place, the seal is confirmed. Replace the rings, screwing them on firmly, then wipe the jars clean and label each one with the name and date. If any of the jars fail to

seal properly, store in the refrigerator and use within 2 weeks. Store the sealed jars in a cool, dark place in your pantry for up to 1 year.

To use the oven canning method: Preheat the oven to 250°F (120°C).

Wash your jars and lids in hot soapy water and rinse well. Place the lids in a bowl and set aside. Stand the jars right side up on a baking sheet and heat them in the oven while you make your jam (or for at least 15 minutes). Remove the baking sheet of jars from the oven only when you are ready to can; leave the oven on.

Ladle the hot jam into a heatproof pitcher. Working quickly, so that the jam does not cool down too much, pour the jam into the prepared jars, using a canning funnel. Leave ¼ inch (6 mm) headspace at the top of each jar. If you have any jam left over that will not fill a jar, label and store it in an airtight container in the refrigerator; use it within 2 weeks.

Wearing gloves, use dampened paper towels to clean the rims of the jars, then secure the lids. (Be careful—the jars will be hot!) Screw on the lids, just to the point of resistance known as "finger-tight," but not too tight.

Place the jars upright on the baking sheet, place in the oven, and heat for 15 minutes.

Remove the jars from the oven and set on a wire rack to cool, leaving at least 1 inch (3 cm) between them. As the jars come to room temperature, the button in the canning lid will become concave. This is a sign of a safely preserved jar. Listen for the popping sound; if you still see the button on the top of the lid, that means the jar has not properly sealed. If any of the jars fail to seal properly, label them with the date and store in the refrigerator to use within 2 weeks. Store the sealed jars in a cool, dark place in your pantry for up to 1 year.

Some canning tips to keep in mind. Following a few rules will keep your canning safe and easy.

- If you don't have access to fresh fruits, you can use good-quality frozen (or freeze your own). You can use them straight from the freezer.

- Old-time jammers swear by this way of finishing the perfect pot of jam. Stir a small dab (½ teaspoon) of butter or neutral oil into the finished jam to absorb and disperse any remaining foam that formed during cooking. You won't taste the butter or oil, but it will add a slight sheen and clarity to the jam.

- If after storage, you see mold on the top of a jam, throw it out!

Basics

Buttermilk Whipped Cream

PICTURED ON PAGE 370

Buttermilk whipped cream provides a nice balance to desserts that could otherwise be cloyingly sweet, such as Bill Smith's Famous Atlantic Beach Pie (page 211), Key Lime Pie (page 210), or Chocolate Honey Pie (page 218). It's also nice with a bowl of macerated fruit.

MAKES ABOUT 2½ CUPS (592 ML)

1 cup (237 ml) heavy cream
2 tablespoons confectioners' sugar
A pinch of fine sea salt
¼ cup (59 ml) buttermilk

In the bowl of a stand mixer fitted with the whisk attachment (or in a large mixing bowl, using a handheld mixer), whip the cream, confectioners' sugar, and salt on medium speed until the cream starts to thicken. Add the buttermilk and beat until the cream holds nice soft peaks. Use immediately.

Whipped Topping

This is a homemade version of the store-bought whipped cream that comes in the blue tub. The addition of gelatin stabilizes it for traveling to gatherings, and it holds up to the Southern heat much better than regular whipped cream.

MAKES ABOUT 2 CUPS (473 ML)

1 teaspoon (3 g) unflavored powdered gelatin
4 teaspoons cold water
1 cup (237 ml) heavy cream
2 tablespoons confectioners' sugar
1 teaspoon pure vanilla extract

In a small saucepan, whisk together the gelatin and water and let stand for about 5 minutes to soften the gelatin.

Place the saucepan over low heat and heat the mixture, stirring occasionally, until the gelatin has dissolved, about 2 minutes. Let cool for 2 to 3 minutes, but do not let stand until the gelatin starts to set; it still needs to be pourable.

In the bowl of a stand mixer fitted with the whisk attachment (or in a large mixing bowl, using a handheld mixer), beat the cream on low speed, gradually increasing the speed to medium as it thickens slightly. Beat in the confectioners' sugar and vanilla. With the mixer running, slowly pour in the gelatin mixture and beat until the topping has reached stiff peaks, about 2 minutes; scrape down the sides and bottom of the bowl with a rubber spatula as necessary.

The topping can be stored in an airtight container in the refrigerator for up to 2 days.

Crème Fraîche

Creamy, silky, and tangy, crème fraîche can be incorporated into sweet or savory dishes, and the best part is, it's easy to make it from scratch at home. You can swap it out in recipes that call for sour cream or yogurt. Fold some crème fraîche into freshly whipped cream to add a bit of tang to a sweet dessert, or spoon a dollop on top of a rich slice of pie or bowl of fresh berries.

ABOUT 2¼ CUPS (532 ML)

2 cups (473 ml) heavy cream
¼ cup (59 ml) buttermilk

Pour the heavy cream and buttermilk into a 1-quart (1 L) Mason jar. Give it a good stir, and place it in a cool place (not the refrigerator) out of direct sunlight for at least 12 hours, and up to 24 hours, until it thickens to the consistency of sour cream.

Stir the cream well and use immediately, or cover the jar and refrigerate for up to 10 days.

Chantilly Cream

Chantilly cream is sweetened whipped cream flavored with anything from vanilla to bourbon. Making perfectly whipped cream takes more patience than you might think. Some folks just turn the speed up to high and then end up with either a curdled mess en route to butter or whipped cream that deflates on your plate like melted ice cream. Perfectly whipped cream is not grainy, and it has a nice shine to it when dolloped onto the plate. For best results, chill the bowl for at least 15 minutes before whipping the cream, which will help the cream whip faster.

MAKES ABOUT 2 CUPS (473 ML)

1 cup (237 ml) heavy cream
2 tablespoons confectioners' sugar
1 teaspoon pure vanilla extract, ½ teaspoon rose water (see Resources, page 389), a few drops of Angostura bitters, 1 tablespoon cooled brewed coffee, 1 tablespoon liqueur, 2 tablespoons bourbon, or your favorite flavoring

In the bowl of a stand mixer fitted with the whisk attachment (or in a large mixing bowl, using a handheld mixer), whisk the cream, confectioners' sugar, and flavoring on medium-high speed until the cream starts to thicken. Reduce the speed to medium and beat until the cream holds soft, shiny, medium peaks, 2 to 3 minutes; do not overbeat. Lift the whisk out to check it out, and then give it a good stir.

Use the cream immediately, or refrigerate for up to 5 hours; it will start to separate as it sits, so rewhip it briefly before using.

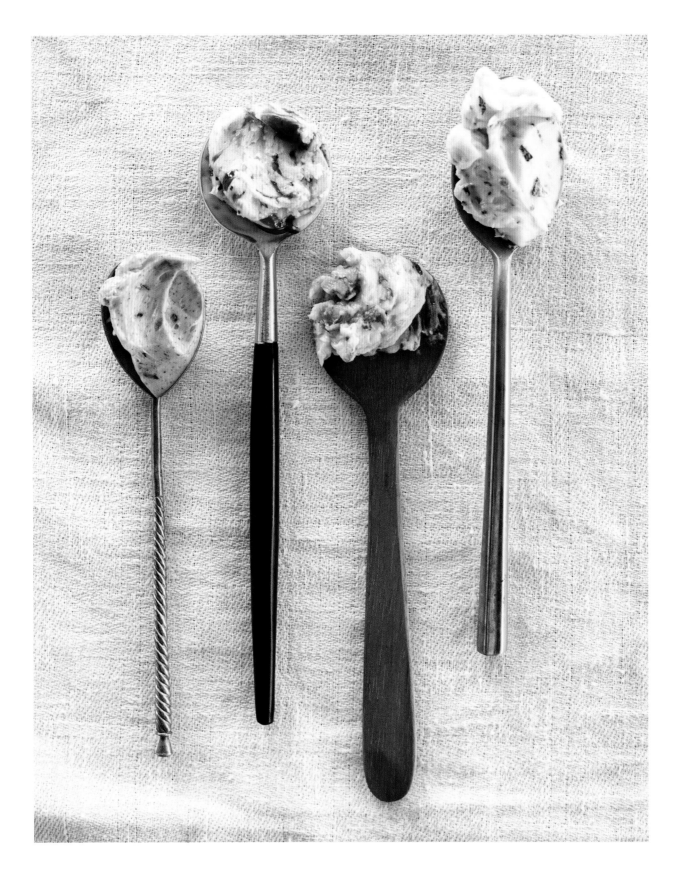

Sweet and Savory Butters

To create different flavored butters, simply combine a stick of softened unsalted butter with preserves or fresh herbs or spices. You can whip the butter and flavorings in a mixer, or simply blend them together in a bowl with a spoon. Once the add-ins are well incorporated, transfer the flavored butter to a piece of parchment or plastic wrap and form it into a log, then wrap well and label and date it. Refrigerate the butter for at least 2 hours before using. You can store these butters in the refrigerator for up to 2 weeks or in the freezer for 6 months.

Here are some great combinations, but be creative and come up with new flavors of your own. All of these make about ¼ pound (113 g) flavored butter.

HERBED BUTTER

Combine 8 tablespoons (1 stick/113 g) softened unsalted butter with:

2 tablespoons minced fresh herbs, such as parsley, rosemary, lavender, and/or thyme

½ teaspoon kosher salt

½ teaspoon freshly ground black pepper

STRAWBERRY BLACK PEPPER BUTTER

Combine 8 tablespoons (1 stick/113 g) softened unsalted butter with:

2 tablespoons strawberry preserves

½ teaspoon freshly ground black pepper

SMOKED PAPRIKA ROSEMARY BUTTER

Combine 8 tablespoons (1 stick/113 g) softened unsalted butter with:

1 tablespoon minced fresh rosemary

1 teaspoon smoked paprika

½ teaspoon kosher salt

SORGHUM PECAN BUTTER

Combine 8 tablespoons (1 stick/113 g) softened unsalted butter with:

2 tablespoons sorghum syrup

2 tablespoons finely chopped pecans

PLUM FLOWERING THYME BUTTER

Combine 8 tablespoons (1 stick/113 g) softened unsalted butter with:

2 tablespoons plum jam

1 tablespoon minced fresh thyme

CITRUS HONEY BUTTER

Combine 8 tablespoons (1 stick/(113 g) softened unsalted butter with:

1 tablespoon honey

1 teaspoon grated orange zest

1 teaspoon grated lemon zest

Flavored Sugars

Flavored sugars are simple to make, but they will add deep flavor to muffins, scones, cakes, pies, cookies, and cobblers. The flavors of these sugars are very pronounced, so use them as a topping or garnish, rather than substituting them for the sugar in a recipe. You can keep flavored sugars indefinitely in airtight jars in your pantry.

CINNAMON SUGAR

1 cup (200 g) granulated sugar
1 cup (200 g) turbinado sugar
3 tablespoons ground cinnamon
2 cinnamon sticks

In a 1-quart (1 L) Mason jar, combine both sugars and the ground cinnamon. Close the jar and give it a good shake to combine. Bury the cinnamon sticks in the sugar.

FRESH HERB SUGAR

1 cup (200 g) granulated sugar
1 cup (200 g) turbinado sugar
1 rounded tablespoon small fresh lemon verbena, thyme, or rosemary sprigs, washed, dried well, and roughly chopped

In the bowl of a food processor, combine both sugars and the herbs and pulse until the sugar is flecked with the herbs and fragrant. Transfer to a Mason jar and let stand for 2 weeks before using.

After 2 weeks, the sugar will be infused with the flavor of the herbs. Strain the sugar through a fine-mesh sieve into another jar and discard the herbs. The sugar will keep in a cool, dry place for up to 1 year.

CARDAMOM SUGAR

1 cup (200 g) granulated sugar
1 cup (200 g) turbinado sugar
½ cup (48 g) whole green cardamom pods

In a 1-quart (1 L) Mason jar, combine both sugars and the cardamom pods. Close the jar and give it a good shake to combine. The flavor will be more pronounced if you can wait 2 weeks before using.

ROSE OR LAVENDER SUGAR

1 cup (200 g) granulated sugar
1 cup (200 g) turbinado sugar
1 tablespoon dried edible rose petals or lavender flowers (see Resources, page 389)

In the bowl of a food processor, combine both sugars and the rose petals or lavender flowers and pulse until the sugar is flecked with the floral herb and fragrant. Transfer to a Mason jar to store.

VANILLA BEAN SUGAR

Don't ever—*ever*—discard vanilla beans after using them. Rinse and dry them and add them to your vanilla sugar jar to give them renewed life.

1 cup (200 g) granulated sugar
1 cup (200 g) turbinado sugar
2 vanilla beans

In a 1-quart (1 L) Mason jar, combine both sugars. Split the vanilla beans lengthwise in half and scrape out the seeds. Stir the seeds into the

sugar and bury the beans in it. The flavor will be more pronounced if you can wait 2 weeks before using the sugar.

When the pods have started to dry out in the sugar, transfer them to the bowl of a food processor and pulse until you are left with tiny flecks of vanilla—and lots of flavor. Then add these bits to the vanilla sugar.

Hot Fudge Sauce

Rich and decadent, this is the perfect hot fudge sauce for dipping fruit or adorning an ice cream sundae.

MAKES 2 CUPS (473 ML)

½ cup (118 ml) heavy cream

½ cup (100 g) granulated sugar

2 tablespoons Dutch-processed cocoa powder, sifted

½ teaspoon fine sea salt

¼ cup (59 ml) corn syrup

½ cup (85 g) finely chopped unsweetened chocolate

½ cup (85 g) finely chopped dark chocolate (60 to 70% cacao)

½ teaspoon pure vanilla extract

In a medium nonreactive saucepan, combine the cream, sugar, cocoa, salt, and corn syrup and bring to a gentle boil, stirring frequently, until the sugar is completely dissolved, 3 to 5 minutes. Remove from the heat.

Add both chocolates and stir until the chocolate is completely melted. Add the vanilla and stir until smooth and silky.

Serve immediately, or store in an airtight container in the refrigerator for up to 2 weeks. Reheat over low heat, stirring, before serving.

Berry Sauce

This versatile sauce comes together quickly and can be served with a slice of pie or other dessert or as an ice cream topping.

MAKES 1 CUP (236 ML)

2 cups (240 g) fresh raspberries, blueberries, or blackberries

⅓ cup (67 g) granulated sugar

In a small nonreactive saucepan, combine the berries and sugar and cook over medium heat, stirring frequently, until most of the liquid the berries release has evaporated and the mixture has a jam-like consistency, about 15 minutes. Remove from the heat and let cool slightly.

Transfer the mixture to a blender or food processor and puree until smooth. Strain through a fine-mesh sieve set over a bowl, pressing on the mixture with a spoon to extract as much liquid as possible. Let cool completely.

The sauce can be stored in an airtight container in the refrigerator for up to 5 days.

Custard Hard Sauce

This traditional custard sauce has a silky-smooth texture and quite a punch. Use it to top Apple Brown Betty (page 333) or Ginger Cake Squares (page 146).

MAKES ABOUT 2½ CUPS (592 ML)

5 large (95 g) egg yolks

6 tablespoons (75 g) granulated sugar

3 tablespoons cornstarch

¼ teaspoon fine sea salt

1 cup (237 ml) whole milk

1 vanilla bean, split lengthwise, seeds scraped out and reserved

1 cup (237 ml) heavy cream

3 tablespoons rum, brandy, or bourbon

In a heatproof bowl, whisk together the egg yolks, sugar, cornstarch, and salt. Set aside.

In a medium heavy-bottomed saucepan, combine the milk and vanilla bean and seeds and bring to just under a boil. Remove from the heat and remove the vanilla bean.

Gradually whisk about ½ cup (118 ml) of the hot milk mixture into the yolks to temper them, so they won't curdle, and then, whisking constantly, add the rest of the milk mixture in a steady stream. Transfer the egg mixture to the saucepan and cook, whisking constantly, until the mixture thickens and coats the back of a spoon, 5 to 7 minutes.

Remove from the heat and stir in the heavy cream and rum. Pour the sauce through a fine-mesh sieve set over a bowl to remove any lumps, then refrigerate for at least 30 minutes before serving.

The hard sauce can be stored in an airtight container in the refrigerator for up to 3 days.

Salted Caramel Sauce

Making caramel sauce doesn't need to be scary. This recipe is easy, but it does require three qualities: patience, caution, and fearlessness. The cream of tartar adds acidity, preventing crystallization (i.e., nasty clumps of sugar) and producing a smooth, creamy sauce. You can kick it up with a shot of bourbon or leave it family-friendly.

MAKES ABOUT 1½ CUPS (355 ML)

1 cup (200 g) granulated sugar

⅛ teaspoon cream of tartar

3 tablespoons water

4 tablespoons (57 g) unsalted butter, cut into 1-inch (3 cm) cubes

½ cup (118 ml) heavy cream, at room temperature

1 teaspoon fine sea salt

1 tablespoon bourbon (optional)

In a medium deep heavy-bottomed saucepan, combine the sugar, cream of tartar, and water and bring to a boil over medium heat, stirring until the sugar is completely dissolved. Once the sugar mixture has reached a boil, stop stirring, reduce the heat to medium-low, and cook, swirling the pan occasionally to distribute the heat evenly and check the color, until the caramel is a golden amber. Watch carefully, as caramel can quickly transform from golden to burnt. As soon as you have patiently reached a golden caramel color, carefully remove from the heat.

Add the butter one piece at a time, stirring until smooth. Slowly and carefully add the cream (it will sputter a bit), stirring constantly until the sauce is shiny and smooth. (If the cream is too cold, the caramel may seize up, so that you get

some lumps of hardened caramel, but don't panic: Just return the pan to low heat and stir until the caramel is completely melted and smooth.) Stir in the salt and the bourbon, if using.

The sauce can be stored in an airtight container in the refrigerator for up to 1 month. Set the container in a bowl of warm water and stir until liquefied before using.

Citrus Paste

Tired of throwing away lemons, limes, or oranges after you have zested them for a recipe? Here's how you can stop that waste. Wash and dry the fruit. Cut it into quarters and remove the seeds. Throw the fruit (yup, including the peel) into the bowl of a food processor and process for about 1 minute, until pureed into a thick paste.

Use the paste in baked goods, frostings, and glazes, or add to drinks instead of citrus zest to pep them up. Store the paste in an airtight container in the freezer for up to 3 months.

Simple Sweet Glaze

Here's a cozy blanket of glaze for pastries and loaf cakes. You can make a plain version with water or use a citrus juice for more flavor. Be creative—add a pinch of ground spice, maybe cinnamon or cardamom, to the glaze if you're using it to top a cake.

MAKES ABOUT 1 CUP (236 ML)

2 cups (250 g) confectioners' sugar
2 tablespoons water or fresh lemon, lime, or
    orange juice, or as needed
1 teaspoon pure vanilla extract, or any other flavoring
    you like (optional)
¼ teaspoon fine sea salt

In a medium bowl, whisk the confectioners' sugar, water or citrus juice, vanilla (if using), and salt together until very smooth and creamy. Add a little more water if needed to reach a honey-like consistency. Use immediately.

Burnt Honey Glaze

"Burnt" honey imparts a deep caramel color and a complex nutty, sweet/bitter flavor that is unique and delicious. Pour this glaze over anything from loaf cakes to ice cream.

MAKES ABOUT 1½ CUPS (355 ML)

10 ounces (284 g) white chocolate, finely chopped, or white chocolate baking wafers, such as Guittard (about 1⅔ cups)
5 tablespoons (75 ml) honey, such as orange blossom
⅔ cup (158 ml) heavy cream, at room temperature
1 teaspoon fine sea salt
2 tablespoons unsalted butter, at room temperature

Put the white chocolate in a heatproof bowl. Set aside.

Pour 4 tablespoons (59 ml) of the honey into a small saucepan and cook over medium-high heat, swirling the pan occasionally for even cooking, until the honey is a dark caramel color, about 3 minutes.

Remove the saucepan from the heat and slowly pour in the cream—be careful; the hot mixture will bubble and steam. With a heatproof spatula or spoon, stir the cream until it is completely incorporated. Add the remaining 1 tablespoon honey and the salt, stirring until the honey is completely dissolved.

Pour the hot honey cream over the white chocolate and whisk until the glaze starts to emulsify. Add the butter and stir until melted and thoroughly combined. Set aside to cool slightly before using.

The glaze can be stored in an airtight container in the refrigerator for up to 5 days. Reheat over low heat, stirring, before serving.

Lemon Curd

Sweet lemon curd has a silky, custardy texture and bright fresh flavor. Use it to fill the Lemon Cheese Layer Cake (page 156), or just enjoy it by the spoonful, perhaps with some berries.

MAKES ABOUT 1 CUP (236 ML)

7 large (133 g) egg yolks
1 cup (200 g) granulated sugar
½ cup (118 ml) fresh lemon juice
4 tablespoons (57 g) cold unsalted butter, cut into ½-inch (1.5 cm) cubes

In a medium heavy-bottomed nonreactive saucepan, whisk together the egg yolks, sugar, and lemon juice and cook over medium heat, whisking frequently, until the mixture is thick and glossy, 8 to 10 minutes.

Remove the curd from the heat and strain through a fine-mesh sieve into a bowl to remove any remaining pesky bits of egg. Let the curd cool for 5 minutes.

Whisk the butter into the curd until melted and incorporated. Place a piece of plastic wrap directly on the surface of the curd so that a skin doesn't form and let cool to room temperature.

Use the curd immediately, or store in an airtight container in the refrigerator for up to 2 weeks.

Pastry Cream

Use this custard to fill pastries, pies, and cakes or the Profiteroles (page 340). You can infuse the milk base with cardamom, coffee, rose petals, or chamomile.

MAKES 2½ CUPS (592 ML)

5 large (95 g) egg yolks
6 tablespoons (75 g) granulated sugar
3 tablespoons cornstarch
¼ teaspoon fine sea salt
2 cups (473 ml) whole milk
1 teaspoon pure vanilla extract
2½ tablespoons unsalted butter

In a heatproof bowl, whisk together the egg yolks, sugar, cornstarch, and salt. Set aside.

In a medium heavy-bottomed saucepan, combine the milk and vanilla and bring to just under a boil over medium heat. Remove the pan from the heat.

Whisk about 1 cup (237 ml) of the hot milk mixture into the egg yolk mixture to temper the egg yolks, so they won't curdle, then add the remainder of the milk mixture in a steady stream, whisking constantly. Transfer the mixture back to the saucepan and cook over medium heat, stirring frequently with a heatproof spatula and making sure to scrape the bottom of the pan to prevent sticking, until thickened, 4 to 6 minutes. Add the butter in two additions, stirring until just melted and incorporated.

Pour the pastry cream into a bowl and place a piece of plastic wrap directly on top of it so that a skin does not form. Let cool for 30 minutes, or until it reaches room temperature, before using. (If you are in a hurry, set the bowl in a bowl of ice water and stir until the pastry cream is chilled.)

The pastry cream can be stored in an airtight container in the refrigerator for up to 3 days.

Milk Jam

This jam is made by simply boiling milk and sugar low and slow, with a big pinch of patience—it has to cook for 2 hours or so. Also known as dulce de leche, milk jam gets its flavor when the milk proteins brown and caramelize. You will want to eat it with everything from cookies to ice cream. Start with the Milk-Jam Shortbread Sammies (page 259).

MAKES 2 CUPS (473 ML)

4 cups (946 ml) whole milk
1¼ cups (250 g) granulated sugar
¾ teaspoon (4 g) baking soda
¼ teaspoon fine sea salt
½ vanilla bean, split lengthwise, seeds scraped out and reserved

In a medium heavy-bottomed saucepan, combine the milk, sugar, baking soda, salt, and vanilla bean and seeds and bring to a boil over medium-high heat, stirring frequently to dissolve the sugar. Reduce the heat to low and simmer, stirring frequently with a heatproof spatula and making sure to scrape the bottom of the pan to prevent sticking, until the mixture is a dark caramel color and has a jam-like texture: This will take time, 2 to 2½ hours.

Remove from the heat and let cool, then refrigerate until ready to use.

The milk jam can be stored in an airtight container in the refrigerator for up to 2 weeks.

Brown Butter

When butter browns, it takes on a whole new flavor: rich, nutty, and toasty. It's delicious in all sorts of baked goods from cookies and cakes to piecrust. Just be sure to add about 15 percent of the weight called for when swapping it for regular butter, as the butter reduces in volume as it evaporates during the cooking process. You can use browned butter for any recipe that calls for melted butter. For room-temperature butter, make sure that it has solidified first before using, then measure the amount you need according to your original recipe. Browned butter keeps well, so you might want to make a big batch to keep on hand.

Use a saucepan that is light in color so you can watch the butter browning. For best results, start with at least 8 tablespoons (1 stick/113 g) of butter. Cut the butter into tablespoon-sized pieces and melt it over medium heat, stirring with a heatproof spatula as it begins to foam up. Then keep stirring to make sure that the flavorful brown bits do not stick to the bottom of the pan, and swirl the pan to look for a light golden color. Watch carefully, because once the butter reaches a certain point, the color can change quickly, going from golden to burnt in the blink of an eye. Pour the butter into a heatproof bowl. It will continue to cook from the residual heat and can overcook; to prevent this, stir for about 2 minutes to cool it down quickly.

The brown butter can be stored in an airtight container in the refrigerator for up to 2 weeks or in the freezer for up to 3 months.

RESOURCES

APRONS

White Bark Workwear
whitebarkworkwear.com

CAKE DECORATING

Afloral
afloral.com

Gourmet Sweet Botanicals
gourmetsweetbotanicals.com

Layer Cake Shop
layercakeshop.com

CHOCOLATE

Acalli Chocolate
acallichocolate.com

Guittard Chocolate Company
guittard.com

CULINARY BITTERS, EXTRACTS, SPICES, VANILLA, WATERS, AND MORE

Beanilla
beanilla.com

Burlap & Barrel
burlapandbarrel.com

Diaspora Co.
diasporaco.com

Heilala Vanilla
heilalavanilla.com

SOS Chefs
sos-chefs.com

Spicewalla
spicewallabrand.com

HEIRLOOM SEEDS

Social Roots
socialrootsseeds.com

HOSPITALITY AND PARTY GOODS

Layer Cake Shop
layercakeshop.com

Oh Happy Day
shop.ohhappyday.com

KITCHEN GOODS, CERAMICS, AND SUCH

Back in the Day Bakery
backinthedaybakery.com

Bon
bon-boutique.com

Clove & Creek
cloveandcreek.com

Crate & Barrel
crateandbarrel.com

Fishs Eddy
fishseddy.com

Gjusta Goods
gjustagoods.com

Herriott Grace
herriottgrace.com

Janie Q Provisions
janie-q.com

Nordic Ware
nordicware.com

Preserved
preservedgoods.com

PW Short
pwshort.com

Star Provisions
starprovisions.com

Williams Sonoma
williams-sonoma.com

ACKNOWLEDGMENTS

With love to Griffith Day, my best half. Thank you for always supporting me and giving me the courage to create the dreams I dream. My cup runneth over, and it's all because of you. I love you more and more every day.

To my editor and dear friend Judy Pray. Words truly can't express how grateful I am for your guidance for more than a decade now (and counting!). Thank you for your dedication to this book and for bringing it to life page after page after page. You bring out the very best in me.

Thank you, Lia Ronnen and Dan Reynolds, for saying yes again and again. This project is a dream come true.

To the amazing team at Artisan: Suet Chong, Nina Simoneaux, Sibylle Kazeroid, Zach Greenwald, Elissa Santos, Nancy Murray, Erica Huang, Allison McGeehon, Theresa Collier, and Bella Lemos. I appreciate the level of detailed attention you put into every page, which allows me to have this beautiful book that I am so proud to share. Your hard work behind the scenes makes it all possible.

To Judith Sutton, the best copy editor on the planet. Thank you for teaching me so many new things all the time. I appreciate your expertise. Thank you to Zachary R. Townsend for reading the recipes as well.

My dear friend (and the daughter I never had) Haylie Waring, you are the creative director of my life. Thank you for your artistic vision and for telling my story in the best way possible. I heart you forever.

Angie Mosier, you are an incredible Southern baker and a phenomenal photographer, and your talent is awe-inspiring. Thank you for your creativity and magic in making these beautiful images. I love spending time with you.

Courtney Culver Colangelo, baking with you is such a joy. Thank you for standing by me in full support day after day as we laugh, dance, and bake to our hearts' content. You are one of the most talented bakers I know. I could not have done this book without you, sweet friend.

Afton Boultinghouse, thank you for saying yes to absolutely everything for seventeen days straight, and for doing it all with a big smile. You spread joy wherever you go.

To my lifelong friend and mentor Jane Thompson. Thank you for giving me the encouragement to take the leap from home baker to professional. I will always be grateful.

To Jennifer Garner, Jessica Harris, Sean Brock, Mashama Bailey, Julia Turshen, Anne Quatrano, and Lisa Donovan, a big thank-you for the kind words of endorsement that grace the jacket of this book.

To all of the librarians and booksellers, thank you for your support over the years. Your enthusiasm means the world to me!

Thank you to my greatest treasures:

Bill Smith, for sharing your expertise about Southern food. Thank you for letting me ask a million questions and for answering them all. I adore you.

(Continued)

Sarah Ross, for allowing me to share a day in the life of your world of historic preservation seed by seed and for shining light on the work of my ancestors; it was a day of reflection like no other. Someday I will get that chicken coop.

Karen Clay, my official advisory committee. Your early-morning calls and texts have gotten me through the best and worst and everything in between for more than forty years. (Can you believe it?!) Thank you for the years of friendship. I love you.

Osayi Endolyn, thank you for sharing your insightful feedback whenever I called on you. You are a real one.

Grace Bonney and Julia Turshen, for always being in my corner every step of the way and putting my name and voice out in the world. You inspire me.

Our extended Savannah family: Bryan, Davida, and Jonah Robinson. I love making Sunday pancakes with you!

Robin Cook, the most dedicated recipe tester. You're the best!

Ginger Waring, for your words of encouragement and always sharing your special treasures with me, especially Afton and Haylie.

The Waring family and Cedar Tree Farms for the most beautiful and delicious eggs.

Anne Quatrano, I cherish your friendship and appreciate your mentorship and encouragement so much. You always make everything seem possible.

LaRaine Papa Montgomery, thank you for your loving spirit and hospitality.

Infinite gratitude to all the folks who have enjoyed my cookbooks over the years; I'm so grateful you are holding this one in your hands.

INDEX

Note: Page numbers in *italics* refer to illustrations.